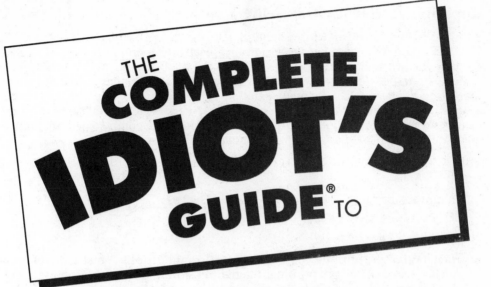

THE COMPLETE IDIOT'S GUIDE® TO

Italian History and Culture

by Gabrielle Euvino
with Michael San Filippo

ALPHA

A member of Penguin Group (USA) Inc.

D1119676

Copyright © 2002 by Gabrielle Euvino

International Standard Book Number: 0-02-864234-1
Library of Congress Catalog Card Number: 2001094737

06   05   04   8   7   6   5   4   3

Interpretation of the printing code: The rightmost number of the first series of numbers is the year of the book's printing; the rightmost number of the second series of numbers is the number of the book's printing. For example, a printing code of 02-1 shows that the first printing occurred in 2002.

Printed in the United States of America

Publisher
Marie Butler-Knight

Product Manager
Phil Kitchel

Managing Editor
Jennifer Chisholm

Senior Acquisitions Editor
Randy Ladenheim-Gil

Development Editor
Suzanne LeVert

Senior Production Editor
Christy Wagner

Copy Editor
Michael Dietsch

Illustrator
Jody Schaeffer

Cover Designers
Mike Freeland
Kevin Spear

Book Designers
Scott Cook and Amy Adams of DesignLab

Indexer
Angie Bess

Contents at a Glance

Contents

Appendixes

Foreword

When I was growing up, I was often enamored of stories from my family about a beautiful and majestic land called the "Old Country," which is how my father referred to Italy. Any time family members talked about the Old Country, they had a twinkle in their eye and a smile on their face. At times, the stories they told me made me laugh and smile. I often wondered why they ever left this beautiful place. Then there were stories that made me sad, and it was these stories that helped me understand why my parents sacrificed everything to come to America. They hoped to secure a better life for the family they would soon have. It was a struggle for them, but they overcame all obstacles and prejudices toward Italians to make their dream come true. I don't think there ever was a time in my life that I wasn't proud of them. It wasn't easy to leave their family behind and enter a world that was new and different from what they were accustomed to. They may have left Italy, but Italy never left them. It is in their blood, heart, and soul. Everything they did could be traced back to Italy. Their traditions, customs, and beliefs came with them, and in turn, were taught to us.

I used to think that everyone was Italian and that everyone lived as I did. I soon realized as I attended school that this wasn't the case. I was surprised to find that my friends didn't have gardens with fig trees, their parents didn't make homemade wine, they never heard of bocce, and they didn't eat the same foods we did. They didn't even celebrate holidays the same way my family did. I was also amazed to learn how Italians were thought of in the rest of society. It disheartened me to think that people felt so negatively toward us.

A major problem facing Italian Americans is the negative stereotypes they encounter in everyday life. The nation as a whole is romantically involved with the notion that Italians are gangsters connected to organized crime, for instance, which is hardly the case. In fact, Italians have contributed far more to our civilization than they have corrupted it.

One way to help dispel the stereotypes surrounding Italians is to inform people just how much Italians have given to the world. This book does just that. It gives people a better understanding of the history and culture of our beloved Italy. There are many facets of our culture that are relatively unknown to a vast majority of people.

Indeed, I was always told to be proud of who I am and where my ancestors came from, and it would be extremely difficult for me not to be proud. Many of the world's great works of art were created by Italians. The laws that governed ancient Rome still have an influence on the modern-day legal system. The radio and telephone are just two of the inventions attributed to Italians. Italian Americans have founded many businesses like Barnes and Noble, The Bank of America, and Tropicana—and this is just the beginning. There is so much for Italians to be proud of—and thanks to this book, you'll soon have an understanding and appreciation of our rich culture and heritage.

Each day I learn more and more about Italian culture, and it makes me that much more proud to know that my family and I are blessed to be a part of this wonderful heritage. As our children grow older, my wife and I look forward to sharing with them the same traditions, customs, and beliefs that our parents taught us. Who knows, maybe they will see a twinkle in our eyes and a smile on our faces when we share with them the same stories our parents told us. Sit down and enjoy as you read and learn more about the wonderful history and culture of Italy and get a better understanding of who Italians really are.

Anthony Parente
Guide to Italian Culture at About.com
italianculture.about.com

Introduction

In *The Complete Idiot's Guide to Italian History and Culture,* we'll show how much of the Italian spirit has become part of your daily life. Whenever you sip an Italian wine or bite into a delicious bit of pasta, you are participating in the Italian legacy. When you bring your child to the doctor, you're probably taking advantage of medical advances made by Italian thinkers and scientists. Every time you watch a movie, read a book, sip an espresso, drive a car, ride a boat, get dressed, or sing a song, you are probably benefiting from a contribution made by an Italian.

Not only have the Italians been instrumental in shaping the course of Western civilization, they helped nurture its birth. Among other things, this book discusses art, literature, politics, language, architecture, food, saints, heretics, the Catholic Church, explorers, opera, immigration, emigration, and integration.

Our hope in writing this book was to help you draw your own map, design your personal course, and find your own way through the vast and fertile cultural and historical Italian landscape. We've planted the seed, and it is up to you to nurture the plant.

Within These Pages

This book is divided into six parts that explore Italian and Italian American culture and history.

Part 1, "A Portrait," introduces the Italians and talks about their origins. Learn why notable visitors such as the English poet Henry Wadsworth Longfellow, Florence Nightingale, and others adopted Italy. Understand the origins of the Italian language. From the northern Alps to the emerald waters of the Costa Smeralda, become acquainted with Italy's varied geography. Discover why so many Italians left their homeland. And just what is Italglish anyway?

Part 2, "Tota Italia," discusses the many layers that make up Italian history. What happened in Rome and why did the great republic fall? Who was Constantine and what was the Byzantine Empire? What were the key events during the Middle Ages that led to the artistic blossoming of the Renaissance?

Part 3, "Quantum Leaps," offers an overview of the Renaissance, arguably one of the most interesting periods of history. You know the names, you've seen their work; who were the masters? What inspired such genius? Who paid for it all? Why did the Renaissance end?

In **Part 4, "Redshirts, Blackshirts, and Greenshirts,"** you'll learn about Napoleon and how the French Revolution affected Italy's politics. Learn more about Giuseppe Garibaldi and his Thousand Redshirts. Understand what led millions of Italians to leave their homeland in search of a better life. See how the words of an Italian philosopher influenced the Declaration of Independence. Understand how Mussolini and his black-shirted Fascists came to power. Find out how the Italian Americans living in America felt about the Fascists and World War II.

Part 5, "Pizza, Pasta, and Fantasia," celebrates the Italian women whose contributions deserve special mention. In addition, it looks at wine, spaghetti, Camevale, film, fashion, fairytales, miracles, and mysteries.

Part 6, "Italy's Exports," acknowledges achievements and contributions made by Italy's sons and daughters. Here we offer you a brief directory of notable Italian Americans. Learn more about some of your favorite entertainers and stars. The list of Nobel Prize winners, teachers, writers, philosophers, politicians, and industry leaders is long. (See how many more you can come up with!)

A Garnish

To garnish the meal, each chapter is enhanced with helpful sidebars that offer interesting and helpful information to assist you in your study of Italy. Take advantage of the tips and suggestions; visit your library to see what they offer. When you're online, take advantage of the suggested Web sites.

Biografia

Interesting individuals are highlighted in a mini-biography designed to be read in a blink.

La Bella Lingua

Expand your vocabulary with these interesting language-related tidbits.

Di Interessa

These sidebars offer snippets of information that are relevant to the chapter. They will often guide you to a place or further reference.

"Italia"

In Italics

This sidebar draws attention to important anniversaries and dates that warrant mention.

Acknowledgments

This book is dedicated to the memory of the author Anne Bianchi, founder of the Toscana Saporita Cooking School. I owe a great deal of my success to her guidance and support. *Mille grazie,* Anne.

This book is truly the result of a collaborative effort and would be quite different had it not been for the generous contributions made by *studenti,* colleagues, friends, family, and readers.

For his attention to detail, follow-through and creative insights, special thanks are extended to Michael San Filippo, writer, entrepreneur, and idea-smith, without whom this book could not be what it is; a special *grazie* to the technical editor, Cristina Melotti, for the *colore* she helped add to these pages, and for her fact-checking and cultural savvy. And special thanks to Arlyse and Gil McDowell for their research, encouragement, and *amore* of Italy.

Special thanks to my agent, Jessica Faust of BookEnds, friend to writers and canines alike, and to Amy Zavatto for being my literary compass.

Gratitude is extended to the individuals whose eyes helped make this book a better read, including development editor Suzanne LeVert, acquisitions editor Randy Ladenheim-Gil, senior production editor Christy Wagner, copy editor Michael Dietsch, editorial coordinator Krista McGruder, and everyone on the Alpha production staff ... thank you!!

Photo contributions were generously made by Anna Andersson, Giancarlo Cammerini, and Marissa Palmisano.

And a sincere thanks to the following individuals for sharing their time with me: my brother Robert, Frank Duncan, Andrea Euvino, Clara Kaye, the Kushner family, Frank, Kara, and Sara Euvino; Anne Richter, Flo Ceravolo, Tricia Tait, Cathy Scarillo, Doug Hatschek, Kim Hornberger and Andy Malcolm, Jessica Mezyk, Richard Smith, David Stoltz, Peter Cooper, Scott and Teal Hutton, Lisa Reisman, Frannie "Rosie" Little, Margaret, Tony, and Marc Salamone, Gloria Rivera, Karen White, Christine Neiman, "Hera," Pia Alexander and the Woodstock library, Catherine Callahan, Carla Smith, Marcel Nagele, Lou Pollack, Rhonda Olinsky, Bruce Dobozin and Devorah Sperber, and everyone at the Woodstock Guild; Gioia Timpanelli, Fred Gardaphé, Stefano Spadoni, the New York offices of Seyfarth, Shaw, and special thanks to the offices of Governor Mario Cuomo.

And a special prayer is extended to Lyn and Kim Schneider with thoughts of their beloved Jim Roarabaugh.

From Michael San Filippo:

Many thanks to my wonderful family and friends for their hearty encouragement and continued support. A huge *abbraccio* to the Marletta, Leoncini, and Zotti families for their heartwarming hospitality and enthusiastic cultural exchange. And a special thanks to Arlyse and Gil for their hard work and infectious passion for the topic.

Trademarks

All terms mentioned in this book that are known to be or are suspected of being trademarks or service marks have been appropriately capitalized. Alpha Books and Penguin Group (USA) Inc., cannot attest to the accuracy of this information. Use of a term in this book should not be regarded as affecting the validity of any trademark or service mark.

Part 1

A Portrait

Every journey begins somewhere, so it may as well be where you are now, in this moment. Part I serves as the launching pad for anyone interested in studying Italy and the Italians. Who are the Italians? What makes Italy unique? Why learn about Italy?

You'll begin the viaggo (journey) with a taste of interesting facts and tidbits related to Italy's history and geography. Study the various regions and you'll begin to realize how diverse and multicultural the Italians are. Learn about the immigrants who made their way to American shores, bringing with them their rich heritage, traditions, and dialects. Compare Italian to English and see how much the two languages influence each other.

The Magic of Italy

Italy. The substance of dreams, romance, and ruins. A country steeped in tradition, filled with contradiction. A place where the edges of legend and reality often blur.

Italy is heir to the Roman legacy, a source of pride she wears like a crown. She is host to the Vatican, the heart of the Roman Catholic Church. Her language is among the most beautiful ever developed. Her architecture spellbinds. The loveliness of her people dazzles. The quality of her wine intoxicates. The sumptuousness of her food nourishes both the body and the soul. Whether you're talking about art and architecture, literature, music, design, business, science, mathematics, olive oil, or wine, there is no limit to the bounty of Italy.

Sibling Rivalry

It has been said that the fiercely independent and heterogeneous national character of the Italians reflects the thousands of years Italy suffered foreign invasion and domination.

The invaders came from all directions: The Greeks arrived from the south, the Gauls stormed from the north. The Phoenicians, the Carthaginians, and the Lombards were followed by the Ligurians, Siculi, and Sards. Then came the Egyptians and the Latins, the Goths, the Vandals, followed by the Franks, the Spanish, the Arabs, the French, and as recent as World War II, the Germans.

Biografia

The Guelphs and the Ghibellines came to represent opposing political factions in Italy during the long struggle between popes and emperors in the turbulent Middle Ages. The terms were first used in thirteenth-century Florence to designate the supporters of the Guelph Pope Otto IV and the Ghibelline Hohenstaufen Frederick II; later the Guelphs generally came to support the pope while the Ghibellines supported the Holy Roman Emperor.

When there was no outside enemy, Guelphs marched against Ghibellines, the Milanese quarreled with the Florentines, and the Emperor fought the Pope. (Perhaps this explains why the Italians continue to love to argue!)

"Italia"

In Italics

Italy was not a unified country until the middle of the nineteenth century. Prior to 1861, the peninsula and Sicily that we now know as *La Repubblica Italiana* (The Republic of Italy) was essentially a cluster of city-states, each with its own language, customs, and government.

Italy has been ruled by emperors, popes, kings, and despots and has suffered plagues and pestilence. What was all the fighting about? And how could a relatively small peninsula located in the heart of the Mediterranean inspire legions to traipse over mountains and sail the high seas?

Italy Yesterday and Today

To find the answers to these questions, one must look at the details. To reveal the secrets of Italy, you must peel away the layers of time. The history of Italy is like a patchwork quilt, each square representing a unique culture; sewn together they create something greater. By studying the specifics and how they connect, you'll discover the bigger picture. For example, to understand the Italians, you need to begin with the Romans; you must study their roads, read their words, visit their places of worship and homes. To appreciate the perspective of the Middle Ages, you must study the role of the church, its impact on society, and the function it served during a very troubled time.

To understand Michelangelo's day, you must consider the revival of classical ideas and how this "rebirth" led to the creative explosion that is now defined as the *Renaissance*. You can then begin to see how the Renaissance helped pave the way for the trade and seafaring that eventually led to the discovery of the New World.

A Land of Old and New

Time is relative, especially for a culture that has so much history behind it. Keep in mind that during the Renaissance, Michelangelo considered himself to be as modern as you consider yourself to be today.

Italy is a study of contrasts between past and present. Standing beneath the shadow of Mount Vesuvius, the infamous volcano that erupted in 79 B.C.E. and buried the inhabitants of Pompeii in a layer of ash, mud, and lava, one can easily imagine the life that once populated what are now stone ruins, covered by vines and surrounded by tourists. In central Rome, vendors sell colorful, glossy guidebooks alongside the great Colosseum, the colossal stadium that showcased the bloody games of the gladiators. Driving north through the Umbrian hills, it's hard not to imagine how life must have been back before automobiles and electric lights when these medieval fortress towns were constructed some eight or so centuries ago.

From the bleached sand beaches of the Italian shores to the snow-capped peaks of the Alps, the bounty and beauty of *Italia* is as varied as her people. Where the ghosts of lives come and gone whisper among themselves, the rolling hills and magnificent walled castles and palaces of Tuscany are often compared to fairytales. (In fact, many of

La Bella Lingua

The term **renaissance** literally means "rebirth" or "revival" and refers to the resurrection of previously forgotten ideas and culture. Italy inspired the greatest artistic and intellectual flowering in history from about 1350 to 1650. During this expressive time called the Renaissance, every known idea would be questioned and old paradigms discarded. The age of discovery had begun.

La Bella Lingua

The modern name **Italia** derives from the word *Vítelú,* the Oscan term for the Italian peninsula and probably connected to the word for calf (seen in Latin *vitulus,* and Umbrian *vitlu*). Originally used to refer to the Greek colonies in Italy, the word eventually became associated with the entire peninsula.

today's favorite fairy tales derive from Italian folktales that were eventually written down.) Thousands of sunflowers, called *girasole* ("turn toward the sun"), point in the same direction. Cyprus trees seem to have been painted against the cloudless sky.

The well-preserved medieval city of Labro rises up from the rocks.

The Italy of Today

Italy is a country of contrasts. You can visit the Pantheon, one of Rome's oldest buildings, and then stop by McDonald's for a burger. You can still walk along the ancient Roman roads, but you had better keep an eye out for traffic. Along with gondolas, you'll also see speedboats coursing down the narrow canals of Venice, and buses parked alongside the Leaning Tower of Pisa.

The modern mingles with the traditional as young, fashionable mothers push strollers along cobblestone streets. Where invaders pressed against the confines of Italian borders, thousands of tourists now flock to witness the spectacle of Italian life, traditions, festivals, and history, many seeking long-lost ties to their Italian heritage. Maybe you're one of them..

Why Learn About Italy?

The ideas and creative genius of the Italians have been influencing the world for centuries. To study Italian history and culture is to learn more about your own cultural heritage, whether you are of Italian descent or not. From the Romans to the Medici, from the Punic Wars to World War II, the panorama of Italy's contributions to the world and to the creation of Western civilization is inexhaustible.

Ask anyone to name 5 prominent Italians, and they will have no problem listing 10, 20, even 100. From Leonardo to Donatello, from Cristoforo Colombo to Amerigo Vespucci, from Caruso to Pavarotti, from Sophia Loren to Isabella Rossellini, the list goes on and on.

In fact, wherever history has been made, an Italian was probably present. Whenever you write a check, you are using a device invented by the Florentines during the Renaissance. Pick up the telephone and you're paying tribute to a contribution made by Italian inventor Antonio Meucci. Switch on a light and you can thank Alessandro Volta. Turn on the radio and you honor Guglielmo Marconi. No one says it better than Luigi Barzini in his book, *The Italians:*

> There would be no pistols but for the city of Pistoia; no *savon* in France but for the city of Savona; no faience anywhere but for the city of Faenza; no millinery but for the city of Milan; no blue jeans but for the city of Genoa, *Gênes*, where the blue cotton cloth was first produced, and no Genoa jibs, no Neapolitan ice cream, no Roman candles, no Venetian blinds, no Bologna sausages, no Parmesan cheese, no Leghorn hens. Italians have discovered America for the Americans; taught poetry, statesmanship, and the ruses of trade to the English; military art to the Germans; cuisine to the French; acting and ballet dancing to the Russians; and music to everybody. If some day this world of ours should be turned into a cloud of radioactive dust in space, it will be by nuclear contrivances developed with the decisive aid of Italian scientists.

What Turns You On?

Does your heart swoon when you listen to the music of Verdi? Are you an incurable romantic looking for company? Do you get weak-kneed when you hear Italian spoken? Think for a moment about the things that you love best about Italy. Do you melt at the sight of Botticelli's *Venus?* Are you moved by Leonardo da Vinci's *Last Supper,* Michelangelo's sculpture of David, Brunelleschi's dome?

Are you a history buff looking to see the past come alive? Are you an amateur photographer hoping to capture that perfect image? Do you love to cook and want to know how to prepare homemade pasta? Are you of Italian origins searching for your roots?

Whatever your reasons for wanting to know more about the uniquely enchanting Italian culture, you'll find yourself in good company.

A Love Affair

The dignity, nobility, and achievements of Italy have drawn some of the greatest minds to her soil. Italy has long been a muse to writers and artists seeking inspiration. Shakespeare set the plots of his enduring plays—*Julius Caesar, Romeo and Juliet, The Merchant of Venice, Othello, The Taming of the Shrew*—in Italy.

Di Interessa

The English nurse Florence Nightingale was born in, and named after, Florence, Italy.

The American poet Henry Wadsworth Longfellow studied in Italy, spoke Italian like a Roman, and translated Dante Alighieri's *Divine Comedy*. The German philosophers Wolfgang Goethe and Friedrich Nietzsche contemplated while in Italy. German Richard Wagner composed, Briton George Sand wrote, and Dutchman Hans Christian Andersen created some of his infamous fairytales while traveling through Italy. Mark Twain haunted Florence while Henry James preferred Rome.

La Dolce Vita

No doubt these visitors were charmed by the Italian way of life. Whether drawn by art or love, poets, painters, and connoisseurs have always been fascinated by the Italian language, history, and culture. And who could blame them? The magnificence of the varied Italian landscapes—the azure sea and its secret lagoons, the Mediterranean sun sparkling off calm waters, the abundant fish and wildlife, the ripe fruit trees, the fresh vegetables—all lend themselves to the sweetness of living in the moment. Perhaps what draws us to the Italian countryside is the appearance of a simpler existence, a way of life that esteems unhurried meals accompanied by fine conversation and good wine.

While this is still to be found, it occurs in tandem with the technological inventions of the modern world, the most obvious example being the Italian's love affair with the cellular phone. Indeed, cities such as Rome and Milan are bastions of modern Italian culture. Among the hustle and bustle, you'll find people from all walks of life, shops showcasing the latest fashions, brightly illuminated chrome and glass bars, clubs, movie houses, restaurants, and theaters. Traffic jams are a daily event for commuters, and endless appointments, play dates, and social or professional obligations are part of modern life. It is the casualness with which the Italians live in between the past and the future that makes them so compelling, as individuals and collectively.

Often, it is the celebration of the ordinary that makes Italy so extraordinary. Wherever you go, life in Italy is made of daily activities that, repeated over time, have formed the habits and customs of the Italians. Even if you're not fortunate enough to call yourself Italian by birth, you can still enjoy the Italian way of life. It could be as simple as taking *una passeggiata* (a stroll) on a summer's evening, or two lovers embracing on a street corner. It might be a long nap in the middle of the afternoon or a face pointed up toward the warmth of the sun, a cool breeze on a hot day, a light rain over a parched earth.

What's Hot in Italy Today?

Alongside the deep-rooted traditions that help define Italian culture, modern Italy has once more become the trendsetter, reflected in the fads and fashions of the times. To grasp the trends is to understand a culture; what's hot and what's not says volumes about contemporary culture, whether you agree with the current tastes or not.

Here's a quick sample of what Italians are tuned in to today (obviously, trends are subject to change!):

1. SMS by mobile—text messaging using the keypad of cellular phones—is so popular in Italy that they've created their own language for it.

2. Drinking San Simone or *limoncello* after dinner.

3. Breil watches. The tagline in print ads reads: "Toglietemi tutto, ma non il mio Breil!" (Take everything, but not my Breil!)

4. Playing Lotto "Se non giochi, non vinci." (If you don't play, you don't win.)

5. The Vineria; similar to a wine bar, it's the place young singles go to mingle, and it's very *di moda* (trendy).

6. Giovanni and Giacomo Aldo from the movie *Tre uomini e una gamba* (*Three Men and a Leg*), presently two of Italy's most beloved comedians.

7. Having your hair done with sunstreaks "colpi di sole" (women and men, too).

8. Pizza with rucola (a bitter red lettuce).

9. Vanity license plates.

10. Colored sunglasses (those retro glasses that are also popular in the United States).

How to Approach Italy and Her Story

The purpose of this book is to whet your appetite to sample for yourself the many treats Italy has to offer. Through the ages, Italy has meant many different things to different people, so there is no one "correct" way to learn about Italy. You can approach Italy as you would a buffet table piled high with gastronomical delights. You can nibble a little of this, taste a little of that, stick with what you love, or try something new.

What is your *passione?* What do you adore? Do you go mad for Michelangelo? Start with the Renaissance. Do you love *la bella lingua* (the beautiful language)? Begin with Dante. Are you a film fanatic? Rent every Fellini film you can find. The journey starts with you. Use this book to help quench your thirst. You can read as much or little as the mood strikes you, skipping to the chapters that interest you most. Or, you can read it from cover to cover.

From grapes to grappa, from pilgrims to *putti,* from mamma to the *madonne,* countless volumes have been written about Italy and countless more will continue to be written because Italy is, and always will be, *di moda* (in fashion). After all, it has been setting the standard for some time.

Italy is like a river that continually renews itself, constantly evolving, always changing, yet somehow eternal. To get a complete picture of Italy, one must start at the beginning, with the Italian. What is it that makes an Italian an Italian? To answer this question, it might help to know a little more about that high-heeled boot standing in the middle of the Mediterranean. That's what we'll explore in the next chapter.

The Least You Need to Know

➤ Italy is a crossroads of history, culture, communication, and technology.

➤ Italy is a country of contrasts.

➤ Italy has always been a popular haunt for writers and artists.

➤ Italians have long been trendsetters in everything from fashion to food.

Che Panorama!

Take a look at Italy on a globe, in an atlas, or in Appendix D, "Map of Italy." What is its most distinguishing aspect? It's wonderful shape—the shape of the boot.

The Boot

If you took a picture of the Earth from the Moon, you would see that Italy looks just like a horseback rider's boot, right down to the little spur jutting out from the ankle. For this reason, Italy is probably one of the most easily identified countries in the world. Show any child a map of the high-heeled boot, and he or she will recognize it as *Italia*.

Divided by the Alps, Italy shares its northern borders with Austria, France, Switzerland, and Slovenia. A peninsula located in southern Europe, Italy is surrounded by water on three sides, extending 708 miles (1,139 kilometers) down into the Mediterranean Sea to northeast of Tunisia.

As if the country were destined to play soccer, the toe of the boot seems to be kicking the large island of Sicilia (pronounced *see-chee-lyah*). The knee of the boot points toward the similarly massive island of Sardegna (pronounced *sar-den-yah*), located a stone's throw south of the French island of Corsica. The Italian coastline, if spread out, would run 4,7290 miles long and is dotted with over 60 smaller islands.

From Puglia to Friuli-Venezia Giulia

Like the geographical and political divisions in the 50 states of the United States, there are 20 regions in Italy, within which several provinces are grouped. Five of those regions (Valle d'Aosta, Trentino-Alto Adige, Friuli-Venezia Giulia, Sardegna, and Sicilia) are given special autonomy for ethnic and historical reasons.

Within each region, you'll find individual provinces. For example, the region of Tuscany includes the provinces of Florence, Pisa, Lucca, and Siena. In the greater region of Sicily, you'll find the provinces Taormina, Siracusa, Agrigento, Messina, and others.

Refer to the map in Appendix D to see these regions in relation to one another. When the name of a region has been anglicized, it is offered in parentheses.

The regions are as follows:

L'Abruzzo	Il Molise
La Basilicata	Il Piemonte (Piedmont)
La Calabria	La Puglia (Apulia)
La Campania	La Sardegna (Sardinia)
L'Emilia-Romagna	La Sicilia (Sicily)
Il Friuli-Venezia Giulia	La Toscana (Tuscany)
Il Lazio (Latium)	Il Trentino-Alto Adige
La Liguria	L'Umbria
La Lombardia (Lombardy)	La Valle d'Aosta
Le Marche	Il Veneto

The City-States Within

Within Italian borders exist two independent city-states, the Republic of San Marino and Vatican City.

As one of the world's smallest countries, *La Repubblica di San Marino* covers 24 square miles (roughly the same size as New York City's Manhattan island) and is a landlocked independent city-state located on the slope of Mount Titano near the Italian city of

Rimini. Like any self-respecting nation, San Marino has a capital, also called San Marino, and football team (that's the Italian term for "soccer team").

Vatican City is an independent sovereignty located within the city of Rome. A papal residence since 1377, the Vatican also has its own postal system, and citizens carry separate passports. You'll learn more about the Vatican and the many people that make up its vast, international network in Chapter 8, "Popes, Politics, and Power."

Home Is Where the Heart Is

The distinct cultures and myriad dialects found throughout the country are largely a result of Italy's landscape. Let's go back to a time before highways, cars, and tunnels, when the only way to get past the mountains was to go over them by foot or on the back of some poor beast. Travel was at best uncomfortable and slow, and people generally did not venture much farther than their own *paese,* an Italian word used to signify both "village" and "country" and used in many different idiomatic expressions that include *il Bel Paese* and the term *paesani.*

Even in today's fast-paced world, a strong regional pride often keeps inhabitants close to their birthplace. Deriving from the word campanile (bell tower), the Italian term *campanilismo* refers to a strong attachment to one's village or birthplace, something profoundly felt by Italians and their ancestors.

Get High!

At least three quarters of Italy consists of hills and include two mountain ranges that dominate the landscape. Running from west to east, the Alps (and the slightly lesser-known Dolomites) create a natural boundary between Italy and her alpine neighbors of France, Switzerland, and Austria. Aside from having made it difficult for barbarians to storm Italy from the north, the Alps serve as a physical natural barrier, protecting Italy from the colder weather of northern Europe. Just below the Alps are the rich and fertile plains of Lombardy and Emilia-Romagna and the Po Valley.

"*Italia*"

In Italics

September 3—The Sammarinesi celebrate the founding of the San Marino Republic with festivities that include a crossbow competition that dates back to the seventeenth century.

La Bella Lingua

paese: country; nation; land; place

il Bel Paese: Italy (the beautiful country)

i paesani: country folk

Paese che vai, usanza che trovi: When in Rome, do as the Romans do.

13

Then come the Apennines, which run along the length of the boot and divide Italy in two. As a result of the location of these mountain ranges, the Italian climate varies greatly from north to south, east to west.

Sea That!

From the Amalfi coast to the Costa Smeralda, there is no escaping the sea. Long before there were established borders, foreign invaders such as the Greeks bombarded Italy's coastlines, establishing trading posts and camps. Later, the Romans used the seas to expand their empire. Explorers like Colombo and Vespucci, Caboto and Verrazano traveled by sea. Emigrants looking for a better life left by the sea. Their sons and daughters returned by the sea. This tie to *il mare* might explain why so many Italian immigrants settled in cities near large bodies of water like New York, Boston, San Francisco, and Chicago.

Fed by rivers such as the region of Lathium's Tiber and Tuscany's Arno, Italy is surrounded by five different seas. Near the city of Genoa and along the Italian Riviera lies the tiny Ligurian Sea. South of the small island of Elba one hits upon the Tyrrhenian Sea, which runs down to the north coast of Sicily. To the east lies the larger Adriatic sea. Beneath the sole of the boot rests the Ionian Sea. All these seas run into the larger Mediterranean Sea.

Di Interessa

Italy's highest peak is Monte Bianco (Mont Blanc) at 4,807 meters above sea level. The Dolomites are a group of 30 or so massifs in a wide arc that reaches from Lake Garda to the Austrian border. The pinkish-orange limestone is a vestige left over from ancient coral reefs.

Di Interessa

The maritime region of Liguria is home to Italy's largest port, Genoa, which was the birthplace of none other than Cristoforo Colombo, also known as Christopher Columbus.

In the Middle of the Earth

The temperate Mediterranean climate has been drawing visitors for centuries. The word Mediterranean literally means "in the middle of the earth," and for many people the mere mention of the word Mediterranean evokes images of baskets of bread and fountains of wine. Barring the natural disasters that occasionally besiege the country, under ideal conditions one finds plenty of sunshine, blue skies, sparkling azure waters, and a gentle breeze. It rains just enough, but not too much. Fig, orange, and lemon trees blossom in spring, grow heavy with fruit, and are harvested in fall. The sea provides fish. The sheep produce wool. The goats provide meat and milk and cheese. At special times, the earth graciously offers truffles and other delicacies. The gnarled branches of olive trees extend their arms with munificence and oil drizzles from ceramic vases. Sounds like *paradiso,* no?

Then there's the other side of the coin. Visit Florence during the rainy season in November and you can feel the chill seep through your bones. Drive through the thick forests and wild countryside of the Dolomites and you'll be hard-pressed to find an olive tree. As a result of the hot siroccos that travel from Africa, the climate of Sicily can be unbearably hot and dry. And the beautiful beaches of the Costa Smeralda (the Emerald Coast) on the island of Sardinia do little to mitigate the effects of a rainless sky.

How Far to Rome?

The centrally located city of Rome neatly divides the country into north and south. It's a surprise to many to realize that the cities of Rome and New York are practically on the same latitude. But unfortunately for New Yorkers, they won't see any palm trees growing on Park Avenue as they would in Piazza di Spagna, one of Rome's more elegant districts.

Di Interessa

The Republic of Italy (population 58,000,000) covers 116,332 square miles (301,300 square kilometers), roughly the same as the state of Arizona (population 5,000,000).

Di Interessa

Many Italian cities are spelled and pronounced differently in English and Italian. Here are a few of them:

Florence	Firenze	Rome	Roma
Genoa	Genova	Turin	Torino
Naples	Napoli	Venice	Venezia
Padua	Padova		

Along with the varied landscape, Italy's regions all possess their own traditions, customs, recipes, and dialects. (In Chapter 5, "The Sound of Music," you'll learn more about the many different dialects spoken up and down the peninsula.) Tuscany's sophisticated charms give way to the more rustic quality of Umbria's hills. The combed and cosmopolitan beaches along the Italian Riviera stand in stark contrast with the grottos nestled along the Sardinian coast.

Di Interessa

Who says you have to go to Italy to see Italian cities? California has its own Venice. New York has a Rome, and New Jersey has a Florence.

Di Interessa

In the Italian northern region of Trentino-Alto Adige just outside the Austrian border, the majority of people speak both Italian and German. Not surprisingly, German is taught in schools and used in legal documents.

Water, Water Everywhere

The gods weren't crazy when they made Italy their home base. The Romans saw the natural harmony between the wet mountains and the parched plains. Although wells and cisterns provided ancient Rome's citizens with enough water, it was the construction of massive public works projects such as the aqueducts that allowed towns to build the elaborate bathhouses and public fountains that came to be the cornerstone of Roman society.

Under the direction of Appius Claudius, who was Rome's censor in 312 C.E., the ingenious Romans enlisted a few thousand slaves and hauled huge blocks of stone to create the first aqueduct, called the Aqua Appia. Remnants of this enormous public works project can still be seen throughout the Sabine Hills just north of Rome, and down to Rome itself.

What began as a necessity was soon elevated to an art form as Roman baths became the rage both inside Rome and in party towns like Pompeii and seaports like Ostia Antica. More than 2,000 years later, visitors from around the world come to the many hot springs scattered up and down the peninsula for their therapeutic properties.

Today, remnants of the ancient waterways and fountains can be found throughout the Sabine hills and in Rome proper. Numerous spas dot the countryside where—in true Roman fashion—visitors can have a mud bath and rinse off in the steaming hot springs!

In Italics

November 4, 1966—Venice found herself under three feet of water as a result of gale-force winds, an earth tremor, and two successive high tides. Miraculously, there were no injuries and no artwork destroyed by water damage. Not so for Florence, who on that same day suffered a similar plight when the Arno River overflowed its banks and flooded many ground-level buildings that included museums and storage areas. As a result, countless manuscripts and paintings were destroyed.

Natural Disasters

Italians are no strangers to the whims of nature and the peninsula has seen its share of tidal waves, volcanoes, earthquakes, mudslides, and flooding. In fact, it was a series of natural disasters in Italy that forced many southern Italians to sell everything they owned, leave their families, and endure great hardships to find a better life. (You'll learn more about these immigrants in Chapters 4, "From Shore to Shore," and 18, "The Island of Tears.")

"Italia"

In Italics

August 24, 79 C.E.—The volcano Mount Vesuvius erupted, transforming the southern city of Pompeii from a vibrant, crowded city into a ghost town. The victims included the Roman historian Pliny the Elder, whose nephew Pliny the Younger escaped harm and recorded the horrific event in great detail. In describing the catastrophe and its aftermath, he wrote, "We were terrified to see everything changed, buried deep in ashes like snowdrifts." Its inhabitants were frozen in place until excavations in the seventeenth century led to the discovery of the buried city.

Di Interessa

Italy is a tectonic hot spot, which accounts for the number of hot springs and volcanoes that dot the peninsula. Aside from Mount Vesuvius, you may have also heard of Mounts Etna and Stromboli. It even has a volcano called Mount Vulcano.

La Bella Lingua

Lo zoccolo refers to the platform shoe worn by Venetian ladies during the Renaissance.

Earthquakes, for instance, continue to shake things up, including the one that occurred in 1997 in Assisi—where St. Francis was born—when the city suffered a series of tremors that caused billions of lire in damage. (Unfortunately, a priceless fresco by the painter Cimabue also was destroyed, though several others painted by Giotto managed to survive.)

Today, although Italians may be able to mobilize much faster than they could during Pliny's time, they're still just as vulnerable to the whims of Mother Nature (and what a fickle creature she is) as were her ancestors. Avalanches continue to steal lives every year high up in the Alps. Excessive rain causes devastating landslides, high tides cause flooding in the plains. Fires wipe out entire forests.

Save Venice!

Venetians are veterans at enduring floods. During the Renaissance, they even invented a special shoe called *lo zoccolo,* a type of platform clog designed to keep their feet above the muck. Unfortunately, the heavy impact local industry has had on the water tables below Venice has significantly exacerbated the flooding. Steps are being made to see how to arrest the slow and steady deterioration of the floating city, but there is nothing that can be done to control the force of the winds and the power of the Adriatic Sea lapping against the sides of the gondolas that grace Venice's canals.

Trouble in Paradise

Venice is not the only city struggling against modern "progress." Perhaps not so apparent but just as alarming, Italy faces another problem: pollution. Milan has one of the highest levels of recorded sulfur dioxide pollution in the world. The Coliseum is slowly crumbling from the constant vibration of Rome's incessantly heavy traffic. Excessive fishing and inadequate industrial waste treatment facilities have polluted the Adriatic. Acid rain is damaging lakes like northern Italy's Lago di Como and Lago di Garda.

There's Hope

It's not all gloom and doom, however. Today, the Italians are mobilizing to begin the arduous task of righting these wrongs before it's too late. Legambiente is an Italian organization dedicated to the preservation of the environment and conservation matters. The Green political party has utilized a popular party slogan *ambiente, agricoltura, alimentazione* ("environment, agriculture, food") to oppose the introduction of "Frankenfood," any bioengineered or genetically modified food currently being sold in the European Union market.

And throughout Italy, in cities like Florence, cars are banned from the city center during "car-less Sunday"—a new measure being introduced to counter the effects of car pollution and to make people more aware of alternative transportation solutions.

Di Interessa

Many of Italy's florists get their flowers from Liguria. Due to its mild winter, flowers of all varieties grow in neat rows of brightly colored blooms throughout the year, including February.

Festa Anyone?

Meanwhile, life goes on. The Italians, ever mindful of the preciousness of the moment, find ample opportunity to celebrate. If not on holiday such as the cherished *Ferragosto*, almost every city, town, and village has a special celebration traceable to the past. Whether a festival, regatta, or religious procession, these events are an integral part of Italian life and one way in which the multitude of traditions and customs of Italy endure. You'll learn more about the many ways Italians celebrate in Chapter 21, "Life Is a *Carnevale*."

In addition, to the major holidays of Christmas and Easter, where just about every village in every province does something special to celebrate, there's a plethora of opportunities to party. These celebrations are one of the things that define the Italians like nothing else, and without a doubt what draws millions of tourists from all over the world.

La Bella Lingua

Coinciding with the religious feast of the Assumption of Mary on August 15, *Ferragosto* refers to the vacation taken during the month of August, when Italy's highways are jammed with scores of vacationing Italians from the cities heading toward the sea and leaving the cities to the tourists. Many businesses, museums, and churches have limited hours during this time.

Often linked to a religious tradition, with roots stemming back to pagan times, many of these festivals have found their way abroad. The San Gennaro feast in New York City, for example, is a weeklong festival filled with colorful banners, games, and Italian foods in honor of San Gennaro, the patron saint of Naples. The occasional liquefaction of a vial of the saint's blood is considered an amazing miracle that is dealt with in more depth in Chapter 24, "Weeping Statues and the Blood of San Gennaro."

A Sampling of Feste

Visit the seaside town of Viareggio or the city of Venice during the cold and bleak month of February and witness the spectacle of revelers dressed in elaborate costumes during *Carnevale* (carnival). Otherwise, if you happen to find yourself in Venice in September, you can witness *la Regatta,* a historical boat race that takes place on Venice's Grand Canal.

Rome participates in the *Festa della Primavera* (Spring Festival), a citywide folk festival that offers typical Roman cuisine, music, and dancing. In the medieval city of Siena, villagers celebrate the Palio, a traditional event that pits one neighborhood against the other in a colorful, boisterous, and hotly contested horse race. Florence hosts the annual *Maggio Musicale* celebrating Renaissance music and culture, costumes, and of course, food.

Filled with traditional costumes, hand-painted carts, and the classic Sicilian puppets called *I Pupi,* the city of Taormina on the island of Sicily is famous for its *Raduno del Costume e del Carretto Siciliano* (Festival of Costumes and Sicilian Carts), a lavish event that commemorates the Knights of the Round Table and the paladins of Charlemagne.

Sometimes, the festivals are more outlandish and include events like the noted *Festa della Arance* (Orange Festival), where villagers from the town of Ivrea pelt one another with—take a wild guess—oranges. On October 4, Assisi honors Italy's patron saint during *la Festa di San Francesco* (the Feast of Saint Francis), with religious ceremonies and singing.

What makes these festivals so interesting? The Italians themselves, as you will soon learn in Chapter 3, "Who Are the Italians?"

The Least You Need to Know

➤ Italy is a land insulated on three sides by water like a castle surrounded by a moat. As a result, Italians are naturally drawn to the sea.

➤ The climate in Italy varies greatly from north to south.

➤ There are 20 regions in Italy, each having its own distinct customs, traditions, and languages.

➤ Almost every Italian town celebrates a special day with a festival.

Chapter 3

Who Are the Italians?

In This Chapter

➤ Italians come in many shapes and sizes

➤ The family comes first

➤ Italian names say something

➤ Italian Americans trace their roots

Who are those Italians anyway? What makes an Italian Italian? Is it because he speaks Italian? Because she was born in Italy?

You probably have a picture in your head of what an Italian looks and acts like, which may or may not be accurate. There are quite a few stereotypes floating around, but how close to the truth are these images?

What Makes an Italian?

Some might say that an Italian is someone who lives in Italy and eats spaghetti every night. While it is true that most Italians do eat a lot of pasta, as you may recall from Chapter 2, "*Che Panorama!*" the different regions are more than lines drawn on a map. Each region has its own traditions, customs, and unique history, resulting in myriad distinct cultures within the wider Italian borders. One sees this clearly enough in the dialects, where a girl in Rome might be called *ragazza,* and in Florence *fanciulla.* Nevertheless, she is still *Italiana.*

Let's make things clear here: Italy is a culture, not a race. If ever there were a melting pot, it would be Italy. In fact, all Italians are descendants of immigrants, an amalgam of all the cultures in Europe, the Middle East, and North Africa. You'll learn more about some of these influences in Chapter 6, "Rome Wasn't Built in a Day."

Prior to its unification in 1861, there was no Italy per se. Rather, the peninsula was a patchwork of city-states, each with its own history, customs, traditions, and languages. You'll learn more about how Italy was unified in Part 4, "Redshirts, Blackshirts, and Greenshirts."

Even after they achieved political unity, Italy's rulers still had to figure out a way to forge a national identity. This was not an easy task considering the tensions between north and south, the lack of a common language (because of the different dialects), and contrasting views among the people about how to run the country, who should run it, and for how long.

La Bella Lingua

The Italian language has endless variety among the various Italian regions. Just consider the different ways of expressing the word "girl." In Rome, they say *la ragazza;* in Florence, *la fanciulla;* and in slang, *la bimba.*

Di Interessa

The separatist *Lega Nord* (Northern League) political party promotes the idea of the "Northern Republic of Padania" and strongly supports secession from Italy.

A World of Italians

Think of it this way: The Piedmontese probably relate as much to their French brothers as they do to their Swiss sisters. Italians living in the northern regions of Lombardy and Trentino-Alto Adige, which border Switzerland and Austria, study both Italian and German and official documents are generally written in both languages. Often, it is not much different than the relationship between two neighboring states such as New Jersey and New York. No doubt we can all agree that there's a world of difference between the fast pace of New York and sun-kissed state of California. Wear a Stetson outside of Texas and you'll get some strange looks. Yet, all these people still consider themselves first and foremost American.

Similarly in Italy there are Jewish Italians and Hindu Italians and Muslim Italians and Buddhist Italians and Protestant Italians and Jehovah's Witness Italians, and plenty of atheist Italians. Not to mention the communists, the socialists, the Christian Democrats, the anarchists, and all in between. Add to this number the Italian expatriates who live around the world, as well as the millions of Italian descendents, who—in spite of the fact that they don't even speak Italian—consider themselves of Italian origin, and do so with great patriotism, regardless of their citizenship.

I'm Not Italian, I'm Siciliano

Allegiances naturally reflect all this diversity. Someone from the southern island of Sicily would first be *Siciliano,* then Italian. A *Fiorentino* from the central region of Tuscany would sooner declare allegiance to *la Toscana* than he would to a *Calabrese* (someone from the region of Calabria, located in the toe of the boot), who in turn would distinguish himself from a northerner *Milanese.*

Interestingly enough, if you were to pit an Italian soccer team consisting of players from Palermo to Parma, you would find a unified front against, say, the English, but once the battle was over, everyone would go back to their first allegiance, *la famiglia,* their second being one's *paese* (hometown).

There's an old Italian saying, *stessa faccia stessa razza* (same face same race) that alludes to the loose definition of what constitutes the notion of "Italian-ness." Essentially, the expression strives to communicate the idea that if you look like us (dress like us, speak like us, feel like us), you must be one of us.

Biografia

Until the Spanish Inquisition, nearly 10 percent of Sicily's population was Jewish. Often, the names were vaguely Hebrew, such as Mosa or di Mosa (of Moses), and Palumbo (the direct translation of Jonah). Other names reflected typically Jewish professions, such as Ferro (iron monger) and Orifice (goldsmith).

Paper Cut-Outs

It is difficult to describe the Italians without resorting to using stereotypes, quite a feat when you're talking about a *cultura* made up of so many unique individuals. Stereotypes simplify, illustrate, and generalize. They allow us to distinguish ourselves from "others" (meaning anyone other than one's immediate clan), provide an image we can all easily identify, and often contain a grain of truth. Just as often, however, they can limit our perceptions and hinder the ability to see things clearly. Today's media-driven images of Italians and Italian Americans make it hard to separate fact from fiction (although sometimes the lines do blur).

Whether Latin lovers, mobsters, singing peasants, widows dressed in black, or mischievous children, the images fed to us by the media are often too flat to adequately describe the Italian. One stereotypical image we have is of the hard-working, self-sacrificing Italian immigrant, ready to work himself

Di Interessa

The Palio horse race takes place every year in the Tuscan city of Siena where various *contrade* (teams) use different mascots such as the *il porcospino* (porcupine) and *la giraffa* (the giraffe) to represent competing neighborhoods. Although the competition can be fierce, everyone shares in a huge citywide celebration after the races.

to death in the hopes of improving conditions for his children. Then there's the happy-go-lucky, singing, passionate, and burly Italian male, as full of himself as a rooster (or a *pappagallo*) and ready to sire a nation. There's the educated thinker, the dark-eyed gangster, the Latin lover, the tortured artist, the broken-hearted poet, the skilled athlete, the smooth-talking politician, the happy chef, the despot ... the list goes on.

Is he Marcello Mastroianni or Roberto Benigni? Benito Mussolini or Federico Fellini? Mario Cuomo or Molto Mario? Al Pacino or Frank Sinatra? (You'll learn more about famous Italians in Part 6, "Italy's Exports.")

The Italian female is just as elusive. In the old days, you could flip through a copy of *National Geographic* and find her dressed as a peasant, cheerily carrying a basket of grapes on top of her head somewhere in the countryside. (Picture, if you will, vineyards in the background, a pair of oxen lumbering up a hill, a castle perched atop a hill.) If you're of Italian descent, you could sit on a sofa and peruse your family albums. There you might see your great-grandmother dressed in black wearing a scarf over her head, surrounded by solemn-faced children (one of whom is your father) on the open deck of an old ship.

Today you can open a copy of *Vogue*, and she's barely dressed in Versace, strutting down a catwalk. Turn on the television and you'll see her standing at a podium daring to break down every stereotype of the "weaker sex."

So who is the Italian female? Is she Caterina de Medici, or Santa Caterina da Siena (St. Catherine of Siena)? Is she the painter Artemesia Gentileschi or artist Georgia O'Keefe? Eleonora Duse or Geraldine Ferraro? Sophia Loren or Camille Paglia? You'll learn more about amazing Italian women, and their ancestors, in Chapter 23, "Mamma and the Madonna."

"*Italia*"

In Italics

1990—10,500 feet above sea level, the oldest and most well-preserved mummy ever discovered was found frozen in the Alps between Italy and Austria. Experts believe that the mummy is about 5,300 years old.

Di Interessa

The term *pappagallo*, which literally means "parrot," is actually used to refer to Italy's wolf-whistlers, those young men often found lounging near popular tourist destinations.

Ciao Gorgeous

Is it the food? The Mediterranean sun? Something in the air? The clothes? Is it the olive skin and dark, soulful eyes? The slender build? The graceful walk? The glitter of a gold chain dangling casually off a slender wrist?

Are they born that way? Or is it something created? That may be part of the Italian way, a combination of good luck and a natural sense of style. With all those travelers passing through Italian soil, some were bound to stick around, resulting in a melting pot of different tribes, races, cultures, and creeds. Although Italians often do possess olive skin and dark hair and eyes, there are plenty of fair-skinned, blue-eyed, blond Sicilians. (A glance back in time shows years of occupation by the northern Normans and German descendants, the *Longobardi* [Lombards], named as such for their long beards.)

La Famiglia È Sacra

Ever wonder why Italians are so loyal to their families? You can't watch a movie without seeing the importance of *la famiglia* expressed in every frame. From *The Godfather* to *Life Is Beautiful*, the Italian attachment to the family is inescapable.

Nothing beats love, and surely the Italians love their families, but there's also a slightly more practical reason (if slightly less romantic) that also contributed to the strong loyalties Italians feel toward their families. Dating back to Roman times, where legal heirs were sometimes obtained through adoption, and later during the turbulent Middle Ages, in a world of constantly shifting political allegiances, if you didn't stick close to the family, you were asking for trouble. This concept is so ingrained in the Italian psyche that it continues to be a sacred institution. The notion of family is the thread that runs beyond national borders and extends to Italians wherever they may roam. (This explains why many Italian Americans are so warmly received when retracing their roots.)

In spite of a long family tradition, however, the idea of a family name, or surname, did not come until the Renaissance.

Di Interessa

In ancient Roman society, the Vestal Virgins were by far the most powerful women (outside the imperial family). It was considered a great honor to be chosen for the job, which included helping prepare the religious sacrifices and tending the sacred fire.

La Bella Lingua

The expression "*La famiglia è sacra*" (the family is sacred) reflects the respect, love, and loyalty most Italians feel toward their family.

What's in a Name?

Prior to the thirteenth and fourteenth centuries, most individuals had only a "Christian" or first name. The only way to distinguish between two people with the same name was through further description. For example, imagine you have two friends named Leonardo and you're talking to your mother. She asks, "Which

La Bella Lingua

Feudalism refers to the political and social system that existed in Italy and Europe from the ninth century to about the fifteenth century based on the relationship between landowning lords (hence the term "landlord") and their vassals.

Leonardo?" You respond, "You know, Leonardo from Vinci." She says, "Oh, that one!"

By the time *feudalism* ended and everyday people started to acquire a certain degree of autonomy and wealth, however, the need for surnames became a necessity.

Names were not simply picked from a hat. You've probably never realized how many Italian names are descriptive. For example, Mr. Rosso may be a descendent of a redhead. Mr. Bianchi's relative may have had very pale skin, whereas the Longo family was more than likely long-limbed and tall. Mr. Tedesco probably came from German extraction. Mr. Iovino was probably a vintner.

Biografia

In Italy, you won't find too many children named Moon Unit or Dweezil, two Italian Americans best known as the children of the late Frank Zappa. Generally, the first son is often named after his paternal grandfather, while the second son is named after his maternal grandfather. The first daughter is named after her paternal grandmother, while the second daughter is named after her maternal grandmother. Subsequent children are named after the parents or a favorite aunt or uncle.

Can Anyone Be Italian?

If you were born outside Italy but are of Italian descent, you may also be eligible to be considered an Italian citizen if any of the following situations pertains to you:

1. Your mother or father was an Italian citizen at the time of your birth, and you never renounced your right to Italian citizenship.

2. Your paternal grandfather was an Italian citizen at the time of your father's birth, and neither you nor your father ever renounced your Italian citizenship.

3. Your maternal grandmother was an Italian citizen at the time of your mother's birth, and neither you nor your mother ever renounced your Italian citizenship.

Tracing Your Genealogy

Think you're related to nobility? If you're of Italian extraction, you may want to research your roots. Even if you are not, the following information can help you re-discover your past.

➤ **Interview your relatives.** Find out the official first and last names of any ancestors. Keep in mind that Italians often took on nicknames that reflected their professions or personal attributes, such as Lucky Luciano, Salvatore "Sammy the Bull" Gravano, and John "Dapper Don" Gotti. (My own grandfather, Louis Euvino, was nicknamed "Lou Reno" during his boxing days.)

➤ **Find official records.** After you've collected a few stories, it's time to get into the attic and dust off the family records your grandmother may have meticulously kept. (If your grandmother was anything like mine, she was a pack rat.) Inside, look for birth certificates, marriage certificates, death certificates, and passenger records from Ellis Island. Perhaps you'll find a newspaper clipping or an old photograph that will help you in your search.

Di Interessa

Contrary to the stereotype of the large Italian family, Italy currently owns the record for the lowest birthrate in Europe.

This passenger record was found during a search of the Ellis Island Web site, www.ellisislandrecords.org.

Name:	SANFILIPPO, FILIPPO
Ethnicity:	ITALIAN SOUTH
Place of Residence:	AGIRA', SICILY
Date of Arrival:	14 APR 1909
Age on Arrival:	22
Gender:	M
Marital Status:	S
Ship of Travel:	MANUEL CALVO
Port of Departure:	Naples, Campania, Italy

➤ **Perform some research.** If you have no family records, you'll have to do a little sleuthing. Officials at Ellis Island have recently made public all records used to keep track of the scores of immigrants that flowed onto its shores. A call to your local Italian Consulate can help you locate vital census records.

➤ **Use the World Wide Web.** Type in the word "genealogy" and see what comes up. There are several sites devoted to assisting descendants retrace their lineage. (Check out the helpful directory offered in Appendix B, "Web Resources.")

➤ **Create a family tree.** Doing so will help you keep track of the many ancestors whose blood you share. The deeper you dig, the more you'll discover.

Share the information with your family members. You never know what memory might be triggered. You see, once an Italian, always an Italian!

Di Interessa

Many famous Italian Americans anglicized their Italian names, including the following:

Charles Atlas (Angelo Siciliano)

Tony Bennett (Anthony Benedetto)

John Cabot (Giovanni Caboto)

Dean Martin (Dino Crocetti)

In addition, many individuals' names were altered when passing through Ellis Island. (A simple vowel change was enough to alter the author's family name from Iovino to Euvino.)

The Least You Need to Know

➤ Italians identify as much with the region they come from as they do with their country.

➤ Prior to the thirteenth century, most people did not have surnames.

➤ If you've got the paperwork to prove it, you may be eligible to become an Italian citizen.

From Shore to Shore

They came in groups, bedraggled and tired and poor, sometimes with nothing more than the clothes on their backs, a tattered Bible, hearts filled with hope, minds occupied with fear, and with a strong determination to survive.

The typical Italian immigrant was neither wealthy nor educated. The men were mostly hard-working laborers from the southern cities and regions such as Calabria, Naples, Sorrento, and Sicily, often speaking dialects that even their own Italian compatriots could not understand. They had little if any formal education, and few prospects. Many left families behind, hoping to send much needed money back home or to save enough to bring them over to America. They were risk-takers willing to sacrifice personal comfort in order to provide a better life for their families.

Even if a majority of the Italians who left would never again step foot on Italian soil, their hearts and loyalties remained attached to the families and traditions they had left behind. These ties were so strong to *la madre patria* (the motherland) that three generations later, Italian Americans continue to uphold the traditions of their ancestors through stories and the passing on of recipes and photographs.

Who were these brave spirits? What compelled them to leave the earthly paradise most people think of when conjuring images of Italy?

Searching for Something Better

Prior to the 1880s, few Italians left their native country. Those who did—mostly migrant workers or political exiles such as Giuseppe Garibaldi—had little intention of remaining so far away from their homeland for very long. They traveled as far as Australia, the United States of America, Argentina, and Brazil.

"*Italia*"

In Italics

1855 to 1900—Castle Garden, an old fort located on the Battery in Manhattan, was the predecessor to Ellis Island.

Biografia

Mother Frances Cabrini (1850–1917) was the first American saint. Born in Lombardy, she arrived in New York in 1889 at the request of Pope Leo XII. She founded the Missionary Sister of the Sacred Heart in 1881 to help combat the desperate conditions of the immigrants. She was canonized in 1946.

What were the immigrants looking for and why did they leave Italy? As you may recall from Chapter 2, "*Che Panorama!*" Italy's varied geography lent itself to the creation of regional, cultural, and linguistic differences between east and west, north and south.

North of Rome, the opulent court culture that defined the Renaissance had given cities like Venice and Mantova a sheen never again replicated. The banking centers of Tuscany, including Pisa, Siena, and Florence, promoted trade and fostered economic growth. A thriving intellectual and cultured life contributed to an educated population. Although not everyone lived like a member of the wealthy Medici family, who were patrons of the arts, if you were resourceful, you could make ends meet.

South of Rome, it was a different story. The typical southern Italians were less educated than their northern cousins and possessed little chance of stepping out of the poverty that defined their existence. Up at dawn, many laborers walked miles to the fields, returning late at night. Food was scarce. Old feudalistic arrangements continued to keep the wealthy landowners prosperous while the landless remained poor. So it had been for centuries, and so it appeared it would remain until stories began circulating about opportunities in the New World. While many of the stories were exaggerations, the desperate conditions of the south offered little comfort. Things could not be much worse, many said, and soon, southern port cities like Naples were inundated with thousands of Italians hoping to find voyage across the Atlantic to *L'America*.

In Chapter 18, "The Island of Tears," you'll learn more about the challenges Italians faced and about the conditions that compelled them to leave in the first place.

They Came in Waves

What began as a trickle soon became a torrent, as wave after wave began to flood the New World.

The largest waves of immigration occurred after 1880. Most were *contadini* (peasant farmers) from the south and Sicily after a series of natural disasters—from tidal waves to earthquakes to crop disease—wiped out their only sources of income. Emigration was the only solution that offered a ticket out of centuries of oppression and poverty. Between 1901 and 1910 more than two million Italians arrived in the United States.

Another wave of immigrants arrived around World War I. A majority of those who came to these shores were fleeing the war and evading the draft in Italy. Others were coming for the same economic reasons their predecessors had: a better life than the one the ever war-struck Italy could offer. You'll learn more about the affects war had on Italy in Chapter 19, "The World at War."

New Land, New Problems

It's probably hard to imagine now how difficult it must have been then to leave everything familiar and start a new life in a foreign land. Compare how easily and inexpensively we travel today— booking our flights online, driving our cars to the airport, sitting on a plane where we are served a hot meal and a glass of wine, and several hours later, calling home via satellite. The immigrant from Southern Italy had it much harder. He spent whatever life savings he had on the boat ticket to *L'America*. Once on board, he and his family spent almost two weeks on a crowded vessel tossing and turning as the boat made its way across *l'Atlantico*.

Most of the earlier ships making the trans-Atlantic voyage had simply changed their cargo from live-stock to people. Although the newer and more spacious ships that came later certainly improved conditions, the majority of Italians going to America traveled in third-class steerage; forced to pass most of the trip below the water line, even the most hearty were affected by the foul air and

"*Italia*"

In Italics

1848—The discovery of gold in the American West lured Italians to leave the East Coast and head for California.

Di Interessa

The American classic "Home Sweet Home" was inspired by an Italian love song overheard by John Howard Payne while visiting Sicily.

crowded accommodations. Having long been city-dwellers, most of the immigrants were headed off to the crowded cities of New York, Chicago, New Orleans, and San Francisco.

Home Is Where the Heart Is

Once on American shores, the average immigrant faced a number of challenges. He or she had to find a place to live, secure work, and learn a new language. Often the plan was simple: make enough money to send back home and eventually return to Italy, once things got better. (More likely, the immigrant did not return to Italy for the simple reason that things were better—why fix something if it isn't broken?)

Millions of immigrants possessed skills that had little or no value in America. If they were lucky, the men found work on railroads and pick and shovel gangs, digging, hauling, and building. (These hard workers would help construct many American buildings, bridges, and roads still being used today.) The women worked in sweat factories, or with the help of their children, performed tedious piece work sewing at home.

The typical immigrant home consisted of a cramped tenement apartment that was probably shared with aunts, uncles, grandparents, and children in a predominantly Italian neighborhood. Unmarried men lived in crowded boarding houses with other Italians, often from the same village.

Di Interessa

The tomato, central to the Italian diet, did not reach Italian shores until traders brought them over to Europe from South America. Tomatoes were seldom eaten in North America until the Italian immigrants helped develop a taste for the *pomodoro* (apple of gold). It's hard to imagine a world without tomato sauce for your pizza and pasta!

"Italia"

In Italics

1910—The U.S. Immigration Commission documented that the average Italian male earned $396 a year. Compare that to the national average of $666. Even so, Italians were glad for the work.

The Italian Community

Village boundaries expand when you are 5,000 miles from home. One of the greatest compliments an Italian could pay to another was to consider him *paesano* (countryman), a common term of endearment used to refer to someone from the same region or province. The Italian community in the United States grew dramatically, with most immigrants settling in Italian colonies and forming tight knit communities in cities such as New York, Boston, and Chicago.

While the immigrants were glad for the work, they sacrificed their health, their youth, and their dreams in order to offer their children the chance to climb out of poverty. If you are of Italian descent, you may remember hearing stories about your grandfather, or his father, and how hard those years were. In Part 6, "Italy's Exports," you'll read more about how the Italian spirit prevailed, eventually bringing the success these visionaries projected.

Go Back Where You Came From

The majority of Italians emigrating to the United States, Australia, Brazil, and other parts of South America came from southern Italy. They spoke regional dialects, little English, and, by American standards, often had peculiar habits—such as using a cloudy, greenish oil (olive oil) on all their food, sending their children to school wearing garlands of garlic to ward off illness, etc.—that made them easy targets for discrimination.

As more Italians began to call America their home, anti-immigrant sentiment grew. Not-so-friendly neighbors did not think twice about throwing out snipes such as "wop," "dago," or "macaroni."

A group known as the Know-Nothing Party, whose slogan was "America for Americans," was particularly anti-Catholic, and thus the heavily Catholic Italians and Irish were targets. By 1856, the Know-Nothing Party had enough political strength to nominate former President Millard Fillmore as its candidate. Although its distorted values of bigotry and prejudice were never wholly embraced by the rest of the country, by 1896, the party had a million members promoting the idea of a Catholic-free United States.

Further impeding immigrant's assimilation into American society were Darwinian notions of racial superiority. In 1916, books like Madison Grant's *The Passing of the Great Race* asserted that anyone coming from the "lowest stratum of the Mediterranean" was "human flotsam." Italians were not alone in this classification, but Grant's words demonstrate how pervasive was the idea of racial superiority.

As a result, many Italians changed their names for the sake of success. Jim Flynn, the only boxer to knock out Jack Dempsey, was born Andrea Chiariglione. (Try saying that three times fast!)

La Bella Lingua

The disparaging term "wop" was used to describe the southern Italian who arrived at Ellis Island without proper documentation and therefore was labeled with the letters W.O.P. (without official papers). Other disparaging terms used to call the Italians include dago, duke, ghini, macaroni, or spaghetti.

Biografia

In 1933, Fiorello La Guardia (1882–1947) was elected mayor of New York. Known affectionately as the "Little Flower" (the translation of his first name), La Guardia worked tirelessly for workers' rights. Born to Italian immigrants, La Guardia is regarded as one of the New York's greatest leaders.

Considering the political climate and anti-immigrant sentiment of the times, is it any wonder the Italians stuck together? Here was a group that had come from the bed-rock of Western civilization, whose ancestors included the world's most brilliant artists, writers, architects, and philosophers. These were the children of the De Medici family and the ancestors of Michelangelo. Yet they were spit upon, exploited, and derided.

Biografia

Geraldine Ferraro (1935–) was the first woman and the first Italian American to ever run for Vice President of the United States. In spite of a stellar record, Ferraro's campaign was riddled with anti-Italian sentiment. She continues to be a trailblazer for women and Italian Americans.

In Italics

1905—The Sons of Italy was founded by Dr. Vincenzo Sallaro.

The Little Italys

In New York, Boston, Chicago, San Francisco, and other cities, Italians (as many groups before and since) formed communities and mutual benefit societies that helped workers get through the tough times. As the Italians improved their economic status, these societies eventually lent their talents to fighting defamation and stereotyping.

Little Italy formed near Mulberry Street in lower Manhattan due to its proximity to the ferry that dropped them off after being processed at Ellis Island. In time, Mulberry Street became the heart of Little Italy in New York and continues to be so to this day. Most New Yorkers—regardless their heritage—are familiar with the annual Feast of San Gennaro, a two-week-long celebration honoring the patron saint of Naples, the port from which so many Italians left their homeland forever.

By 1890, South Philly was the second largest Italian-American community in the United States. In Boston, it was the North End. In Chicago, the Near Westside became known as Little Sicily. Baltimore's Little Italy was near the port. In St. Louis, an Italian enclave was located at Dago Hill. San Francisco's Little Italy was located in North Beach.

Spaghetti and Bullets

While most Italian immigrants were forming civic groups and organizing benevolent societies, another organization was giving Italians a bad name. Indeed, few bad guys have been portrayed with such exaggerated romanticism as Al Capone and Lucky Luciano. From Francis Ford Coppola's rendition of Mario Puzo's novel *The Godfather* to the television show *The Sopranos* the big-bad-tough-guy image has proliferated in the media.

Although we cannot imagine living that way, we love watching these bad boys, whose power is such that, with one simple gesture, scores are settled and wrongs are righted, and the world is as it should be. Whatever the reason, the flip side of these depictions is that many Americans have the mistaken notion that these shows exemplify the typical Italian-American experience.

The origins of the secret society known as the Mafia or the Cosa Nostra go back to ninth-century Sicily, when foreign invaders forced a group of partisans to seek "Mafia," the Arabic word used to signify "refuge." The success of the organization rested on its strong commitment to its members, based on the values of loyalty and respect. Structured like a family, the head of every chapter was called a don—his word was not to be questioned.

By the eighteenth century, wealthy citizens were paying Black Hand notes to ensure protection. The protection was a sham, since the biggest threat came from the so-called protectors. By the late nineteenth century, the Mafia had grown to be a vast underground society. No authority was greater. Few attempts by the Italian government were successful in wrestling control from these Sicilian bullies.

It was natural that many Mafia members would find their way to American shores since it allowed them to avoid potential persecution. America presented ample opportunity for these opportunists to offer their "protective services" to the poor Italian immigrants living in American cities.

Some Mafia members became "bosses" by sponsoring a group of immigrants' trip to America. Once they arrived, these immigrants were forced to fulfill unfair contractual promises made before the naive immigrant understood what he was signing. Often this meant he was forced to work in gangs for little wages under slave-like conditions.

By the 1900s, the Mafia had shifted its focus to other means, including racketeering, gambling, and prostitution. The Prohibition era of the 1920s allowed them to amass huge amounts of wealth selling

Di Interessa

Prior to becoming the mayor of New York in 1994, Rudolph Giuliani prosecuted several organized crime leaders while serving as a United States attorney.

Di Interessa

During the 1880s, New Orleans contained the largest Mafia base in the country.

Di Interessa

Jimmy Hoffa, the former Teamsters union president, was probably the most corrupt union leader until he mysteriously disappeared in 1975.

bootleg liquor. The Mafia had its hand in just about every aspect of business, controlling criminal rackets as well as legitimate businesses. You'll learn more about the Mafia in Chapter 20, "Myth and Magic."

The Dream Lives On

Early immigrants made incredible sacrifices in order to give their children and their grandchildren a better life, and to a large extent, they were successful. Today, most Italian Americans are proud of their heritage and do honor to their new homeland, but never forgetting where they come from. If you're of Italian descent, pat yourself on the back and thank whichever of your relatives brought your family here. If it weren't for them, you would not be reading this book!

The Least You Need to Know

➤ The Italian immigrants came in several waves. Many fled poverty.

➤ Italians experienced a great deal of anti-immigrant sentiment.

➤ The Italians formed community organizations such as the Sons of Italy and the Missionary Sisters of the Sacred Heart.

➤ Almost every great city has a Little Italy.

➤ The Mafia began as a secret society in ninth-century Italy. Its influence on American life began with immigration.

The Sound of Music

Even without understanding a word, it is possible to be seduced by a voice, especially when that voice is speaking Italian.

When you put several Italian voices together, you have a *concerto*. This symphony of language is what I call *la bella lingua* (the beautiful Italian language).

Express Yourself

If it wasn't the food that first attracted you to the Italian culture, then it was probably the language. Listening to Italians speak is truly a musical experience. There's the effortless rolling of Rs, the tender vowels, the occasional exaggerated tone, the melodious cadence. Most important, of course, is the *espressione*. As we all know, the Italians are masters of expression, whether artistic, musical, or linguistic.

Languages are not born, they evolve. The history of the Italian language begins with classical Latin, the literary language of ancient Rome. Latin originally developed in central Italy in the area known as Latium. Eventually, Latin became the official language of Rome.

There's a Write Way and a Wrong Way

Around the time of Julius and Augustus (60 B.C.E.–15 C.E.), through the efforts of writers such as Cicero, Virgil, and Horace, a codified version of the Latin language was developed that had fixed rules of grammar, syntax, and meaning. The creators of these rules held them to be perfect, establishing that there was a "write" way and a wrong way to write Latin. (This was not necessarily the case with the spoken language because of the many variations that were used throughout the vast Roman Empire.)

As you may recall from Chapter 2, "*Che Panorama!*" the Italian peninsula was as well-traveled in Caesar's era as it is today. After the fall of the Roman Empire, while the educated elite and the members of the Church wrote classical Latin, the spoken form of the language took a life of its own. This "*vulgar*" language came to be replace Latin as the single language used in the peninsula.

Influenced by the constant stream of invaders, traders, and barbarians, each region began to develop its own vernacular, which furthered the split between classic Latin and Vulgar Latin. Eventually the verbal use of Latin waned and finally died down. The language that had once been used by the Roman leaders Caesar, Augustus, and the scholar Pliny the Elder only existed in written form. You'll learn more about these important players in Chapter 6, "Rome Wasn't Built in a Day."

Today's Romance languages (including French, Spanish, Portuguese, and Rumanian) all derived from vulgar Latin, and Italian is the Romance language closest to Latin, sharing many common roots and terms used in Latin. For example, the Italian word *carnevale* (carnival) dervies from the Latin stem *carn*, meaning "flesh." The word *verbo* (verb) finds its origins in the Latin word *verbum* (word). As you might have noted, many English words also share these common Latin roots.

In Chapter 2 you learned about the different regions, all of which possess their own variations of Italian. Primarily because this was the language used by the great

Di Interessa

Prior to the Romans, some of the larger ethnic groups living within the Italian peninsula included the Etruscans (giving Tuscany its name), Faliscans, Oscans, and Umbrians. Combined with Latin, these Italic languages gave birth to what we now call Italian.

La Bella Lingua

In linguistic parlance, the term **vulgar** refers to a form of language spoken by ordinary people. Vulgar Latin was the language spoken across the peninsula, eventually transmuting into the language we now call Italian.

medieval writers Dante, Petrarca, and Boccaccio. Tuscan Italian is the standard language read in newspapers, heard on the radio, and listened to on television. It's the language used in official documents and what is taught to schoolchildren.

In the Beginning: Dante

One of the first to write down the spoken language of the people was a Florentine named Dante Alighieri (1265–1321). A philosopher and man of letters, Dante is considered one of the most important poets that ever lived. As an educated man, Dante was quite familiar with classical Latin.

The classical Latin used by the Church was not, however, the language used when Dante went to the *taverna* for a glass of *vino* and a bite of *pane*. Through the narrow, crowded streets of Florence, the Florentines had their own language. It was the language that mothers spoke to their children and that merchants used with customers.

An instant bestseller, Dante's masterpiece, *The Divine Comedy,* was a long vernacular poem written in the Tuscan dialect that recounted the tale of the poet's journey through Hell, Purgatory, and Heaven. Composed during Dante's exile from Florence, the book was written in *terza rima,* a complex verse form in pentameter with interlocking triads rhyming aba, bcb, cdc, etc. The highly symbolic and imaginative poem offers readers insight on the medieval perspective as it follows the poet on his trip. In fact, modern educated Italians continue to study Dante's fourteenth-century poetry without too much difficulty, and his book has been translated into dozens of languages. (Imagine the royalties he would have collected!)

Dante was not the only one to transcribe the language of everyday life; others like Boccaccio and Petrarca would follow Dante's example, and soon, Tuscan Italian became the rage. You'll learn more about these important literary figures in Chapter 9, "Leaving the Middle Ages." Their works eventually came to be used as models of grammar, assisting in the development of a fixed standard for the Italian language.

Today, Latin is only used during Mass.

"Italia"

In Italics

Thirteenth century—The use of the vernacular in literature begins with the "Stil Novo" ("new style") poets from Sicily and Tuscany. For the first time, the spoken language was put into written form, allowing for the development of a specific set of rules.

Di Interessa

Although there were many regional vernaculars used during the thirteenth and fourteenth centuries, the Tuscan city of Florence's superior cultural, artistic, and political status led to the predominance of the Florentine dialect. More than any living language, Tuscan Italian most resembles Latin.

Kissing Cousins: Dialects

A *dialect* is a variation of a language, usually particular to a region and often quite different from the standard spoken and written language. Italy's culture and history is a fusion of different influences that have resulted in the development of several regional dialects.

Through television, radio, and efforts by the government to linguistically unite the peninsula, Tuscan Italian is the official standard language used. However, the dialects continue to be spoken and most Italians are familiar with at least one, if not two, dialects.

Take Gianni, for example. An Italian born in Rome whose *mamma* was born in Sicily and whose father was born in Milan, Gianni speaks Italian to his teacher, Roman to his friends, Sicilian to his mother, and Milanese to his father.

Ciao!

La Bella Lingua

A **dialect** is a regional variation of a language that differs from the standard in vocabulary, grammar, and pronunciation; a form of language spoken by members of a particular social class or profession; a nonstandard spoken language.

Some dialects actually sound and work like different languages altogether. Up north in Lombardia, a region once ruled by Austria, you can hear a distinctly German accent and a softening of the Rs. In the Piedmont, you can hear French influences. The colorful Napoletano dialect possesses traces of Spanish and French. Down in Calabria, Greek can be detected.

There are many regional dialects. Some of the main dialects used in the peninsula include Ligurian, Lombardian, Milanese, Napoletano, Piedmontese, Romano, Siculo, Umbrian, and Veneto. Both Sicilian and Sardo are considered by many to be languages in their own right. For example, during news coverage of an earthquake in Sicily, Italian television stations used Italian subtitles beneath the emotional testimonials of the Sicilian-speaking locals.

The Most Important Phrases You'll Ever Need to Know

For those of you interested in learning the Italian language, you may want to take an Italian class or pick up a book or two. For now, the following (extracted from *The Complete Idiot's Guide to Learning Italian*) should get you started.

The stressed syllable is in **bold**.

Italian	Pronunciation	English
Salve.	*sal-veh*	Greetings.
Buon giorno.	*bwon jor-noh*	Good morning/day.
Buona sera.	*bwoh-nah seh-rah*	Good evening.
Buona notte.	*bwoh-nah noh-teh*	Good night.
Ciao! (familiar)	*Chow*	Bye!
Sì.	*See*	Yes.
No.	*No*	No.
Per favore.	*per fah-**voh**-reh*	Please.
Grazie.	***grah**-tsee-yeh*	Thank you.
Mi scusi.	*mee skoo-zee*	Excuse me.
Prego.	*preh-goh*	You're welcome.
Mi dispiace.	*mee dees-pee-**ah**-cheh*	I'm sorry.
Aiuto!	*ah-**yoo**-toh*	Help!
Dov'è ...?	*doh-**veh***	Where is ...?
Quanto?	*kwahn-toh*	How much?

Di Interessa

If you want to express you have (or have not) understood something, in Italian you would say:

Capisco.	*kah-pee-skoh*	I understand.
Non capisco.	*non kah-pee-skoh*	I don't understand.

Gestures

I would not be doing justice to the Italian language if I did not mention the language of gestures. How efficient is this language? If you were to turn the sound off of an Italian movie, I wager that you would have no problem identifying the emotions being expressed.

There are enough Italian hand gestures to fill books, and some of them are truly vulgar, while others are more sentimental. Indeed, although the Italians are by nature theatrical, their gestures are not just for show, but rather signify a natural aspect of the collective expression. To see young children gesticulate (ever emulating their parents) in this manner is almost too cute for words. It's as if the Italians punctuate with their hands. This mini-glossary of gestures will help you get started.

➤ **Way back when.** A hand flipped over the shoulder indicates something that has happened in the past.

➤ **You idiot!** Raise the index and pinkie fingers of a clenched fist—commonly used by school children in the United States as a gesture for a bunny rabbit's raised ears—and you have the Italian gesture for *cornuto* ("cuckold"), another way of saying fool.

➤ **Who cares?** With your palm towards your chest, flip the tips of your fingers beneath your chin and you have just express your indifference.

➤ **È buono! That's good!** To express that something is good or nice, raise your eyebrows while poking your cheek with your index finger. Rotate finger.

La Bella Lingua

La Commedia dell'arte refers to "the art of comedy," a type of outdoor theater that began during the sixteenth century and lasted until the early eighteenth century. Given the vast number of dialects used throughout the Italian peninsula, performance troupes needed to find ways to communicate to their audiences that did not rely on language. Often, the players spoke in their native tongue while relying on physical cues.

What's in a Name?

The English language shares a great deal with Italian, since a great deal of English finds its origins in Latin. Some words that have made their way into English from Italian are shown in the following table.

English	Derivation
America	Amerigo Vespucci
Ancona hen	comes from the town of Ancona

English	Derivation
ballet	from the word *ballare* (to dance)
bankrupt	from the words *banca rotta* (broken bank)
burlesque	Burla
cappellini	literally "thin hair" otherwise known as "angel hair"
Dantesque	from Dante (Italy's version of Shakespeare)
draconian	from Draco, a Greek legislator in the seventh century B.C.E.
Fallopian tubes	named after Fallopio, the man who first identified them
florins	from Florence, minted in 1252
Galvanometer	named after the scientist Luigi Galvani
gazette	from Gasetta
Lippizaner horses	named after the northern town of Lippiza
Pall Mall	short for *palla maglia* (ball and mallet)
Marconigram	named after Marconi, the man who first discovered radio
sardines	named after the island of Sardinia
sequins	comes from *zecchino,* meaning "a small coin"
spaghetti	comes from *spago,* meaning "string"
volt	refers to Alessandro Volta

Italglish

If you are of Italian descent, you can probably remember your *nonno* mixing English and Italian to form what has been dubbed "Italglish." The speech of most immigrants was generally a combination of Italian, dialect, and English. Although the children of these immigrants would speak and understand the dialects of their parents, this rich tapestry would soon be lost as the new generation assimilated into American culture.

While you may know that many words commonly used in English find their origins in Italian, you may not have known how many Italian words find their origins in English. Italian immigrants often spoke English while applying their native language rules.

Modified English words included verbs such as *spiccare* (to speak), *giumpare* (to jump), and *boxare* (to box). Other expressions included *azzorrait* (that's all right), *orriope* (hurry up), and the irreverent *sciaddappa you mauta!* (shut up your mouth!).

Sometimes, the English word used by the Italian immigrant in a colony would translate quite differently in Italian. Often this had to do with the pronunciation of the English word, such as the Italglish word *uomene* (woman), which sounded remarkably like the Italian word *uomini* (men). Imagine the confusion when the immigrant returned to his homeland!

Some of those confusing Italglish words are listed in the following table.

Italglish	English	Italian Significance
arte	heart	art
boia	boy	executioner
fessa	face	fool
genitore	janitor	parent
omaccio	how much	big ugly man
rendita	rent	income
stinco	stink	shin bone
sciarpa	shop	shoe
uliveta	elevated train	olive grove
uomene	women	men

I Scream for Ais Scrim!

Often due to the immigrant speaker's inability to properly pronounce the strange English words he heard around him, words evolved into a melodic mutation of English and Italian. As is the case with most Italian words, you may notice that most of the Italglish words end in a vowel. (Doesn't this help you understand how Italian derived from Latin?)

Italglish	English
ais scrim	ice cream
alò	hello
aigacciu	I've got you; I understand
A micci	how much?
ausa	house
avaia	how are you?
azzorrait	that's all right
baccausa	backhouse, toilet
baisicle	bicycle
bossa	the wife of the boss
bosso	boss
botta	boat
Broccolino	Brooklyn
ciunga	chewing gum
cuccio	church
farma	farm

Italglish	English
grignollo	greenhorn, newcomer
guarda bene	good looking
gubbai	good-bye
iasse	yes
iu	you
lova	lover
menne	men
mia ghella	my girlfriend
naise	nice
olda faesce	old fashioned
pezzo	dollar
pis vuorche	piece work
prominenti	important people
sannemagogna	son of a gun
scudo	dollar
sobuè	subway
ticcì	teacher
trocco	truck
vischi	whiskey

Especially in parts of New York City and other centers of Italian immigrants, it is still possible to hear vestiges of this hybrid language, especially in the slang and idioms of the local neighborhoods. Like many forgotten words and languages, many of these Italglish words will never again be used. Their legacy however, lives on.

Places where Italglish was spoken included Broccolino (Brooklyn), Coneiland (Coney Island), Gerserì (Jersey City), Obrochen (Hoboken), and Toidavenue (Third Avenue).

When Speaking Italian Was a Crime

On the night of December 7, 1941, just after the bombing of Pearl Harbor, U.S. immigration agents rounded up Italian nationals suspected of disloyalty. Most of them were immigrants in the process of becoming U.S. citizens; others had been in America for decades but had not been naturalized.

Di Interessa

Refer to the book *La Merica* by Michael La Sorte for a fascinating and in-depth chronicle of the Italian immigrant experience.

For the next two years, many Italian Americans lived under strict curfew and some were even imprisoned. Eventually, 600,000 Italian Americans would be branded as "enemy aliens."

The impact these measures would have on Italian Americans is difficult to overstate. Many immigrants made a point of not using Italian in public or in clubs and stores, while others stopped teaching it to their children. The government surely encouraged this trend by its posters proclaiming "Don't Speak the Enemy's Language! Speak American!" The message was clear: not only was the Italian heritage considered alien, but inimical to the American way. It seemed best to abandon both, and thousands did just that. If you're of Italian descent, perhaps this will help you understand why your grandparents did not teach their children how to speak Italian. (Or was it because they didn't want their children to know what they were talking about?)

The Least You Need to Know

➤ The history of the Italian language starts in Rome with classical Latin.

➤ Tuscan Italian became the standard language used throughout the peninsula.

➤ Dialects are used throughout the peninsula.

➤ Italians use gestures as another way to express themselves.

➤ Many English words such as "bankrupt" find their origins in Italian.

➤ Italglish is a hybrid of English and Italian.

Part 2

Tota Italia

In Part 2, you'll gain an insider's look at the major historical movements that defined Italy from ancient times up until the Renaissance.

Read the story about two abandoned twins adopted by a wolf, and you have the birth of Rome. Learn about St. Francis of Assisi and the Franciscans. Study the different architectural styles that left Italy with so many magnificent cathedrals and castles. Understand the pope's rise to power during the tumultuous period known as the Middle Ages. Read the works of Dante, the father of the Italian language as we hear it today. Study the bawdy words of Boccaccio and see how his writings marked the beginning of the modern short story. Muse over the love poetry of Petrarca and find out just how romantic the Italians can be.

Chapter 6

Rome Wasn't Built in a Day

In This Chapter

➤ The Etruscans, tribes, and Greeks

➤ The Roman Empire

➤ Peter and Paul

➤ Constantine and the Byzantine Empire

All roads, if they were worth their salt, led to Rome. The study of Rome, the "Eternal City," is a convenient starting place for studying Italian history, if only because that is the place where Western civilization begins.

Thankfully, we know a great deal about the Romans because of the many wonderful records, ruins, and remains that give insight into how the Romans lived, governed, and died. But there is a history that goes back even further, and to really understand Italy, you'll want to begin there.

Your Mother Was a Wolf

When you're talking about a history that stretches back 2,700 years, it's sometimes difficult to separate the fact from the fiction. As one legend has it, Roman history began in the year 753 B.C.E., when the twins Romulus and Remus were born out of wedlock to a Vestal Virgin and Mars, the God of War.

At this point, the legends differ as to how and why the infants were abandoned. Some say that they were left on a mountaintop, while others claim they were set adrift in a basket on the Tiber River in a story that is highly reminiscent of the biblical story of Moses. Whatever the case, all the legends seem to confer that the two infants were found by a she-wolf who suckled them and raised them as her own. Told of their destiny, the sons of Mars founded Rome in 753 B.C.E. on the very spot where they had been discovered.

And what would they call their new city? In a dispute over whether to call the city Rema or Roma, Romulus—provoked by his brother—ended up killing Remus. So the story goes, Romulus went on to found Rome as the first of seven kings until the city became a republic in 509 B.C.E.

The famous symbol of Rome—a wolf suckling two infants—is located in Rome's Capitoline Museums in the Palazzo dei Conservatori. It is of notable interest that the fifth-century B.C.E. Etruscan bronze statue of the she-wolf originally did not possess the human twins, which were added sometime during the fifteenth century.

Livy Said …

A great deal of what we know about ancient Rome is due to the extensive writings handed down by the Roman historian Livy of Patavium (59 B.C.E.–17 C.E.). In his *History of Rome* (which took 40 years to complete), Livy suggested that the babies were actually saved by a "common whore who was called 'Wolf'" by the shepherds of the area. Today, Italians sometimes use the word "lupa" as a slang term for "whore."

According to Vergil ...

Another legend comes from writings by an important Roman poet named Vergil (also spelled Virgil). The son of a farmer, Vergil (Publius Vergilius Maro; 70–19 B.C.E.) was born near the northern city of Mantua, Italy. Educated in philosophy, Virgil is best known for having composed the epic poem the *Aeneid*. Written during the last 11 years of his life, from 30 to 19 B.C.E., it is considered the greatest epic poem in Latin literature and was a source of inspiration for later European literature, especially during the revival of ancient Roman texts during the Renaissance.

Essentially, the *Aeneid* celebrates the founding of Rome through the legend of a Trojan prince named Aeneas. In the adventure story, after the fall of Troy, Aeneas wanders the Mediterranean for seven long years before being shipwrecked off the coast of North Africa, where he falls in love with the Queen of Carthage. Aeneas leaves the queen and leads his tribes to the Tiber Valley (the Tiber is the river that runs through Lathium and down into Rome), where Rome was settled. The rest is history.

Before There Was Rome

Supported by archeological findings, we know that early in the first millennium B.C.E., the Italians living on the peninsula were an amalgamation of people loosely gathered in organized tribes, each with its own culture and history.

Tribes across the peninsula included the Etruscans (giving Tuscany its name), the Phoenicians, the Latins (giving the region, Latium, its name), the Sabines (located in the Sabine hills outside Rome, they were eventually absorbed by the Latins), the Siculi (see where the word Sicily comes from?), and the Sards (located on the neighboring island of Sardinia), to name a few.

Magna Grecia

La Magna Grecia (meaning Great Greece and pronounced *mahn-yah greh-chah*) is the name given to the expansion of Greek tribes into Southern Italy and Sicily from the eighth to the fifth centuries B.C.E. The early Greek colonies were consistently placed in strategic positions along coastal vantage points, and exerted a strong influence upon the Etruscans and the Romans, as evidenced in their art, religion, and traditions.

The Etruscans

Of equal influence on early Rome were the enigmatic Etruscans. At the height of its power, this ancient civilization presided over the Italian regions we now call Tuscany and Umbria. Called *Etrusci* by the neighboring Latins, they were referred to by the Greeks as *Tyrrhenoi* (whence the Tyrrhenian Sea). As such, they were a highly sophisticated society that evolved around 800 B.C.E. and lasted for almost seven hundred

51

years, before the last traces of Etruscan independence were eradicated in 88 B.C.E. with the Social War of Sulla, a Roman general whose dictatorship was notorious for its butchery and cruelty.

Unlike Roman history, which was well-documented by a number of reliable sources, the Etruscans left no written history to tell us their story. What we do have—inscriptions that utilized letters from the Greek alphabet and another, still unrecognized and yet-to-be translated, language—has led to speculation that the Etruscans may have been Greek immigrants, or perhaps had come from as far away as Phoenicia (currently Lebanon) and Mesopotamia (currently Iraq and Syria). The strong possibility of Eastern influences is especially evident when one studies their art.

Etruscan tombs have revealed an obsession with death that produced a highly developed sepulchral art. Indeed, much of what we know about the Etruscans comes from the art that had been stashed away in tombs and unearthed by archeologists, including medallions, terracotta statues, and reliefs. This art shows us that the Etruscans were a matrifocal (we know that they were a culture whose women enjoyed a great deal of power and freedom), highly sophisticated, civilized people familiar with a number of technologies that were later adopted by the Romans, one of the most notable of which was the chariot. Their wealth stemmed from the rich deposits of metals found in the region that included iron ore, copper, lead, tin, and gold, which was made into jewelry by skilled craftsmen.

These factors combined to help make Etruria one of the chief export markets of Greek and Phoenician traders and allowed it to expand its boundaries to as far as Umbria and into Latium. Consisting of a loose confederation of city-states whose allegiances were probably based more on religious rather than political ties, they were also a strong maritime power and established colonies on Corsica, Elba, Sardinia, and as far as Spain.

Di Interessa

Rome's Villa Giulia is home to the Museo Nazionale Etrusco and houses a fascinating collection of Etruscan artifacts and relics including pottery, jewelry, and statues.

In fact, Etruscan authority was significant enough that early Rome was ruled by several kings from the royal Etruscan Tarquin family. It was during this time that the Sabines and all of Latium were subjugated by Rome.

Things changed in 510 B.C.E. when the heads of Rome's most influential families—threatened by the Etruscan influence and growing in strength themselves—expelled the last Etruscan king, Lucius Tarquinius Superbus (Tarquin the Proud) from the throne. In what reads like the plot of Shakespeare's play *Rape of Lucrece*, legend has it that the reason behind Tarquin's expulsion had to do with the rape of a noblewoman Lucretia (who subsequently committed suicide) by his son Sextus. To avenge her, Lucretia's husband, Lucius Tarquinius Collatinus, and the Brutus family (to which Lucretia belonged) raised a rebellion and drove the Tarquins out of Rome.

The Roman Republic

With the expulsion of the last Tarquin king, the first Roman Republic (509–27 B.C.E.) was established. In order to prevent all the power from being placed in the hands of one king, a government was created that would consist of two consuls to be elected annually by a popular assembly and a Senate.

Now, although Rome was a republic, the power remained firmly in the hands of Rome's privileged patricians (the military and political elite), something that did not please the plebeians (ordinary citizens) who were not a mass you'd want to rile. Concessions were demanded, eventually leading to the creation in 450 B.C.E. of the Twelve Tables—Rome's earliest codified laws.

Essentially, the Laws of the Twelve Tables marked the first time that the principles governing legal disputes were written down. Seeing the words inscribed on the wooden tablets made it much more difficult for Rome's patricians to discriminate against the plebeians with impunity.

The Romans Are Coming

The next 200 years were defined by increased Roman expansionism, first into the Etruscan territories and then into southern Italy, an area that continued to be dominated by the Greeks. The incredible speed with which the Roman armies conquered new territories continues to be studied by military experts today. Eventually, this brought Rome's armies to the edges of the powerful North African city of Carthage (currently Tunisia).

In the Punic Wars, a series of three distinct conflicts between Carthage and Rome, the Romans continued their domination of the Mediterranean. It was during this time that they faced the Carthaginian general Hannibal, best known for crossing the Alps with elephants and a full baggage train. Hannibal's reputation as a soldier and strategist were legendary, but even his legions were not enough to stop the Romans, and by the war's close in 146 B.C.E., Carthage had surrendered its Spanish province to Rome. Rome's territories now included the entire Mediterranean, stretching as far as Jerusalem and Asia Minor. With Carthage under its thumb, Rome was now the greatest power west of

Di Interessa

The structure of the Electoral College currently used to elect the president of the United States can be traced to the Roman republic. Under their system, the adult male citizens of Rome were divided, according to their wealth, into groups of 100.

"Italia"

In Italics

279 B.C.E.—King Pyrrhus of Greece is quoted as saying, "If we win one more victory against the Romans we shall be totally ruined," leading to the use of the phrase *Pyrrhic victory*, used when a winner's losses are greater than his gains.

China. The population of Rome swelled with the peasants, slaves, and freedmen all looking for work, which they found in massive public works projects that included the construction of roads, aqueducts, markets, and temples, paid for with taxes from Rome's expanding trade.

Biografia

Spartacus (d. 71 B.C.E.) was an ex-slave who broke out of a gladiators' school in Capua and fled to Mt. Vesuvius, where he was joined by many other fugitives. In the Gladiator's War, Spartacus was killed in battle and several thousand captured slaves were crucified along the Capua-Rome highway. Although the slaves had ultimately lost, the war served to caution landowners against mistreating their slaves.

Things were not all rosy, however. The money that flowed into Rome remained in the privileged patrician hands of the Senate. They had forgotten the importance of ensuring the support of the plebeians, who were becoming increasingly disenchanted and dispossessed. Uprisings and revolts became standard, and it was clear that in spite of all their good intentions, Roman politicians had moved away from the ideals that had once defined the Republic, until a man named Gaius Julius Caesar came along.

Caesar Isn't Just a Salad Dressing

Much has been written about the man who was immortalized in Shakespeare's play *Julius Caesar*. Without getting too mired in detail, suffice it to say that Gaius Julius Caesar (100–44 B.C.E.) was a Roman statesman born into one of the oldest patrician families in Rome, yet he allied himself with the popular party (making him an interesting link between the people and the patricians). His life was marked by a series of wars, dramatic victories, and most memorably, a relationship with the queen of Egypt, Cleopatra. In what is considered one of the greatest romances in history, Caesar's alliance with Cleopatra (69–30 B.C.E.)—who was married to her younger brother—resulted in the birth of a son, Caesarion, in addition to a revolt, and ultimately, Egypt becoming a vassal of Rome.

A controversial historical figure, Caesar's greatest contribution was unifying the Roman Empire after a century of disorder and revolt. A gifted diplomat and popular general, Caesar established his reputation as a champion of the people. His ability to remember personal details about the men, as well as his willingness to endure the same hardships they did, made him an idol to his legions. He also created the Julian calendar, which, with minor modifications, is still used today. It replaced a system that had 10 months with the current 12-month year by adding the months July (for Julius) and August (for Augustus).

After years of war, in 47 B.C.E., Julius Caesar—alongside his protégé, the Roman soldier Marc Antony (83–30 B.C.E.)—defeated Syria and Pontus with such ease that his report simply stated the often quoted, "Veni, Vidi, Vici" ("I came, I saw, I conquered"). With the defeat of his enemies, in 48 B.C.E. Caesar was elected consul and soon had himself appointed dictator for life. As dictator, Caesar's power was unparalleled but his increasing popularity with the Roman people had aroused great resentment among his enemies, including much of the Senate. As a result, a small group of conspirators that included friends of Caesar—fearful of his ever-growing power and hoping to restore the republic without a dictator at the helm—murdered him on March 15, 44 B.C.E., which has come to be referred to as The Ides of March. In his will, Caesar had left everything to his 18-year old nephew and adopted son Octavian, later to be known as Augustus.

Gaius Julius Caesar (100–44 B.C.E.).

Help Wanted: Emperor

With Caesar's death, Rome had no ruler, bringing a period of anarchy and mayhem. Who would replace Caesar? As the dead emperor's nephew and heir, the young Octavian (63 B.C.E.–14 C.E.) was the true successor. Having been the recipient of Caesar's generous tutelage, Octavian (later Augustus) understood Roman politics like no other, but he would first prove his mettle in a series of wars, the final of which has gone down in history as one of the greatest battles ever recorded. In the Battle of Actium (31 B.C.E.), Octavian defeated none other than Marc Antony and Cleopatra. With it came the fall of Egypt—a dramatic victory that left Octavian in control of all of the Roman territories. The seizure of Cleopatra's treasure made Octavian wealthier than the city of Rome itself (needless to say, this was no small prize!). In 28 B.C.E. Octavian was declared emperor of Rome and honored by the Senate with the name Augustus ("revered one").

Di Interessa

There's little wonder that the legendary Cleopatra remains one of the world's greatest heroines. The daughter of a Pharoah and mistress to Caesar and later to the Roman soldier and politician Marc Antony, her ambition and charm have been portrayed in Bernard Shaw's comedy play *Caesar and Cleopatra* and in Shakespeare's *Antony and Cleopatra*.

After Julius Comes Augustus

Augustus' rule began a long period of peace (200 years) referred to as the Pax Romana ("Roman Peace"), during which time the Empire swelled to include all the territories of the Mediterranean extending east to the Rivers Rhine and Danube.

During his reign, Augustus purged the Senate of unworthy members, reorganized the army, and brought constitutional rule back to the city. A supporter of the arts, Augustus was patron to the Roman poets and scholars Virgil, Ovid, Livy, and Horace. An intelligent administrator, he reformed taxation laws, worked on improving Rome's roads, created a postal system, and developed police and fire services.

Built to Last

It was during the Pax Romana initiated by Augustus' rule that ancient Rome flourished magnificently, advancing in size and majesty far beyond the examples set by the Greeks and Etruscans. The Romans gave us cement when they developed mortar made from volcanic ash. They fine-tuned the arch and, as mentioned before, constructed monumental buildings, and public works projects funded by taxes paid by citizens.

Completed in 25 B.C.E. by Marcus Agrippa, Rome's Pantheon is considered the oldest building in Rome. For more than 100 years, this magnificent building was used for common purposes and neglected by the state, until Emperor Hadrian ordered it repaired in 118 C.E. It was consecrated as a church in 609 C.E.

An example of one of their most impressive achievements was the Baths of Caracalla. And make no mistake, the Romans loved their baths. Used for both hygiene and exercise, the baths offered Romans an opportunity to put their feet up, scrape off some dirt, and gossip. The Baths of Caracalla had a capacity of nearly 1,600 bathers and had areas used for playing sports, auditoriums for music, lecture theaters, libraries, gardens, fountains, and public toilets. Afterward, many Romans enjoyed a light bite and a glass of wine.

An important Roman city was Ostia Antica, originally founded at the mouth of the Tiber River to serve as a military outpost and a port to supply Rome. Food reserves destined for the capital arrived there from all over the Empire and were stored in great warehouses. They were then moved to Rome on barges that floated along the banks of the Tiber.

That's Entertainment, Folks

When they weren't at the baths, Romans enjoyed the games. There were three kinds of entertainment: theatrical performances (*ludi scaenici*), chariot races (*ludi circenses*), and gladiator fights and beast hunts (*munera*). At first these events were staged together to form a whole day's entertainment. By imperial times each event could be seen separately, often in its own specially designed building.

Gruesome deaths were not an uncommon sight in Rome. To mark an important event like a battle victory, wealthy individuals often put on gladiator games. The gladiators were prisoners, criminals, slaves, or paid volunteers who fought for the public's entertainment in huge amphitheaters such as the Colosseum. A successful gladiator received money, a crown, and great adulation. After many victories he might be awarded a wooden sword, which signified his freedom. Many freed fighters became trainers at special schools for gladiators.

The custom of gladiatorial fights had its origins in the practice of slaughtering slaves on a chieftain's grave. It was introduced into Rome in 264 B.C.E. and continued until the fifth century C.E. The emperor Trajan presided over a show that lasted 117 days in which 10,000 gladiators took part.

Di Interessa

To better understand Roman times and get a picture of the power behind the Roman legions, check out the movie *Gladiator* (2000), directed by Ridley Scott and starring Russell Crowe.

The Slaves

If owning gladiators and putting on public spectacles was a mark of a man's power and wealth, so, too, was owning slaves. It is doubtful that Rome could have built her magnificent cities and expanded so far without the forced labor of slaves.

Most slaves were non-Romans, such as prisoners of war and their descendants. There were household slaves, slaves who worked the fields, slaves who built the cities, slaves who fought in the armies. Both individual citizens and the state owned slaves, who were bought, sold, and taxed like any other property. They had no rights or privileges, and were forced to work at any jobs their masters gave them.

Educated Greek slaves—considered the cleverest by their Roman owners because they were well-read and articulate—were the most expensive. They worked for the wealthiest Romans, often holding positions such as doctors, tutors, musicians, goldsmiths, artists, and librarians. Other slaves received wages for their work, and if they saved enough, they could buy their freedom back from their masters. Favorite slaves might be freed as a reward for good service.

By the height of the Imperial Era, freed men were a large, rich sector of the population. Many became businessmen, administrators, artists, civil servants, engineers, and architects.

The Early Christians

It was during the Pax Romana that Rome began to be affected by a completely new element as the first Christians entered the picture. Although they posed no direct threat to Nero (37–68 C.E.), Rome's emperor at the time, their refusal to acknowledge the divine honors of the emperor resulted in a clash of values that led to officially sanctioned persecution. Among the earliest martyrs were St. Peter and St. Paul.

St. Peter

Rome's famous St. Peter's Cathedral was built in honor of St. Peter, who died around 64 C.E., one of Jesus Christ's twelve apostles and considered the first bishop of Rome. As a leader at the council of Jerusalem that had met in order to discuss the integration of non-Jews into the Christian movement, according to stories, St. Peter left Antioch for Rome where he was crucified in the most horrible way imaginable, with his head pointed downward. Since then, Vatican Hill has always been designatedthe place where his martyrdom occurred. Three hundred years later, Constantine erected a church over the supposed burial place of St. Peter. When it fell into disrepair, the huge St. Peter's Cathedral was built, where it remains to this today, visited by millions of tourists and pilgrims hoping to catch a glimpse of what many believe to be the bones of St. Peter.

St. Paul

Like Peter, St. Paul was an apostle and a Jew, but was born to a Roman father of some means. Educated in Jerusalem, Paul became a zealous nationalist who was at first quite anti-Christian. So the story goes—in around 33 C.E. Paul was traveling to Damascus, where he had received a commission to assist the chief priest in suppressing the growing Christian movement. On his way, he was temporarily blinded by a flash of light, during which time he heard Jesus ask, "Why persecutest thou me?" To be sure, upon recovering, Paul immediately began preaching and spent the next thirteen years studying the faith, visiting Jerusalem twice. From there, Paul set out on his first missionary journey, a practice that consisted of going to synagogues and marketplaces, setting up churches, and moving on to the next city.

It was after his last visit to Jerusalem that Paul was arrested for provoking a riot and imprisoned for two years before being brought before the Roman officials Herod Agrippa and Festus. As a Roman citizen, Paul was sent back to Rome where he was again imprisoned. While in prison, Paul continued to conduct his ministry as Jews and Roman Christians visited him.

Although the stories differ on the exact circumstances of his death, it is generally agreed that Paul was beheaded, making him one of Rome's earliest Christian martyrs. St. Paul's tomb and shrine are located at the Roman Basilica of St. Paul's Without the Walls.

You're Great, Constantine!

The beginning of a new era came with the arrival of Constantine, also known as Constantine the Great. As one of the four contenders for the throne of Rome, legend has it that he saw a cross in the sky and the words *"In hoc signo vinces"* ("You will conquer with this sign") before an important battle. After his victory, in the Edict of Milan in 313 C.E., Constantine not only granted freedom of worship to Christians, but he gave people special privileges if they adopted the religion. (He himself converted to Christianity before his death in 337 C.E.)

In 330 C.E., Constantine moved his court and his armies to a new city whose position made it an ideal link between Europe and Asia. The new capital would aptly be called Constantinople (now Istanbul) and in it the Eastern Church (as the church was now called) became almost as influential as its Roman cousin, giving birth to the Greek Orthodox Church, among others.

Meanwhile, the unprotected city of Rome, already susceptible to being raided, once more became a target for invasions and attacks. In 455 C.E., the Vandals sailed to Italy, invaded Rome, and destroyed it. The city's administrative services collapsed, and chaos and famine followed. Rome's population fell from over one million to about 20,000. What had been a thriving metropolis was now reduced to ruins. The Roman Empire had come to an end.

Constantinople became a great and powerful city at the center of a huge empire, preserving many of the traditions of the western Romans, including their administrative skills and military system and the Christian religion. Fending off attacks from foreign invaders, Constantinople remained an imperial capital for 1,000 years. In 1453, it finally fell to the Muslim armies, marking the point at which all remaining political links with Rome were finally broken.

Rome Today

Rome is a complex city that has changed, and changed dramatically, throughout its long history. There's Caesar's Rome, and the Rome of Augustus. There's Constantine's Rome, Napoleon's Rome, Garibaldi's Rome, Mussolini's Rome, and Fellini's Rome.

Today, if you're looking for one city to meet all your needs, try Rome. There is the Rome of Italy's parliament and there is the Rome of Cinecittà, Italy's version of Hollywood. There is the Jewish Rome, where one of the first *ghettos* was created. There is the decadent Rome of *La Dolce Vita* and there is the holy Rome, seat to the papacy. There is the Rome of the Romans and the Rome of the tourists.

Indeed, Rome has always attracted the attention of foreigners. Notables drawn to Rome include the German religious reformer Martin Luther, and later, his country-man poet and philosopher J. W. von Goethe; the French painter Jean Auguste Ingres; the English poets Lord Byron, John Milton, and Percy Bysshe Shelley; the Spanish painter Diego Velazquez; and the American writers Ezra Pound and Henry James.

If you ever get the chance, pack a picnic and go sit in the ancient ruins of Rome's magnificent Forum. If you listen very carefully, you may still be able to hear the voices of those who came before, long, long ago.

The Least You Need to Know

➤ Before Rome, the Italian peninsula was an amalgam of tribes and cultures that included the Etruscans, Sabines, and Greeks.

➤ Julius Caesar was Rome's first consul. Augustus was the first emperor of Rome.

➤ Peter and Paul were among the earliest Christian martyrs.

➤ Constantine the Great granted freedom of worship to Christians and became one himself.

The Medieval Minestrone

The Dark Ages. The total collapse of civilization. Barbaric tribes sweeping down on the Italian peninsula, destroying everything in their path. Fire, flood, earthquake, and volcanic eruptions foretelling the end of life as we know it.

Was it really all doom and gloom during the long stretch of time called the Middle Ages? Was the world actually dangling at the end of its rope?

The Middle of What?

The Middle Ages in Europe occurred between the fall of the Roman Empire in the fifth century C.E. to the Renaissance (about 1500). What were the various trends and political movements that, when taken together, made up the "medieval minestrone"? Although the Middle Ages were a violent and disruptive period of political fragmentation, it also resulted in some real achievements.

Let's start with the political chaos. From the forth to ninth centuries, a succession of hostile Teutonic tribes (peoples originating from southern Sweden, the Danish peninsula, and northern Germany) invaded northern Italy, taking advantage of the breakdown of Roman authority. The Visigoths, under Alaric I, sacked Rome in 410.

As you read in Chapter 6, "Rome Wasn't Built in a Day," the Vandals (also a Germanic tribe) sacked Rome in 455. The devastation caused by the Vandals gave rise to the term "vandalism." Originally migrating southwards from Scandinavia and the southern Baltic coast through Europe, the Vandals established a kingdom in Spain and Africa in 429.

The Ostrogoths, a branch of the Goths, frequently invaded northern Italy in the sixth century. Between 493 and 526 their leader Theodoric the Great (454–526) ruled Italy. Following his death, the Eastern Roman Empire, after a long struggle, destroyed the Ostrogoths in 562.

That wasn't the last of the German tribes in Italy, though. The Lombards (also known as *Longobards*, "long beards") also invaded the peninsula and established a kingdom in 572 with Pavia as its capital. The Lombards would continue to rule for two centuries until they lost their independence to Charlemagne in 774.

The Lombards left their name to the central northern Italian region of Lombardy (*Lombardia* in Italian), between the Alps and the River Po. They also left behind the iron crown of the Lombard kings, which was used for the coronation (951) of Otto I (the first Holy Roman Emperor) as king of Italy and for the crowning of several succeeding emperors, including Charlemagne, Charles V, and Napoleon I. According to tradition, the crown was made from a nail of Christ's cross and is kept in the cathedral at Monza, founded in the sixth century by the Lombard queen Theodolinda.

Di Interessa

Gotland (or Gothland or Gottland) is the largest of the Swedish islands in the Baltic Sea. Germanic peoples such as the Goths originated there.

"*Italia*"

In Italics

800 C.E.—Charlemagne was crowned Holy Roman Emperor. The king of the Franks (768–814) and the Lombards (774–814), Charlemagne's reforms and wide-ranging interests revolutionized European life.

An Architectural Primer

If you're looking for visible evidence in Italy of the Goths, Visigoths, and Ostrogoths, you won't find it in Italian Gothic architecture. In fact, Italian Gothic architecture does not refer to churches and castles built by the Goths during the Middle Ages. And the Romans didn't erect Romanesque buildings like Trajan's Arch either. That's the reason for this idiot-proof overview.

If you visit Italy, you may become overwhelmed by all the monuments, old buildings, and statues, so consider this a head start on figuring out what you're looking at. Keep in mind that there are very few buildings that feature just one pure architectural style. Sometimes a church would be partially built in the Gothic style, only to have a new architect build parts of it (after a fire, for instance) in the Renaissance style.

➤ **Roman** (to the fifth century C.E.). The arch—a curved structure spanning an opening—and the vault—an arched roof—are among the Romans greatest contributions to architecture. These were first used in engineering constructions such as bridges, aqueducts, and viaducts, and were later used in palaces, theatres, and bathhouses. Two of the most famous Roman-style buildings are in Rome: the Colosseum and the Pantheon.

Rome's Colosseum was an architectural wonder.

➤ **Byzantine** (fourth to mid-fifteenth century). Byzantine architecture developed in the ancient city of Constantinople after 330 C.E. It is religious, highly stylized, and notable both in the blueprint form of the Christian basilica and the domes and vaults atop these churches. Ravenna is a veritable treasure trove of Byzantine architecture, especially the church of San Vitale.

➤ **Romanesque** (fifth to mid-thirteenth century). The name, of course, gives it away. The style developed from late Roman architecture, but with certain differences. Buildings in this style are easily identified by arcades (a passage with an arched roof), carved capitals (the top of a column), and rounded arches. The cathedral of Pisa, San Ambrogia's basilica in Milan, the cathedral of Massa Marittini, and the church of San Miniato in Florence are all Romanesque-style buildings.

➤ **Gothic** (thirteenth to mid-fifteenth centuries). The combination of the pointed arch and the flying buttress—an arch abutting a building and anchored on a pier—supported the heavy roof and allowed the Romanesque wall to be replaced by the glorious Gothic window. The abbey of San Galgano, the church of Santa Maria della Spina in Pisa, and the Duomo of Siena are prime examples.

➤ **Renaissance** (fifteenth and sixteenth centuries). Wedge-shaped masonry around semi-circular window arches and classical cornices are characteristic of Renaissance buildings. The Florentine architect Filippo Brunelleschi is the father of Renaissance style, whether it be *il cupola* over Santa Maria del Fiore, the loggia of the Spedale degli Innocenti, or the church of San Lorenzo (all in Florence).

➤ **Mannerism** (bridged Renaissance and Baroque). Mannerism was a short-lived link between the Renaissance and Baroque periods. The great architect Andrea Palladio designed buildings known for their classical, centralized proportions, such as Villa Capra at Vicenza and Il Redentore in Venice. The inner courtyard of Palazzo Pitti, by Bartolomeo Ammannati, is also a terrific example of Mannerist architecture.

➤ **Baroque** (late sixteenth and seventeenth centuries). Think theatrical, bold, exuberant! Popes favored the curved pediments, highly ornamented window surrounds, and intricate moldings. Palazzo Barberini and the church of Saint Carlo alle Quattro Fontane are examples of Baroque, as are the ornate columns of St. Peter's. For over the top Baroque architecture, visit Lecce, where the buildings drip with excessive ornamentation.

Di Interessa

If you're inspired to learn more about art and architecture in Italy, check out the official Web site for the Uffizi Gallery in Florence. As one of the oldest museums in the world, the Uffizi Gallery offers photos, engravings, biographies, and explanations of artistic movements at www. televisual.it/uffizi/.

Know Your Parts

Even if you don't pray, chances are you'll find yourself in at least a few churches if you visit Italy. Here's a mini-glossary of architectural terms in Italian and English to get you started.

abbazzia abbey

anfiteatro amphitheater

arco arch

battistero baptistery

campanile bell tower

cappella chapel

cenacola Last Supper

chiesa church

cortile galleried courtyard or cloister

loggia a covered gallery or balcony

lunette semicircular space in vault or ceiling

nave the central body of a church

portico covered entrance to a building

santuario sanctuary

torre tower

Laying the Foundation for Scholarship

During the Middle Ages the creation of Christian monasteries kept scholarship alive. Monasteries and abbeys were not only places of religion but centers for the preservation and spread of culture. St. Benedict of Nursia (480–543), for instance, established a monastery on Monte Cassino that combined spiritual training with agricultural activity.

In addition, the monasteries took an important economic role due to their plans for the drainage and use of lands devastated and depopulated by constant war. The papacy, monasteries, and other ecclesiastical institutions found themselves in possession of huge estates, often enlarged by further donations from benefactors, who contributed to strengthen their political authority and power.

Biografia

Umberto Eco (1932) is a professor at the University of Bologna and a novelist best known for his fictional work *The Name of the Rose* (1981), a murder mystery set in a medieval monastery.

Light Bright

Architecture was not the only bright spot to light up the gloom of the Middle Ages. Another was the art of illuminated manuscripts, first practiced by monastic scribes. These were manuscripts of gospels, books of hours, and prayers, written by hand and decorated with designs in opaque or transparent watercolor and frequently gold leaf.

The word "illuminated" came from a usage of the Latin word *illuminare* in connection with oratory or prose style, where it meant "adorn." Although it began as the elaboration of capital letters and decoration of margins, by the time printing was invented it had become a form of miniature painting, perfected by professional illuminators.

The movie *The Name of the Rose* (1986; from the book of the same name written by Umberto Eco) beautifully depicts the work involved: Monks in what appear to be drafty and candle-lit libraries are stooped over their workbenches, squinting as they paint letters and borders on parchment paper.

Monks from the Franciscan Sanctuary of Poggio Bustone take a break from their studies.

Family Feudalism

Feudalism originated during the eighth and ninth centuries after the collapse of Charlemagne's empire. Those in power—kings and lords—gave access to farm land in return for promises of loyalty and military service, as well as a portion of the crops tilled from that land.

Landowners—also known as feudal lords—certainly had the upper hand in the feudal system. In fact, a hereditary law passed work obligations from father to son, forcing peasant laborers to work for the lords and leaving them no choice in where they could work. Serfs—tenant farmers—were tied to the land that they tilled. Although they had their own homes, plots, and livestock and enjoyed customary rights that distinguished them from slaves, serfs were not free to move from the land on which they worked.

The deal was simple: Serfs farmed part of their lord's estate for their own benefit, keeping the profits and fruits of their labors. In exchange, they worked the land without pay for a certain number of days and additionally gave the lord a share of their produce. Interestingly enough, most of the land owned by the Church had feudal obligations.

In the countryside during the tenth and eleventh centuries, the feudal system begin to decline. In the north, cities began to assert their power through stronger government and organized militaries. This promoted the end of feudalism in northern Italy, replacing it with a deeply rooted identification with the city as opposed to the larger region or the country.

Feudalism was finally abolished in northern Italy during the Napoleonic regime. The south, on the other hand, was a different story. Feudalistic arrangements continued to persist well into the nineteenth and twentieth centuries and were one of the contributing factors in the great wave of emigration to the United States from the south after 1880.

Di Interessa

The term "feuding" originally referred to armed conflicts between feudal lords and the exploited peasants who toiled for them.

Apocalypse Then

Fireballs dropping out of the sky. Economic disaster, worldwide hunger, and gangs of heavily armed bandits looting and pillaging their way across the countryside. Dire predictions for the millennium just past? Or fear-mongering in the year 1000? If you're reading this book, then you survived the Y2K bug, and the world survived the first millennium, too.

But what did people in Italy worry about with the turn of the millennium in the year 1000? How did they prepare for the doomsday scenario just as widely spread among its people as ours was just a few years ago? Obviously, around the year 1000 there was no Internet, no 24-hour cable news stations, no books, newspapers, or magazines to create the overwhelming, inescapable crush of media hype that surrounded the recent new millennium change-over. Indeed, only monks and priests were literate one thousand years ago, and other than the agricultural seasons and the cycle of Christian feast days, most peasants had little awareness of calendrical time. And the New Year wasn't celebrated on January 1 but on Easter, the most important holiday in Christian tradition.

People in the Middle Ages struggled every day. They were concerned with harvests and livestock, with finding clean water and having a place to sleep at night. They didn't have to bother with life-threatening situations like their personal computer not functioning after midnight on January 1, 2000, during a Y2K disaster or the ATM not dispensing cash.

But even though there weren't any Y1K T-shirts for sale, or huge televised celebrations planned in every national capital in the world, some people started paying attention to the date. They were getting panicky, too, because of rumors that the new year would bring the Last Judgment. From all over the world, pilgrims flocked to the Sepulcher of the Savior in Jerusalem, on the spot where tradition says Jesus was crucified and buried. Some sought salvation, others hoped to witness the Second Coming of Christ.

Biografia

During the sixth century C.E., Dionysius Exiguus (c. 556), a Roman monk and scholar, was the first to use the present system of reckoning a date for the birth of Jesus. Unfortunately, he made a mistake of between four to six years that was never corrected. Astronomers now generally agree that the Bible's description of the celestial skies at the time of Jesus' birth correspond to a period several years before the date that Dionysius established.

Unquestionably, big things were expected to happen. People just didn't know if these events would be positive or negative. Even natural occurrences like a thunderstorm or eclipse were thought to portend the end of the world and sent people into a tailspin of panic.

One particularly vivid account of the medieval millennium, based only on conjecture, imagined a throng of worshippers huddled in the flickering candlelight of St. Peter's Basilica in Rome, weeping and trembling as they awaited the turn of the millennium. Many were certain it would unleash the holy terror of Christ's Second Coming and the end of the world.

So convinced were some Christians that the apocalypse was upon them that they gave away all their possessions and fled to the magnificent Vatican sanctuary clothed in sackcloth and ashes. As Pope Sylvester II calmly intoned the familiar Latin phrases of the Midnight Mass on that dreaded millennium eve, fearful believers prostrated themselves on the polished marble floor, their eyes closed in anticipation of the trumpet blast that in a moment would herald the arrival of Judgment Day.

It mattered little to the anxious worshippers in Rome that the pope and other Church leaders apparently did not share in such urgent apocalyptic expectations. There were plenty of other priests and abbots who had expounded for years on how the turbulent events of the late tenth century fit perfectly with the Bible's vivid descriptions of Earth's final days.

As the pontiff concluded the sacred liturgy, the crowd remained rooted, motionless, transfixed, barely daring to breathe, not a few dying from fright, giving up their ghosts then and there.

Even though the final fretful moments of the year 999 did not result in the long-dreaded apocalypse, the French medieval monk Radulfus Glaber (c. 980–c. 1045) reported in his book *Historiarum Libri Quinque* an outbreak of heresies in France and Italy around the year 1000. He interpreted these heresies as signaling the unleashing of Satan as prophesied in Revelation. Glaber noted other portentous signs and wonders—earthquakes, comets, famines, and volcanic eruptions. As a result of all the concern about the new millennium, the end of the tenth century saw a marked decline in artistic and cultural activities in monasteries. But then the year passed, the world was not destroyed, and the peasant masses continued to scratch out a meager living.

All Roads Lead to Rome

The Middle Ages were marked by pilgrimages to three destinations: Jerusalem; Santiago de Campostela, Spain; and Rome. The "Romei" were pilgrims heading for Rome driven by the desire to visit the tombs of St. Paul and St. Peter and to be physically close to the tombs of the other Roman martyrs.

Pilgrims to Rome also wanted to observe the reputed image of Christ's face (Veronica's Veil) and to admire all the other wonders of the holy city of Rome. Many of them specifically wanted to tour all four basilicas in the city (San Pietro, San Paolo Fuori le Mura, Santa Maria Maggiore, and San Giovanni in Laterano) to receive and to obtain "forgiveness"—otherwise known as an indulgence. Pilgrims believed an indulgence would cancel punishment in purgatory for sins committed on earth.

The obsession with pilgrimages to holy shrines was the impetus behind the Crusades, in which thousands of Christian knights went to Palestine to fight the Muslims and convert them to Christianity. The first Crusade (1095–99) was launched with the support of the papacy. Several other holy wars were fought in the twelfth century, but none of them was successful. Italy benefited greatly from the resultant growth of trade, though, and the introduction of eastern concepts into medieval culture.

Di Interessa

Currently in the Basilica di San Francesco, St. Francis' tomb was buried in secrecy to prevent his remains from being stolen (medieval society placed enormous value on relics). It was not discovered until 1818 after two months of excavations.

St. Francis of Assisi

One of the most important religious figures of the Middle Ages was St. Francis of Assisi (1181–1226). The patron saint of Italy, friend to the animals, and official saint of ecology, St. Francis was born as Giovanni Francesco Bernardone to a wealthy cloth merchant of Assisi.

As a young man, Francis lived the cheerful and carefree life of a nobleman until war broke out with the neighboring city of Perugia. Captured, Francis lingered in a dungeon for almost a year before being released; the experience would change Francis' perspective immeasurably. When he was 25, Francis heard a voice tell him "Repair my falling house." Taking a vow of poverty and devoting himself to the service of others, Francis interpreted the message literally and, using his father's money, set about to repair the remains of the semi-derelict church of San Damiano in Assisi. Francis' associations and actions soon led his father to legally disinherit his son. The fact that Francis—a man born to prestige and power—would decidedly choose to live a life of poverty was practically inconceivable.

In 1208, Francis gathered 12 disciples devoted to prayer and helping the unfortunate, including the lepers who lived nearby. In 1210, Pope Innocent III gave Francis and his companions the official authority to spread the good word. By 1219, the Franciscan Order had over 5,000 friars within its ranks. Much of the success behind Francis' successful movement toward a life of humility, chastity, and poverty was in large part due to Francis' ability to gain the support of the papacy.

Di Interessa

The cappuccino you love so much was named after the brown, hooded frock that became the signature uniform of the Capuchin monks.

St. Francis is attributed with having created the first Christmas crèche of Mary, Joseph, and Jesus in the small town of Greccio. He wrote numerous musical works, including "The Canticle of the Creatures," a beautiful hymn venerating all living things.

In 1224, after 40 days of fasting, the nearly blind and impoverished Francis received the stigmata, the marks of the crucifixion of Christ. Bleeding from his hands and feet, St. Francis' final years were marked by great physical pain and almost total blindness. He died in 1226 and only two years after his death, he was canonized. In 1980, Pope John Paul II proclaimed him the patron saint of ecologists.

Santa Clara

The literate and noblewoman Clare of Assisi (c. 1194–1253) was another ray of hope during the Middle Ages. Born of a noble Assisi family, she refused two offers of marriage and, under the influence of St. Francis, decided to devote herself to a religious vocation. Secretly leaving home at the age of 18, she went first to a Benedictine house. When it appeared that other women wanted to live in the Franciscan way, St. Francis set up a separate community in Assisi with Clare as Abbess (a position she occupied until her death). Clare was soon joined by her mother, sisters, and others.

Clare's great hope was to persuade successive popes to grant her community of "Poor Clares" the "privilege of poverty" so that they could live entirely on alms; the austerity of their order went far beyond any that women had previously undertaken. She was canonized two years after her death, and in 1958 Pope Pius XII declared her the patron saint of television alluding to a story of her telepathically experiencing the Christmas Midnight Mass being held in the remote Church of St. Francis in Assisi while on her deathbed.

Miracles attributed to St. Clara involved curing the sick with the sign of the cross, rainbow "auras" encircling her while she meditated, and the uncanny ability she appeared to have to communicate with animals.

Di Interessa

Not only is Umbria the birthplace of St. Francis but also a number of other saints, including St. Rita, St. Valentine, St. Clare, and St. Benedict. Look for depictions by the artist Giotto of the great St. Francis.

The Least You Need to Know

➤ Teutonic tribes repeatedly invaded Italy during the Middle Ages.

➤ Many Christian monasteries were founded during the so-called Dark Ages.

➤ Many peasants were virtual prisoners of the land they farmed during the period of feudalism.

➤ Military expeditions organized to convert Muslims to Christianity were unsuccessful.

Chapter 8

Popes, Politics, and Power

> ### In This Chapter
>
> ➤ The papacy and the Church get top billing
>
> ➤ Tradition and rituals are part of Italian culture
>
> ➤ Papal patronage of Renaissance artists

It is impossible to separate church from state in a country like Italy, where its religious and cultural traditions are so deeply entwined. The influence of the Vatican is particularly felt in Rome, the seat of the papacy. The high dome of St. Peter's Basilica—the center of the Roman Catholic faith—overlooks the city, reminding its citizens and the millions of pilgrims who come to its doors that the Church is here, and it is here to stay.

Rome: Seat of the Vatican

Rome is a city of churches in a country where churches are built on top of churches, and the *campanile* rings on the hour. At her heart is the Vatican, a separate state within the city.

As seat to the central government of the *Roman Catholic* Church, the papacy has its work cut out. Over the centuries, an elaborate bureaucracy has developed to manage its vast interests in both temporal and spiritual matters. In pursuing its mission, the Vatican requires an enormous engine to manage the huge job of administering to the

La Bella Lingua

The term **Roman Catholic** was first coined in nineteenth century Britain to distinguish it from other (non-Roman) Catholics. When used officially, the term refers to THE Roman Catholic, the Archdiocese of Rome.

millions of Catholics around the world; to this end it is equipped with its own newspaper, post office, army, fortress, prison, and radio show.

Indeed, the Vatican City State probably packs more power per square meter than any other independent nation in the world. Think of it—a region just a few city blocks wide, with a population of approximately 1,000 people, has direct spiritual reign over one billion people and, of course, considerable influence on Christians and non-Christians alike the world over.

That kind of clout attracts all types of visitors, including religious pilgrims, clergy from around the world, art lovers, and tourists. The most popular attractions inside Vatican City include Piazza San Pietro, St. Peter's Basilica, and the Vatican Museums.

In Italics

Second century c.e.—The fortress Castel Sant'Angelo was originally built by the Roman emperor Hadrian as a mausoleum for himself and his family. Popes have used it as a fortress, prison, and hideaway. It was here that Pope Clement VII took refuge during the 1527 Sack of Rome by the troops of Charles V before he surrendered. Today, the castle contains a museum of arms and artillery, with unmatched views of the city and the Vatican.

The Pope's Cabinet and the Curia Romana

The pope's cabinet consists of the Sacred College of Cardinals, whose job it is to assist the pope in making decisions and running the government. Reporting directly to the pope, the Curia Romana is the administrative body responsible for running the show and implementing the scores of rituals and ceremonies connected to the pope during his reign. They are also in charge of the various missions and goals (including the upkeep of monasteries, convents, orphanages, and hospitals) of the Church.

The Swiss Guard

Founded in the 1505 by Pope Julius II, the Swiss Guard essentially serves as the pope's bodyguards. Today that role is more symbolic, as tourists snap photographs during the changing of the straight-faced guards, which is the only time you'll get to see the dapperly dressed fellows move. Michelangelo is often credited with designing the elaborate costumes of the Swiss Guard.

Peter Picked a Pope

Electing a new pope can be a strenuous task. It took almost three years to elect a successor to Pope Clement IV, who died in 1268, since no one could poll the two-thirds majority vote necessary for a new pope to be selected. Hoping to force a vote, the cardinals were confined within their living quarters and even their daily food allowance was reduced.

These days, choosing a pope isn't quite as harsh. The College of Cardinals meets in a secret conclave in the Sistine Chapel after the death of the previous pontiff. The election is by secret ballot. After each session the paper ballots are burned; if the vote is inconclusive, straw is added to produce black smoke. White smoke signifies that the cardinals have chosen a new pope.

The Popes

All in all, there have been 265 popes recorded by the Church (not including the so-called anti-popes). While some popes have been great thinkers and reformers, for about a thousand years—roughly from the eighth century to the nineteenth century—the pope was also the political and military leader of the independent territories under the rule of the Papacy. Needless to say, that's a big job.

"*Italia*"

In Italics

1929—Vatican City as we know it today was established.

"*Italia*"

In Italics

Spring 2001—With Pope John Paul II's health in serious decline, several TV networks reportedly paid large sums of money to secure the best view of the Vatican in Rome. Anticipating a papal election, they planned to film the white puff of smoke indicating a new pope from rooftops, apartment terraces, and hotel windows.

Biografia

Peter and Paul, two disciples of Christ, went to Rome in 55 C.E. to establish a church. The Emperor Nero crucified Peter, and it was in his honor that St. Peter's Church was built in the Vatican.

1. St. Peter (32–67)
2. St. Linus (67–76)
3. St. Anacletus (Cletus) (76–88)
4. St. Clement I (88–97)
5. St. Evaristus (97–105)
6. St. Alexander I (105–115)
7. St. Sixtus I (115–125)—also called Xystus I
8. St. Telesphorus (125–136)
9. St. Hyginus (136–140)
10. St. Pius I (140–155)
11. St. Anicetus (155–166)
12. St. Soter (166–175)
13. St. Eleutherius (175–189)
14. St. Victor I (189–199)
15. St. Zephyrinus (199–217)
16. St. Callistus I (217–222)
17. St. Urban I (222–230)
18. St. Pontain (230–235)
19. St. Anterus (235–236)
20. St. Fabian (236–250)
21. St. Cornelius (251–253)
22. St. Lucius I (253–254)
23. St. Stephen I (254–257)
24. St. Sixtus II (257–258)
25. St. Dionysius (260–268)
26. St. Felix I (269–274)
27. St. Eutychian (275–283)
28. St. Caius (283–296)—also called Gaius
29. St. Marcellinus (296–304)
30. St. Marcellus I (308–309)
31. St. Eusebius (309–310)
32. St. Miltiades (311–314)
33. St. Sylvester I (314–335)
34. St. Marcus (336)
35. St. Julius I (337–352)
36. Liberius (352–366)
37. St. Damasus I (366–383)
38. St. Siricius (384–399)
39. St. Anastasius I (399–401)
40. St. Innocent I (401–417)
41. St. Zosimus (417–418)
42. St. Boniface I (418–422)
43. St. Celestine I (422–432)
44. St. Sixtus III (432–440)
45. St. Leo I the Great (440–461)
46. St. Hilarius (461–468)
47. St. Simplicius (468–483)
48. St. Felix III (II) (483–492)
49. St. Gelasius I (492–496)
50. Anastasius II (496–498)
51. St. Symmachus (498–514)
52. St. Hormisdas (514–523)
53. St. John I (523–526)
54. St. Felix IV (III) (526–530)
55. Boniface II (530–532)
56. John II (533–535)
57. St. Agapetus I (535–536)—also called Agapitus I
58. St. Silverius (536–537)
59. Vigilius (537–555)
60. Pelagius I (556–561)
61. John III (561–574)
62. Benedict I (575–579)
63. Pelagius II (579–590)
64. St. Gregory I (the Great) (590–604)
65. Sabinian (604–606)

66. Boniface III (607)
67. St. Boniface IV (608–615)
68. St. Deusdedit (Adeodatus I) (615–618)
69. Boniface V (619–625)
70. Honorius I (625–638)
71. Severinus (640)
72. John IV (640–642)
73. Theodore I (642–649)
74. St. Martin I (649–655)
75. St. Eugene I (655–657)
76. St. Vitalian (657–672)
77. Adeodatus II (672–676)
78. Donus (676–678)
79. St. Agatho (678–681)
80. St. Leo II (682–683)
81. St. Benedict II (684–685)
82. John V (685–686)
83. Conon (686–687)
84. St. Sergius I (687–701)
85. John VI (701–705)
86. John VII (705–707)
87. Sisinnius (708)
88. Constantine (708–715)
89. St. Gregory II (715–731)
90. St. Gregory III (731–741)
91. St. Zachary (741–752)
92. Stephen II (752)
93. Stephen III (752–757)
94. St. Paul I (757–767)
95. Stephen IV (767–772)
96. Adrian I (772–795)
97. St. Leo III (795–816)
98. Stephen V (816–817)

99. St. Paschal I (817–824)
100. Eugene II (824–827)
101. Valentine (827)
102. Gregory IV (827–844)
103. Sergius II (844–847)
104. St. Leo IV (847–855)
105. Benedict III (855–858)
106. St. Nicholas I (the Great) (858–867)
107. Adrian II (867–872)
108. John VIII (872–882)
109. Marinus I (882–884)
110. St. Adrian III (884–885)
111. Stephen VI (885–891)
112. Formosus (891–896)
113. Boniface VI (896)
114. Stephen VII (896–897)
115. Romanus (897)
116. Theodore II (897)
117. John IX (898–900)
118. Benedict IV (900–903)
119. Leo V (903)
120. Sergius III (904–911)
121. Anastasius III (911–913)
122. Lando (913–914)
123. John X (914–928)
124. Leo VI (928)
125. Stephen VIII (929–931)
126. John XI (931–935)
127. Leo VII (936–939)
128. Stephen IX (939–942)
129. Marinus II (942–946)
130. Agapetus II (946–955)
131. John XII (955–963)
132. Leo VIII (963–964)

133. Benedict V (964)

134. John XIII (965–972)

135. Benedict VI (973–974)

136. Benedict VII (974–983)

137. John XIV (983–984)

138. John XV (985–996)

139. Gregory V (996–999)

140. Sylvester II (999–1003)

141. John XVII (1003)

142. John XVIII (1003–1009)

143. Sergius IV (1009–1012)

144. Benedict VIII (1012–1024)

145. John XIX (1024–1032)

146. Benedict IX (1032–1045)

147. Sylvester III (1045)

148. Benedict IX (1045)

149. Gregory VI (1045–1046)

150. Clement II (1046–1047)

151. Benedict IX (1047–1048)

152. Damasus II (1048)

153. St. Leo IX (1049–1054)

154. Victor II (1055–1057)

155. Stephen X (1057–1058)

156. Nicholas II (1058–1061)

157. Alexander II (1061–1073)

158. St. Gregory VII (1073–1085)

159. Blessed Victor III (1086–1087)

160. Blessed Urban II (1088–1099)

161. Paschal II (1099–1118)

162. Gelasius II (1118–1119)

163. Callistus II (1119–1124)

164. Honorius II (1124–1130)

165. Innocent II (1130–1143)

166. Celestine II (1143–1144)

167. Lucius II (1144–1145)

168. Blessed Eugene III (1145–1153)

169. Anastasius IV (1153–1154)

170. Adrian IV (1154–59)

171. Alexander III (1159–1181)

172. Lucius III (1181–1185)

173. Urban III (1185–1187)

174. Gregory VIII (1187)

175. Clement III (1187–1191)

176. Celestine III (1191–1198)

177. Innocent III (1198–1216)

178. Honorius III (1216–1227)

179. Gregory IX (1227–1241)

180. Celestine IV (1241)

181. Innocent IV (1243–1254)

182. Alexander IV (1254–1261)

183. Urban IV (1261–1264)

184. Clement IV (1265–1268)

185. Blessed Gregory X (1271–1276)

186. Blessed Innocent V (1276)

187. Adrian V (1276)

188. John XXI (1276–1277)

189. Nicholas III (1277–1280)

190. Martin IV (1281–1285)

191. Honorius IV (1285–1287)

192. Nicholas IV (1288–1292)

193. St. Celestine V (1294)

194. Boniface VIII (1294–1303)

195. Blessed Benedict XI (1303–1304)

196. Clement V (1305–1314)

197. John XXII (1316–1334)

198. Benedict XII (1334–1342)

199. Clement VI (1342–1352)

200. Innocent VI (1352–1362)

201. Blessed Urban V (1362–1370)
202. Gregory I (1370–1378)
203. Urban VI (1378–1389)
204. Boniface IX (1389–1404)
205. Innocent VII (1406–1406)
206. Gregory XII (1406–1415)
207. Martin V (1417–1431)
208. Eugene IV (1431–1447)
209. Nicholas V (1447–1455)
210. Callistus III (1455–1458)
211. Pius II (1458–1464)
212. Paul II (1464–1471)
213. Sixtus IV (1471–1484)
214. Innocent VIII (1484–1492)
215. Alexander VI (1492–1503)
216. Pius III (1503)
217. Julius II (1503–1513)
218. Leo X (1513–1521)
219. Adrian VI (1522–1523)
220. Clement VII (1523–1534)
221. Paul III (1534–1549)
222. Julius III (1550–1555)
223. Marcellus II (1555)
224. Paul IV (1555–1559)
225. Pius IV (1559–1565)
226. St. Pius V (1566–1572)
227. Gregory XIII (1572–1585)
228. Sixtus V (1585–1590)
229. Urban VII (1590)
230. Gregory XIV (1590–1591)
231. Innocent IX (1591)
232. Clement VIII (1592–1605)
233. Leo XI (1605)

234. Paul V (1605–1621)
235. Gregory XV (1621–1623)
236. Urban VIII (1623–1644)
237. Innocent X (1644–1655)
238. Alexander VII (1655–1667)
239. Clement IX (1667–1669)
240. Clement X (1670–1676)
241. Blessed Innocent XI (1676–1689)
242. Alexander VIII (1689–1691)
243. Innocent XII (1691–1700)
244. Clement XI (1700–1721)
245. Innocent XIII (1721–1724)
246. Benedict XIII (1724–1730)
247. Clement XII (1730–1740)
248. Benedict XIV (1740–1758)
249. Clement XIII (1758–1769)
250. Clement XIV (1769–1774)
251. Pius VI (1775–1799)
252. Pius VII (1800–1823)
253. Leo XII (1823–1829)
254. Pius VIII (1829–1830)
255. Gregory XVI (1831–1846)
256. Blessed Pius IX (1846–1878)
257. Leo XIII (1878–1903)
258. St. Pius X (1903–1914)
259. Benedict XV (1914–1922)
260. Pius XI (1922–1939)
261. Pius XII (1939–1958)
262. Blessed John XXIII (1958–1963)
263. Paul VI (1963–1978)
264. John Paul I (1978)
265. John Paul II (1978–)

Biografia

Charlemagne (742–814), also known as Charles the Great, is considered one of the greatest European rulers of the Middle Ages. Best known for having founded what is known as the Holy Roman Empire. Charlemagne revived the title of Roman Emperor in the west and, on Christmas Day in 800, was crowned "Emperor of the Romans" by Pope Leo III, a gesture that resulted in centuries of conflict between the northern emperors and the popes.

In Hoc Signo Vinces

As discussed in Chapter 7, "The Medieval Minestrone," the Roman Empire began its final decline after Constantine abandoned Rome to move the center of imperial rule to Constantinople. This move eventually shifted the power and wealth associated with the Church away from Rome. The Holy Roman Empire refers to the successor state founded in 800 by Charlemagne after he defeated and conquered the invading Lombards.

Based on the "Donation of Constantine," a document many historians now believe was a forgery, additional papal territories were acquired in the ninth century. Wealthy landowners hoping to gain appointments to prestigious Church positions bequeathed and donated additional lands.

"Italia"

In Italics

Fourth century—The Emperor Constantine erected a basilica over the supposed burial place of Peter. After the original basilica fell into disrepair, the huge St. Peter's Church was built on the same location in the sixteenth century.

Monasteries and Abbeys Become the Rage

During the Middle Ages, monasteries and abbeys were built throughout Europe and developed into important centers of learning and peaceful arts. Often, they became the nuclei of future towns. Wherever churches were built, towns soon grew around them. As you will soon see, the Church continued to have an important role during the Renaissance.

By the thirteenth and fourteenth centuries, the single most powerful institution in Europe was the Roman Catholic Church. The Church affected almost every facet of life, political, cultural, social, and economic. Indeed, for many centuries the papacy was not only a spiritual stronghold but also a position of great political power. After all, Rome was in the center of the peninsula and had many advantages, including a port that provided access to the rest of the world.

As a result, there were regular attempts made by rival groups to sit on the "Throne of St. Peter." The stakes were high, for whoever ruled the papacy also controlled the vast wealth and territories that came with it. As a result, it sometimes occurred that an *antipope*—someone who attempted to assume the role of pope without the support of the Church—would claim the papacy, especially during a disputed papal election. (All in all, there have been approximately 35 to 40 antipopes.)

In what became known as the Great Schism of 1378 to 1415, there were actually two popes. Under pressure by the Romans to ensure the papacy remained in Rome (and not Avignon), by threat of death, the Cardinals were forced to elect the Roman Urban VI (previously Barolomeo Prignano) as pope. Five months later, in a split between the College of Cardinals, Urban's election was declared null and void, and in his place, Clement VII (previously Robert of Genova) was declared pope. During this time, the hostile political climate of Rome made it a very dangerous place for Clement, who moved his papacy to the safer grounds in Avignon.

Who was the real pope? The ensuing political and spiritual confusion surrounding this question lasted for an entire generation before the papacy was reunited in Rome in 1415.

By the sixteenth and seventeenth centuries, the peninsula was a patchwork of city-states, each with its own histories and traditions, kings, and *duchies*. The Papal States are one such example, with the pope serving as the head of state. By 1859, the Church controlled 16,000 square miles, from the Adriatic to the Tyrrhenian Sea.

Rites of the Church

The rites of the Church form the basis of many celebrations and festivals in the life of an Italian Catholic. Beginning with baptism only days after a baby's birth, the first communion at the age of seven or eight, confirmation soon thereafter,

"*Italia*"

In Italics

1309–1377—With the election of Pope Clement V, the papacy was moved from Rome to Avignon for what came to be known as the Avignon papacy.

La Bella Lingua

A **duchy** refers to a county or territory ruled by a signore who happens to be either a duke, a baron, or a count.

marriage, and the last rites and funeral, the rites of the Church mark the passages of a life.

To mark these occasions, Italians feast. A party or festival includes not only family and close friends but also the community at large. Regional, communal, and family traditions are passed down from generation to generation, century after century. In Italy, rich and poor alike commemorate these events with equal reverence and celebration.

Regardless a person's spiritual inclination, holidays are appreciated as opportunities to spend time with family. In between the official national *feste* (holidays), Italians have their agendas full of engagements, parties, post-parties, regattas, ceremonies, festivals, carnivals, and—not to rain on anyone's parade—funerals. In between are birthdays, saints's days (at least one saint for each day of the year), *Carnevale* (Mardi Gras), and Ferragosto (August holidays).

Italy has nine official holidays, six of which are based on Roman Catholic holy days, which are generally tied to important events in the Bible.

Di Interessa

The seven rites of Catholicism include:

1. **Baptism:** A religious ceremony that traditionally happens at birth, in which the child is sprinkled with holy water to symbolize purification.

2. **Penance:** "Forgive me Father, for I have sinned ..."

3. **Communion:** Occurs around the age of seven and is considered an important event in a Catholic's life, who is now permitted to receive "the body of Christ" in the form of the host during Sunday Mass.

4. **Confirmation:** After communion, confirmation marks a Catholic's formal acceptance into the Roman Catholic Church.

5. **Marriage:** The ceremony in which two people are joined together in wedlock.

6. **Ordination:** Marks the official investiture as a Catholic priest. Most priests discuss the "calling."

7. **Last Rites:** A priest blesses you before your death.

Just about every Italian town has its own personal saint. The Saints' Days are another occasion in which the Church influences communal life. Many villages and cities commemorate their saint's day with religious and nonreligious celebrations, such as the San Gennaro feast that occurs in Naples as well as New York City.

Strong Enough to Suspend Time

All those celebrations take place pretty much at the same time every year, in part because of the development of a common calendar. For a variety of astronomical reasons, the calendar used in the western world since the time of Julius Caesar was incorrect. By the sixteenth century, the vernal equinox—crucial to the calculation of Easter—had slipped from March 21 to March 11.

In 1582, Pope Gregory XIII (1572–1585) modified the calendar to bring it closer to conformity with the natural course of the seasons. It was decided to cancel 10 days beginning with October 4, 1582, which was followed the day after by October 15, 1582. The pope, in all his infinite power, simply said, "Today is October 4, and tomorrow will be October 15!" And so it was. Now the calendar is much closer to the astronomical calendar, with minor tweaking necessary (leap days) to account for the fact that there are approximately 365.25 days in the year. The change was accepted immediately by Catholic states and adopted by Protestant nations soon afterward.

> **Di Interessa**
>
> "Peter's pence" was an annual tax for the support of the papacy levied from the early tenth century at the rate of a penny on every English householder. It was abolished in England in 1534 during the Reformation. Today the term refers to a voluntary payment by Roman Catholics to the papal treasury.

Popes Patronize Painters

So now you can see how the Catholic Church has influenced your world, even if you are not Catholic. Another consequence of the popes' influence involved the arts.

Often belonging to important families of the ruling classes, during the Renaissance, many popes (including Julius II and Leo X) lived like kings and were avid patrons—supporters—of the arts. Julius II (1503–1513) came from an impoverished noble family in Liguria and is best known for having laid the cornerstone to the magnificent St. Peter's Church. Also a great patron of the arts, he supported the artists Raphael, Michelangelo, and Bramante, three great painters living at the time. (You'll learn more about the masters in Chapter 12, "*Putti*, Painters, and the Arts.")

Leo X (1513–1521), born a Florentine named Giovanni de' Medici, was the son of the powerful Lorenzo de' Medici, part of the great Medici family you'll learn more about in Chapter 11, "Strange Bedfellows." Leo was made a cardinal when still a boy. Although a good enough pope, Leo's real claim to fame was through his patronage of the artist Raphael, best known for his sweet-faced Madonna and mythological and biblical figures painted throughout the Vatican.

Another member of the Medici family and cousin of Leo X, Clement VII (1523–1534) was also a patron of Raphael and of Michelangelo, whose great fresco of the Last Judgment in the Sistine Chapel was undertaken by his orders. Grandnephew of Pope Paul V and member of the Chigi family from Siena, Alexander VII (1672–1678) did much to beautify Rome. He hired the sculptor, painter, and architect Gian Lorenzo Bernini (1598–1680) to design the colonnade that encloses the piazza in front of St. Peter's Basilica. Bernini also designed the magnificent Throne of St. Peter, a gilt-bronze cover for the medieval wooden throne of the pope.

Di Interessa

In the 1500s, monks living in a medieval monastery in the northern Italian village of Lucedio mysteriously went crazy and committed unspeakable acts of evil. The locals believe that the devil came and conspired with witches to curse the town and the monastery. The monks were excommunicated from the Catholic Church. Reportedly, the ghosts of the depraved, unholy men—and those they tortured—have haunted the area ever since.

Best to Conform

The Church's patronage belied another, far more destructive policy known as the Roman Inquisition. At its height during the late sixteenth and early seventeenth centuries, the local and Roman inquisitions were active against both famous intellectuals and village eccentrics. Anyone not fitting into the prescribed models of behavior became vulnerable to an "inquiry."

Those people accused of heresy who refused to confess were tried before an inquisitor and jury. Punishments were harsh and included the confiscation of goods, torture, and death.

Among the victims of the Inquisition's investigations during this period were the philosophers Francesco Patrizi, Giordano Bruno, and Tommaso Campanella, and the scientist Galileo Galilei. Galileo ended his days under house arrest (you'll read more about Galileo's ordeals in Chapter 13, "Great Discoveries: Here We Come!"), and Campanella spent many years in prison. Condemned to death by the church, Bruno was burned at the stake.

Today, it's hard to imagine that the Vatican—so beloved by millions of pilgrims and tourists—might have been behind such brutal methods, especially when you look at the current pope.

Pope John Paul II

Pope John Paul II was born as Karol Wojtyla on May 18, 1920, in Wadowice, Poland. He was voted in a *Time* magazine poll as "The most tireless moral voice of a secular age, he reminded humankind of the worth of individuals in the modern world."

His Holiness has authored several titles, including *For the Children: Words of Love and Inspiration from His Holiness Pope John Paul II; The Way to Christ, Spiritual Exercises;* and *Breakfast with the Pope: Daily Readings*, among others.

Have a look at the resumé of Pope John Paul II:

1946	Ordained as priest
1956	Named professor of ethics at Lublin University
1958	Became auxiliary bishop of Cracow
1963	Appointed archbishop
1967	Named to the College of Cardinals
1978	Elected pope
1979	Made papal visit to his homeland
1981	Wounded by assassin
1998	Met Castro and celebrated Mass in Cuba

Biografia

According to a legend widely believed in the Middle Ages, Pope Joan (c. 1000) was a woman in male disguise. The story may be connected to the power-hungry Theodora the Senatrix and her daughter, Marozia, who completely controlled the elections of the popes from 901 to 964, and whose sons and grandsons kept the papacy in the family's possession.

Pope Trivia

Indeed, the pope is a powerful figurehead. Here are a couple of popular pope-related tidbits:

➤ The bulletproof, glass-enclosed vehicle that Pope John Paul II rides in (aptly called the "popemobile") is a target for a popular local joke: The papal license plates, SCV1, stand for *Stato della Città del Vaticano* (Vatican City State), but many Romans consider them an acronym for "Se Cristo Vedesse"—if only Christ could see this.

➤ The skullcap worn by popes is called a *zucchetto* (not to be confused with a *zucchino*, which is an Italian squash).

➤ The chartered jet that Pope John Paul II used during his 1999 U.S. visit was code-named "Shepherd One."

The Least You Need to Know

➤ For over two millennia, the papacy has played a pivotal role in the political, spiritual, and social life of the Italian peninsula.

➤ The Roman Catholic Church and religious tradition permeates every level of Italian culture.

➤ The Papal States, governed by the pope, were an independent territory in and around Rome that existed for over 1,000 years and were once the mightiest power in Europe.

➤ The papal court made Rome a brilliant Renaissance capital, enriched by some of the finest art of the West.

➤ The Vatican City State is an independent, sovereign state.

Leaving the Middle Ages

On the one hand, the Middle Ages were marked by disasters such as famine and the plague and represented a period of discord and political instability. On the other hand, the first signs of the unique and highly creative period that would become known as the Renaissance were becoming evident. Led by creative geniuses such as Dante and Giotto, Italy was making real progress in the artistic and literary fields.

Famine

Times were tough, make no mistake. Between 1339 and 1375, there were four major famines which would not have been more disastrous than those of the previous century had they not been accompanied by many wars filled with large mercenary armies that left a wake of destruction behind them.

Bigger Weapons, Bolder Warlords

Military technology never seems to lag, regardless of the political situation or social conditions of a period. Humans always seem to find a way to upgrade their fighting machines, and this period of history was no different.

The crossbow became widely available, a weapon that far surpassed the piercing power of the longbow, which it replaced. Because of the crossbow's superiority, knights had to wear heavier armor for better protection, which demanded stronger and more numerous horses upon which they could ride. The result of all these technical developments was that waging war became more expensive, and mercenary troops began to replace the citizen militias.

Biografia

Sir John Hawkwood (d. 1394), an Englishman, was one of the most legendary *condottieri*. He was the leader of the body of English mercenaries known as the White Company and fought for Italian cities, popes, and princes, from 1360 to 1390. He was made commander-in-chief of the Florentine forces. He died in Florence and was buried in the Duomo. Paolo Uccello (1396–1475) painted a fresco of him in Florence's main church.

During the fourteenth century, these troops increased in size and became a force in their own right. Many city-states employed bands of mercenary soldiers to protect them or attack their adversaries (sometimes the best defense is a good offense). These *condottieri*—from the Italian word *condotte,* or contracts—studied war as art and relied mainly on cavalry armed with lances.

An example of this was Venice, where in the early 1500s over 30,000 *condottieri* were employed. It wasn't unusual for some mercenary bands to prolong the wars they fought in order to continue collecting a paycheck.

Black Death and Bankruptcies

One manifestation of economic decline was the bankruptcies of great Florentine banking houses—the Peruzzi in 1343, the Acciaiuoli in 1345, and the Bardi in 1346. In Chapter 10, "Can You Spare a Florin? Banking and Commerce," you'll learn more about the Italian banking system and bankruptcies around the time of the Black Death.

Famine and wars were minor affairs compared with the horror of the Black Death of 1348, which struck when the resistance of Italians had already been lowered. Later, in the seventeenth century, historians applied the term "Black Death" to the plague of 1348, but in the fourteenth century, it was simply referred to as "the plague" or "la peste."

It is believed to have begun in China in the early 1330s in one of the main trading ports. In October 1347, Italian merchant ships returned to Messina, Sicily, with most of the crews dead. By January 1348, it reached Genoa and Pisa; by February, Venice. From these ports it spread throughout the peninsula and on to the rest of Europe.

Government, trade, and commerce came to a virtual halt. Embargoes were put in place to help prevent the spread of the disease, but they also prevented the movement of goods and people. There was no medical science worthy of the name that could handle the crisis. Doctors considered it a scourge of God or the result of unusual constellations in the sky. We now know, of course, that it was spread by fleas on the bodies of black rats that were transported aboard trading ships.

Di Interessa

In the wake of the first plague infestations, there were physical attacks by citizens on women lepers and Jews who were thought to have deliberately spread the plague or to have polluted society and brought God's vengeance.

By the end of the fourteenth century, years of instability and war had induced famine, blights of Black Death, and natural disaster, wreaking havoc upon the increasingly unsanitary and overcrowded cities of Italy. The Black Death eradicated one third of the population in Italy, causing fear and havoc throughout the country and devastating the economy.

> Ring around the rosies
> A pocket full of posies
> Ashes, ashes
> We all fall down!

We used to dance in a circle while reciting this seemingly innocent nursery rhyme. But these four lines refer to the single most devastating epidemic in recorded history.

The roses actually refer to rosary beads that were used for prayers asking for divine intervention. The buboes and abscesses of the illness emitted a putrid odor, so flowers (or posies) were carried to mask the smell. Ashes resulted from burning the corpses and the expression "fall down" refers to people dying.

During times of war, the metal roofs of many churches were used to create artillery like this one at San Galgano.

(Photo by Anna Andersson)

Let There Be Light

It sometimes happens in the history of art that a transitional period between two great schools or styles produces single works of immense worth. In the late thirteenth century in Italy, a transition from medieval traditions—Byzantine or Gothic—to the first glimmerings of the Renaissance took place, and a new spirit and new techniques combined to produce one of the great phases in the development of painting and architecture.

Byzantine artists in Italy in the mid-thirteenth century had become heavily formalized in their work. One of the first to take a new direction was Cimabue. Cenni di Peppi (1240–1302), known by his nickname Cimabue (meaning "bullheaded") was a painter and mosaicist. Little is known about his life, and his only documented work is the mosaic figure of St. John in the apse of Pisa Cathedral in 1302.

Cimabue's reputation as the first artist of the Italian Renaissance rests upon his mention by Dante in a famous passage which, literally translated, states that "Cimabue believed he held the field in painting, but now the cry goes out for Giotto so that the fame of the former is obscured."

Nevertheless, Cimabue is now generally recognized as heralding the coming of the Renaissance and as the most important artist in Italy before Giotto. Later scholars, such as Lorenzo Gilberti and Giorgio Vasari, recognized Cimabue as the artist who marked the divide between the art of the Middle Ages and that of the Renaissance. Vasari's *Lives of the Most Excellent Painters, Sculptors, and Architects* (1550) even begins with an account of Cimabue's career.

Cimabue probably painted the *frescoes* in the choir of the upper church and of the *Madonna Enthroned with Four Angels and St. Francis* in the lower church at Assisi. The *Crucifix* (c. 1287–1290) in the church of Santa Croce, Florence, and the large *Madonna and Child Enthroned,* in the Uffizi, are also attributed to him.

La Bella Lingua

A **fresco** (Italian for "fresh") is a method for painting walls and ceilings in which powdered pigment is mixed only with water and applied directly to unset ("fresh") plaster. Artists apply only enough plaster to finish in one day before the plaster dried. Each of these areas is called a *giornata* ("day's work").

Ringing in the Renaissance

Although Cimabue's painting hinted at the flowering that was to come, the man most often cited as the first Renaissance painter credited is the Florentine, Giotto (Giotto di Bondone, 1266–1337). Giotto was a painter and an architect who was the first to break with the formulas of Byzantine painting and gave new life to the art of painting in Italy. His strongest influence had been the work and teaching of Cimabue.

Bell Towers

Giotto is credited with building the *campanile*—bell tower—of the cathedral at Florence, but it was as a painter that he made his biggest impact. His contemporaries recognized Giotto's artistic originality, and the author Boccaccio wrote that "his work was so perfect that a man standing before it would

"*Italia*"

In Italics

November 4, 1666—Torrential rains throughout Italy caused a national emergency. In Florence, the Arno River overran its banks and inundated the city with water, wreaking untold damage. Cimabue's *Crucifix* was the flood's worst victim. Although restored, much of the original paint was lost.

often find his visual senses confused, taking for real what was only painted," in his renowned book *The Decameron*.

Where Is Giotto Today?

Where can you see Giotto's work today? His fresco cycle in the Arena (or Scrovegni) Chapel in Padua completely covers the interior wall surfaces. In Florence, he painted the bell tower that's part of Florence's main church, as well as the frescoes in the Bardi and Peruzzi chapels in the church of Santa Croce. And in the Uffizi, you can see his majestic altarpiece, the *Ognissanti Madonna* (c. 1305–1310).

The Emergence of Tuscan

In addition to the changes taking place in the art world, literature was undergoing major new developments as well. As we'll discuss in more depth later in the chapter, Florentine culture produced the three literary artists who best summarized Italian thought and feeling of the late Middle Ages and early Renaissance: Dante, Petrarch, and Boccaccio. Known as the "Tuscany Trinity," they were also the first Italian writers to make literary use of the Tuscan dialect spoken in Florence, Siena, and other north-central Italian towns. In the meantime, it's important to understand how the language of Italy was developing and changing at this time.

Until the thirteenth century, Latin remained the literary language of Italy. At that point, poets at the Sicilian court of Frederick I (later Emperor Frederick II) began to imitate the poetry popular in Provence, France, in their native Italian. The style was referred to as the Sicilian school of poetry. During his reign, Frederick attracted poets such as Giacomo Pugliese and Rinaldo d'Aquino from many parts of Italy. With his death in 1250, the cultural center of Italy slowly began to shift to Florence.

The *dolce stil nuovo* (Italian: "sweet new style") was a style of love poetry founded by the Bolognese poet Guido Guinizelli (c. 1240–1276) and perfected by the Florentine poets Guido Cavalcanti (c. 1250–1300) and Dante. It was characterized by a spiritualization of courtly love, the use of the vernacular, and the sonnet, ballad, and canzone verse forms. An example of this style is Dante's lyrics to Beatrice in his *La Vita Nuova*. The style influenced Petrarch, Pietro Bembo, Dante Gabriel Rossetti, and Ezra Pound.

During the fourteenth century, the Tuscan dialect began to predominate, thanks to the region's central position as well as the aggressive commerce of its most

"*Italia*"

In Italics

Easter Monday, 1282—The massacre of 2,000 French residents of Palermo marked the beginning of a revolt called the Sicilian Vespers. Following the uprising, the island passed to the House of Aragon, and the Italian peninsula south of the Papal States became known as the Kingdom of Two Sicilies until it fell to Giuseppe Garibaldi in 1860.

important city, Florence. Also, of all the Italian dialects, Tuscan differs the least in morphology and phonology from classical Latin, and so it harmonizes best with the Italian traditions of Latin culture. This was the beginning of change in Italian literature. The medieval themes gave way to voice and traditions of modern society and were the beginning of what was to be called the "Italian style" in writing.

Dante

Dante Alighieri (1265–1321) towers over Italian literature just as Shakespeare does over English literature. Until Dante, Italians had no written vernacular language that all literate Italian could understand. Dante's poetry virtually created the Italian language.

Dante's early work consisted mainly of courtly love poetry; his first book, *La Vita Nuova* (c. 1290–1294), consists of 31 poems linked by a prose narrative and tells of his love for Beatrice Portinari. However, Dante's international renown and reputation as the founding figure of Italian literature rests on *The Divine Comedy,* an epic poem that tells of his spiritual journey that takes the form of an imagined visit to Hell and Purgatory. The poet Virgil is his guide until he reaches Paradise, where Beatrice, now a blessed spirit, takes over.

Revenge Served Up in Hell

The Divine Comedy allowed Dante to take a little revenge on his political enemies, who had exiled him from Florence during the Guelph–Ghibelline conflict in 1302. He took this revenge by describing his enemies' torments in Hell. Dante's judgments on a number of people and issues are reflected in the historical persons who populate Hell and in the imaginative punishments he metes out to them there. Some sinners are condemned to a life of pushing heavy weights with their chests, others are naked in a snake pit, still others are terrorized by monsters, while some particularly unlucky ones have flesh that melts as they step on searing, burning sand.

The action takes place in the year 1300, starting on Holy Thursday. The poet is lost in the woods and unable to escape. *La Divina Commedia* is structured in terza rima, with three cantiche (*Inferno, Purgatorio, Paradiso*), each having 33 *canti* (plus an introductory canto to the *Inferno*), and with each of the regions having nine subdivisions.

Inferno

The first part of Dante's great poem describes the poet's journey through Hell under the guidance of Virgil, the celebrated Roman poet. In the dark, fiery underground, imagined as a conical funnel reaching to the center of the earth, Dante encounters a variety of former friends and enemies.

Purgatorio

Emerging from the Inferno, Dante, still accompanied by Virgil, follows a spiral up to the Mount of Purgatory, where they encounter various groups of repentant sinners on the seven circular ledges of the mountain. On its summit is the Earthly Paradise where the poet meets Beatrice, who is to guide him through the spheres of Heaven.

Paradiso

Now Dante's guide is Beatrice, the woman who had inspired his love. Paradise is divided into spheres: the sphere of the Moon, of Mercury, Venus, the Sun, Mars, Jupiter, Saturn, the Fixed Stars, and the Primum Mobile, or First Mover. In each sphere Dante has conversations on spiritual matters with historical characters.

Dante first met Beatrice during a party. They were both nine years old. In *La Vita Nuova* he wrote this about the initial encounter: "Love ruled my soul … and began to hold such sway over me …" When Beatrice died in 1290, Dante was inspired to write a series of love poems that dealt with his love for her and his grief at her death.

The woman loved by Dante also features in Dante's *Divine Comedy*. Toward the end of the second book, *Purgatorio*, Dante meets Beatrice, who replaces Virgil as Dante's guide through Paradise in the final book, *Paradiso*. Unfortunately for Dante, his love for Beatrice went unreturned since her family arranged for her to marry Simon dé Bardi. She was married in 1283, only to die a few years later.

Di Interessa

In 1880, French sculptor Auguste Rodin (1840–1917) was commissioned to produce a set of portals for the new Museum of Decorative Arts in Paris based on Dante's *Divine Comedy*. Titled *The Gates of Hell*, the project occupied the rest of Rodin's life and inspired a number of his most famous individual works, including *The Thinker*, *The Three Shades*, and *The Prodigal Son*. The doors were never cast in bronze in his lifetime but two copies were made from his original casts in 1917 for the Philadelphia Museum of Art and the Musée Rodin, Paris.

Greed, Pride, Weakness, Sin!

Dante's epic poem was recognized almost immediately for its significance. Boccaccio composed an account of Dante's life and was the first to deliver a series of public lectures on the text of the *Divina Commedia*. It confirmed the literary authority, prestige, and influence of the work and its author.

Chaucer, the first English poet to name Dante in his work, has quotations from the *Divina Commedia* throughout his later work. Nineteenth-century poets, especially Byron, Shelley, and Thomas Carlyle, much admired Dante's work and thus revived interest in the medieval poet, and the twentieth-century writer T. S. Eliot in particular was profoundly influenced by Dante's work.

Painting by Numbers

Hundreds of artists, from Botticelli to William Blake, from Gustave Doré to Salvador Dalì, have produced cycles of illustrations for Dante's work. Giovanni di Paolo, a fifteenth-century Sienese painter, created an illustrated edition of the Paradiso.

His vision of Hell has proved enormously influential. Michelangelo's Last Judgment (1536–1541) in the Sistine Chapel at the Vatican seems capture Dante's Inferno precisely. Minos, the judge of the damned, his tail wrapped around his body, looks on while Charon, the infernal ferryman, drives the damned into Hell with his oar. Dante's tortured sinners and their terrible fate later attracted the Romantic imagination and provided Delacroix with the subject of his first large-scale painting, *The Barque of Dante* (1822), which is now in the Louvre in Paris.

Bawdy Boccaccio

Another important writer emerging in the late Middle Ages was Giovanni Boccaccio (1313–1375). Boccaccio was the first to write a commentary on Dante, and he was also a friend and disciple of Petrarch. Around him gathered enthusiasts of the new humanism.

Boccaccio was instrumental in the development of the Italian language. His *Il Decamerone* consists of 100 stories told by characters that are also part of a story that provides the setting for the whole, much like *The Arabian Nights*. Regarded as a masterpiece and a model for Italian classical prose, Boccaccio's influence on Renaissance literature was enormous and continues even in contemporary times.

Boccaccio's writings were used for plots and characters by writers in other countries. For example, his epic poem "La Teseida" (c. 1341) was used by the fourteenth-century English poet Geoffrey Chaucer as the basis for his "Knight's Tale" (1387) and by the seventeenth-century English poet John Dryden in his poem "Palamon and Arcite."

The Decameron

Boccaccio's most famous work was *The Decameron*. In it, he gathered 10 young, attractive men and women who are seeking to escape the ravages of the Black Death and put them in a beautiful Tuscan villa outside the city of Florence. Then, to while away the time and to escape the epidemic, he let each of them take turns telling bawdy stories. Each day ends with one of the storytellers singing a song accompanied by lusty, vibrant dancing.

At first blush, the tale of ten Florentines sounds like a pitch for the latest reality-based TV show screenplay. But in fact, it's the framework for *Il Decamerone*, written by Boccaccio almost 650 years ago. Regarded as his masterpiece and a model for Italian classical prose, its influence on Renaissance literature was enormous.

The storytelling takes up ten days of the fortnight (the other days were reserved for religious devotions and personal adornment) and provides the title of the book, *Il Decamerone*, or *Ten Days' Work*. The stories total 100 in all and explore a wide range of moral, social, and political issues, with a candor and wit that may astound the modern reader. The problems of corruption in high office, sexual jealousy, and the differences between the rich and the poor figure prominently in a substantial number of *The Decameron's* tales.

Di Interessa

You can readily pick up a copy of Boccaccio's *The Decameron* at a bookstore near you, or watch Pier Paolo Pasolini's bawdy film, *Il Decamerone*.

The Beds Confused

The titles alone of some of Boccaccio's tales would be enough to send TV producers, religious fundamentalists, and media critics scrambling. These include: "Masetto da Lamporecchio Pretends to be Deaf and Dumb in Order to Become a Gardener to a Convent of Nuns, Where All the Women Eagerly Lie with Him," and "Two Men Are Close Friends, and One Lies with the Other's Wife. The Husband Finds It Out and Makes the Wife Shut Her Lover in a Chest, and While He Is Inside, the Husband Lies with the Lover's Own Wife on the Chest."

Boccaccio's gift for humor and wit are also evident in "The Beds Confused," a precursor to the modern-day bedroom farce. Two young men lodge at an inn, and before the evening is over, a hilarious round of musical beds ensues that includes the host, his wife and daughter, and the two guests hopping from room to room.

Then there's the lascivious "Story of Patient Griselda." This tale, told on the tenth day, is one of trust, betrayal, and mistaken identity, when a marquis who has two children by his wife, Griselda, stages their deaths and an act of infidelity (with one of his daughters, no less) before finally accepting his wife again and bestowing the title of marchesa upon her.

Famous Women

After writing the *Decameron,* Boccaccio spent the last decades of his life compiling en-cyclopedic works in Latin. One of these was *Famous Women,* the first collection of biographies in Western literature devoted exclusively to women. *Famous Women* in-cluded the life stories of 106 women, from "Eve Our First Mother" to Queen Joanna of Naples, from vestal virgins to Minerva, the goddess of wisdom. It was one of the most popular works at the end of the era of manuscript books.

The Modern Man

The third member of the literary trinity from Tuscany was the humanist scholar and poet Petrarch (Francesco Petrarca, 1304–1374), born in Arezzo because his father was in exile from Florence. Petrarch was a passionate admirer of an-cient Roman civilization and one of the great early Renaissance humanists, creating a Republic of Letters.

Di Interessa

You can visit Petrarch's house in Padua. Built in the fourteenth century, it's open to the public as a museum with historical ex-hibits. The interior walls are dec-orated with scenes inspired by *Il Canzoniere.*

His literary criticism was highly respected, as were his translations from Latin into the Vulgate and his own Latin works. Petrarch helped to restore classi-cal Latin as a literary and scholarly language and to discredit the use of medieval Latin, which had served as an international medium of communica-tion. But it is his love poetry, written in the vulgar tongue (the everyday language spoken by ordinary people), that keeps his name alive today.

Head Over Heels in Love

Before card stores and chocolate manufacturers all conspired to commercialize the true spirit of love, passion, and romance, Petrarch literally wrote the book on infatua-tion. The collection of Italian verses, *Rime in vita e morta di Madonna Laura* (after 1327), translated into English as *Petrarch's Sonnets,* were inspired by Petrarch's un-requited passion for Laura (probably Laure de Noves), a young woman Petrarch first saw in church. Also known as *Il Canzoniere* (*Songbook*), the sonnets had enormous influence on the poets of the fifteenth and sixteenth centuries.

Head-over-heels in love with Laura, Petrarch wrote 365 sonnets, one passionate poem a day, dedicated to his true love. Considered the first modern poet because of his in-terest in individuality, the Italian poet perfected the sonnet during the fourteenth century.

Here's a passage from one of the sonnets that Petrarch composed demonstrating the intensity and inwardness of his feelings:

> Oh blessed be the day, the month, the year,
> the season and the time, the hour, the instant,
> the gracious countryside, the place where I was
> struck by those two lovely eyes that bound me …

The Least You Need to Know

➤ Plague, famine, and war destabilized Italy during the 1300s.

➤ The transition of art from the Byzantine and Gothic styles to the Renaissance was largely a result of innovative artists like Cimabue and Giotto.

➤ Dante Alighieri's three-part epic, *La Divina Commedia,* is one of the great works of world literature.

➤ Boccaccio's 100 witty tales provided escape fiction from the terrible world of the Black Death.

➤ Petrarch, one of the great early Renaissance humanists, wrote love poetry in the vulgar tongue.

Part 3

Quantum Leaps

The Renaissance was essentially a rebirth of classical ideas that ranged from the intellectual to the sensual. In Part 3, you'll learn more about this artistic explosion.

Count your blessings as you study the development of the complex and highly functioning banking system that helped finance the great works of art and architecture. Read about the opulence and majesty of the great city-states and their rulers. Get a crash course on the Italian masters Leonardo da Vinci, Michelangelo, Raphael, and Titian. Who were the major players of the time? What was humanism?

See how the Renaissance paved the way for the scientific Golden Age that brought us thinkers like Galileo Galilei and paved the way for the discovery of the New World, an accident that would have profound and far-reaching consequences.

Study how the Inquisition forced men like Galileo to renounce their words, yet contemporaneously nurtured the musical phenomenon known as opera during the Baroque.

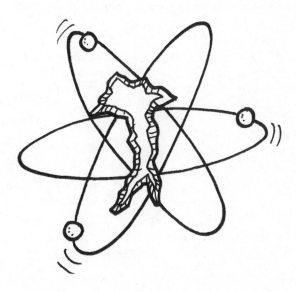

Chapter 10

Can You Spare a Florin? Banking and Commerce

> ## In This Chapter
>
> ➤ Paper wealth and modern banking
>
> ➤ Florins, ducats, and sequins
>
> ➤ The check's in the mail
>
> ➤ Renaissance art commissioned by wealthy families

Think of Renaissance Italy, and what comes to mind? Probably sculpture by Michelangelo, marble-clad churches, Botticelli's *Birth of Venus* and *Primavera*. Raffaello's frescoes in the Vatican, huge palaces filled with artwork, and Titian's fantastic paintings in Venice. The amount and quality of artistic work produced during this era is mind-boggling.

Although art may now be priceless, where did the money come from to pay for artists to produce it? Who commissioned the paintings, sculptures, and architectural designs, and why? In this chapter, you'll learn about the new banking system created and developed by Italians and how the wealth generated from this industry helped to finance many of the great works of Renaissance art.

Banker's Hours

Roberto Benigni's latest film is playing and you need some cash to buy a couple of tickets. So you head to the nearest branch of your bank and make an ATM withdrawal. Or you're planning a trip to Italy and write out a check to the travel agency. Easy, everyday financial transactions that we take for granted, but centuries ago there were no banks, and the idea of writing a slip of paper that stood for money was unimaginable.

Silver and Gold

It's difficult to imagine a world without money. The earliest written records of human activity makes mention of money. Money is the basis for trade, the "medium of exchange," and enables both buyer and seller to trade what they have in order to get what they want.

Before coins were used, the Romans made payments with cattle and lumps of copper. During the third century B.C.E., Romans got the idea for coins after traveling to Greek cities in southern Italy and Sicily, where coins had been in use for hundreds of years. The early Roman coins were variations of the Greek coins.

In the days when money was made of precious metals such as gold and silver, heavy chests of coins were shipped around the world in trade. Dragging that *sacco di soldi* around was both tiring and cumbersome, so a system of credit that used coins and bills to represent specified values began to develop. Starting in the thirteenth century, Italian city governments began to issue gold coins. In Venice they were called ducats, or sequins. Florentines used florins.

Di Interessa

During the prosperous Renaissance, more emphasis was placed on one's personal appearance and hygiene; money to bathe was considered a regular part of a man's wages.

Ciao!

La Bella Lingua

To express that someone is wealthy in Italian, you would say they had *un sacco di soldi* (a sack of money), perhaps a remnant from the days before paper money.

The Commercial Revolution

Banking and trade go together. Since the twelfth and thirteenth centuries, several Italian innovations nurtured what is referred to as the "Commercial Revolution." The development of insurance for goods in transit, credit, paper money, letters of credit, and the creation of new accountancy methods enabled Italians to dominate international trade and banking throughout Western Europe.

Nowadays, large corporations can get financing from national banks. They've developed sophisticated methods of transacting large loans and payments. During the Middle Ages, however, there were no credit cards, no electronic debit, and no mortgage officers. Savvy merchants, concerned about being swindled during money-changing transactions, had to weigh out the coins being spent.

The Church forbade charging interest, and compelled Italian merchants to devise ways to sidestep the rules. By using foreign currency to buy and sell goods, they could take advantage of exchange rates. Or they might, for example, lend to English sheep farmers or wool merchants in return for lower prices on the goods that they provided.

The Merchants of Venice

Gold, silk, spices, and coffee. The Venetians dominated Eastern trade for several centuries—how else could they pay for all those gold mosaics in the Basilica di San Marco? Along with Genoa and Florence, Venice was at the center of Europe's trading networks. Their gold coins were used throughout Europe and the Eastern Mediterranean.

In the twelfth century, the Venetians also organized one of the first banks of public debt. The government, in order to finance military operations, forced all its citizens to invest in war bonds, which could be sold or transferred. The Bank of Venice lasted until 1797, when the city of Venice was taken over by Napoleon, whom you'll read more about in Chapter 16, "Parlez-Vous Français?"

Break the Bank

The Italian Jews of Lombardy were among the first to make a business dealing in money. Shakespeare's Shylock character, in fact, was fashioned after the racist stereotypes of the era. They had benches—*banchi*—on which they exchanged money or bills. If the banker failed, his bench or bank was broken, hence the word bankrupt—*bancarotta*.

Italian merchants had to make long journeys by land and by sea in order to carry out their business. It was dangerous and inconvenient to carry

"Italia"

In Italics

1472—The world's oldest bank, Banca Monte dei Paschi, is founded in Siena.

Di Interessa

The Rialto, an island and district in Venice, was once the center of trade for the Venetian Republic.

Biografia

Francesco Datini (1335–1410), a merchant from Prato, invented the bill of exchange for banking transactions.

large amounts of gold coins, so from the beginning of the thirteenth century they began to use bills of exchange. The bill was a legal document that was signed before witnesses.

Using bills of exchange allowed for a very versatile system. Merchants could obtain credit, transfer funds, buy and sell, and deal with bills whose value could differ from one location to another. Italian bankers and businessmen also invented other forms of financial techniques during this time, including life insurance and double-entry bookkeeping.

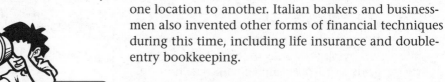

Di Interessa

In addition to the Medici family, the fourteenth century featured several other financial and political family dynasties throughout the peninsula that included the Visconti in Milan, Este in Ferrara, Della Scala in Verona, Carrara in Padua, and Montefeltro in Urbino.

In Italics

1904—In the tradition of his ancestors, the Italian American Amadeo Pietro Giannini opened his Banca d'Italia inside an old saloon. Giannini offered loans to earthquake victims and people with no collateral but their good names. Later, he developed branch banks in different areas to make it easier for customers.

Plagued by Debt

Nevertheless, there were some serious bankruptcies between 1342 and 1346. For instance, one of the biggest of the Italian banks' customers, Edward III of England, could not repay his huge debts from the Hundred Years' War in France, which led great Florentine bankers such as the Bardi and the Peruzzi to go bankrupt.

In the midst of the banking industry turmoil, one Florentine family in particular rose to prominence. The Medici became powerfully prosperous through its interests in cloth and silk manufacturing. Giovanni di Bicci de' Medici (1360–1429), considered the first in a line of great Medici, inherited the family business.

Giovanni managed a bank in Rome before moving to Florence and setting up the family bank in 1397. The Medici bank, like any modern one, held deposits and made loans, dealt in bills of exchange, changed money, and conducted business abroad. Until 1455, each of its branches was a partnership under a central holding company.

The bank grew rapidly and had nine branches outside Florence. Under Cosimo de' Medici, the bank became so successful that it was put in charge of papal finances. Until 1434, more than half of the bank's revenues came from its Rome branch (which followed the pope around on his travels). Its connections with Rome and the Vatican's reliance on it gave the bank tremendous clout both with other customers and with the Church itself.

The institution lasted until 1494, when it collapsed due to a depression, internal strife, and French aggression.

Starving Artist—Will Work for Money

We've answered half the riddle on how all that Renaissance art was financed and created—Italian bankers beginning in the 1200s created a thriving banking system with procedures that are still used today. They also became well-off because of the power they had as bankers to popes, kings, and governments. What to do with all that money?

Patronage is the influence or financial support of an artist—so it benefits both people. The patron gets to rub elbows with the creative types, and the artists can afford a place to sleep and meals to eat. What was unusual in cities like Florence, Naples, Rome, and Venice during the Renaissance was the concentration of wealth, generous patrons, and creative genius that all came together.

> ## "Italia"
>
> ### In Italics
>
> **1252**—The first gold florin was minted in Florence. The coins were minted in the Zecca (mint), which was next to the Palazzo Vecchio in the center of the city.

M as in Medici, Money, Magnificent, Michelangelo

The Medici clan reached its height in sponsoring artists with Lorenzo il Magnifico (1449–1492), who broadened the family's activities from traditional banking and politicking to patronizing artists and sculptors. He spent large sums of money commissioning paintings, sculptures, and architectural designs from artists like Botticelli, Donatello, and Michelangelo.

Lorenzo was instrumental in the development of Florentine artistic genius during the second half of the fifteenth century (even at the risk of depleting his bank account). Besides commissioning artists, Lorenzo also opened a school of sculpture in his garden at San Marco, where Michelangelo studied when he was a teenager.

The Uffizi Museum, a shrine to Renaissance art and architecture, contains many artworks commissioned by the Medici. The building itself was designed by the family architect Giorgio Vasari. Inside, the Tribunale contains a collection of portraits such as Bronzino's *Bia de' Medici* and Vasari's *Lorenzo il Magnifico*.

Ticket to Heaven

Most artistic commissions were for religious works. Many banking families considered the funding of altarpieces and chapels as a kind of penance for usury (the lending of money at an exorbitant rate of interest), an act that, while condemned by the Church, was inherent to the banking industry. To spend eternity in the most fashionable company, many wealthy merchants commissioned family chapels.

Consider the church of Santa Maria Novella in Florence. Around the perimeter are chapels named after the families that commissioned them. The Cappella di Filippo Strozzi contains frescoes painted by Filippo Lippi, and the Tornabuoni Chapel has a cycle of Domenico Ghirlandaio frescoes. They include a portrait of Giovanni Tornabuoni and his family, friends, and clients.

Di Interessa

The Medici coat of arms features several red balls, which may represent coins, to show that they were bankers. It is similar to that of the Guild of Moneychangers, to which the Medici belonged.

"*Italia*"

In Italics

1605—Bank of the Holy Spirit of Rome set up by Pope Paul V, Europe's first national bank.

Not to be outdone, the Medici family lent the city the funds to build the Basilica di San Lorenzo but retained artistic control over its construction. Designed in 1419 by engineer and architect Filippo Brunelleschi (1377–1446), the church features the Medici coat of arms everywhere, and tombs holding Medici ancestors fill both the sacristies and the Cappella dei Medici behind the altar.

The Medici also commissioned Michelangelo to design the Sacrestia Nuova in 1524, with two impressive tombs for Lorenzo and Giuliano, a gesture implying—it was believed—that money could buy anything, including eternal paradise.

And Florence wasn't the only Italian city where patronage led to incredible works of art. The Church (the chief patron of many works in Rome) commissioned works from great artists in Rome and the Vatican. Raffaello's frescoes in the papal apartments, painted in the 1510s, was paid for by Pope Julius II. The same pope hired Michelangelo to paint the stupendous fresco on the ceiling of the Sistine Chapel in the Vatican.

Power in Numbers: The Guilds

By the Middle Ages, the creation of social and economic guilds began to appear, offering membership by profession or craft to merchants and craftsmen. The primary function was to establish standards and alliances that helped protect businesses from competition. The merchant guilds also found their collective numbers served to protect them from feudalistic governments.

Italy's high standards of excellence are founded on a tradition that goes back centuries. By the Renaissance, each guild set the terms for its craft, determining methods of sale, quality control, and production. The guild structure in Florence was comprised of two distinct ranks: the upper "greater" guild and the lower "lesser" guilds.

The Greater Guild

The Greater Guild consisted of doctors, lawyers, importers, wool and silk manufacturers, furriers, and bankers. These were the power players of the day, and while they were the minority, their power on the economic and political life of Florentine society was undisputed. If a loan needed to be made—such as for the dowry of a hopeful bride or if one needed a political favor—one could approach a member of the greater guild. Similar to a few notable associations today, membership had its privileges.

Di Interessa

Serving as an example for all of Europe, the first foundling hospital was created in Milan in 787 by the archpriest. This hospital was designed to shelter unwanted children and the poor. Throughout Italy, unwanted children were left at *la ruota,* a sort of lazy Susan built into the thick monastery walls and designed to protect the identity of the mother. The child was left exposed to the elements until his cries were heard, leading the nuns to give these children the name Esposito (exposed).

The Lesser Guild

The Lesser Guild was comprised of innkeepers, shop owners, bakers, butchers, carpenters, blacksmiths, weavers, and master craftsmen. The Lesser Guild had even more members than the Greater Guild, but got its name because it had less power than its wealthier counterpart. Nevertheless, membership in the guild gave the average working "giovanni" a voice he might not otherwise have had.

Funny Money

The word *lira* comes from the Latin word *libra,* the unit of weight used to establish the value of early Roman copper money. In the mid-nineteenth century, after Vittorio Emanuele II became King of Italy, the lira was officially made Italy's national currency. Italian money has always been beautiful. Much larger than dollars and printed with any number of Italian notables, the bills were art in themselves.

By January 1, 2002, Italy—along with much of Europe—will have switched its national currency to the euro as part of the European Union's design to implement a common banking system.

Sadly, the unique and colorful national bills and coins will disappear, to be replaced with the European Union currency. The coins will have a common EU face on the front and a nation-specific design on the back, but the bills will be the same from nation to nation.

The Least You Need to Know

➤ The modern banking system began in Lombardy, Italy in the fourteenth century.

➤ The great banking families of the Italian Renaissance lent money to popes, European monarchs, and international traders.

➤ Bankers and businessmen thought the quickest way to paradise was to commission religious art and architecture.

➤ The Medici of Florence, an influential banking family, were patrons of Renaissance artists such as Michelangelo, Donatello, and Brunelleschi.

Chapter 11

Strange Bedfellows

In This Chapter

➤ La signoria

➤ Magnificent Medici

➤ Power marriages and ruling families

➤ Savonarola: trial by fire

➤ Machiavelli writes a manual for rulers

Italy during the Renaissance was a time of opulent celebrations and grand courts, of dashing soldiers and elegantly dressed princesses. Rich bankers and merchants spent their fortunes on paintings, sculptures, medals, and bronzes to decorate their stylish villas and palaces.

The Italian Renaissance began in the late fourteenth century and spread to the rest of Europe in the fifteenth century. It was a time of tremendous achievement in the arts, architecture, politics, and the study of literature, when creative superstars produced prodigious pieces of art. You'll learn more about the intellectual and artistic movement and the artists themselves in Chapter 12, "*Putti*, Painters, and the Arts."

Cities? States? City-States!

If you lived on the Italian peninsula during the Renaissance, you would not call yourself an Italian. Italy was not a single country; instead, it was split up into small, independent city-states, each with their own government. You would be a citizen of the Republic of Venice, or the Duchy of Savoy, or the Kingdom of Naples, for instance.

Many of the Italian city-states came to be dominated by single families, such as the Visconti and then the Sforza in Milan. The Medici created a dynasty in Florence that lasted for 300 years. New political alliances were often made through marriage, resulting in a complicated and interconnected network of power players.

During the Renaissance, independent city-states dominated the north, the Papal States ruled central Italy, and the Kingdoms of Naples and Sicily ruled over the southern regions.

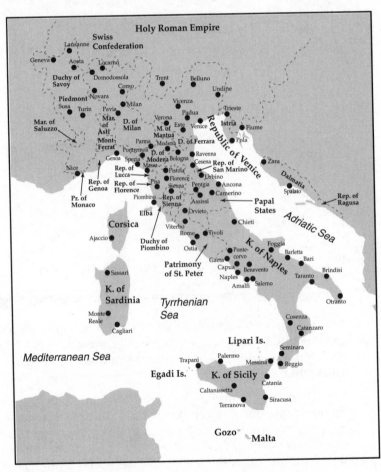

The city-states had a type of government they called *la signoria*. The name derives from the term *signore* (lord) used to describe a strong ruler. The *signori* promised efficient government and peace while promoting civic pride through magnificent public works and generous patronage of arts and letters. This created a significant demand for craftsmen, writers, and musicians (not unlike today's multi-billion dollar advertising industry). *Signori* established dynasties, especially in northern Italy (e.g., the Visconti and Este), and the *signoria* also led the way for the modern nation-state.

Di Interessa

During the Renaissance, Venice—often called *La Serenissima* (the most serene and lovely)—was renowned for its banks in the Rialto, the site of Europe's first bank in the twelfth century. Similar to Florence, Venice's government was also a form of *signoria,* with a *doge* who was appointed for life. With little formal power but immense informal influence, the doge provided continuity and experience.

Florence: The Medici

The Medici name is inseparable from Renaissance Italy. Volumes have been written about the Medici family, known for their powerful presence and generous patronage of the arts during the Renaissance. They were a highly influential family of bankers and merchants whose members effectively ruled Florence for much of the fifteenth century. Cosimo and Lorenzo de' Medici were notable rulers and patrons of the arts in Florence.

During the sixteenth century, the Medici were regarded as wise and tolerant rulers whose passionate love of the arts made Florence one of the most magnificent artistic centers in European history. The Medici family provided four popes (including Leo X) and two queens of France (Catherine de' Medici and Marie de' Medici) before the last male heir, Gian Gastone, died in 1737.

"Italia"

In Italics

1571—The first public library was opened in Florence. The *Biblioteca Medicea-Laurenziana* housed the collections of Lorenzo il Magnifico.

Medici Family Tree

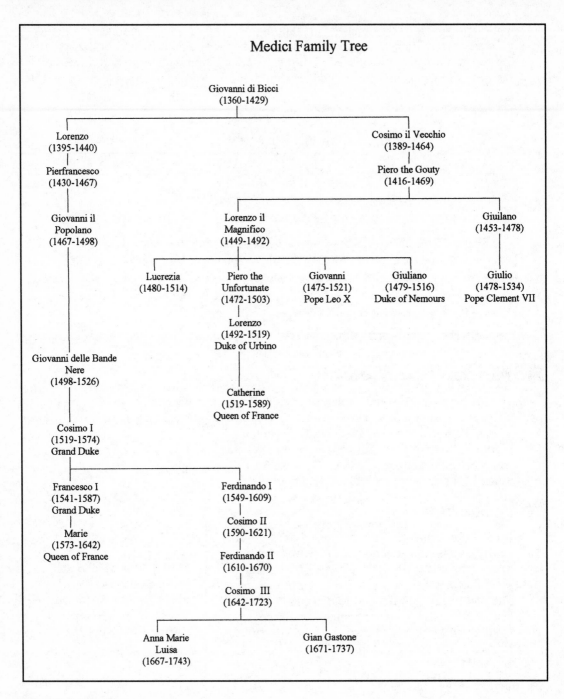

The Medici family tree.

Florence: Art in the Square

The Piazza Signoria (named for the Florentine *signoria*) was located in the center of Florence and served as the hub of political life. The Palazzo Vecchio, which dominates the square, was originally called the Palazzo della Signoria since the local government assembled there (and still does today).

The entire complex is the epitome of art commissioned by government leaders to beautify their surroundings and to convey specific political messages. Just to name a few of the many artworks (many of which were commissioned by the Medici) in and around the square:

➤ Michelangelo's statue of *David* standing outside the front door of the Palazzo Vecchio. (This is now a copy; the original is in the Galleria dell'Accademia.)

➤ Donatello's *Judith and Holofernes* in front of the Palazzo Vecchio's façade. (This is also a copy; the original is inside the Palazzo Vecchio in the Sala dei Gigli.)

➤ The equestrian statue of Cosimo I, cast in bronze by Giambologna.

➤ The *Studiolo* of Francesco I inside the Palazzo, a tiny room literally encrusted with paintings.

➤ *Hall of the Five Hundred* covered with frescoes representing Florence's victories in battle.

The Loggia dei Lanzi, across the square from Palazzo Vecchio, is an open-air sculpture gallery with works by Giambologna and Benvenuto Cellini (1500–1571). And last but not least, the Uffizi is just a few steps away. You could spend a lifetime in and around Piazza Signoria and still not have enough time for all the incredible artwork.

Milan: The Sforza Family

During the Renaissance, the northern city of Milan was ruled by the Sforza family (the name means "force" in Italian). In 1450, Francesco Sforza (1401–1466), a mercenary soldier, became the duke of the city-state. He earned a reputation as a strong and peace-loving prince by giving Milan great public works and throwing lots of lavish parties.

Ludovico il Moro, who ruled starting in 1480, and his wife Beatrice d'Este (whose brother was Alfonso and whose sister was Isabella from Ferrara) promoted the musical arts and were known for their extravagant musical festivities that included sets and stage machines designed by none other than Leonardo da Vinci.

Ferrara: The Este

The city of Ferrara was also located in the north (east of Milan) and represented another prime example of a powerful city-state. Ruled by the Este family for more than three centuries, Ferrara featured palaces and churches built by the family, who also were prominent patrons of art and literature. Ferrara was also notable for its music and theater.

Of particular interest is Isabella d'Este (1474–1539) who, at the age of 16, married the soldier and scholar Francesco II Gonzaga (1466–1519), Marquis of Mantova. Encouraged by her father, she was trained in the arts of singing, dancing, and playing musical instruments and was educated as any man of her time, speaking both Greek and Latin.

Di Interessa

One of the greatest of Italian romantic literary epics features Ruggiero, a legendary ancestor of the Este family. *Orlando Furioso* (1532) tells the tale of Orlando and other knights of Charlemagne. It was written by the poet Ludovico Ariosto (1474–1533), who studied law in Ferrara and served the Este court starting in 1503.

As the duchess of Mantova, Isabella helped the city become a center of culture and learning. Isabella's tastes ran from the fanciful to the serious. Her friends included Titian and Leonardo da Vinci (both painted her portrait), Raffaello and the writer Castiglione. When her husband Francesco was captured in battle in 1509, Isabella ruled the city on her own. You'll learn more about the leading women of the Renaissance in Chapter 23, "Mamma and the Madonna."

Through marriage, the Este family allied themselves with other leading families of Italian city-states to reinforce their control. In what must have been the Renaissance equivalent of a soap opera, Isabella's sister Beatrice d'Este (1475–1497) married Ludovico Sforza of Milan and their brother Alfonso I (1476–1539) married Lucrezia Borgia.

Mantova: The Gonzagas

The Gonzaga family ruled the northern Italian city-state of Mantova for almost four hundred years. The Gonzaga supported the Holy Roman Emperor Charles V and fought against Charles VIII of France at the Battle of Fornovo in 1495. The family included several cardinals, *condottieri,* many patrons of the arts and scholarship, and a saint (St. Aloysius Gonzaga).

During the Renaissance the Gonzaga court was a glittering center for the arts where some of the greatest artists and architects of the period, such as Leon Battista Alberti (1404–1472) and Giulio Romano (1499–1546), worked under the patronage of the family.

Bridal Chamber Bliss

The Gonzaga family commissioned one of the most romantic and extravagant honeymoon suites ever created. Painted by Andrea Mantegna (1431–1506), the *Camera degli Sposi* (*Wedding Chamber*) was completed in 1474 and is located in the Palazzo Ducale in Mantova.

Inside, there are group portraits of the Gonzaga family and medallions of the Caesars. Most remarkable, however, are the fresco decorations that line the room. The painted architectural elements on the walls and ceiling create a three-dimensional, lifelike effect. Directly above the center of the room is a painted opening to the sky, with cherubic angels and elegant ladies gathered around a balustrade in dramatically foreshortened perspective. It was a technique that created the illusion of a total environment, not seen since antiquity and which led to similar ceiling decorations during the Renaissance.

Federico II Gonzaga commissioned Giulio Romano (1499–1546) to design the opulent Palazzo del Tè for his mistress. The principal rooms included the *Sala di Amore e Psiche,* which portrayed erotic and playful frescoes of the classical gods, and the floor-to-ceiling *Sala dei Giganti*, a painting that shows the giants storming the mythological god Olympus. For a tryst by the pool, there was the *Appartamento del Giardino Segreto* (*Apartment of the Secret Garden*) with its secluded grotto. Naturally, in true Renaissance style, having the good taste to commission such fine works reflected well on the Gonzaga family.

Di Interessa

The Castello Sforzecso was originally a fifteenth-century fortress that served as the barracks for Duke Francesco Sforza's soldiers. Today it is a museum where Michelangelo's last work, the unfinished *Pietà Rondanini,* can be seen.

Urbino: The Montefeltros

The Montefeltros were a noble family that ruled the city of Urbino (the birthplace of the great Renaissance painter Raffaello) between the thirteenth and sixteenth centuries. The best-known member of the family was the Duke of Urbino Federigo da Montefeltro (1422–1482), who distinguished himself both as a military leader and as an art patron, especially to the Renaissance painter known for his court portraits, Piero della Francesca (1420–1492). Federigo da Montefeltro was easily recognized after having lost his right eye and part of his nose in a jousting tournament. As a result, paintings such as Masolino and Masaccio's *Healing of the Maimed* (Brancacci Chapel, Santa Maria del Carmine Florence), always portrayed him from the left.

Di Interessa

Aldo Manuzio (1450–1515) was a printer who founded the Aldine Press in Venice in the 1490s. The press, through Manuzio's efforts, was instrumental in spreading learning throughout Europe and also pioneered the widespread use of *italic* type.

115

Although Federigo da Montefeltro was an outstanding soldier who served both the papacy and Lorenzo de' Medici as a *condottiere,* his true passion was for the arts and scholarship. He abhorred the new fashion of printing books and in response, collected one of the biggest libraries of handwritten manuscripts—which were as unique as paintings—in Europe. These manuscripts are now part of the Vatican Library in Rome, which has extensive archives of many private collections and is accessible only to church officials and scholars.

A Picture Is Worth a Thousand Words

The various governing parties were closely watched by citizens, statesman, and artists. In what was still a highly illiterate world, social commentary was often expressed through paintings (not unlike the story told through today's cartoons) that told a story or attempted to make a point.

Biografia

It's one of those terms that's become a cliché: the "Renaissance man," the scholar, artist, scientist, and diplomat, all rolled into one. And usually the first image is of Leonardo da Vinci or Michelangelo. But what about all those accomplished, intelligent women of the era?! Popular medieval and Renaissance Italian female writers whose works merit mention include:

St. Clare of Assisi (1194–1253)

Angela of Foligno (1248–1309)

St. Catherine of Siena (1347–1380)

Cassandra Fedele (1465–1558)

Laura Cereta (1469–1499)

St. Catherine of Genoa (1447–1510)

In Siena's Palazzo Pubblico, for instance, there is a huge fresco titled *Good and Bad Government,* painted in the fourteenth century by the brothers Ambrogio and Pietro Lorenzetti. In the area representing good government, people are seen dancing in the street while artists create wonderful designs and farmers tend fertile fields. The bad government scenes depict, not surprisingly, thieves, devils, and total ruin. Citizens are clearly being reminded of the importance of good government.

Many paintings, such as the portrait artist Pisanello's (1395–1455?) depiction of *Saint George and the Princess of Trebizond,* illustrated the consequences of ill-doers who dared go against the local authority. In his painting, the decayed corpses of hanged men were left as a warning to others.

Festivities

Special occasions offered the gentlemen and ladies of the court time to gossip and mingle. While party-goers clinked glasses, alliances were made and friendships forged, some of which developed into clandestine affairs that are the favorite topic of many of today's movies such as *Lucrezia Borgia,* directed by John Copley. (To see a list of popular films, consult Appendix C, "Suggested Films and Books.")

Part of Italy's charm today stems from the pervasiveness of festivals, carnivals, and holy days that re-create the grand banquets of the Renaissance.

> **Di Interessa**
>
> The Madonna was unquestionably the most popular subject for prints and paintings during the Renaissance. Paintings of the Madonna were religious, they depicted woman in her perfect, idealized state, and they were a sure sell.

What's for Dinner?

The banquets held during the Renaissance were true feasts. Long tables were piled high with sweet meats and pastries, candied apples, minced chicken livers, and gilded oranges. Duck, geese, and game such as rabbit, deer, pheasant, and wild boar were decorated with the reds of berries and the yellows of lemons and accompanied by the beverage of choice, *il vino.*

While the lavishly dressed guests gorged on food and wine, minstrels and court jesters accompanied by four-stringed lutes, fifes, and harpsichords danced and sang ballads of love and longing. Secular themes were made more popular by the fact that new printing techniques allowed the first sheet music to be printed and distributed.

What's Playing Tonight?

Inside the palaces beneath lavish sets, theater groups performed religious-based scripts from the notable writers of the time, including Machiavelli's play *Mandragola,* and the poet Angelo Poliziano (1454–1494). Poliziano's belief that the Greeks "sang" their lines resulted in the first opera, *Orfeo.* You'll learn more about opera in Chapter 15, "Violins and Lace: The Baroque."

Produced during Isabella d'Este's time was the popular play *Calandria,* adopted by Cardinal Bibbiena. In this upside-down comedy, a boy and a girl—both twins—are depicted in several gender-defying circumstances that reflect the rather salacious tastes of the Vatican and its alleged harem.

A Taste for Gambling

Gambling and dice throwing were also popular during the Renaissance, and marked cards and loaded dice were popular items. Betting was also a common pastime; participants guessed on the life-expectancy of a nobleman or the length of time a particular family might rule. Other favorite pastimes included chess, *tarocchi* (tarot cards), and the lottery.

Historians have found evidence that as early as the sixteenth century, Venetians enjoyed trying their luck (perhaps this is why we call it good "fortune"?) by participating in small lotteries with prizes that included money, fine clothing, jewelry, carpets and real estate. The idea of contributing a small amount of money in exchange for the possibility of winning big appealed to members from every social class. Gamblers invented all sorts of methods for predicting the winning numbers.

Di Interessa

The Palio horserace founds its origins in Medieval times and continues to this day. Held in Siena, the entire city closes down to watch the various *contrade* (districts)—each represented by a flag and often an animal such as *il porcospino* (porcupine) or *la giraffa* (the giraffe)—vie for their own jockeys as the horse race around the town square.

Di Interessa

Several weapons of war, such as the multi-barreled gun, mortar bomb, and rapid-fire cannon, were engineered by Leonardo da Vinci.

Cover Your Assets

It may seem that the formation of Italian city-states implied peaceful times. Not quite. In fact, the *signori* could count on an enemy threatening to wage war or take control of fertile farmland at the ring of a *campanello*. With aggressive neighbors, how were the city's businessmen and craftsmen able to continue their work?

As a solution, city-states hired bands of mercenary soldiers to protect them or attack their adversaries (sometimes the best defense is a good offense). These *condottieri*—from the Italian word *condotte,* or contracts—studied war as art and relied mainly on cavalry armed with lances.

An example of this is Venice, where in the early 1500s over 30,000 *condottieri* were employed. It wasn't unusual for some mercenary bands to prolong the wars they fought in order to continue collecting a paycheck.

Golden Age of Rome

The Papal States, in central Italy, didn't have a *signoria,* but it certainly had its own powerful head of government. And like the ruling families in city-states, the popes understood how the fine arts and grand architecture could boost their status and improve the image of the Papacy.

Pope Julius: Friend to Artists

During his reign, Pope Julius II (1503–1513) expanded the Vatican Library, collected ancient sculpture, and laid the cornerstone of St. Peter's Basilica. Craftsmen journeyed to the city in hope of a papal commission, and great artists such as Michelangelo, Raffaello, and Bramante all created masterpieces under Pope Julius II's employ. (You'll learn more about them in Chapter 12.)

Nipotismo

Papal nephew? That was the term used for children considered to be those of the pope's siblings, but which were understood to be the pope's own illegitimate children. During the Renaissance, especially under corrupt popes such as Pope Sixtus IV, the position of the papal nephew rose to new heights, as nephews were given influential positions and high salaries. This practice of *nipotismo* (*nipote*) means nephew in Italian) was one way in which the Church became morally discredited during the Renaissance.

Bedroom Politics

For bedroom politics and palace intrigue during the Renaissance, there was no figure more notorious than Lucrezia Borgia (1480–1519), the daughter of Rodrigo Borgia (better known later as Pope Alexander VI).

In 1491, the 11-year-old Lucrezia was already betrothed to two Spanish nobles. Her ever-enterprising father then sought an alliance with the Milanese, and in 1493, at the age of 13, Lucrezia married Giovanni Sforza, duke of Milan. The political winds quickly shifted, and as pope, Alexander annulled the union in 1497 in order to arrange a marriage between Lucrezia and the 17-year-old Alfonso, at that time the nephew of the King of Naples.

The mysterious *Infans Romanus* (*Roman Infant*) (1500–1548) has always been the subject of much speculation and used as "proof" of Lucrezia Borgia's

Di Interessa

Watch Joan Sutherland bring the Renaissance to life in *Lucrezia Borgia* directed by John Copley (1980).

decadence and depravity. Named Giovanni, he first appeared around 1503 in the papal courts and was passed off as Lucrezia's illegitimate child.

In fact, the pope wrote two papal bulls, the first a public statement that recognized the child as Cesare Borgia's, and the second a secret document that recognized the child as his own. The purpose of the papal bulls was to give Alexander an excuse to name the young Giovanni the heir to the small duchy of Nepi, a property important to the Borgia family. Otherwise, there may never have been any acknowledgement whatsoever about the parentage of the Infans Romanus.

Love and Politics Don't Mix

Three years after marrying Lucrezia Borgia, Alfonso was murdered in 1500 by his bodyguard on orders of Lucrezia's brother Cesare. The next year, Lucrezia married Alfonso d'Este, the duke of Ferrara. It was another arranged union, this time to solidify Cesare Borgia's power base in Romagna.

Fortunately for Lucrezia, it was the last time she had to be a pawn in her family's power games. She went on to become an influential member of the Este court in Ferrara and an avid patron of the arts.

Dastardly Deeds

If Lucrezia was the Borgia family *femme fatale,* her brother Cesare (1475–1507) was the prototype of the cunning political ruler portrayed in Machiavelli's book *Il Principe* (1532). He was well-schooled, having studied law at the University of Perugia. He became the bishop of Pamplona in 1491, the archbishop of Valencia, and was named cardinal at the age of 18 when his father became pope.

A successful soldier, Cesare became duke of Romagna in 1501 and for a short time even employed Leonardo da Vinci as his inspector of fortresses. Notorious for his licentious habits and bad temper, he was unscrupulous, treacherous, and cruel toward his political rivals.

How to Be a Prince

Niccolò Machiavelli (1469–1527) served the Florentine republic as a diplomat from 1498 to 1512, when the restoration of the Medici family forced him into exile. Due to his experience as a statesman and his acute observations of the rapidly changing political landscape, while living in exile Machiavelli wrote *Il Principe* (*The Prince*). It became the definitive political guide for the governing of a forcefully united Italy freed of foreign domination and an instruction guide for machiavellian leaders everywhere.

Machiavelli's influence became such that it has been incorporated into the English language as an adjective—*Machiavellian*. Other quotes you may or may not have known were written by Machiavelli include:

"Is it better to be loved than feared, or the reverse? The answer is that it is desirable to be both, but because it is difficult to join them together, it is much safer for a prince to be feared than loved, if he is to fail in one of the two."

"Since a prince is necessitated to play the animal well, he chooses among the beasts the fox and the lion, because the lion does not protect himself from traps; the fox does not protect himself from wolves. The prince must be a fox, therefore, to recognize the traps and a lion to frighten the wolves."

"And if sometimes you need to conceal a fact with words, do it in such a way that it does not become known, or, if it does become known, that you have a ready and quick defense."

"It is necessary for him who lays out a state and arranges laws for it to presuppose that all men are evil and that they are always going to act according to the wickedness of their spirits whenever they have free scope."

La Bella Lingua

Il Principe was condemned by the pope, but its viewpoints gave rise to the well-known adjective **Machiavellian,** now a synonym for political maneuvers marked by cunning, duplicity, or bad faith.

How to Be a Gentleman

The soldier, statesman, and writer Baldassare Castiglione (1478–1529) is best known for having written *Il Cortegiano* (*The Courtier*), a treatise instructing the inquiring Renaissance man on deportment, etiquette, and other fine point of behavior. This handy little guide offers a vivid portrait of court life in Urbino and describes the qualities of the perfect courtier: a connoisseur of cultivated tastes and sensibility who excelled at a variety of civilized pursuits with effortless grace.

Savonarola: Prophet of Doom

With all the revelry and animated social climbing going on during the Italian Renaissance, there had to be a spoilsport. He came in the form of a robed Dominican friar in Florence. The narrow-minded and puritanical Italian religious reformer Girolamo Savonarola (1452–1498) preached against the vice and corruption of Pope Alexander VI and openly attacked what he believed were the excessive material inclinations of the Medici family by leading bonfires of "vanities" to destroy works of art considered wicked and profane. This brings to mind Tom Wolfe's book, *The Bonfire of the Vanities.*

Savonarola was uncompromisingly opposed to what he thought were the cataclysmic evils of Humanist thinking. He made many prophecies during his sermons (some of which, including the death of Innocent VIII, turned out to be true), exercised strict control over religious art, and tried to outlaw gambling and licentious dress and behavior.

In 1495, irritated and fearful of Savonarola's growing power, the pope forbade him to preach and summoned him to Rome. Savonarola refused to comply with these orders and eventually was excommunicated, declared guilty of heresy, and sentenced to death. On May 23, 1498, in Florence's Piazza Signoria, he was hanged and his body burned at the stake.

The Renaissance wasn't over, but the heat was on as power struggles made city-states up and down the peninsula even more vulnerable to attack from both foreign armies and rival neighbors.

The Least You Need to Know

➤ Powerful and independent city-states ruled Italy during the Renaissance.

➤ The astonishing artistic achievements of the Renaissance were a product of the extraordinary economic and social environment of the city-states.

➤ Great ruling families accelerated the cultural and artistic activity of their cities.

➤ The courts of the ruling families were places of outstanding art, music, and scholarship.

Putti, Painters, and the Arts

Most of us know when we have viewed a masterpiece, even if we can't describe why we know. Seeing the secretive smile of the *Mona Lisa*, you can't help but wonder what she is thinking. Standing at the foot of the Sistine Chapel it can be difficult to breathe—how *did* he do that?

The Renaissance represents more than a flourishing of ideas. Through the imagination of the artist, what had only lived in the realm of dreams and nightmares was given a form. From Botticelli's prancing virgins to Michelangelo's writhing stone captives to the seductive, come-hither expression of Titian's *Venus,* a masterpiece shows us what can be brought out from deep within.

Bravissimo! The Renaissance

The *Renaissance* provided more artistic masterpieces than any other period of history. You're probably already familiar with many names associated with this time, including Caravaggio, Leonardo da Vinci, Michelangelo, Raphael, Tintoretto, Titian … the list goes on.

While you may not have time to properly appreciate the vast array of accomplishments associated with the period of the Renaissance, you can begin by familiarizing yourself with some of the key thinkers and *artisti* of the time.

But first things first. Let's try to figure out just what inspired this tremendous spate of scholarship and creation.

Titian's Venus of Urbino, *Uffizi Gallery, Florence.*

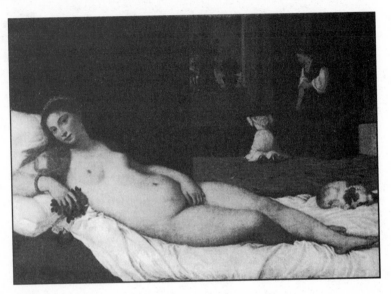

Materially Speaking

As you remember from Chapter 9, "Leaving the Middle Ages," the Black Death of 1348 was one of the greatest and most terrifying catastrophes to strike the world. Italy was particularly devastated. This event, combined with the development of the city-states, the emergence of a market economy, and the creation of the guilds in Florence, led men and women to question their existence and challenge the revered authority of both divine and human laws. Was the plague a result of God's wrath? Or was there another explanation?

The search for truth and a rendering of the "real" material world began a revolutionary shift in consciousness. The humanists, in reviving Plato, taught that there is an ideal world, and our own real world. Reflecting this shift, artists now struggled to render the world they inhabited in as "realistic" a manner as possible. The study of theology was replaced with accounting, anatomy, astronomy, botany, and mathematics, eventually giving way to the golden age of science.

> **Ciao!**

La Bella Lingua

The term **Renaissance** means "rebirth" and is used to describe the period of European history from roughly 1400 to 1600.

Humanists Are People, Too

Obviously, when you're talking about humanism, you're talking about people. In this case, Humanism with a capital H refers to the cultural and intellectual movement during the Renaissance as a result of the rediscovery of the art, literature, and civilization of the ancient Greeks and Romans.

While writers such as Dante and Boccaccio had experimented with the spoken vernacular of the times, most people outside the church and aristocracy did not read at all; if they did, it was in Latin.

A large part of the humanists' work involved the careful translation and editing of ancient Latin and Greek works. For the first time, many ancient texts were translated from Greek and Hebrew into Latin, the language of scholars.

The Platonic Academy

Instituted in Florence by Cosimo de' Medici at his villa in Careggi, the Platonic Academy was an informal body of scholars and humanists who met under the leadership of Marsilio Ficino to discuss philosophy and study the classics. The villa hosted many great minds that included the philosopher Pico della Mirandola and artists such as Brunelleschi, Donatello, and Michelangelo.

Marsilio Ficino

The Italian philosopher Marsilio Ficino (1433–1499) became one of the most influential thinkers of his time. Under the patronage of Cosimo de' Medici, Ficino translated several Greek classics into Latin, including the Greek philosopher Plato's dialogues and the writings of an earlier philosopher, Plotinus. Ficino was the first to completely translate Plato's works into any European language. In fact, many of the ideals espoused during the Renaissance were based on the newly translated and edited epistles of Plato and Socrates.

In 1462, Ficino became head of the Platonic Academy in Florence. Ficino taught that man distinguished himself from lower animals through

La Bella Lingua

Humanista (humanist): (1) a Renaissance student or follower of classical learning; (2) one concerned with the welfare of human beings; (3) originally referred to a teacher of Latin and Greek.

Di Interessa

The Florentine architect Filippo Brunelleschi (1377–1446) and the architect, painter, and humanist Leone Battista Alberti (1404–1472) both visited Rome to study the ruins and incorporate ancient principles into their own work, forming the basis for the study of architecture as a science in and of its own.

religion and the possession of a soul. In one of his most noted commentaries, "Symposium," Ficino saw a parallel between the Platonic and Christian concepts of love. The highest form of human love and friendship was based, he explained, on the soul's love for God. This theory of "Platonic" love dominated European poetry and literature during the Renaissance.

Biografia

The ruling families such as the Este of Ferrara, the Medici in Florence, the Sforza of Milan, along with the dukes of Urbino and the doges of Venice, hired humanists to teach their children classical morality and how to write letters and histories. Children of merchants were taught basic grammar and how to use an abacus.

Plato

The Greek philosopher Plato (427?–347 B.C.E.) was a friend and pupil to what many call the father of modern philosophy, Socrates (469–399 B.C.E.). Plato lived for some time in the court of the tyrant Dionysius the Elder in Syracuse (current Sicily). Plato's goal was to show the rational relationship between the soul, the state, and the cosmos. The methods used in the Socratic philosophy *dialectic* were meant to reveal the truth through constant questioning. In his work *Republic*, he asserts that the philosopher is the only one capable of ruling the just state through his understanding of the intricacies of the universe. In his republic, each social class contentedly performs the work for which it is best suited; the philosopher leads, the peasant farms, the warrior fights.

Pico della Mirandola

The Italian scholar and Platonist philosopher Giovanni Pico della Mirandola (1463–1494) was well regarded by his peers for both the prowess of his mind and the beauty of his expression.

Drawing from Hebrew, Greek, Latin, and Arabic philosophies, Pico opened his manifesto "De hominis dignitate oratio" (Oration on the Dignity of Man), with an examination on what makes human beings so universally unique and remarkable. Pico became the first scholar to use Kabbalistic doctrines to support Christian theology. After a papal commission denounced many of his ideas, Pico was forced to flee to France where he was captured and imprisoned for a brief period. Pico settled in Florence where he became associated with the Platonic Academy.

His notable collection of texts led to the establishment of the first libraries, broadening the intellectual scope of universities and academies.

Leonardo da Vinci

The illegitimate son of a Florentine notary and a peasant girl, Leonardo da Vinci (1452–1519) was born in 1452 near the town of Vinci. While coming from what might have been a disadvantaged position, Leonardo came to epitomize the ideal Renaissance man. Although best known as a painter, in his 67 years of life, Leonardo da Vinci excelled as an artist, sculptor, architect, musician, engineer, inventor, scientist, and writer.

Leonardo's abilities were not limited to solely one craft. Always a charming and precocious child, he moved to Florence at age 14 and entered an apprenticeship with the sculptor and painter Andrea del Verrocchio (1435–1488). There he came into contact with other artists such as Sandro Botticelli (1444–1510), Domenico Ghirlandaio (1449–1494), and Lorenzo di Credi (1459–1537).

By 1472, Leonardo was registered in the painters' guild in Florence, where he completed the *Adoration of the Magi* (located in the Uffizi gallery in Florence), commissioned by the monks of San Donato. In 1482, at the invitation of the patron of the arts the duke Ludovico Sforza, he remained in service for the next 16 years. It was during this time that he composed the *Trattato della Pittura* and detailed notebooks that demonstrate the breadth of his curiosity.

Leonardo's scope saw no limits. In the course of his lifetime, he was exposed to the best minds of the Renaissance. His contemporaries included Niccolò Machiavelli (who later became a good friend); the Medici pope Leo X and his brother Giuliano; the artists Michelangelo, Bramante, and Raffaello; the patrons Cesare Borgia and Francesco Sforza (Ludovico's father); and the French kings Louis XII and Francis I, among others. Leonardo was one of the first to take a scientific approach towards understanding the world we live in.

Throughout his life, Leonardo made incredible headway in the area of science. He sketched out amazing drawings for working machines and technology that would take another four centuries to be realized. Some of his sketches clearly show plans for a flying machine that markedly resemble today's helicopter. Another machine was designed to carry one passenger by a self-generated means strongly resembles today's bicycle. He even established the principles for a *camera oscura* (dark room) that laid the foundation for the first camera.

Di Interessa

Leonardo's notebooks are filled with the scribblings, illustrations, and thoughts of genius. As a leftie, Leonardo's writings are particularly unique for the fact that they were written perfectly backward. Was he dyslexic or trying to keep his ideas a secret?

Di Interessa

The painting of *St. Anne, Mary, and the Child* (located at the Louvre in Paris), is an example of Leonardo's handling of *sfumato*, a term used to describe the gradual blending of one area of color into another without a sharp outline.

*This anatomical study
was drawn by Leonardo.*

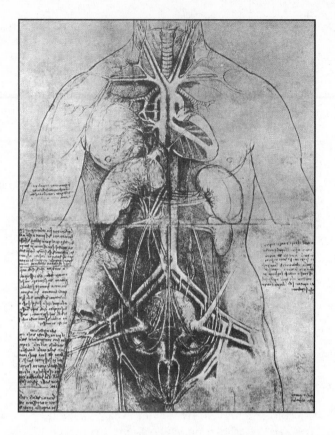

Leonardo also had amazing powers of observation and skill as an illustrator, which enabled him to notice and re-create the effects he saw in nature, and added a special liveliness to his portraits. Using the techniques of the day, Leonardo's mastery of shadow effects and textures gave works such as *La Gioconda* (known by most as the *Mona Lisa*), *The Last Supper,* and *Madonna of the Rocks,* almost lifelike appearances.

At the invitation of Francis I of France, Leonardo was invited to spend the rest of his days pursuing his own research at the castle of Cloux (near Amboise). As the in-house court artist, Leonardo entertained guests with his witty aphorisms, observations, and ideas until his death.

The elegant man later known for his long, curly beard and soulful eyes was as curious as he was observant. Interestingly, while the great genius had a keen eye and quick mind that led him to make important scientific discoveries, Leonardo never published his ideas. His work as a military engineer and weapon designer contrasted with a love of animals so great that he was a vegetarian. Considered one of the greatest painters of the Italian Renaissance, he left only a handful of completed paintings.

Michelangelo Buonarroti

Michelangelo Buonarroti (1475–1564) was undoubtedly one of the world's greatest talents who requires little introduction.

The second of five brothers, Michelangelo was born March 6, 1475, at Caprese in Tuscany. After insisting on becoming an artist, the young Michelangelo was placed under the tutelage of the Master painter Ghirlandaio in 1488 when he was thirteen years old. After about one year of learning the art of fresco and other techniques and traditions, Michelangelo was invited into the household of Lorenzo de' Medici where he was further schooled by the best teachers Florence had to offer, including a pupil of the great master Donatello. While staying with the Medici, Michelangelo had an opportunity to converse and mingle with the younger Medici, two of which later became popes (Leo X and Clement VII).

La Bella Lingua

The word "cartoon" derives from the Italian word *cartone* (cardboard) and refers to the full-scale drawings used by painters such as Michelangelo to prepare for a painting.

Certainly contact with such important figures of the Renaissance must have been auspicious for the young and extremely gifted artist. By the time he was 23, Michelangelo had accepted a commission for what would become one of his most famous sculptures. Located in St. Peter's church in the Vatican, Rome, *La Pietà* depicts an adult Christ laying in Mary's lap with such exquisite execution, it is as if the rock has been caressed to life.

Just days after the legendary statue was placed in Saint Peter's, Michelangelo overheard an observer's remark that the work was done by Christoforo Solari, a compatriot from Lombard. That night in a fit of rage, Michelangelo took hammer and chisel and placed the following inscription on the sash running across Mary's breast in lapidary letters: *Michel Angelus Bonarotus Florent Facibat* (Michelangelo Buonarroti, Florentine, made this). This is the only work that Michelangelo ever signed.

In a world where art was commissioned by patrons, Michelangelo found himself torn between the whims of the Medici family in Florence and the Papacy in Rome. In April 1508, Julius II summoned Michelangelo back to Rome to start work on the papal tomb. In addition, Julius II had a new job for the artist; he was doing a little remodeling and wanted Michelangelo to paint the apostles on

Di Interessa

Produced between 1501 and 1504, Michelangelo's famous *Davide* (David) depicted a model of heroic courage. The gigantic marble statue was so lifelike, Michelangelo is known to have tapped the statue with a hammer and ask, *Perché non parli?* (Why don't you speak?)

the ceiling of the Sistine Chapel. Working high above the chapel floor on scaffolding, for four years Michelangelo painted scenes from the Old Testament, leaving behind some of the finest pictorial images of all time.

Michelangelo's Pietà *in San Pietro.*

In 1534, Michelangelo left Florence for Rome where he could count on the esteem, protection, and affection of Pope Clement VII who, shortly before his death, commissioned Michelangelo to paint the fresco of the Last Judgment in the Sistine Chapel. Completed in 1541, it was the largest fresco of the Renaissance.

Michelangelo's crowning achievement as an architect was his work at St. Peter's Basilica, where he was made chief architect in 1546. The building was being constructed according to Donato Bramante's plan, but Michelangelo ultimately became responsible for the altar end of the building on the exterior and for the final form of its dome.

By the time Michelangelo died at the ripe old age of 89, he had left a core of work that would be admired by both peers and visitors for centuries. In his will, he purportedly left his soul to God, his body to earth, and his personal belongings to his family. He is buried in the church of Santa Croce in Florence.

Raphael

Raphael, born Raffaello Sanzio (1483–1520), was the youngest of the three artistic giants of the High Renaissance. He was born in Urbino, and at the age of 17, his father sent him to Perugia to become an apprentice under the highly regarded Perugino (1445–1523?). In the four years he spent in Perugino's workshop, Raphael learned all that his master could teach him, namely a clear organization of the composition and the avoidance of excessive detail.

Raphael began to modify the style he had learned, gradually assimilating the new techniques of Leonardo and Michelangelo. In 1504, Raphael went to Florence, bearing a letter of recommendation from the Duchess of Montefeltro. The intensive debates surrounding the new directions being taken in art at that time must have made a forceful impression on the young 21-year-old.

It was a period in which Leonardo, just returned from Milan, was astounding the public with his *Mona Lisa*; Fra Bartolommeo (1475–1517) was exhibiting his *Last Judgement*; and Michelangelo, who had come back to Florence from his first trip to Rome three years, previously, had completed his *David*.

Located in the Vatican in Rome, Raphael's most famous painting is *The School of Athens*. Portraying the secular sciences of philosophy, Aristotle and Plato are seen in conversation at the center of the picture. Like Michelangelo in the Sistine Ceiling, Raphael also incorporates a number of his contemporaries into his fresco. His portrait of Plato is probably modeled from the legendary Leonardo da Vinci, while Archimedes may be recognized as the great Renaissance architect Donato Bramante (1444–1514).

After the death of Bramante in 1514, Raphael was appointed architect of St. Peter's. He also became increasingly involved with the excavations and surveys of ruins in Rome.

La Bella Lingua

The Italian term *contrapposto* translates to "set against." Often used by the masters, it refers to a method derived from the ancients, whereby parts of the body are set in opposition to each other around a central vertical axis.

Di Interessa

For a wonderful novel that dramatizes Michelangelo's life, read *The Agony and the Ecstasy*, by Irving Stone.

131

Titian

By the dawn of the sixteenth century, the republic of Venice reigned as one of the wealthiest and most powerful city-states in Europe. The preeminent artist during this period was Tiziano Vecellio (1485–1576), also known as Titian.

Born in the town of Cadore in the Dolomite Mountains, Titian received brief training with the Venetian mosaicist Zuccato before he studied painting with both Giovanni Bellini and the innovative Giorgone. By 1510 he had established himself as an independent master.

While his influence is clearly evident in the works of his Venetian contemporaries Tintoretto, Veronese, and Bassano, Titian's work also exerted a strong impact on Rubens, Rembrandt, Velázquez, and other artists of the seventeenth century.

Titian was known as the greatest portraitist of his time. An excellent colorist (a major preoccupation of the Venetian School) he was also known for flowing lines and the relaxed mood evoked in his paintings. On Titian, the writer Vasari stated, "there was almost no famous lord, nor prince, nor great woman, who was not painted by Titian."

Di Interessa

The imaginative Teenage Mutant Ninja Turtles are named after some of the innovative artists of the Renaissance: Donatello, Leonardo, Michelangelo, and Raffaello.

Following a succession of commissions for the courts of Ferrara, Mantua, and Urbino, Titian's fame spread internationally. His patrons included such prominent figures as the German Emperor Charles V, Philip II of Spain, Francis I of France, and Pope Paul III. After a brilliant career spanning more than 66 years, Titian died in 1576.

Throughout his long and prolific career, Titian explored many pictorial challenges. Titian's compositions and brushwork were tremendously influential on later artists. Painters from Velázquez to Balthus studied and valued the work of Titian. His influence is perhaps felt more strongly in the twentieth century than that of any other Renaissance artist.

A Brief Renaissance Who's Who of Italian Artists

There are far more artists than covered here. Use this list to begin your study of High Italian Renaissance artists. Any library will have books on the Renaissance, or you can do a search online.

Pick one you love and study everything you can, or become a generalist; either way, it will help you develop your own latent genius!

Leon Battista Alberti (1404–1472)

Giovanni Bellini (1430–1516)

Sandro Botticelli (1444–1510)

Donato Bramante (1444–1514)

Filippo Brunelleschi (1377–1446)

Michelangelo Buonarroti (1475–1564)

Vittorio Carpaccio (1460–1525)

Michelangelo da Caravaggio (1571–1595)

Raffaello de Sanzio (1483–1520)

Leonardo da Vinci (1456–1519)

Piero della Francesca (1420–1492)

Donatello (1386–1466)

Giorgione (1478–1510)

Masaccio (1401–1428)

Andrea Mantegna (1431–1506)

Angelo Poliziano (1454–1494)

Jacopo Tintoretto (1518–1594)

Tiziano Vecellio (1485–1576)

Paolo Veronese (1528–1588)

Biografia

The Italian Renaissance painter Paolo Uccello (1396–1475) developed a system of perspective and foreshortening that paved the way for artists to paint with greater realism.

The Least You Need to Know

➤ The Renaissance reached its peak during the fifteenth century.

➤ The Humanists revived many ideas from classical times when ancient texts were translated from Greek, Hebrew, and Arabic into Latin.

➤ The Platonic Academy in Florence was created by Cosimo de' Medici and served as an informal meeting place for the great minds of the time.

➤ Leonardo da Vinci, Michelangelo Buonarroti, Raffaello (Raphael), and Tiziano (Titian) were key figures during the Renaissance.

Chapter 13

Great Discoveries: Here We Come!

In This Chapter

➤ Europeans head west in search of the Far East

➤ Marco Polo, Christopher Columbus, and Amerigo Vespucci

➤ The "discovery" of the New World

➤ The golden age of science

How did Christopher Columbus end up in the New World? Why isn't the United States of America the United States of Columbus? Who was Amerigo Vespucci, and why did his name end up on the maps? Where does Marco Polo fit in?

The search for spices and a shortcut to the Far East led the way for many Italian explorers. Italians also paved the way for the scientific explosion that resulted from the Renaissance.

We Like It Spicy

Back before supermarkets offered us just about every spice conveniently packaged in small glass jars, during ancient times spices from the Far East were quite in demand. Carried by caravan and ship across China and India to Rome and other cities, spices were used for the preservation of food (especially meat) and for the simple improvement in taste.

By the Middle Ages, when overland trade routes were cut off by the Mongols and Turks, the establishment of new trade routes became essential. The bitter rivalries and feuds between the European powers can be partially attributed to the race to find these hot commodities. As you can imagine, the expenses connected with obtaining the spices were enormous.

It was this demand for goods from the Far East that set the stage for the discovery of the American continents.

Marco Polo

The discovery of the "New World" is historically credited to the Spanish but was very much an Italian affair. In 1271, at around the age of 16, the Venetian Marco Polo (1254?–1324) accompanied his father Nicolo, his uncle Maffeo, and two Roman Catholic missionaries on their second journey to the Court of Kublai Khan. The missionaries soon abandoned the party, which reached Cambuluc (today's Peking) in 1275.

Di Interessa

Marco Polo's book, *Divisament dou Monde (Description of the World)* was first published in French and is probably the most famous travelogue ever written. In it, Mr. Polo described marvels such as paper money, coal, and other Oriental splendors virtually unknown in Europe. It was the basis for the first accurate maps of Asia and later helped Christopher Columbus in his explorations.

Some skeptics claim Marco Polo never made it to China and that his memoirs were more likely copied details from Persian or Arabic guidebooks on China, since no reference to Marco Polo (or any other Italian) has been found in Chinese sources describing the court of Kublai Khan.

Back when it took four years to travel to China, the tendency was to stay for a while. Most people don't realize that Marco Polo spent close to 20 years serving the Khan, who employed him on business throughout China, Southeast Asia, and India. Marco Polo may also have ruled the Chinese city of Yangchow for three years.

Legend often (incorrectly) claims that Marco Polo brought spaghetti back from China when in fact it was a chef who plainly knew how to cook a mean noodle. By 1295, Marco Polo was back in Venice, fighting along with other Venetians against the forces of Genoa, where he was taken prisoner. It was during his time in captivity that he dictated an account of his journey titled *Divisament dou Monde* to a writer with whom he shared his jail cell.

Marco Polo died in 1324 when he was 70 years old. On his death bed, he was reported saying, "I didn't tell half of what I saw, because no one would have believed me."

Di Interessa

There was a time when spices were worth their weight in gold, such as when Alaric I apparently demanded pepper as part of the ransom for raising the siege of Rome in 408.

Unsung Heroes

Italians continued to dominate in exploration and seamanship with accomplishments such as the circumnavigation of Africa by the brothers Ugolino and Vadino Vivaldi in 1291. This feat was not properly documented, explaining why Ugolino and Vadino are lesser known than other contemporaries.

Until 1302 when Flavio Gioia developed a working compass, it would be especially difficult to travel far without a map, and that's just what early adventurers did. The Italian dominance in the sciences of cosmography, astronomy, and geography, set the stage for the likes of Christopher Columbus, Amerigo Vespucci, Giovanni Caboto (better known as John Cabot), and Giovanni da Verrazano to discover and make the "New World" a reality.

Christopher Columbus

Christopher Columbus (1451–1506) (known to Italians as Cristoforo Colombo) was but one of many who believed one could reach land by sailing west. While engaged as a sugar buyer in the Portuguese islands off Africa by a Genoese mercantile firm, Columbus met pilots and navigators who believed in the existence of islands farther west.

There is enough evidence to support the possibility that Columbus, though undeniably a devout Catholic, might also have been the descendent of Spanish Jews. Evidence includes his adopted Spanish name "Colon" (a commonly used Jewish variation of the Italian name Colombo). Additionally, while scheduled to depart from Spain on August 3, 1492, Columbus apparently insisted on leaving a day earlier. August 2, 1492, was the day that had been ordained for the last Jews of Spain to

depart the country. Ironically, it coincides with the Ninth of Av, the Jewish fast of mourning for the destruction of the Jerusalem temples.

While seeking support for his "Enterprise of the Indies," Columbus was repeatedly rebuffed. No one was particularly interested in pursuing a pipe dream; certainly the Italians were not, nor were the Portuguese. It would take another eight years before Columbus finally convinced the Spanish monarchy (who were in an expansionist mood) to outfit the necessary ships for the trip.

In 1492, Columbus Sailed the Ocean Blue

On August 3, 1492, Columbus, armed with the compass and charts by the famous Florentine cosmographer Paolo dal Pozzo Toscanelli, sailed from Palos, Spain, with three small ships, the *Santa Maria*, the *Pinta*, and the *Niña*. What he didn't realize was that Toscanelli's charts erroneously showed the location of Japan to be within the sailing distance of the ships of the day (about 3000 miles).

After 34 days at sea, hysteria began to seize the hearts of the brave sailors. Surely they were about to fall off the edge of the world! In October, Columbus arrived at the Canary Islands and after changing course and quelling a mutiny, finally landed on Watling Island (near the Bahamas).

In the Name of Spain, I Hereby Proclaim ...

Columbus believed he had reached the East Indies. He claimed the "new" land for Spain and continued to sail around exploring neighboring lands where he discovered Cuba and Hispaniola. On Christmas Eve, the Santa Maria was wrecked off the north coast of Hispaniola.

Leaving his men to found a colony, Columbus quickly made his way back to Spain where he was given a hero's welcome and made "admiral of the ocean sea."

By October 1493, he was returning to the new lands with a fleet of 17 ships and 1,500 colonists. By the time they got back to Hispaniola, the original colonists were dead.

Undeterred, Columbus founded another colony. Conditions were wretched and Columbus' strict administration led some of the colonists to seize a ship and sail back to Spain to complain, with Columbus hot on their trail. By the time Columbus made his third trip, the only colonists he was able to bring were convicts. While Columbus had proven it was possible to cross the Atlantic, he died in relative obscurity, still believing that he had reached the Orient.

Way to Go Amerigo

The Florentine Amerigo Vespucci (1454–1512), in whose honor the Americas were named, was educated as a businessman and worked as a representative for the Medici family's affairs in Spain.

Enamored by the art of navigation and an avid student of cosmography (a theoretical science that encompassed physics, geography, and astronomy), he also collected maps and books. A contemporary of Columbus, he became influential in Spain and may have even helped in the financing of Columbus' second voyage.

In 1499, when the second voyage of Columbus failed to return any goods from the Orient, Amerigo organized and signed onto an expedition as astronomer with Captain Alonso de Hojeda. They reached the coast of Brazil where they explored much of the coast and sailed up the Amazon River.

A second and third voyage under the flag of Portugal made it possible for Vespucci to chart much of the new continents (from the Gulf of Mexico) to 35 degrees south of the equator. While Columbus was given credit for his discovery, it was Amerigo's scientific applications and calculations that led to the declaration that South America was not India, but in fact a New Land (Mundus Novus). Furthermore, he concluded that another ocean, larger than the Atlantic, must exist beyond this new mainland.

Di Interessa

One of Vespucci's greatest contributions was a method by which he was able to determine longitude to accuracy within two degrees. His method became the standard for the next 300 years. Vespucci also calculated the earth's circumference just 50 miles (80 kilometers) shy of the correct measurement.

Di Interessa

As a result of Amerigo's excellent cartographic abilities, cosmography was radically altered. In 1507 the name "America" was first applied to the continent with the publication of Martin Waldseemüller's *Cosmographiae introductio*.

Giovanni Caboto

The Italian explorer Giovanni Caboto (1450?–1499)—better known by his English name John Cabot—was born in Gaeta, around 1450. During his youth, he became a citizen of Venice and married his wife Mattea.

Like Columbus and Vespucci, Cabot believed the riches of the Far East could be obtained by sailing west. To make the exploratory voyages to the Orient, he needed sponsorship. Unsuccessful in Portugal and Spain, he followed the advice of English merchant friends and became a resident of Bristol, England where he changed his name.

La Bella Lingua

In Italian, *caboto* means "coastal seaman" and was often the name given to navigators and sailors in the seafaring cities of Italy.

Di Interessa

Named in honor of the Italian explorer and located in the heart of New York Harbor, the Verrazano-Narrows Bridge links the boroughs of Staten Island and Brooklyn. Completed in 1964 by O. H. Ammann, it is one of the longest suspension bridges in the United States with a span of 4,260 feet (1,298 meters).

In England, he was able to find backing from his merchant friends and obtained a "Letter of Patent" from Henry VII to "... discover and claim a New World." In 1497 he set out with one ship and a small crew of 18 men on the *Matthew*.

It was Cabot's intention to sail west to Japan. He found, instead, the eastern coast of what is now Canada, which he claimed by planting the banners of King Henry VII of England, St. Mark (the patron saint of Venice), and the Pope of Rome.

Returning to England as a hero, Cabot was granted a pension and given 300 men and several ships for a second voyage. In May of 1498, he sailed from Bristol where accounts differ about the nature of the voyage. One account says he sailed to the east coast of Greenland and that his crew mutinied because of the extreme cold. Another account says he sailed down the coast of North America to the Chesapeake Bay before returning to England.

In any case, the English claims in North America were based on his discoveries. Cabot died shortly after his return to England. Following in his father's footsteps, his son Sebastian Cabot (1483?–1557) continued to sail the seas in search of spices.

Verrazano Bridges the Gap

The Italian navigator Giovanni da Verrazano (1480–1527) was born in Val di Greve (near Venice), Italy. Verrazano is best known as the first European explorer to enter New York Harbor.

Verrazano made a name for himself in the service of the French as a "Corsair" (pirate) against the Spanish. Commissioned by the King of France (Francis I) to sail west in search of the nebulous Far East, in 1524 he reached the shores of present day North Carolina. From there he explored the shores north as far as Nova Scotia. During his second voyage, while exploring the West Indies, Verrazano was killed by natives.

Read All About It: Native American Discovers Italy!

The Europeans' right to claim parts of already occupied territories was supported by the Vatican through a *Papal Bull* titled the Doctrine of Discovery.

La Bella Lingua

A **Papal Bull** is a written statement formally issued by the pope and bearing an official seal.

Fortunate Eagle

In 1973, an educator, activist, and artist named Fortunate Eagle was invited as the only Native American representative to be a delegate at an international conference in Rome, Italy. Fortunate—actively involved with natives' rights to lands—decided to lay his own Claim of Discovery in response to Columbus' "discovery" of the New World, a land already inhabited for millennia by Native Americans. In keeping with the spirit of things, an Alitalia airplane was renamed *Chief Joseph* and served as Fortunate's discovery ship.

I Hereby Claim ...

Dressed in full native regalia, Fortunate was greeted by photographers and newspapers eager to record this monumental event. Upon exiting the plane, the leader made the claim, "In the name of the American Indian people, and pursuant to the Doctrine of Discovery, I hereby lay claim to this land called Italy."

The good-humored native was later introduced to the pope, whose audience included several bishops, cardinals, and priests. When the pope raised his bejeweled hand to be kissed, much to the surprise of all in company, the native (also wearing a beautiful ring) mirrored the gesture. Whose ring would be kissed after all? The point had been made, and the pope and Fortunate became instant friends.

"*Italia*"

In Italics

Galileo Galilei was born in 1564, the same year that Michelangelo died. Sir Isaac Newton was born in 1642, the year of Galileo's death.

Galileo Figaro Magnifico

The single characteristic shared by the men and women of the Renaissance was the belief that they were capable of understanding anything. Like much of the Renaissance, this era of scientific discovery was influenced by many factors.

The invention of moveable type brought about the printing press in the middle of the fifteenth century. The result was akin to opening a Pandora's box of knowledge. Since the Dark Ages, most of the knowledge had been the province of the Church. Printing made information available to all that were curious.

The golden age of science is exemplified by the accomplished works of the great men of the Renaissance. While Leonardo da Vinci may have optimized this era, many others also made great contributions to the revitalization of the sciences.

Di Interessa

You may be familiar with the famous song that mentions Galileo titled "Bohemian Rhapsody" by the rock legend Queen. Listening to it in a new light, the listener will realize that this number-one hit was done in a pseudo-operatic Italian style.

"*Italia*"

In Italics

1610—Galileo was invited to Florence to serve as philosopher and mathematician to Florence by another important figure of the times, Cosimo II de' Medici, patron to the arts.

Galileo Galilei (1564–1642) is known as the founder of modern mechanics and experimental physics. Most remember him for stating, in scientific terms, the argument of Copernicus: The Earth and other planets revolve around the Sun. As an astronomer, mathematician, and physicist, Galileo's curiosity concerning natural laws laid the foundation for today's experimental science.

Until Galileo's earth shattering writings—supporting those of Copernicus—it was commonly believed that the earth was a stationary entity located in the center of the universe, an idea established by the Greco-Egyptian astronomer Ptolemy (Claudius Ptolemaeus).

In 1611, Galileo visited the papal court in Rome to display the telescope he had created. Finally, Copernicus' ideas would be proven! Not so, said the papacy. Galileo's discoveries and ideas were so contradictory to the beliefs of the time that Galileo, once more summoned to Rome, was warned not to uphold or teach the system of Copernicus, since it was denounced as dangerous to faith.

For 20 years, Galileo worked on his experiments until 1632 when he wrote and published (contrary to Rome's directive) *Dialogo … sopra i due massimi sistemi del mondo* (*Dialogue concerning the two chief world systems*). Written for the layman, it did not take long for the church to call Galileo back to Rome for an inquisition. Given the choices—take back your words or die a horrible death, it is no wonder that in 1633, Galileo renounced all his beliefs and writings supporting the Copernican system of the solar system.

E Pur Si Muove

Legend has it that after his inquisition, the impious Galileo is purported to have said sotto voce, *E pur si muove* (and yet it moves), referring to the earth. He was banished to the town of Arcetri, just outside Florence, where he continued to conduct experiments while living under house arrest until his death.

Galileo's Firsts

The following list illustrates some of Galileo's achievements in what is quite a resumé:

Di Interessa

The famous story in which Galileo is said to have dropped weights from the (still straight) Leaning Tower of Pisa is untrue. The actual experiment was conducted by Simon Stevin several years earlier.

Galileo Galilei (1564–1642) ...

➤ Invented the lens and the microscope
➤ Discovered the true oscillation period of the pendulum
➤ Discovered that acceleration occurs in a straight line
➤ Invented the thermoscope (an early version of the thermometer)
➤ Stated that heavy and light objects fall at the same rate
➤ Proved that air has weight
➤ Discovered and observed the four largest satellites of Jupiter
➤ Constructed and used the first practical telescope
➤ Discovered that Mars is round
➤ Defined the Law of Freefall
➤ Observed Saturn and began to study the phases of Venus
➤ Extended the theory of Bonaventura Cavalieri into the Law of Parabolic Fall
➤ Established the concept of Energy
➤ Analyzed the principle of "odds" in dice
➤ Discovered and explained the solar phenomena of sunspots
➤ Carried out a controlled chain reaction
➤ Revised and improved on Da Vinci's hygrometer

Other Italian Scientists

The Italian contributions to the sciences includes some of these notables.

Table of Firsts: 1350 to 1600

Scientist	Year	Discovery	Contribution
Giordano Bruno	1535	Discussed the universe as infinite	Philosophy
Luigi Alvise Cornardo	1558	Created long-life formula	Longevity
Giovanni da Fontana	1420	Sketched jet-propelled animals	Physics
Giovanni de Dondi	1364	Invented astronomical clock	Astronomy
Scipione del Ferro	1510	Discovered solution to cubic equation	Mathematics
Francesco di Giorgio	1490	Invented ball and chain centrifugal governor	Physics
	1495	Designed jet-propelled petards	Physics
Girolamo Fracastoro	1530	The Father of Epidemiology; described syphilis	Epidemiology
	1538	Proposed germ theory of disease	Epidemiology
	1538	Published idea of Solar System	Astronomy
	1546	Published textbook of contagious diseases	Epidemiology
Alvisio Luigini	1566	Published treatments for syphilis	Medicine
	1599	Published treatise on venereal disease	Medicine
Luca Pacioli	1450	Republished: *Libra Abaci* by Leonardo Fibonacci	Mathematics
	1494	Developed Lucas Sequence of Numbers	Mathematics
Nicolo Tartaglia	1512	Discovered solution to quartic equation	Mathematics
Bernardino Telesio	1565	Adopted empirical criteria	Philosophy

Copernicus

Although he was not Italian, the Polish mathematician Nicholas Copernicus (1473–1543) received part of his schooling in Bologna, Italy. Educated in mathematics and optics before studying Canon Law, Copernicus lived his life as a canon of the cathedral of Frauenburg.

An avid astronomer, Copernicus spent most of his time making observations from the walls surrounding the cathedral—and without the aid of a (yet to be invented) telescope.

In 1530, he wrote down his ideas and observations in a treatise called *De Revolutionbus Orbium Coelestium*. Dedicated to Pope Paul III, his findings would be known as the Copernican System, creating the foundation for modern astronomy.

Until Galileo put "scientific" weight behind them, few knew of Copernicus' findings.

The Least You Need to Know

➤ The demand for spices set the stage for the discovery of the American continents.

➤ The writings of Marco Polo became the chief source of information about China until the nineteenth century.

➤ Christopher Columbus, Amerigo Vespucci, John Cabot, and Giovanni Verrazano were all Italian explorers.

➤ Galileo Galilei wrote *Dialogue Concerning the Two Chief World Systems* supporting the ideas of Italian-educated Copernicus.

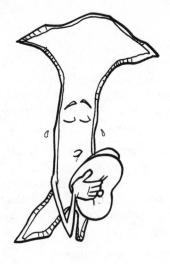

The Day the Music Died

As much as the Renaissance was a time of open-mindedness, tolerance, and experimentation, the Inquisition that soon absorbed the country was severe, rigid, and hardly tolerant.

Perhaps humanity, like Icarus, had flown too close to the sun and burned its wings. The rich and fertile period that had nurtured the mind of Galileo during the Renaissance soon turned barren, resulting in a period of stagnation and reform. Suddenly, men like Galileo were being told that their brilliance was no longer necessary since so many of the scientific ideas ran counter to the teachings of the Church.

How did fear and loathing overtake the humanistic, high-minded ideals of the Renaissance?

Pope Paul III

Let's go back to the popes, since it's with the Church that this all begins. A member of the Farnese family, Paul III was a key figure. During the time of his reign (1534–1549), this patron of the arts worked with artists such as Michelangelo in the construction of the beautiful Palazzo Farnese. Clearly, the humanist-educated Paul III valued the attributes we associate with the Renaissance.

The development of the printing press in Germany tremendously expanded the Protestant cause supported by thinkers such as John Calvin and Martin Luther. More of these writings began to come through the peninsula via Venetian book dealers and small manuals such as the *Beneficio de Cristo*.

Alarmed by the spread of Protestantism and its penetration into Italy, this same pope would in 1540 issue the bull that approved the founding of the Order of the Jesuits by Ignatius Loyola. In the first half of 1500, the success of the counter-Reformation was successful in Italy because of the Catholic Church's ability to respond to demands for the reform of the Church.

"Italia"

In Italics

1527—Daily life in Rome was disrupted after the city was sacked by Charles V of Spain. Countless works of art were destroyed by unruly troops. Pope Clement VII found refuge in the fortress of Castel Sant'Angelo located in the center of Rome.

The Holy Office

One of Paul III's advisors was Giovanni Carafa, a Neapolitan Cardinal. When in 1555 the fanatical Carafa became Pope IV himself, he immediately took steps to stamp out heresy and the growing Protestant movement.

Biografia

Alessandro Tassoni (1565–1635) spent much of his life in the service of Charles Emmanuel I of Savoy and Francesco I of Modena. In 1602, he wrote a sharp letter of defense against accusations by the Italian Inquisition that he was as a polemist of high order. Tassoni is best known for the mock-heroic poem "Secchia Rapita" (1622), which ridicules the war between Bologna and Modena.

Through the "Holy Office" (also known as the Roman *Inquisition*), the long-defunct institution of the Inquisition was resurrected under the guise of keeping Italy free of the heresy that had spread across Europe. (Others saw it as an attempt to counterbalance the severe Spanish Inquisition when Italy was under Spanish rule.)

La Bella Lingua

The word **inquisition** derives from Latin *inquiro* ("inquire into") and refers to the organization founded in the thirteenth century by the Roman Catholic Church to seek, interrogate, and sentence citizens whose ideas did not coincide with the orthodox religious beliefs of the time. The organization was later revived in an attempt to stamp out the growing Protestant movement.

From the end of the sixteenth century to the beginning of the seventeenth century, a succession of popes, from Pius V (1567–1572) to Urban VIII (1623–1644), imposed the decrees of what came to be known as the Council of Trent.

The Council of Trent

The Council of Trent (1563) defined the differences between Catholic and Protestant positions and formalized the ideals, doctrines, and laws of the Church. Essentially, the council held that both the Bible and the traditions of the Church were the Word of God. Furthermore, the council argued, only the Catholic interpretation of the Bible (called the Vulgata) was the "correct" and official version. They stressed that "salvation should be sought by faith and good works, not by faith alone"; they also affirmed the seven sacraments. On the other hand, the Protestants argued that the Bible was the only true Word of God.

The Holy Office was a by-the-book kind of organization whose chief concerns centered on the proper interpretation of doctrinal truth. If you

Di Interessa

The Inquisition officially came into existence with the constitution "Excommunicamus" of Pope Gregory IX (1227–41). The office of the inquisitor was a job entrusted almost exclusively to the Franciscans and especially the Dominicans because of their supposed indifference to worldly concerns.

were not in concordance with the way the church viewed things, whether because you happened to dress funny or act eccentrically, you could be accused of being a heretic. Conformity was the rule, and anyone could be accused of heresy.

Bruno Giordano: Victim of the Inquisition

The Italian Renaissance philosopher Bruno Giordano (1548–1600) was born near the city of Naples. Born as Filippo, Giordano changed his name when he joined the Dominicans who trained him in Aristotelian philosophy. At the age of 28, in 1576, the free-thinking Giordano was forced to flee the sanctuary to avoid a trial based on doctrinal charges.

Bruno's travels lasted for many years as he wandered throughout Europe, including Geneva, Toulouse, Paris, and London, where he spent time writing and in company with the English poet Sir Philip Sidney among others. During his most productive period, he wrote several works which included "Ash Wednesday Supper" (1584), "On the Infinite Universe and Worlds" (1584), "On the Cause, Principle, and Unity" (1584), and a poetic dialogue that praised Platonic love in *Gli eroici furori* (1584).

Di Interessa

The Index of Forbidden Books was a list of books thought to be offensive to the faith and morals of the Church. The writings of Galileo were to be added to this list, in addition to the works of several prominent thinkers of the time.

In 1585, Bruno returned to Paris before moving on to Frankfurt where he arranged the printing of many of his writings. Invited back to Italy by the Venetian nobleman Giovanni Mocenigo to serve as a private tutor, Bruno was denounced in 1592 and tried for heresy on charges of blasphemy, immoral conduct, and heresy. Turned over to the authorities in Rome, Bruno was repeatedly tortured and interrogated for eight years. He was burned at the stake on February 17, 1600, in Rome's flower market *Campo dei Fiori*.

Regarded as a champion for free thinking, Bruno's writings and philosophical theories expressed his belief that the universe is infinite, God as we know it is a universal world-soul, and that material things are manifestations of the one infinite principle.

Baby Boom

Meanwhile, between 1500 and 1600, Italy's population almost doubled, making the peninsula one of the most densely populated regions in Europe. All those new mouths required feeding and measures were made to clear fresh areas of land for large-scale farming, much of which included crops such as wheat and the production of olive oil and wine. Additional land was cultivated when large marsh areas were drained in the Po Valley and throughout the Tuscan and Roman Maremma.

The textile industry grew in response to the population increase. The production of wool doubled and silk manufacture began to be seen in the north.

In addition, the construction of beautiful palaces and buildings during the High Renaissance was made possible because of the evolution of an available credit system. Sponsored by the Spanish, explorers such as Columbus and Vespucci searched the seas using the same monies being spent on the elaborate public works projects, ship building, and art commissions, all paid for by rich banking families such as the Genoese Doria, Grimaldi, Spinola, and Pallavicino.

It seemed as though it could last forever, but it wouldn't.

> ## "*Italia*"
>
> ### In Italics
>
> Prior to the Black Death of 1348, Italy's population has been estimated to be around 11 million. By the mid-sixteenth century, Italy's population finally recovered, reaching 13.3 million.

The Beginning of the End

At the end of the sixteenth century, a recession began to take place in Italy that sharply contrasted with the facade of prosperity. Due to the Crown's inability to repay its debts, the rich banking families soon found their investment in the Spanish monarchy was going to cost them more than they had bargained for, often to their ruin.

Historians differ on the exact reasons behind the recession, but many speculate that it was a combination of events. The merchant entrepreneurs that had been central to the Italian economy since the Middle Ages were less interested in the trade and commerce that had made so many of them rich. It was far more intriguing to spend their money on the arts than industry.

Cheap Imports Steal the Market

The guilds may also have contributed to the recession. Cheaper goods were pouring in from the North, making it difficult for Italian artisans and craftsmen—bound by the standards established by the guilds—to compete. Soon, instead of being a producer, Italy was a consumer, and by the end of the seventeenth century, she imported more finished goods from France, Holland, and England than she exported.

Since the majority of the population continued to be too poor to afford the manufactured goods enjoyed by their aristocratic cousins, domestic demand was weak; the heralded discovery of the New World further shifted energies away from a Mediterranean market to the Atlantic.

Bandits

Rising unemployment combined with a food crisis triggered widespread banditry that began to appear in the countryside. Bandits often terrorized a town with little fear of consequence. The problem was pervasive enough that watch towers were built in Naples and brush fires started to "smoke" out the bandits in the shrub-covered terrain of Campagnia.

Disaster Strikes Again: Mo' Plague

As if rising employment, roaming bandits, and hunger weren't enough, in 1630 the Plague struck in a year-long epidemic that wiped out between one third and one half of the population. Naturally, the northern cities were more affected than the rural countryside, with Venice, Milan, Florence, Verona, and Florence suffering enormous losses. In 1656, a similar outbreak occurred in the southern city of Naples (the most populous city at the end of the sixteenth century) and spread across the mainland.

Di Interessa

In *I Promessi Sposi* (*The Betrothed*), the devastating plague of 1630 is immortalized in Alessandro Manzoni's historical novel that describes life in Milan under Spanish rule in the seventeenth century.

The rise in population that had defined the sixteenth century quickly plummeted. The plague did not respect borders, and in the wake of the tornado came world recession.

The act of war is expensive and everyone, from Naples to Rome to Madrid to Mantua, struggled to scrape together enough to keep the engine running. Taxes were rising while production had decreased. To raise capital, the governments and the papacy sold crown lands, titles, privileges, and monopolies (and probably their daughters) in exchange for a few *scudi* (ducats).

War exaggerated the effects of the recession, along with constantly shifting alliances that resulted in rising hostilities. For example, Venice fought against the Austrian Hapsburgs (1615) before it was involved in a 30-year dispute over the Alpine region of Valtellina (1620) that would last until 1659. In the meanwhile, the Republic of Genoa was caught in a web of dependency due to its indebtedness to the Spanish.

The Church Reigns Supreme

The humbling aftermath of the wars and creation of the Council of Trent led to the renewal of Catholic culture throughout Italy and created a social hierarchy that equated peasants and artists with ignorance. The parish priest was now the ideal figurehead, trained through Roman *catechism* to lead the faithful along the perilous and difficult journey of life from birth to death and afterlife. In his sermons, the priest preached the virtues of respect, obedience, and resignation.

The Italian nobility stayed close to the Church. Jesuits educated its children and led the many annual religious ceremonies and processions that were held.

Later, the Baroque churches and sanctuaries of the Catholic Reform were only part of the intense efforts made to reestablish Italian Catholicism. The cult of the saints was spread by the *bizzocche* (Tertiary Sisters) among the women of their neighborhoods. Religious pilgrims and tourists began to come from around the world to cities like Rome, Loreto, and Assisi to visit the reliquaries and saints' bodies. Paintings in the churches of the day served to remind the mortals of their mortality and further the idea of the Church's superiority.

La Bella Lingua

The **catechism** is the instruction in the principles of Christianity that follow a body of basic beliefs.

Burned at the Stake

One of the earliest Christian leaders and author of *De Civitate Dei* (*The City of God*), St. Augustine of Hippo (modern Annaba, Algeria) (354–430) declared that heretics, pagans, and Jews would burn forever in eternal fire unless saved by the Catholic Church. Although he was speaking in metaphorical terms, the bishop's words were nevertheless taken literally, leading to the practice of burning victims to death.

The execution of a witch or heretic was usually a great public occasion and generally took place shortly after the sentencing. The witch was usually strangled first, and then her corpse—or sometimes her unconscious or semiconscious body—was tied to a stake or dumped into a tar barrel and set afire. If the witch was not dead and managed to get out of the flames, onlookers shoved her back in.

The Witch Hunts

As a result of the Inquisition, which lasted roughly between 1400 and 1700, the witch hunts that had swept across Europe were also affecting Italy. It's difficult to know just how many people, mostly women, were killed during this time, but figures range from the high thousands to the millions. Most were burned alive at the stake.

Biografia

The legend of the Werewolf of Pavia begins in 1541 and involves a farmer who, as a wolf, tore many men to pieces. When the bloodthirsty maniac was eventually caught, he explained that there was little difference between himself and a wolf. In response, the magistrate cut off his arms and legs, leading to his death.

Why were these women hunted? Factors may include the Hundred Years' War between France and England (1337–1453); the Black Death (1347) that decimated Europe; and changes in weather patterns that led to widespread famine. But these things alone were not enough to create the level of fear and hatred ascribed to the witch hunts.

The real reason may have to do with the clash of religions that eventually motivated Paul III to resurrect the Inquisition through his Holy Office.

It appears that there will always be scapegoats whenever a society finds itself in trouble. The troubles that had descended over Europe could be easily blamed on the supernatural powers attributed to the witches. Stories arose that spoke of women killing and eating infants, stealing men's sexual prowess, creating spells, and transforming into beasts.

Di Interessa

Women and men born with a caul were believed to have mysterious healing powers and the ability to see witches. Cauls were sometimes saved by these benandanti and worn about their necks as amulets.

One of the main targets of the Inquisition were the *benandanti,* a term that roughly translates to mean "good walkers," and describes members of an ancient agrarian cult in the Friuli region of northern Italy. The *benandanti* came to the attention of Inquisitors in the late sixteenth century.

It was believed the *benandanti* had the ability to contact the dead and to exercise control over the powers of nature for the benefit of society. They saw themselves as protectors of agricultural fertility and went into trances where they envisioned victory over the witches.

Until 1610, the *benandanti* retained their anti-witchcraft stance before they, too, came under persecution by the Inquisition and were identified as witches.

Cagliostro: Potion Maker

Where there are witches, there must be magic. Where there is magic, there must be magicians. Count Alessandro Cagliostro (1743–1795; originally Giuseppe Balsamo) was an Italian magician and alchemist who committed numerous crimes throughout Sicily. After fleeing the island, he and his wife Lorenza Feliciani were among the most distinguished families of the Continent. By the sale of love philters, magic elixirs, and concoctions, Cagliostro amassed great wealth. His constant scandalous behavior led him to travel from one country to another. His declining years were spent imprisoned in the fortress of San Leo. Reputedly, he was successful in necromancy, the practice of attempting to communicate with the dead, and the manufacture of diamonds by alchemy. He was also the founder of an occult society called The Egyptian Lodge.

Giacomo Casanova

If you have every fallen in love, you are familiar with feeling spellbound by the object of your affection. Just about everyone knows that the Venetian Italian adventurer Giovanni Giacomo Casanova (1725–1798) was a notorious ladies' man. What they don't know is that he also apparently practiced witchcraft and divination.

In 1755, the Venetians imprisoned Casanova for impiety and practicing magic. After a sensationally executed escape, Casanova slipped out of Italy and made his way to the friendlier climate of Louis XI, the King of France. Best known as the lover of the Marquise de Pompadour, in 1785, Casanova retired to the castle of a friend to write his memoirs.

When asked, "If witches and magicians had devils and demons at their command, why could they not defeat the prying Church authorities?" Casanova replied, "Because the Church officials commanded more devils and demons than anyone else."

The Least You Need to Know

➤ The popes used their power to turn away calls for change.

➤ The Council of Trent strengthened the Roman Catholic Church in its confrontation with Protestantism.

➤ Italy's population dramatically increased from 1500 to 1600, only to be decimated by the plague in the mid-1600s.

➤ A recession in the 1600s made life miserable.

➤ The Inquisition and witch hunts killed many innocent people.

➤ Several wars on the Italian peninsula cost governments much money and resources.

Violins and Lace: The Baroque

The highly stylized and ornamental style of architecture and art that lasted from the mid-sixteenth to the early eighteenth century is characteristic of the Baroque. No longer convinced the earth was at the center of the universe, artists and writers attempted to process, interpret, explain, and ultimately express the mysteries of the vast universe they lived in during this time.

At the same time, classical music of the seventeenth century was undergoing a revolution as opera spread across Europe with as much drama as a diva during opening night. Opera's intoxicating effects had audiences swooning and the public begging for more.

La "Dramma per Musica"

Webster's defines opera as "a dramatic musical work in which singing takes the place of speech." Ask an opera lover to describe opera and she'll tell you it's about big voices, lavish sets, and lots of drama. The first opera composers simply referred to it as "dramma per musica" (drama through music), for it was in opera that actors began to sing their words to the music instead of simply speaking them.

Opera originated in sixteenth-century Florence, nurtured by musicians and poets who were part of an academy called the *Camerata*. It had been their aim to imitate the ancient Greek pastoral poetry they believed had either been sung or chanted. Since there were no recording devices like we have today, they had to guess at what the Greeks sounded like; along the way opera was invented.

La Bella Lingua

The **Camerata** referred to the sixteenth-century Florentine society of poets, musicians, and scholars who were dedicated to creating an equivalent of ancient Greek drama. Members included the composers Giulio Caccini, Emilio del Cavaliere, and Jacopo Peri.

La Bella Lingua

The word **opera** comes from Italian and simply referred to a work, as in *opera d'arte* (work of art). It later came to refer to the dramatic performance set to music we all now recognize as opera music.

Italian music dominated the late Renaissance and early Baroque periods, with wealthy families and patrons spending huge sums of money on extravagant productions in cities such as Florence, Padua, Mantua, and Ferrara.

Opera achieved an ideal musicians embraced during this period. They held that music should move the listener in an emotional and physical way. This could only have been accomplished through the unique collaboration between musicians, artists, poets, painters, and architects (the original set designers) without whose distinctly different and unique "voices," opera could never have existed.

The First Operatic Giants

Although opera began in the dynastic courts, it was not until the appearance of Venetian dramatic composer Monteverdi in the sixteenth century that this aristocratic art form became available to a wider audience. Monteverdi was followed by Giovanni Pierluigi da Palestrina, whose works came to dominate the opera scene.

Later, in seventeenth and eighteenth century, audiences in Naples applauded to the music of the universally recognized master of Neapolitan Baroque music, Alessandro Scarlatti. In Venice, they applauded Antonio Vivaldi, and in Cremona, they crooned to the violins of the great violin maker Antonio Stradivari.

Claudio Monteverdi

One of the true geniuses of Western music, Claudio Monteverdi (1567–1643) published his first madrigals (love poems that were set to music) at the early age of 15 and was one of the first to use the pizzicato, a technique that involved plucking a stringed instrument. Monteverdi is also said to be responsible for the introduction of *bel canto,* a term that literally translates to mean "beautiful singing" and was characterized by full, even tones and a brilliant display of vocal technique.

Monteverdi always began with the words contained within the *libretto,* the small book used in opera to tell the story; he essentially "translated" the text within the libretto into a tangible and powerful musical experience that became a model for future operatic composers to come.

In 1590 Monteverdi became the choir master for the ducal court of Mantua in 1602. His first opera, *Orfeo,* was performed in 1607, and by 1613, Monteverdi was appointed the prestigious position of choirmaster and conductor for St. Mark's Cathedral in Venice. When the first opera house opened in 1637, Monteverdi wrote a series of operas that included *Il ritorno di Ulisse* (*The Return of Ulysses;* 1640) and *L'incoronazione di Poppea* (*The Coronation of Poppea;* 1642). Today, Monteverdi's operas continue to be performed around the world.

Giovanni Pierluigi da Palestrina

One of Italian opera's key composers was Giovanni Pierluigi da Palestrina (1525–1594). Considered the first "Catholic Church musician," he was the undisputed master of the Mass (of the 105 Masses he wrote, *Misa Papae Marcelli* was his most famous).

Additionally he was known for his elegant madrigals and motets (a vocal composition usually with a religious theme). Palestrina was a legend in his own day and brought opera to a new level through his ability to refine polyphonic techniques.

Palestrina began as a choirboy before he was hired in 1544 as an organist at St. Agapito in his hometown of Palestrina at age 19. Palestrina's big break came after the bishop of Palestrina became Pope Julius III and appointed Palestrina *maestro di cappella* (choirmaster) of the Cappella Giulia in Rome. In 1554, he produced his first Masses, some of which were performed in the Sistine Chapel. After many stints serving some of Rome's greatest churches, in

"Italia"

In Italics

October 6, 1600—Set to music by Jacopo Peri and Giulio Caccini, *Euridice* was the first opera from which any music has survived. It was performed at the Palazzo Pitti in Florence during the wedding celebration of Marie de' Medici and Henry IV of France.

La Bella Lingua

The word **baroque** appears to come from Portuguese and literally means a rough and irregularly shaped pearl—a fitting description for the politically chaotic sixteenth and seventeenth centuries.

1564 Palestrina was invited by Cardinal Ippolito d'Este to oversee the music at his country estate in Tivoli (just outside of Rome).

La Bella Lingua

Bel canto, or "beautiful singing," refers to an operatic style of music that blends beautiful composition with refined vocal technique.

A **pizzicato** is a piece of music. It is also the style of playing in which instead of a bow, fingers are used to pluck the strings of an instrument.

Libretto, literally "little book," tells the story, outlines the plot, and paints the picture that will be expressed so passionately by the singers. Without the libretto, opera loses half its meaning.

Madrigal 1. a song for two or three unaccompanied voices that was developed in Italy in the late thirteenth century. 2. A short love poem set to music. 3. A polyphonic song using a vernacular text that was written for four to six voices that developed in Italy in the sixteenth century.

Biografia

One of the most influential librettists of the eighteenth century was Pietro Metastasio (1698–1782). His 27 librettos were set to music by Mozart, Gluck, Bach, Handel, and the Italian composers Giovanni Pergolesi and Niccolo Jommelli.

With the publication of his work, Palestrina's success continued to increase during the 1560s and 1570s. In 1577, during the Counter Reformation, the Church asked Palestrina to rewrite the Church's main plainchant books in accordance with the Council of Trent's guidelines that dictated the music be written using words that could be readily understood. Palestrina's ability to do so probably preserved Church polyphony from being banned altogether. Palestrina's last years at St. Peter's in Rome were among his most productive.

Alessandro Scarlatti

The composer Alessandro Scarlatti (1660–1725) revolutionized the music scene in Naples when he arrived as the new choirmaster for the royal service in 1684. The first of his 115 operas, *Gli equivoci nel sembiante* (1679), won him the protection of Queen Christina of Sweden, for whom he wrote *L'onesta negli amori* (1680). During the time Scarlatti remained in Naples, he wrote more than 40 operas and musical numbers for the court.

In 1702, Scarlatti left for Florence, and by 1707 he was appointed choir master to Cardinal Pietro Ottoboni in Rome. Scarlatti is chiefly remembered for creating a form of Italian overture allegro-adagio-allegro, a forerunner to classical symphony. His work anticipated the music of much later composers such as Mozart and Schubert.

Antonio Vivaldi

The composer and violinist Antonio Vivaldi (1678–1741) was born in Venice where he was trained by his father, who was also a violinist. In 1703, after being ordained a priest, Vivaldi taught for a year at the Ospedale della Pietà, a conservatory for orphaned girls, where he was associated as music director until 1740.

The irony of teaching music to girls was that until the late eighteenth century, the high female lead parts were sung by men, many of whom were *castrati*. A *castrato* was a male singer who had been castrated before puberty in order to retain a soprano or alto voice. (Perhaps they had taken the biblical statement made by St. Paul in his First Epistle a little too seriously when he said, "Let your women keep silence in the churches.")

During this time, Vivaldi's small recitals and weekly concerts helped establish an international reputation. J. S. Bach was a contemporary of Vivaldi and transcribed some of his concertos and sonatas. In the course of a lifetime, Vivaldi wrote over 45 operas, 70 sonatas, and 500 concertos. Among his many works are the oratorio *Juditha Triumpharus*, and his opus, *The Four Seasons*.

Antonio Stradivari

The great violin maker Antonio Stradivari (1644–1737) was born in Cremona. The father of 11 children, Stradivari brought instrument-making to its finest level, the secret of which remains to be unveiled. Although Stradivari's sons Francesco (1671–1743) and Omobono (1679–1742) carried

Di Interessa

Oratorio differs from opera in that it is customarily based on a religious subject and is performed without scenery, costumes, or stage action.

Biografia

The soprano Italian singer Farinelli (born Carlo Broschi; 1705–1782) is by far the most famous *castrato*. He studied with the noted composer Nicola Porpora and toured throughout Italy, Paris, London, and, at the invitation of Queen Elisabetta Farnese, Madrid where she hoped his voice soothed the moody King Philip V.

on the family tradition, some believe the Stradivari touch had to do with the varnish, but skeptics disagree. Whatever the reason, the sound of a Stradivari is pretty close to magic.

Opera Houses

During the seventeenth century, Venice was to become a center for opera when the first public opera house in the world opened in 1637. By 1700, at least 16 more theatres were built and hundreds of operas produced.

Today, many of Italy's opera houses continue to produce concerts. World-renowned for their technical perfection and detailed magnificence, they are in themselves works of art. But what would an opera be without lavish sets and gorgeous costumes?

➤ **La Scala in Milano.** Constructed by the architect Giuseppe Piermarini in 1778, La Scala premiered with a production of *L'Europa Riconosciuta* by Antonio Salieri. Decorated in a neo-classic style, La Scala was built in a traditional horseshoe shape purported to improve the acoustics. It has four tiers of boxes and two galleries.

➤ **Teatro San Carlo of Naples.** The Neapolitans did not fool around when it came to opera. It was forbidden either to applaud during the performance or to yell for an encore. When opera was at its height, Naples was one of the most vital cultural centers in Europe. Neapolitan opera is most noted for its *opera buffa*. In 1737, the Bourbon King Carlo commissioned Giovanni Medrano to design Naples' Teatro San Carlo, where premiere performances were held using the works of Donizetti, Bellini, and Rossini. (Unfortunately, the beautiful opera house was destroyed by fire in 1816.)

➤ **Teatro Massimo di Palermo.** After 25 years of restoration, the enormous nineteenth-century Teatro Massimo recently reopened its doors. The theater is one of Italy's primary opera houses with the capacity to hold 3,200 spectators. Like Rome, Palermo is a city of layers. Walk down the streets and you'll see vestiges of another time, of Greeks, Moors, Romans, Normans, and Arabs. While much of the old Palermo has been destroyed through neglect and time, a cultural and artistic revitalization program is breathing new life into this important *città*.

Di Interessa

For a wonderful film centered on that fine instrument, the violin, don't miss *The Red Violin* (1998), directed by Francois Girard.

An Opera Glossary

Many people strangely feel dumb when it comes to opera, a musical form that is now making a comeback with sold-out performances by the Three Tenors (Pavarotti, Domingo, and Carreras) and more recently, by the dynamic and popular opera singer Andrea Bocelli.

To begin to appreciate opera, it helps to understand a little about the terms and expressions used to talk about this powerful musical form. What's the difference between *opera seria* and *opera buffa?* What's a *libretto?* To learn more opera terminology, use this quick guide:

a cappella   "In the chapel"; refers to voices without music and no instruments.

aria   A song or melody sung by a single voice.

bel canto   "Beautiful song" in Italian.

cadenza   A passage toward the end of a song designed for the singer alone to strut their stuff in beautiful "cadence."

canzone   Literally "song" in Italian.

coloratura   Describes the "color" in a passage, including those difficult trills and sparkling arpeggios singers train all their lives to sing.

duet   Two people singing simultaneously, often with different words and melodies.

forte/mezzo forte   Loud/not so loud.

piano/mezzo piano   Soft/not so soft.

falsetto   A male voice in an upper register beyond its normal range, coming from the Italian *falso* (false).

fugue   A baroque style passage in which three or more distinct musical lines are tossed from voice to voice, coming from Italian *fuga* (flight).

libretto   Literally "little book" in Italian, the script for the piece.

opera buffa   Comic, "buffoon" opera that uses characters from everyday life. The first opera buffa was originally a musical intermezzo used during the eighteenth century (sort of like comic relief) before it became a complete opera on its own.

opera seria   Common in the seventeenth century, opera seria ("serious opera") was generally much more formal than opera buffa and often used mythological references.

operetta   A cross between opera buffa and opera seria, an operetta is usually very light.

overture   An instrumental composition introducing the entire opera.

prelude   A shorter overture.

prima donna   A female opera star.

recitative   Helps advance the story, sung dialogue between arias.

vibrato   A slight wavering in pitch used to enhance notes.

Highlights of Italian Music

If you want to better understand the musical evolution that resulted in opera, the following timeline gives an overview of the more important musical breakthroughs and what happened in Italian music afterward.

➤ **Roman Empire.** We can speculate, but we're not sure how the music sounded during this time since notation did not exist. Music was generally used during ceremonies, using instruments such as horns and drums.

➤ **The early Christian period.** The Gregorian chants still used today are ascribed to Pope Gregory the Great. Gregorian chant has no meter at all. It is written in neumes, notes on a single syllable. Early musical notations first appeared in manuscripts during the ninth century.

➤ **Medieval period.** The music teacher and theorist Guido d'Arezzo (995–1050) reformed musical notation as we know it today.

➤ **Thirteenth and fourteenth centuries.** One of Italy's first great composers, the fourteenth century composer Francesco Landini (1335–1397) wrote polyphony (many voices), especially the "ballata."

Di Interessa

Opera enthusiasts will enjoy the Museo Teatrale, a small museum located within the annex of La Scala that houses a wonderful collection of Verdi memorabilia, with an extensive collection of scenery backdrops and props.

➤ **The Renaissance (late fifteenth and sixteenth century).** The madrigal was the rage, as composers such as Cipriano de Rore (Parma), Luca Marenzi (Rome), and Don Carlo Gesualdo (Ferrara) wrote lively numbers. The Venetian composers Andrea (1510–1586) and his nephew Giovanni Gabrielli (1554–1612) wrote antiphonal music for organ and brass written to be performed at St. Mark's Cathedral. The sacred music written for unaccompanied voices are best represented by the motets and masses written by Giovanni Pierluigi da Palestrina (1525–1594).

➤ **Early Opera (late sixteenth and seventeenth century).** Claudio Monteverdi (1567–1643) wrote *Orfeo* (Orpheus) in 1607. It was an instant hit and marked one of the most significant moments in operatic history.

➤ **Baroque period (mid-sixteenth to early eighteenth century).** Best represented by the keyboard music performed by Domenico Scarlatti (1660–1725), an early developer of the Sonata style who performed for the Queen of Sweden, Pope Innocent XI, and other nobles. Arcangelo Corelli (1653–1713) and Antonio Vivaldi (1678–1741) work on the opera, operatorio, and chamber music.

➤ **Classical period (1725–1790).** The drama of Opera Seria is the works of Giovan Battista Pergolesi (1710–1736) and Baldassare Galuppi (1706–1785).

➤ **Early Romantic period (1790–1830).** The music of the early Romantic period brought stories such as *The Barber of Seville* by Gioachino Rossini (1792–1868) and *The Puritans* by Vincenzo Bellini (1802–1835).

➤ **Grand Opera (1830–1893).** Here is where you get the whole show for an out-of-body experience. Three composers to begin with include Gaetano Donizetti (1797–1848; *Lucia di Lammermoor, Don Pasquale,* and *L'Elisir d'amore*), Giuseppe Verdi (1813–1901; *La Traviata, Il Trovatore, Rigoletto, Othello,* and *Aida*), and Ruggero Leon Cavallo (1857–1919; *Pagliacci*).

➤ **Modern Opera.** The daddy of modern opera is Giacomo Puccini (1858–1924) who wrote *La Bohème, Madame Butterfly, Tosca,* and *Turandot*.

> **Di Interessa**
>
> To learn more about Italian music and its history, with helpful links and annotated information, visit the Italian Music homepage at www.cilea.it/music/entrance.htm.

An Idiot's Crash Course on the Players

No one needs to know you learned so much from a *Complete Idiot's Guide*. While we're still on the subject of opera, it's a good idea to know a little about those eccentric, artistic, and passionate players. If you're so inspired, take a moment to listen to a recording of one or two of the operas mentioned in this chapter. If you buy a CD, read the libretto that comes with it so you understand the characters and what all the crying is about.

Opera Divas

Divas don't get to be divas by sitting around whining. It takes discipline to sing Puccini's *Madame Butterfly!* Most female roles fall under three major categories:

➤ **Soprano.** The highest female voice; most divas are sopranos. The soprano plays the juicy part (usually a heroine or a martyr) and usually gets the biggest bucks for her high notes and dramatic flair.

➤ **Mezzo-Soprano.** A female voice that ranges between a soprano and a contralto. Mezzos are generally the witches and tramps but they also get to play the so-called trouser roles of adolescent boys, originally played by the *castrati* before women were allowed to sing on stage.

➤ **Contralto.** The lowest female singing voice. A good contralto may be likened to a rich, deep, red wine. Contraltos can sound like men and play comical old women or sympathetic mother figures.

The Gents

In one of the earliest recordings ever made of opera, Enrico Caruso sang the part of Nemorino in Donizetti's *The Elixir of Love* back in 1902. Big men wearing big hats with big voices are a given at the opera.

Di Interessa

The cummerbund on a man's tuxedo was traditionally used as a place to put opera tickets.

➤ **Tenor.** The highest male vocal, usually the lead. The tenor is what makes opera. Luciano Pavarotti, Placido Domingo, and Jose Carreras are all tenors. They get a lot of roses for being able to hit a high C and hold it. They are expected to have healthy appetites for food, wine, and women.

➤ **Baritone.** The most common voice in adult males, the baritone possesses a deep and rich voice lower in range than a tenor.

➤ **Bass.** The lowest of the male voices, the bass singer is equivalent to a human tuba. Bass singers usually play authority figures, such as Dr. Bartolo in Rossini's *The Barber of Seville*.

An Explosion of Creativity

While opera was capturing the hearts of its listeners, artists, writers, and playwrights were wooing appreciative audiences with their ability to evoke emotion and inspire awe. Whether the artist Bernini's exquisite stone sculptures or magnificent architectural wonders, the play of light in bad boy Caravaggio's dramatic paintings, the religious themes of the Venetian artist Tiepolo, or the plays of Goldoni, the art and mastery of the Renaissance had blossomed into the sophisticated, complex, and highly ornate works characteristic of the Baroque.

Caravaggio

In and out of jail several times during his lifetime, the painter Michelangelo Merisi da Caravaggio (1572–1610)—known simply as Caravaggio—was trained in Milan before moving to Rome, where much of his work was conducted. The often politically incorrect, volatile, and tempestuous painter developed a reputation for his wild behavior and sensual portraits, such as the *Young Bacchus* (1595, Uffizi, Florence), depicting the Greek god of wine wearing a wreath of grape leaves.

Influenced by the Renaissance painters, in particular Michelangelo, Caravaggio departed from traditional methods that insisted on lengthy preparations, instead painting directly from his subjects. His paintings are best characterized by the use of foreshortening and a mastery of *chiaroscuro* (in Italian, "light-dark"), a painting style that used light and shadow for dramatic, expressive results.

Caravaggio traveled extensively, during which time he painted commissions such as the *Conversion of Saint Paul* and *the Cruxifixion of Saint Peter* (1601, Santa Maria del Popolo, Rome) in Rome, *The Flagellation of Christ* (1606, San Domenico Maggiore, Naples) in Naples, and *The Raising of Lazarus* (1608, Museo Nazionale, Messina) in Sicily. Caravaggio died from fever on a beach in Port'Ercole, Tuscany after contracting malaria. His impact on the art of his day was profound. If you can't get to Italy anytime soon, you can see his painting *The Musicians* at the Metropolitan Museum in New York City.

La Bella Lingua

The word **chiaroscuro** means "light-dark" and refers to the pictorial art form that emphasizes the relationship between light and shadow.

La Bella Lingua

Mannerism (from Italian *maniera*, "manner," or "style") refers to the predominating artistic style in Italy from the end of the High Renaissance in the 1520s to the beginnings of the Baroque style around 1590. Mannerists works brought painting and sculpture to a new level of complexity, emotional expression, and sophistication.

Gianlorenzo Bernini

The sculptor and architect Gianlorenzo Bernini (1598–1680) is arguably the single most important artist of the Baroque. A sculptor, architect, painter, playwright, designer, and draftsman, Bernini's life was dominated by his work. Having been taught from an early age by his father, Pietro Bernini (also a talented sculptor from what is now referred to as the Mannerist style), a Bernini sculpture makes one want to touch the stone to test if it really is made of marble, and not flesh.

Bernini was the first sculptor to understand the dramatic potential of light in a sculptural composition, such as in his masterpiece *The Ecstasy of Teresa* (1652, Santa Maria della Vittoria, Rome), a sculpture depicting the blissful Saint Theresa whose long flowing dress seems to be sliding off the figure. It is a sculpture that is so moving it'll make a believer out of anyone. Indeed, Bernini's stone sculptures seemed to blend movement with emotion in larger-than-life-sized sculptures that include *The Abduction of Proserpina* (1622).

In architecture, Bernini's hand influenced several churches built in Rome and included the highly decorated Sant' Andrea al Quirinale (Rome). Additionally, he designed the ornamental baldachin (altar canopy) over the high altar of Saint Peter's, a commission he received from Pope Urban VIII, one of seven popes he would work with over the course of his long, prodigious career. A familiar site to most tourists visiting Rome, Bernini also designed the *Fountain of the Four Rivers* (1651), located in Piazza Navona.

Biografia

The painter Gian Antonio Canaletto (1697–1768) is mostly known for his panoramic paintings of Venice. His principal patrons were English aristocrats who bought his small scenes portraying Venetian landmarks such as the Grand Canal and the Basin of St. Mark as souvenirs. His best-known painting is titled *The Marriage of Venice to the Sea.*

Gian Battista Tiepolo

The painter Gian Battista Tiepolo (1696–1770) is considered the last great master of the Venetian School. Greatly influenced by the sixteenth-century master Paolo Veronese, the colorful frescoes of Tiepolo used mythological, biblical, and historical figures in compositions that convey the illusion of vast expanse through the use of steep perspective. Completed in 1750, his decorative frescoes in Palazzo Labia illustrate the lives of Mark Anthony and Cleopatra. His painting *The Triumph of Faith* (1755) can be viewed in the Chiesa della Pietà. You don't have to go to Italy to see a painting by Tiepolo; you can visit his work *Apotheosis of Francisco Barbaco* at the Metropolitan Museum in New York city.

The Playwright Carlo Goldoni

You can't talk about the Baroque without mentioning the narrative plays of Venetian Carlo Goldoni (1707–1793). Goldoni's works dealt with many of the same issues portrayed in modern stories: love, sex, and money. His play, *La Locanderia (The Laundress)*, inspired an opera by Antonio Salieri (1750–1835) and reflected the social mores of his time.

Considered the founder of modern Italian comedy, Goldoni was born in Venice. At the age of 14, he joined a group of traveling players and soon found himself immersed in the world unique to performers.

After having acquired a law degree in Padua, Goldoni returned to Venice where he started practicing law and writing plays. Goldoni's contribution included changing Italian comedy by giving the players a script. The characters were based on the masques of the commedia dell'arte (Pulcinella, Arlecchino, Colombina) and were staged with characters drawn from real people using authentic situations.

Goldoni wrote about 150 comedies. In 1761, he left for Paris where he composed *The Beneficent Bear* for the wedding of Louis XVI and Marie Antoinette. After losing his royal pension during the French Revolution, Goldoni died in poverty, but the richness of his work endures.

The Least You Need to Know

➤ The "dramma per musica" blended music with words.

➤ The early giants in opera included Palestrina, Monteverdi, and Scarlatti. Vivaldi was both a composer and a violinist most noted for his work *The Four Seasons*.

➤ The sculptor and architect Gianlorenzo Bernini is probably the single most important artist of the Baroque.

➤ The painter Caravaggio is best characterized by his mastery of *chiaroscuro* (light–dark).

➤ The playwright Carlo Goldoni is considered the father of modern Italian comedy.

Part 4

Redshirts, Blackshirts, and Greenshirts

Until the Risorgimento resulted in Italy's unification, there was no Italian state. Starting with the French Revolution, in Part 4 you'll learn about Garibaldi and the Thousand and see how this resulted in the long-awaited birth of a nation.

You'll learn why so many millions of Italians chose to leave their beloved homeland and head toward American shores. You'll begin to understand how a dictator like Benito Mussolini could rise to power. What effect would the World Wars have on Italians and Italian Americans? How did the end of Fascism result in the modern Italian state? How does the Mafia fit into all of this? Who were the neorealists and what films can you watch to help dramatize all of these events?

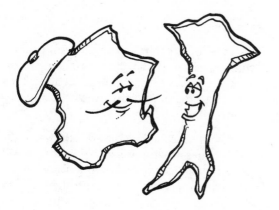

Chapter 16

Parlez-Vouz Français?

In This Chapter

➤ Dichiarazione d'Indipendenza

➤ Little man on a big horse

➤ Loot for the Louvre

➤ Ere I saw Elba

➤ Welcome back Austria

Imagine dominating an era so completely during your lifetime that history and events were named after you. And because of your commanding stature, only your first name would be necessary. You would be, of course, Napoleon Bonaparte (1769–1821), the French Emperor who also reigned over Italy for several years.

How did Napoleon's actions influence Italy? What influence did the French Revolution have on Italy's unification? How did these events impact the United States?

The Napoleonic Empire

Born to Italian parents on the island of Corsica, Napoleon was a man whose actions and accomplishments between 1800 and 1815 so greatly influenced Europe and the New World that it is commonly described as the Napoleonic era. The reverberations of

La Bella Lingua

Napoleon Bonaparte was born on the island of Corsica and originally known by his Italian name, *Napoleone Buonaparte.*

Biografia

Continental Congress members William Paca and Caesar Rodney, both of Italian descent, signed the Declaration of Independence.

this tumultuous time would later open the gates to the long-awaited Italian unification.

Torn in Three

While American colonists were fighting for independence from the English in the 1770s, the Italian peninsula was, as usual, filled with squabbling factions, each desperately trying to maintain control over an increasingly discontent public.

Political alliances changed as often as the tides and depended on such issues as who was in power and who was a contemporary enemy. Supported by the French monarchy and its soldiers, the pope controlled the Papal States—semi-autonomous territories—in central Italy. The Austrians controlled northern Italy's city-states. The Spaniards continued to rule over Southern Italy. Poor Italy was being pulled in three directions.

About the same time that the United States first formed its government, an equally important struggle was taking place in France that would completely transform the Western world, including Italy. Across the Atlantic, the American Revolution had sparked growing nationalistic feelings throughout Europe. The Italians, tired of being constantly ruled by outsiders, and eager for autonomy, found their aspirations for independence rekindled by the radical events of the French Revolution (1789).

In Italics

March 28, 1786—A skilled orator, Napoleon addressed his hungry, ill-equipped troops with this famous "honor, glory, and riches," speech:

> Soldiers, you are naked, badly fed ... Rich provinces and great towns will be in your power, and in them you will find honor, glory, wealth. Soldiers of Italy, will you be wanting in courage and steadfastness?

Name That Republic

Napoleon's armies stormed through the peninsula, igniting Italian nationalistic feelings with every victory. Napoleon would redraw the Italian map several times. His Italian campaign of 1796 and 1797 resulted in several short-lived republics. In 1796, he established the Cispadane and Transpadane Republics which were united to form the Cisalpine Republic in 1797. In 1802, the Cisalpine Republic (consisting of Lombardy and Emilia-Romagna) was renamed the Italian Republic; in 1805, with the addition of Venice, it was again renamed the kingdom of Italy.

In central Italy, the French moved in and took over the Papal States, forcing Pope Pius VI to flee to Tuscany. The French now controlled the entire Po Valley, a strategically significant area that spanned a good portion of the Italian peninsula, and included Bologna and the northern reaches of the Papal States.

The dazzling success of Napoleon's Italian campaign was based on three factors:

1. Brilliant oratory skills. Napoleon had the enthusiasm of a televangelist and the wit of a talk-show host.

2. A never-ending supply system, which he made virtually independent of the practically bankrupt French treasury by permitting his troops to live off the land (and take whatever they wanted, whenever they wanted).

3. A reliance on speed and massed surprise attacks using small, compact units.

From the beginning, Napoleon Bonaparte saw himself as a "man of destiny." This ambitious young man would put his education at French military schools to use; by 1796 the 26-year-old Bonaparte was already commander of the French army in Italy.

Napoleon's visions of grandeur were only just beginning. After his coup d'état of November 9, 1799, in Paris with his control of France firmly in place, Napoleon would once more prove his mettle in battle on Italian soil.

"Italia"

In Italics

March 1796—Napoleon Bonaparte led the French army over the Alps, invading Italy and driving out the pope, the Austrians, and the Spaniards. Decisive victories led to the Treaty of Campoformio (October 17, 1797), a peace settlement between France and Austria that formalized the French conquests.

Di Interessa

According to legend, the delicious dish chicken Marengo was first created and served to Napoleon after his victory over the Austrians in the northern Italian village of Marengo in June 1800.

The ambitious leader crossed the Alps with his armies again and reoccupied Milan on June 2, 1800, as the War of the Second Coalition broke out. A few days later, with his troops outnumbered and Austria threatening to invade France, General Bonaparte narrowly but convincingly defeated the forces of Baron Michael von Melas at Marengo. This crucial victory would lead to a longer-lasting French control over the Italian states. Napoleon was crowned King of Italy at Milan in 1805.

Although opinions vary on Napoleon's place in history, he was beyond a doubt one of the world's greatest conquerors. As emperor of France and king of Italy, Napoleon was now directly in control of northern and central Italy. He promoted the growth of liberalism through his efficient and lasting administrations and legal reforms. He introduced a French Civil Code, a progressive legal reform which served as a model for civil law codes not only in Italy but throughout Europe as well, improved roads, and strengthened education.

Di Interessa

An Italian proverb:

After the game, the king and the pawns all go in the same box.

All in the Family

Napoleon was a family man at heart. During his reign, he bestowed several positions of power to family members throughout the peninsula. He appointed his stepson, Eugène de Beauharnais as viceroy of Italy. He proclaimed his brother—Joseph Bonaparte—king of Naples (a region that included the island of Sicily and all southern Italy). When Joseph would later be made king of Spain, he offered the same job to his brother-in-law Joachim Murat. Like father, like son: He even crowned his newborn son, Napoleon II (the "Eaglet"), by Maria Luisa of Austria, king of Rome in 1811.

Napoleon didn't forget his sisters, either. He offered the duchies of Parma, Guastalla, and Piacenza to his favorite sister, the remarkably beautiful and vain Paolina Borghese, whose second marriage to Camillo Borghese, a member of the Roman nobility, was arranged by Napoleon. His other sister, Elisa Baciocchi (whose original Italian name was Maria Anna Elisa Buonaparte), was made grand duchess of Tuscany.

Certain members of Napoleon's family would also find their way to American shores. After Napoleon's younger brother, Joseph, abdicated the Spanish throne, like any self-respecting ousted king, he left Europe for America where he lived in Bordentown, New Jersey from 1815 to 1841.

Napoleon's youngest brother, Jerome Bonaparte (1784–1860), served in the navy and was sent to the West Indies. While visiting the United States, in 1803

"*Italia*"

In Italics

March 17, 1805—Napoleon, the new king of Italy, proclaimed the Italian Republic a kingdom.

he met and married an American woman named Elizabeth Patterson. They had one son, also named Jerome (1805–1870).

I Just Have to Have It!

Napoleon, in addition to being king and emperor, was an art lover. Napoleon had always been awestruck by the beauty and richness of Italy's artistic patrimony. From the Etruscan pottery to Roman statues, from medieval manuscripts to Mannerist masterpieces, he just couldn't get enough and used every opportunity to add to his collection.

Using the army as his moving men, Napoleon had a number of important works of art carted away as wartime booty. These included major paintings by Rafael, Titian, and other Renaissance masters. New museums, including the prestigious Louvre, were built to house the precious spoils of war, which was partially furnished with stolen goods. Although much of the art has been since returned, a great deal continues to remain in France.

As an educated man, Napoleon understood the value of things. The irreverent French general wasn't satisfied with taking sculpture, paintings, and drawings. In the Vatican library, Napoleon took a liking to the pope's fancy books; wouldn't they make a nice addition to his personal collection? Lacking a papal library card, Napoleon had the rarest of manuscripts and volumes packed up and shipped to Paris. (Although long overdue, eventually most of the books were returned to Rome.)

Napoleon is Pastry

The seemingly invincible Napoleon could not last forever. After a series of military disasters, the tides turned against the emperor. By 1813, deserted by his allies, Napoleon's Grande Armée, once a legion 500,000 strong, was only a fifth of its original size. With his army decimated and his troops ravaged, Napoleon was forced to retreat. In March 1814, Napoleon abdicated, putting an end to the Napoleonic Empire.

Di Interessa

Napoleon had a sweet tooth. By some accounts, it is said that on the eve of Waterloo, Napoleon ate so many of his favorite French pastry (named in his honor) that he lost the battle.

"Italia"

In Italics

December 2, 1804—In the Cathedral of Notre Dame, Napoleon forced the Italian Pope Pius VII to come to Paris to consecrate him as emperor. At the last minute, in an act contrived to demean the pope, Napoleon took the crown from the pope's hands and crowned himself.

Before conceding defeat, Napoleon named his then three-year-old son, Napoleon II, as his successor. The allied leaders refused to agree to such manipulation and put Marie Louise and her son into the custody of her father, the emperor of Austria. Napoleon never saw either of them again.

Napoleon was exiled to the island of Elba, which the Allies gave him as a sovereign principality. A man of such vigor and vision couldn't be expected to retire at the age of 45 on a small island off the coast of Tuscany, and he soon made a dramatic but short-lived comeback. Napoleon escaped from Elba to France on March 1, 1815, and returned briefly to power. About to face a European coalition, his only hope was in attacking before the enemy could attack him.

On June 18, he began a massed attack against the British but was soon defeated when long-awaited Prussian troops finally arrived. After Napoleon's fall, the Congress of Vienna—an assembly of European powers that met in 1814 and 1815—reestablished Austrian control of the Italian peninsula. Once more, Italy's hopes of governing itself were dashed.

True to his original claims of being a man of destiny, Napoleon's ideas, legal code, and maxims on warfare would stimulate the movements leading to national unification throughout Europe.

However, Italy was still not united, disappointing Italian patriots. Frustrated, and ready to take matters into their own hands, many of these thinkers decided to form the secret revolutionary societies that would eventually aid in liberating Italy from foreign dominion once and for all.

One group, the Carbonari, attracted the attentions of two young men that would later lead Italy to her long-awaited unification: Giuseppe Garibaldi and Giuseppe Mazzini. You'll learn more about these men in Chapter 17, "Let's Call It *Italia:* A Nation and a Democracy."

Di Interessa

Three Italian regiments totaling 1,500 men assisted the colonists during the American Revolution.

Red, White, and Green in the New World

Across the Atlantic Ocean, in the land named for the Florentine explorer, navigator, and geographer Amerigo Vespucci (1454–1512), Italians played an important role in the early history of the United States.

While Napoleon's legions spread across Europe, another Italian was busy influencing American politics like no other. A Tuscan scholar, physician, and agriculturist, Filippo Mazzei (1730–1816) fought beside Patrick Henry and formed friendships with both Benjamin Franklin and U.S. president Thomas Jefferson.

Among his many contributions to the fledgling nation, Mazzei is credited with penning the phrase: "All men are by nature equally free and independent." Jefferson, accustomed to translating his friend's work from Italian into English, is said to have paraphrased Mazzei's words, incorporating them into the Declaration of Independence: "All men are created equal."

This concept of freedom was a quantum leap from just a few centuries before. The idea that everyone was entitled to his or her piece of freedom *by nature* was a brand new way of thinking. The power imbalances of feudalism certainly did not promote this idea. Nor did the monarchies, or the popes, or the emperors of Rome. These new principles were heralded by thinkers in both Europe, and across the Atlantic, giving birth to the foundation of the modern democratic world.

Now it's time to learn more about how the efforts of leaders such as Giuseppe Garibaldi and Giuseppe Mazzini would help make real these revolutionary ideas.

Biografia

Other Italians in America devoted to American independence included Giuseppe Maria Francesco Vigo. In addition to being a fur-trader, linguist, colonel, and spy, Vigo also offered financial support toward the cause. Italian officers in the colonial militia included Lieutenant James Bracco and Captain Cosimo de Medici.

The Least You Need to Know

➤ During the Napoleonic Empire the French emperor united much of northern Italy into the Italian Republic. In 1804 Napoleon declared the newly united nation the Kingdom of Italy, with himself as monarch.

➤ The entire Italian peninsula was under French domination between 1796, when troops under General Napoleon Bonaparte invaded Italy, and 1814, when they withdrew.

➤ After two decades of authoritarian rule, profound changes took place in Italy; many Italians began to see the possibilities of creating a united country emancipated from foreign domination.

➤ After Napoleon's fall in 1815 the Congress of Vienna carved up Italy and granted substantial control to Austria.

Chapter 17

Let's Call It *Italia:* A Nation and a Democracy

In This Chapter

➤ Revolution anyone?

➤ Kings, counts, and princes

➤ Italy's national heroes: Garibaldi, Mazzini, and Cavour

➤ *La Miseria* sparks emigration

In this chapter, you'll learn about the pivotal moments that led to Italy's unification through the Risorgimento—a series of political and military events that resulted (*finalmente!*) in the unified Kingdom of Italy in 1861. You'll witness an end to centuries of monarchy and anarchy, and see the beginning of a new era, both politically and artistically.

The Struggle for Unity

In spite of the fact that Napoleon Bonaparte was banished to St. Helena (a small island in the southern Atlantic), where he died in 1821, the charismatic leader's aspirations for a unified Italy lived on. In addition, the Italians, now joined by a sense of national unity, were hungry for autonomy from France and other foreign countries that had ruled their country

The times were turbulent. Napoleonic rule having ended in 1815, the *popolo*—the people—were riled as the different factions along the peninsula labored to find a new political and social framework with which to work. The next 50 years would be filled with a dizzying array of populist insurgencies, local disturbances, and acts of civil disobedience. Yet again the peninsula found its shores stained with the blood and tears of clashing ideologies. Some uprisings quickly faded out, while others ended in death.

Italy, fragmented into city-states, kingdoms, and territories, was suffering from an identity crisis. Throughout its history Italy has had a multitude of sovereigns serve as heads of state, whether it be Roman emperors, popes, Norman kings in Sicily, Bourbon monarchs, or Medici grand dukes. Perhaps there is something unique about the land of olives and grapes that nourishes imperialist dreams.

Italian unification continued to be impeded by the existence of several independent states such as the Kingdom of the Two Sicilies (including the island of Sicily and the entire southern half of the Italian peninsula); the Kingdom of Sardinia (consisting of the island of Sardinia and the northern region of Piedmont); the Duchies of Tuscany, Parma, and Modena; and—not surprisingly—the principality ruled by the pope in Rome.

"Italia"

In Italics

March 17, 1861—The kingdom of Italy was officially proclaimed by a parliament assembled in Turin. On that day, Vittore Emmanuelle II of Savoy, at the age of 41, was proclaimed king.

If you were a prince and could do whatever you wanted, would you hand over the reins for the sake of common good? In each of these states, the monarchs (the Savoy family in Sardinia, the Bourbons in Sicily, and the Habsburgs in the duchies) exercised absolute powers of government. They liked things just as they were. As you'll soon see, Italy would finally achieve national unity, but it would take 50 more years of revolution and war before this would happen.

The Heroes of Italian Unity

Similar to the way Americans celebrate George Washington, Thomas Jefferson, and Abraham Lincoln, Italians have their icons, too. In just about every Italian city, you'll find a via (street) named after Garibaldi, Mazzini, or Cavour, those Italian heroes who led Italy toward the long-awaited Italian unification.

Giuseppe Garibaldi: Italy's Hero

To an Italian, Garibaldi's name represents national pride, often evoking a swelling of the chest, a reverent nod. To the rest of the world, he represents man's universal struggle for freedom and independence. A soldier, idealist, insurrectionist, and revolutionary, Garibaldi was, and continues to be, one of Italy's greatest heroes, and for this reason you'll be hard-pressed to find an Italian town, city, or village without a street named in his honor.

Giuseppe Garibaldi.

Visionary Leader: Giuseppe Mazzini

Another important Italian figure to play an integral role in Italy's unification was Giuseppe Mazzini (1805–1872). A patriot and avid disciple of republicanism, Mazzini was the most influential and significant leader of the national revolutionary movement. As founder of the patriotic group Giovane Italia (Young Italy), he aroused the passions of a new generation with grandiose notions of unity by stressing the importance of revolution and war based on direct popular action.

Mazzini, working closely with Garibaldi, first organized revolts in the 1830s in an attempt to drive the Italian princes from their thrones. The well-armed princes were not about to give up their sovereignty without a fight, and soon Mazzini—condemned to death if found—was forced to flee Italy.

"Italia"

In Italics

July 30, 1850—Giuseppe Garibaldi's ship, the *Waterloo*, landed in New York Harbor. Immediately following his arrival in America, Garibaldi took out citizenship papers to become a fully naturalized American. He landed a job in a Staten Island candle factory before going back to seafaring and organizing insurrections.

Undaunted (as a hero should be), Mazzini headed toward friendlier turf. For the next several years, while living in a London suburb, he published newspapers and pamphlets advocating the ideals of nationalism and republicanism for the Italian people. During the revolutions of 1848, he again returned to Italy, hopeful that the uprisings taking place across the entire peninsula would finally lead to Italy's unification. His prayers were answered after ten more years of insurrections and revolutionary activity.

La Bella Lingua

Risorgimento (rinascita) means revival, renaissance, or rebirth. *Il Risorgimento* is the movement for, and period of, political unification in Italy; it also came to mean "a past Italian greatness awaiting revival."

Political and Diplomatic Mastermind: Camille Benso Cavour

Camille Benso Cavour (1810–1861) was another key figure involved with the *Risorgimento*. First a lieutenant in the Sardinian army, Cavour became interested in politics after traveling widely in Europe. In 1847 he co-founded the newspaper *Il Risorgimento*, a nationalist journal supporting forcing Austria out of Sardinia and unifying all of Italy under a Sardinian constitutional monarchy. In the 1850s Cavour served in important cabinet positions in the Sardinian parliament and sent troops to assist during the Redshirts' invasion of Sicily. As a statesman, Cavour was instrumental in bringing about the unification of Italy.

Cavour was named Italy's first prime minister, although his tenure would be brief. He died in June 1861.

Here are some of the more prominent nationalist movements in the struggle for Italian nationhood during the Risorgimento.

Year(s)	Name/Location	Highlights
1820 and 1821	Revolutions of 1820 and 1821; Kingdom of the Two Sicilies, Milan, Turin	First significant threat to Congress of Vienna; demands for constitutional government and independence from foreign powers fall short
1831	Revolutions of 1831; Parma, Modena, Papal States	Discontent with political leadership and clerical repression temporarily usurps pope's rule
1833	Savoy	First attempts at insurrection by Giuseppe Mazzini's organization Giovane Italia.

Year(s)	Name/Location	Highlights
1848	Revolutions of 1848 (First War for Italian Independence)	Revolt in Palermo spreads to entire mainland; several rulers forced to grant constitutions in their regions; turning point in fight for modern Italian state
War of 1859	Second War for Italian Independence	Liberation of Lombardy from Austrian troops leads to creation of Kingdom of North Italy ruled by King Vittore Emmanuelle II.
War of 1866	Third War for Italian Independence (Seven Weeks' War)	Prussian/Italian coalition defeats Austria; Venetia and Mantua areas liberated.

A Hero Here, a Hero There

After the aborted uprising of 1833, with a bounty on his head, the former chief rebel leader of the Risorgimento left Italy once more. Taking his talents elsewhere, Garibaldi would spend the next 12 years fighting injustices in South America, where similar uprisings were occurring in civil wars across Brazil and Uruguay. Not surprisingly, he was as celebrated a hero in South America as he was in Italy.

Di Interessa

While encountering adventures on land and sea, Garibaldi's private life resembled a *telenovela*. While in Brazil, he eloped with Anna Maria Ribeiro da Silva, a married woman, who remained his companion until her death during an attempted escape from Austrian troops in 1849. Between battles in January 1860, Garibaldi found time to marry Giuseppina, the daughter of the Marchese Raimondi. There was no honeymoon for the heroic soldier; within hours of the marriage he discovered she was five months pregnant. Garibaldi left her immediately. It wasn't until 20 years later that the revolutionary hero was able to have the union annulled so that he could marry his true soul mate, Francesca Armosino, a longtime companion.

Garibaldi returned to Italy in early 1848 and rejoined the movement for Italian freedom and unification. He then organized a group of volunteers to fight against the Austrians in Lombardy and the French in Rome. The following speech illustrates the oratory abilities of this leader as he called upon his fellow countrymen to rally for independence.

> Romans and Countrymen! Whoever wishes to carry on the struggle against the enemy, let him come with me. I can offer him neither money, nor lodging, nor food. I can only offer him, instead, hunger, thirst, forced marches, battles and even death. All who have the name of Italy, not only on their lips, but in their hearts also … let them follow me!

With those words, Garibaldi was able to gain the support of 4,000 men. Unfortunately, they were no match against the enemy's 65,000. In one of the greatest manhunts in history, Garibaldi fled his beloved Italy, sailing to Tunis, Gibraltar, England, and finally to America. He would not touch Italian soil for another nine years until 1859, when King Vittore Emanuelle II, now committed to the unification of Italy, called upon Garibaldi to take charge of the Alpine Infantry against the Austrians. The stakes were high but the Austrians proved to be no match against Garibaldi. In a sweeping victory, Garibaldi's skill as a leader combined with the fervor of a common cause led to the liberation of both the north and all of Lombardy, including the Sardinian kingdom.

With the north unified, Garibaldi now turned his attention to the rest of Italy.

The Expedition of the Thousand

In 1860, the loved and feared honorable Giuseppe Garibaldi led a volunteer force of 1,000 men from Genoa to Sicily. Distinctively clad in bright red shirts, Garibaldi's motley crew became known as the Redshirts and as the Thousand.

Although lacking preparation and possessing few weapons, Garibaldi's impassioned volunteers landed at Marsala on May 11, 1860, and in less than three months conquered the entire island of Sicily. It was Garibaldi's bravery and courageousness as well as the collective pent-up rebellious spirit of his men that accounted for the success of the expedition.

Italy Is Unified at Last!

The tireless Garibaldi and his thousand Redshirts then crossed to the Italian mainland. In a dramatic victory, they soon captured Naples. After the Marches and Umbria regions were annexed from the papal government, Italy was finally unified. It was an event that the Italian peninsula had not witnessed since the Roman Empire's swan song almost 1,500 years previously.

After the frenzied celebrations were over, with Garibaldi's job now done, the hero retired to the small island of Caprera, calling upon the people to support King Vittore Emmanuelle II. His sojourn would not last.

"Italia"

In Italics

July 4, 1861—The 39th New York Infantry paraded before President Abraham Lincoln. Along with the stars and stripes, the dapperly dressed Garibaldi Guard (as they called themselves) carried a flag that had waved at the head of Garibaldi's columns. In the breeze fluttered Mazzini's words "Dio e Popolo!" (God and the People!) Although Garibaldi was unable to come to the assistance of the Union cause, many Italian soldiers crossed the Atlantic to volunteer. In Washington Square Park, a statue of Garibaldi pays tribute to the Italians' role during the Civil War.

We Could Use Your Help

It was during this time that the great Italian commander was beckoned by none other than U.S. president Abraham Lincoln. The Civil War president had always been interested in the Italian peninsula, even having been awarded an honorary citizenship from the tiny Republic of San Marino.

In the fight for human freedom, Lincoln recognized in Garibaldi a kindred spirit, offering him a Major-General's commission in the Army. Garibaldi, committed to the liberation of all men and wholeheartedly opposed to slavery, was eager to help.

As he prepared to leave for America, he was beseeched by his countrymen not to leave until all of the pieces to the Italian unification puzzle were in place. Venice and Rome were still under foreign rule, and Garibaldi's loyalties were first to Italy. Compelled to finish what he had begun, the great commander was forced to decline Lincoln's offer, but not for lack of want, responding:

Di Interessa

Thomas Jefferson and Benjamin Franklin were among America's first Italophiles; both spoke Italian. Thomas Jefferson's vineyards at Monticello (a source of great pride) were inspired by the Italian taste for wine.

I should be very happy to be able to serve a country for which I have so much affection and of which I am an adoptive citizen, and if I do not reply affirmatively and immediately to the honorable proposition which your government through your agency has made to me, it is because I do not feel myself entirely free, because of my duties toward Italy.

Garibaldi's Last Dance

Rome wasn't won in a day, and three separate attempts to conquer the last region were unsuccessful. In 1860, riding the momentum of their victories in Sicily and Naples, the Redshirts marched on Rome. When Cavour persuaded the king to send troops, Garibaldi wisely decided not to confront them.

In 1862, he was halted by the national army of Calabria, and in 1867 was stopped by French and papal troops. Rome was finally captured in 1870 when French troops were distracted by their involvement in war against Prussia, but by then Garibaldi was fighting other battles. Ironically, he fought for the French during the Franco-Prussian War (1870–1871).

After 67 battles on land and sea, Garibaldi returned to the island of Caprera where he would spend the rest of his days. Giuseppe Garibaldi died at the age of 74, in 1882. As one of the greatest masters of revolutionary war who had ever lived, he was mourned by the freedom-loving world.

But the quest for national autonomy was not the only subject for discussion at the Italian family dinner table. In such a pressure cooker of ideas, culture flourished, opera reigned, and several classic works were produced.

> Ciao!

La Bella Lingua

Roma o Morte ("Rome or Death") became Garibaldi's battle cry after his defense of the city against the French in 1849.

Opera: Political Voices Raised in Music

Political upheaval has often been the force behind cultural change (or is it the other way around?). There was great social turmoil and political melodrama during the Risorgimento, so it may not be very surprising that Italian opera flourished during the nineteenth century. Many of the classics that were written then still pack them in at the theatre today.

It was the age of *bel canto* ("beautiful song") and the number of opera houses increased dramatically throughout Italy. Giacomo Puccini (1858–1924) created the masterpieces *Madame Butterfly, La Bohème,* and *Tosca.* Often the works dealt directly with revolutionary themes, such as when Giocchino Rossini (1792–1868) composed *Guillaume Tell.*

Il maestro of nineteenth-century opera however, was Giuseppe Verdi (1813–1901). Just a short list of his many works would satisfy even the most discriminating crowd at Milan's *La Scala.*

Much more than just a great operatic composer, Verdi was a patriotic hero and advocate for human rights. The chorus *"Va pensiero"* from *Nabucco* became the theme song for the Risorgimento, and many Italians today still want it for their national anthem. Much of Verdi's work also promoted national unity and read like the latest headlines in a revolutionary tabloid: taunts at French and Austrian kings, references to political assassinations, and rallying cries against tyranny.

Verdi's Greatest Hits

Nabucco (*Nebuchadnezzar;* 1842)

I Lombardi (1843)

Macbeth (1847)

Rigoletto (1851)

Il Trovatore (1853)

La Traviata (1853)

I Vespri Siciliani (1855)

Simon Boccanegra (1857)

Un Ballo in Maschera (*A Masked Ball;* 1859)

La Forza del Destino (*The Force of Destiny;* 1862)

Don Carlos (1867)

Aïda (1871)

Otello (1887)

Falstaff (1893)

La Bella Lingua

Giuseppe Verdi's last name, ironically, was also an acronym for "Vittore Emmanuelle, Re d'Italia," so *"Viva Verdi"* became a familiar battle cry of the Risorgimento.

A Capital City, a National Language

Having served as the capital of the kingdom of Sardinia starting in 1720 and the political and intellectual center of the Risorgimento, and home to the royal house of Savoy, perhaps it was inevitable that Turin would serve as the first capital of Italy from 1861 to 1865. In June of 1865, the capital was transferred to Florence, and on July 2, 1871, Rome was proclaimed the capital of a united Italy.

Di Interessa

To celebrate Florence's turn at being Italy's capital, in true Italian fashion, a Roman-style triumphal arch was built in Piazza della Republica in the heart of the city's historic center. Originally the main square of the ancient Roman city Florentia, at the end of the nineteenth century the area was home to a lively market and the Jewish ghetto. In the name of civic improvement, the district was destroyed.

In addition to establishing a stable capital, the Italians were also developing a true national language. Indeed, while seamstresses where sewing red shirts for Garibaldi's volunteers and Cavour was plotting a secret war to provoke Austria, the intellectuals, writers, and poets were promoting the implementation of a national language. This basic idea was essential to fostering a sense of national identity throughout the peninsula. As you may remember from Chapter 5, "The Sound of Music," Italy had practically as many spoken languages as it did pasta shapes for much of its history.

Even after unification, though, the Tower of Babel might have been a more apt symbol for the Italian peninsula than the Leaning Tower of Pisa. The first language of most inhabitants was the local dialect, and at least two thirds of the population were illiterate in 1861. This was a major challenge during educational efforts in the last decades of the 1800s, exacerbated by a shortage of schoolteachers who spoke standard Italian in local areas.

To support the cause, the novelist Alessandro Manzoni (1785–1873) effectively rewrote the text of his novel, *I Promessi Sposi* (*The Betrothed*), changing the original Milanese terms and phrases to Florentine. It was the efforts of Manzoni and others that led the language of Dante to become the national language of modern Italians. Manzoni's example inspired similar works from other writers, leading Tuscan Italian to become the standard language used in official documents and taught in schools.

You're Bringing Me Down

Unfortunately, the unification of Italy was not to be the silver bullet that everyone hoped it would be. The bigger the party, the bigger the hangover, and the headaches Italy faced after unification were painful indeed. The legacy of centuries of strife and disunity still plagued the country.

Although Italy was now united, the north was reluctant to share its wealth with the impoverished south, often viewing the south as a strain on its pocket and ball and chain around its ankle.

Times Were Tough

Particularly in the provinces south of Rome—often referred to as the *mezzogiorno*—and including the island of Sicily, people felt no enthusiasm for the new government. And why should they? While the northerners were figuring out how to dot their i's, life in the south continued as usual. A rapidly growing population was depleting precious resources; work was scarce and a large segment of the population barely survived on potatoes and beans. Entire families lived in one room. Powerful and corrupt landowners took advantage of the powerless (and defenseless) peasants.

And, as if it didn't already have enough going against it, the south was barraged by a series of natural disasters. Droughts, earthquakes, volcanic eruptions, and an insect infestation that resulted in the destruction of their carefully tended vineyards added to what the people of the south called *La Miseria*. *La dolce vita* was the stuff of fiction.

We're Outta Here!

The decision to emigrate was not made without a great deal of consideration. Let's not forget the Italian's attachment to his homeland. Poverty alone would not be sufficient cause to take leave of everything familiar to face the hardships of being a stranger in a strange land.

Unwilling to wait for Italy's economy to stabilize, hungry for a full meal, and, more important, eager for the chance to succeed, millions of Italians abandoned their homeland and sought a new life in the New World. *La Merica* was waiting. (Do you see why Italian Americans tend to be so ambitious? It's in their blood!)

In this cartoon that ran in the magazine Punch *in 1870, after the unification of the kingdom of Italy, Pope Pius threatens politically minded Italian Catholics with Excommunication.*

The Least You Need to Know

➤ The Risorgimento was the Italian nationalist movement that resulted in a unified kingdom of Italy in 1861.

➤ The success of the Risorgimento can be attributed primarily to three Italian heroes: Camille Cavour, Giuseppe Garibaldi, and Giuseppe Mazzini.

➤ France surrendered Rome on September 20, 1870, the pivotal date in modern Italian history.

➤ Intolerable conditions forced many Italians to escape to America in the late nineteenth and early twentieth centuries.

The Island of Tears

The story of the Italian immigrants is universal. It's a tale of suffering and sacrifice, fear and courage, dreams and delusions. It shows how the tenaciousness of those early pioneers led the way for their children, and their children's children (maybe that's you) to succeed.

As you learned in Chapter 4, "From Shore to Shore," there were several waves of immigration. This chapter focuses on the mass exodus that occurred after the Italian unification. Why did so many leave? What conditions did they face when they arrived? What options were available to them?

In Search of a Better Life

Unification had made the Italians free, but it had not made them equal. Similar to the experience in the United States, while the north prospered, the rural south lagged far behind.

As you may recall, it had been hoped that conditions would improve in the *Mezzogiorno,* the Italian term used to describe southern Italy, after Italy's unification. Instead, the north prospered while the south struggled against a series of hardships that included overpopulation, disease, a series of natural disasters, and crop failure. For many families, life had become unbearable.

The typical southern Italian immigrant—in contrast with the political exile Giuseppe Garibaldi or the intellectual Filippo Mazzei, both of whom had other aspirations—was simply looking to improve conditions for himself and his family.

Prior to 1890, many immigrants were looking for a place to work, not a permanent home. Both their loyalties and their families remaining in Italy, the majority of those coming to the United States were men between the ages of 16 and 45. Similar to migrant workers traveling wherever there was work, these men often made the journey back and forth across the Atlantic several times a year.

The majority of immigrants had few transferable skills. They found work as day laborers, usually with other Italians on work gangs run by tough, Italian-speaking men they aptly referred to as Bosses. They dug trenches and tunnels, in mines and along roads. What few other jobs there were generally involved construction and other backbreaking work.

Andiamo in America! Let's Go to America!

With new shoes on their feet and money in their pockets, each time the travelers returned from America, they brought stories of success, wrapped in crisp dollar bills. Such success was unheard of in the *Mezzogiorno,* where people scraped by and could barely afford the passage to the New World. When word got out that money was to be made, the rush to America began.

L'Isola Della Lacrime—the Island of Tears—was the name Italians gave Ellis Island to describe the confusion, chaos, and demeaning circumstances that greeted the immigrant upon arrival to New York after the long trip across the Atlantic in what was referred to as *via dolorosa.*

Most of the Italians were bound for New York, where large Italian colonies dominated the entire streets such as Mott and Mulberry. Others were headed for Boston, Chicago, and upstate New York.

> ## "*Italia*"
>
> ### In Italics
>
> **1657**—The very first emigrants to make the voyage from Italy to New York were a group of Italian Protestants seeking asylum in the Dutch colony of New Amsterdam.

> ## *Ciao!*
>
> ### La Bella Lingua
>
> Sadly, one of the first American words a southern Italian immigrant learned was probably *grignoni* (green horn). As far as the immigrant popularity contest went, this was just about the lowest rung on the ladder.

Prior to 1892, although laws regulating immigration existed, the procedure for newcomers consisted of little more than a headcount. The typical immigrant simply had to muscle together the cash to buy a ticket that he used to gain passage on a boat (usually leaving from Naples). At that point, his biggest concern was how to minimize the *mal di mare* (sea sickness) that usually accompanied the long voyage. Once the ship landed, he made his way down the gang plank and into the streets of New York. There were no lines to wait in, no process to go through, no medical examination to pass.

After 1892, all immigrants were required to fulfill certain bureaucratic requirements. Not unsurprisingly, first and second class passengers were processed much more quickly and given direct passage to Manhattan. From there they could go about their business without further delay.

The passengers in steerage, on the other hand, eager to start a new life and exhausted from the long voyage over, were forced to wait another long day. Finally, ferries brought the huddled immigrants to Ellis Island where they were corralled into the Great Hall, a large crowded room with tall, steel cage-like fences. Here they were given a number for identification, and told to wait. Chaos reigned as people shouted in different languages, babies cried, and inspectors instructed new groups to move ahead.

La Bella Lingua

The *via dolorosa,* or "sorrowful way," was how immigrants described the long ocean voyage to America, the worst part of the trip for many. Once they arrived at Ellis Island, many of the immigrants were maltreated and herded like animals; women were slapped, men were prodded and the cries of babies went unheeded.

"Italia"

In Italics

January 1, 1892—Ellis Island opened its doors and was the point of entry for more than 95 percent of all Italian immigrants.

Ellis Island

Once on Ellis Island, the frightened immigrants had to go through a series of inspections, examinations, and interrogations before being allowed into America.

In spite of the confusion experienced by the immigrants, Ellis island was an enormous complex with a rigid and complicated bureaucracy. It was run by efficient staff eager to push through the thousands of immigrants who continued to pour through its doors every day. Healthy immigrants in possession of the proper papers were cleared without much difficulty. (If you recall, the cabin passengers were given direct passage to Manhattan.)

Aside from having to show proper documentation, the first test the immigrant had to pass was the medical examination. Doctors poked and prodded, and interpreters stood by to assist the process. Bodies were searched for deformities. Scalps were checked for lice, eyes for trachoma. Anyone suspected of carrying a disease or possessing a deformity was marked with white chalk and sent down another line. There, they would be further inspected by stern-faced, crisp-shirted officials.

Sometimes, all that was needed was a cough or limp for someone to be sent back to Italy. Mostly, however, passengers were sent through. It would have been too costly to hold them, given the influx of immigrants arriving every day.

Almost There

The last step was the customs inspection. Since most of the immigrants had already been briefed both back in Italy and onboard the ship, they were able to answer the inspector's questions without much difficulty.

They were asked how many children they had, how old they were, what their prospects for work were. Did they have family in America? Were they planning on returning to Italy? Did they have money to sustain them in case they didn't find work immediately?

If an immigrant had no prospects, friends, relatives, or sponsors, but was young and healthy, he was generally allowed to proceed.

Di Interessa

Very few Italians emigrated to the United States before 1870. Between 1820 and 1870, no more than 25,000 Italians made the voyage, most of whom came from northern Italy.

Di Interessa

If you wanted in, you had to have money. In 1907, the sum required for entering America was $20 for those under 40 years of age, $40 for those 40 and up. Although it was unlikely the officials would ask to see the money, if the money was lacking (as it often was), the appropriate amount was borrowed for as long as was necessary to get through the examination.

Help Wanted! Immigrants Welcome!

The immigrants had come to America in search of work. Many Italians were forced to take menial jobs for little pay. Children worked alongside their mothers doing piecework while their fathers combed the streets in search of work. Hunger and humiliation would come hand in hand. For many of these desperate people, the American dream was just that—a dream.

Although many immigrants were given poor wages and worked under brutal conditions, work was still work. Enterprising individuals were eventually able to save enough to buy a small piece of land or buy a business.

The Boss System

In 1864, due to a shortage of unskilled labor at the end of the Civil War, America began to actively recruit migrant contract labor. Agents in Italy seized the opportunity to organize groups of workers and bring them to the United States.

The Boss System offered immigrants the opportunity to work in exchange for a percentage of their wages. Usually, workers lived and worked under the same roof in work camps that migrated around the country. They worked in mines, lumberyards, quarries, and railroads, often performing the work that had previously been the domain of the American slaves. Similarly, many of them were practically held prisoner, since they had no reasonable alternatives and few marketable skills to help them find a way out.

They were further bonded by a particularly vicious system that involved the company store. Here, immigrants were provided with the basic necessities including food, wine, and tools. Prices were two to four times what they would normally be, often beyond the pocketbooks of most workers. No problem, said the Boss. We'll deduct it from your pay next week.

In the end, it was rare that a worker did not find himself working like a dog but somehow more in debt than when he started!

Biografia

Constantino Brumidi (1805–1880), the "Michelangelo of the U.S. Capitol," lay on his back hundreds of feet above the floor to paint the mural on the Capitol dome in Washington, D.C. He also painted the frescoes on the walls, designed bronze staircases, and carved marble statues.

Di Interessa

The 1900 federal census shows 33,000 Italian unskilled laborers worked in New York State alone.

Success Italian Style

But not all Italian immigrants in the early twentieth century were doomed to a lifetime of toil and desperation. Some of them, through a combination of hard work, talent, and ambition, prospered in their new home. The men and women listed in the following table are just some of the Italians who overcame the challenges in the New World and succeeded beyond their wildest dreams.

Person	Accomplishment
Amadeo Pietro Giannini	Established the Bank of America in San Francisco in 1904, which eventually became one of the largest banks in America.
Amadeo Obici, Mario Peruzzi	Founders of the Planters Peanut Company in the beginning of the twentieth century.
Ettore Boiardi	Uh-oh, SpaghettiOs! Chef Boy-Ar-Dee was really Boiardi, an Italian immigrant who began work as a chef's apprentice in the 1920s and opened a restaurant in Cleveland, Ohio, before canning his pastas and sauces.
Mother Frances Cabrini	This Italian American was the first American saint. She founded a multitude of colleges, schools, orphanages, and hospitals, as well as the Missionary Sisters of the Sacred Heart. Mother Cabrini emigrated to the United States in 1889, became a U.S. citizen in 1909, and died in 1917.
Rudolph Valentino	Hollywood's first sex symbol and the first "Latin Lover" of the silver screen. Born Rodolfo Guglielmi in Castellaneta, Italy, in 1895, he immigrated to the United States in 1913 and first worked as a dancer.
Adriana Caselotti	Was the voice of Snow White (*Biancaneve* in Italian), the first full-length animated film, which was released in 1937.
Alfred E. Smith	Born Alfred Emanuele Ferrara, was the first Italian American governor of New York (1919) and the first Italian American presidential candidate.
Charles Joseph Bonaparte	Founded the Federal Bureau of Investigation in 1908, built the U.S. Navy into one of the strongest in the world, and was the first Italian American appointed to a cabinet position.
Enrico Caruso	The world-famous tenor made his American debut at the Metropolitan Opera House in New York City on November 23, 1903.

Birds of a Feather Flock Together

Although thousands of Italians were exploited, they also stuck together, supporting one another on a number of levels. They shared stories, lent money, offered shelter, and exchanged services. Indeed, Italian immigrants knew how to network. They formed their own social clubs and associations, joined trade unions, and became citizens so that they could find patronage jobs from local political organizations such as the first national Italian American organization, the Sons of Italy, founded in 1905.

For a nominal fee, the Society for the Protection of Italian Immigrants offered incoming immigrants the convenience of their escort service. Around this time, other organizations included the Settlement Italiano di Richmond Hill, the Italian Benevolent Institute, the Comitato Soccorso della Italiana e Patronato di Protezione degli Emigranti Italiani, and the Benevolent Aid Society for Italian Immigrants.

Unfortunately, regional rivalries, hatreds, and stereotypes long bred in Italy did not disappear during the Atlantic voyage. There was no love lost between the educated northern Italian and the blue-collar southern Italian. Although northern Italians had immigrated a generation before the *contadini,* they were reluctant to help their southern countrymen.

Centuries-old prejudices, customs, and dialects separated the two groups. The northerners considered themselves more sophisticated than the southerners in their Old World costumes. Likewise, the southerners regarded their northern brothers and sisters with suspicion.

America Shuts the Golden Door

As the stream of immigrants grew larger, the federal government started looking for ways to turn people away. In 1921 and 1924, the United States Congress passed laws setting strict limits on all immigration. These quotas—based on the number of immigrants from each country—actually benefited the Italians. Based on the number of Italians already living in the United States, the Italian quota was relatively high.

La Bella Lingua

The Italian proverb "*Chi esce riesce*" means "He who leaves succeeds."

Di Interessa

Here's a math problem for you. In 1906, the off-peak third-class fare to New York cost 125 lire. If the official exchange rate was 5.45 lire to the U.S. dollar, how much did the ticket cost?

Di Interessa

In July 1900, Gaetano Bresci—an emigrant from Paterson, New Jersey—assassinated the Italian King Umberto.

Between 1870 and 1920, more than four million Italians immigrated to the United States. From the passing of the National Origins Act (1921) until the end of World War II, fewer than 6,000 Italians a year were permitted to enter the United States.

The Least You Need to Know

➤ A mass emigration of peasants and the poorest classes to the United States occurred in the late 1800s and early 1900s.

➤ Ellis Island in New York Harbor was the primary gateway for Italian immigrants.

➤ For many Italian immigrants, finding a job was a grind.

➤ American immigration quotas created in the 1920s severely cut the number of Italians entering the country.

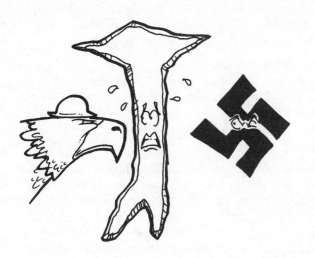

The World at War

Since ancient Rome, war has been a constant feature of Italy's history. The country has had more than her fair share of despots, dictators, and demigods. Five hundred years from now, textbooks will probably regard World War I and World War II as one tumultuous period. Along with the rest of the world, Italy grappled with changes wrought by the Industrial Revolution as conflicting ideologies ripped the country apart. Led by Benito Mussolini, also known as *Il Duce* (pronounced *eel doo-cheh*), fascism grew from the chaos.

The Big Picture

The term *fascio* was first used by the Italian dictator and leader of the fascist movement Benito Mussolini (1883–1945) in 1919, and in Italian simply translated to signify union or league. It also referred to the ancient Roman symbol of power—a bundle of sticks bound to an ax—which represented civic unity and the authority of

Roman officials to punish wrongdoers. This was a powerful image for a nation be-sieged by popular unrest, riots, and strikes and was meant to remind Italians of their powerful heritage; they are heirs of the Roman Empire and proud of it.

To understand *fascism,* and how a totalitarian government could come to exist merely 60 years after Garibaldi and his Redshirts united the peninsula, it's important to understand the crisis facing Italians prior to World War I and how this led to Italy's devastating alliance with Germany during World War II.

The profound changes caused by the Industrial Revolution in Italy led to an economic growth spurt would last from 1896 to 1913. The revolution was marked by technological advances in manufacturing as well as social and political change. The revolution also created a new kind of dependency between worker and employee. Existing disparities in the distribution of the overall wealth were exacerbated, and in many ways, the "haves" (landowners, aristocracy, and fledgling entrepreneurs) continued to have more, while the "have-nots" (mostly the factory workers and landless peasants) found themselves increasingly dependent on the will of their employees.

During the Industrial Revolution, more than half of Italy's industry remained concentrated in the regions of Lombardy, Piedmont, and Liguria, referred to as the "industrial triangle." The north's proximity to the rest of Europe, combined with its historical dominance, made it naturally suited for the revolution.

Technological innovations were changing the face of the country. While Giovanni Agnelli—founder of the car company Fiat—revved and raced the new assembly-line produced cars (modeled off Ford's methods), Camillo Olivetti was introducing the revolutionary *macchina da scrivere* (writing machine)—the first Italian typewriter. Movie theaters had popped up across the country as riveted audiences watched the spectacular epic film *Cabiria*.

Meanwhile, in the agrarian south, tensions were growing between the rich landowners and the peasants who worked the land. Indeed, in sharp contrast to the sweet life being enjoyed by the north, the south struggled with overpopulation, crop failure,

Ciao!

La Bella Lingua

Fascism is a system of government based on a totalitarian philosophy that glorifies state and nation and assigns to the state control over every aspect of national life. It is characterized by repression of all opposition and extreme nationalism, and was practiced by the dictator Benito Mussolini between 1922 and 1943.

"Italia"

In Italics

1913—Universal manhood suffrage was introduced by prime minister Giovanni Giolitti (1842–1928), although women were still excluded. For the first time, the masses were directly participating in national life through elections.

disease, labor strikes, food riots, and inflation. All this led to the mass emigrations that were described in Chapter 18, "The Island of Tears." It also led to the development of a new political movement.

The Origins of Fascism

When World War I began in August 1914, Italy initially remained neutral. Only after signing a secret treaty with the Allies did the country actively take part in the hostilities. During the next couple of years, Italy would fight invading Austrian and German troops. Italy's reluctant participation during World War I (1914–1918), the "war to end all wars," left 600,000 of her young men dead.

Although Italy had been "victorious" in the war, the promises of territory made by the British and French Allies had not been kept. The devastation left in the wake of war combined with the tremendous loss of life seemed a high price to pay for so little in return. In this respect, Italy was no better off than the defeated Germany. Like the poor cousin knocking at the castle door, Italy felt rebuked and bitter. Fascism became the response to the humiliations Italy suffered during World War I. For instance, in the northern Po Valley, tensions were growing between the landless farm-laborers (the *braccianti*) and the capitalist landowners. The growing socialist movement threatened the status quo as workers began to meet and organize. For many of the landowners, the faster the movement could be quelled, the better.

As a political philosophy, fascism developed as a negative response to growing socialist and democratic egalitarianism. Many landowners and middle class were terrified of being dominated by the lower classes being organized by socialist leaders and intellectuals.

No one seemed to be in control of the increasing violence, and things were getting worse, not better. In response, groups of young men began to gather into action squads that went out at night to target specific leaders of the socialist farm-workers' movement. The bands were mainly comprised of ex-combatants, students, and petty bourgeoisie.

Di Interessa

To better understand the conditions facing the peasant farmer at the beginning of the twentieth century, view the film *L'Albero degli Zoccoli (The Tree of Wooden Clogs)* by Ermanno Olmi (1978), which won the Palme d'Or at the Cannes Film Festival.

Ciao!

La Bella Lingua

The term *braccianti* comes from the Italian word *braccia* (arm) and refers to the day laborers that were the "arms" of the land.

Although their intentions were more toward intimidating the victims of their attacks, murder was not uncommon. As uniforms, the armed bands wore black shirts, a color that would later come to symbolize the fascists.

The Italian Dictator Benito Mussolini

Mussolini's followers stood for aggressive nationalism and were violently opposed to any form of communism or socialism. Mussolini first became active in politics as a young newspaper journalist when he published an editorial in October 1914 urging Italy to enter the ongoing battles of World War I. He served in the army, where he attained the ranking of corporal, until he was injured in 1917.

Mussolini's lean toward a more nationalist approach led the Socialist Party to expel him. Instead of being deterred, Mussolini directed his energies to editing the newspaper he had founded, *Il Popolo d'Italia,* a publication the French subsidized to encourage Italy's entry in the ongoing battles of World War I.

But Mussolini aspired to much more than writing an underground newspaper, and in 1919 he launched a new nationalistic movement, the *Fasci di Combattimento,* in Milan. Although the son of a socialist, the young and energetic Mussolini offered a different solution to the violence that was ripping the country apart. Through strict order, stability, and renewed social and cultural life, he promised to rebuild Italy and bring her status back to what she had enjoyed during the Roman Empire. Mussolini's message appealed especially to the lower middle class and the landowners, who were strongly opposed to socialism.

"Italia"

In Italics

June 10, 1924—Italian socialist leader and member of parliament Giacomo Matteotti (1885–1924) was murdered by fascist thugs for his condemnation of the violence used in the elections of 1924. Although Mussolini distanced himself from the killing, the murder showed the true face of fascism and marked the beginning of the dictatorship. Matteotti is regarded as the first martyr of the fascist regime.

The March on Rome

It didn't take long for the determined Mussolini to gather together the force he would need to begin to carry out his vision. On October 28, 1922, Mussolini sent a band of 25,000 militant fascists—most of them former soldiers from the north—wearing the requisite black shirts to march on Rome to demonstrate their force and take power. During the next few days, the fascist squads arrived from all over Italy, traveling by automobile, truck, and train. Using rifles, carbines, daggers, and clubs, the armed and ready militia occupied the municipal and federal offices and took control of the press, railway stations, post and telegraph offices, and telephone.

Di Interessa

Displayed in all fascist barracks were the Fascist Ten Commandments, containing rules of conduct for the perfect fascist militiaman.

1. Remember that the fascist, especially the militiaman, must not believe in perpetual peace.

2. One's country may be served even standing guard over a two-gallon tin of petrol.

3. If you are punished, you have probably deserved it.

4. Your comrades are your brothers because they live with you and because they think like you.

5. Your musket and your uniform have been given to you not to spoil in idleness but to preserve for war.

6. Never say, "It does not matter because the Government pays," because it is you who pay and the Government is one you desire and for which you wear the uniform.

7. Discipline is the sun of the armies; without it there are not soldiers but only confusion and defeat.

8. Mussolini is always right.

9. A volunteer can plead no extenuating circumstances when he disobeys.

10. One thing must be precious above all—the "Duce's" life.

The Blackshirts had mobilized, they explained, with one aim in mind, "the safety and greatness of our country." And who had the most to gain by restoring order? Those that had the most to lose—namely the industrialists and wealthy aristocracy. In addition, the Vatican, feeling threatened by the atheism being promoted by communism, had its own motives for supporting fascism.

The army would have been the only force capable of blocking the Blackshirts, but the king, reluctant to invoke the state of siege, opted instead to invite Mussolini to form his own government. This capitulation to Mussolini would eventually cost the king his throne when the public voted to end the monarchy and create the Italian Republic.

On October 31, 1922, Benito Mussolini formed his first government and was named prime minister. The following year the Blackshirts became the national militia. Mussolini started his reign by redesigning the calendar to show 1922 as Year One. His fascist regime made every effort to control all aspects of daily life. Handshakes were replaced with the "Roman salute" (the right forearm raised vertically). Adults and children were encouraged to join the party and participate in the numerous activities being organized by the state to promote nationalism.

Mussolini's Italian Empire

As you may recall from Chapter 6, "Rome Wasn't Built in a Day," Caesar and his successors created a military dictatorship during the Roman Empire. Similarly, Mussolini hoped to create an "Italian Empire." In reviving the symbols used in ancient Rome, his initiatives were designed to create a common sense of purpose and bolster the Italian economy.

Mussolini commissioned large-scale public works such as the Esposizione Universale di Roma (EUR)—a building complex of offices and apartments—and authorized the draining of the swamps that caused malaria. For a while, it seemed like Italy was finally recovering from the effects of the First World War.

But leading her along her way was the dangerous leader Mussolini—a mesmerizing speaker with a genuine understanding of the power of propaganda. In 1937, the Ministry of Popular Culture was created to coordinate the political propaganda machine and to oversee the press and media. Mussolini's slogans were painted everywhere and like a rock star in concert, the fist-waving, dynamic *Il Duce* gave speeches to huge crowds. Italians hung his photos in their homes and businesses, and many Italian children were named Benito in honor of their leader.

To promote the image of a virile, brave leader to admire and imitate, he had pictures taken of himself swimming, piloting an airplane, riding a horse, and driving a race car. There is even one in which the "Lion of Italy" (as he was sometimes called) can be seen crouching beside a passive lion, as calm as the beast itself.

Mussolinia

In Rome, new government buildings such as the EUR copied classic styles. When the Via dell'Impero, a road built between the Capitol and the Colosseum, it was flanked with maps of the old Roman Empire.

Since the south continued to be plagued by economic and social problems, Mussolini planned a new city called "Mussolinia" in southern Italy as a model of progress. Construction stopped after only a few buildings were erected. Mussolini started a series of initiatives to improve the Italian economy; he called them *Le Battaglie*—"The Battles." Farmers were encouraged to grow more wheat (the Battle for Grain), families were encouraged to have more children (the Battle for Births), and land for agriculture was reclaimed (the Battle for Land).

ROBERT N. ROADCAP
2772 JOSEPH AVE., APT 2
CAMPBELL, CA 95008-6236

He created the "Dopolavoro" (leisure time) institution to promote schemes for the "better employment of the free time of workers of all classes," in keeping with the fascist principles of working with "purpose, method, and order." Through the Dopolavoro Office, thousands of clubs, societies, sporting, educational, and artistic groups were organized.

Intellectuals and Liberals Flee

Under the guise of maintaining order, Mussolini outlawed all opposition political parties. Newspapers and books were censored. Intellectuals and liberals whose ideas did not conform to the fascist ideals were forced to flee the country and become political exiles.

Several of these writers went on to create important works that disputed the ideals promoted by Mussolini and his followers. Among them was a staunch opponent to fascism, the Italian historian and philosopher Benedetto Croce (1866–1952) who wrote, in 1925, *Il Manifesto degli Intellettuali Anti-Fascisti*, in response to Gentile's *Manifesto degli Intellettuali Fascisti*. The intellectual and politician Antonio Gramsci (1891–1937) wrote, in 1927, *Lettere dal Carcere (Letters from Prison)*, describing his experience. In addition, in 1929 the novelist Alberto Moravia (1907–1990) wrote *Gli Indifferenti (Time of Indifference)*, a realistic study of the moral corruption of a middle-class mother and two of her children; it became a sensation.

The Lateran Treaty

While Mussolini was certainly no altar boy, one of his greatest diplomatic triumphs was settling the 60-year-old controversy with the pope. On June 7, 1929, the Lateran Treaty was signed between Italy and the papacy to create the State of Vatican City. As a sovereign state, the papacy was given a large sum of money to compensate for the loss of papal territories in 1860 and 1870.

The gesture did wonders to increase Mussolini's personal prestige both in Italy and abroad. The pope agreed to accept the fascists as long as the Catholic

Di Interessa

A significant achievement of Mussolini's was the elimination of the disease malaria by draining the swamps and marshes near Rome. Another contribution involved the preservation of precious Roman ruins that had been abandoned to time and thieves.

Biografia

Luigi Pirandello (1867–1936) wrote *6 Personaggi in Cerca d'Autore (Six Characters in Search of an Author)* in 1921, the same year the fascist movement became a political party. In 1934, Pirandello won the Nobel Prize for Literature. The central theme of his plays is the search to distinguish between illusion and reality.

religion was taught in every Italian school, thus settling the "Roman Question," the relationship between church and state.

As you may remember from Chapter 7, "The Medieval Minestrone," the monasteries and abbeys, including many of the universities, had been under the province of the Catholic Church, particularly the Jesuits, for ages. Until the Napoleonic invasions in the eighteenth century, the clergy had enjoyed a monopoly in the field of education. The reintroduction of religion as a compulsory subject in elementary education restored the authority of the Holy See and brought its priests back into the schools.

Biografia

While Mussolini was attempting to mold the minds and souls of Italy's children, another Italian—Giovanni Gentile (1875–1944)—was additionally commanding the attention of Americans for his educational reforms. The neo-idealist philosopher believed knowledge served to raise self-consciousness; his philosophy, called actual idealism, derived from ideas inspired by the German philosopher Hegel.

On Making Baby Fascists

Mussolini's political and social machine exempted no one, not even school children. Under the guidance of the Italian Minister of Education, Giovanni Gentile (1875–1944), the Fascist Party began to assume responsibility for the educational, moral, and physical development of the nation's children. The Church would take care of their souls.

Di Interessa

Mussolini levied a "bachelor tax" to encourage Italian boys out of their mothers' houses and into marriage. Families with five or more children received a certificate signed by *Il Duce* himself.

The Gentile reforms aimed to create special schools to respond to the different needs of society. Students were to be judged by their maturity and character as much as they were to be rewarded for being good test takers.

Several organizations were developed to nurture the development of Italy's *bambini*. Boys were expected to become healthy and robust soldiers and urged to join the *Balilla* to learn the value of physical strength, bravery, and above all, obedience and discipline.

Girls, on the other hand, were hardly expected to participate in the nasty business of war. Instead, they attended the *Piccole e Giovani Italiane* (Little and Young Italian Girls), whose function was to prepare them for their future domestic roles as teachers and mothers.

In keeping with the theme of an empire, Roman history was given prominence in the school curriculum. April 21, the traditional date of the founding of Rome, became a public holiday.

The Beginning of the End

Ideology was a poor substitute for bread. Faulty administration and a lack of foresight caused many of Mussolini's grand plans to fail. Campaigns designed to bolster Italy's sinking spirit failed as more and more Italians found themselves worse off than ever. Inflation was rising while wages were falling. Covert anti-fascist organizations began to emerge. At the same time, the world began creeping to the edge of international calamity.

The World at War

While Mussolini was pushing his reforms on Italy, another European dictator, the German chancellor Adolf Hitler, led a campaign for world conquest that would result in World War II.

In the Berlin–Rome Axis of October 1936, Mussolini's alliance with Hitler had atrocious results. Influenced by Nazi racist policies, in November 1938, Italy passed racial laws banning Italian Jews from marrying Aryans and excluded them from holding jobs in civil and military administrations. Despite the fact that the overwhelming majority of Italians were outraged at the new laws, at the hands of the fascists and Nazis, almost 20 percent of Italy's Jews were deported to German death camps during the war. Alongside the Jews were many Italian partisans who had been part of the resistance.

In May 1939, Italy signed the Pact of Steel military alliance with Germany. By June 10, 1940, Italy had declared war on France and Great Britain. The Italian alliance with Germany against the United States shocked Italian Americans who had supported Mussolini who now felt betrayed.

La Bella Lingua

To foster national unity, the fascists tried to "purify" the Italian language. Foreign words were replaced with similar Italian terms, and *Lei*, the polite form of address, was replaced with *Voi*.

Biografia

Primo Levi (1919–1987) was a novelist, scientist, and Italian Jew who was imprisoned at the Nazi concentration camp at Auschwitz after he was captured as a member of an anti-fascist resistance group. He wrote many books detailing his experiences as a survivor and witness to the Holocaust atrocities, including *Se questo è un uomo* (1947; *If This Is a Man*).

Di Interessa

During World War II, the Vatican library became a safe refuge for some of the world's rarest books. In October 1943, German officers gave advance warning to the abbot of the ancient Benedictine Abbey of Monte Cassino that the upcoming battle for the strategic hilltop site would put the abbey's vast collection at risk. As a result, 40,000 rare parchments—including works by Cicero and Augustine—were hurriedly loaded onto trucks and moved to the Vatican.

The Second World War would be an absolute disaster for Italy. The army was poorly trained and outgunned, led by a dictator drunk on power and without any clear goals. In the first of several losses, the Italian army was defeated in Greece in October 1940. The fascist regime was rocked to its foundation, and Mussolini was forced to ask Hitler for help.

Italy Is Invaded ... Again

Allied forces invaded Sicily on July 10, 1943. Days later, Rome was bombed, leading to a large-scale exodus of the Roman population and bringing the political crisis to a climax. Il Duce was arrested, the Fascist government was disbanded, and Pietro Badoglio was named prime minister.

Di Interessa

More than a million Italian Americans fought valiantly for the United States in World War II. Thirteen received the Congressional Medal of Honor and ten received the Navy Cross.

In September 1943, the cowardly King Vittore Emanuelle III and his government fled the country, abandoning Rome to the Germans. Mussolini was rescued, and Italy became a war zone for 18 months as the Allies and Germans fought each other up the peninsula, wreaking untold devastation throughout the land. Italian partisans in Northern Italy fought hand-to-hand combat against those still loyal to the fascists.

After being rescued by the Germans, Mussolini set up the "Italian Social Republic," a puppet government in the north Italy town of Salò that lasted from 1943 to April 1945. The last-ditch effort proved futile. While attempting to escape to Austria, the face that had been printed in books, newspapers, and posters was recognized by partisans. On April 28, Mussolini was captured by Italian partisans, tried in a court-martial, and shot with his mistress, Clara Petacci. Their bodies were brought back to Milan and hung upside down in Piazzale Loreto.

Raising the White Flag

The final Allied offensive in Italy began in April 1945, and by the end of the month the German armies had been completely smashed. Following the end of military action, several provisional governments were created until Italians voted for a political democracy in the spring of 1946. Although Italy was devastated economically, she had been liberated from the manacles of both fascism and Nazism.

While Mussolini had attempted to unite the nation and give Italians an identity, the totalitarian rule of fascism had proven to be a terrible failure. In a twisted way, however, the nation had united; fascism proved to be the common enemy, and as such offered Italy enough reason—after centuries of struggle—to step up to the plate and become a single state under a single banner. On June 18, 1946, the Italian Republic was officially proclaimed.

Italian Americans: Divided Loyalties

For the Italian immigrants living in the United States, both Mussolini's fascism and the two World Wars presented a conflict of interests. On the one hand, many of them had just traveled to America. They received letters from home and families and read newspapers about the dismal political situation, concerned about their native land. But they were Americans, too, and supported the U.S. government, which was often at odds with Italy.

During World War II, an estimated 500,000 captured Italian soldiers were interned in 27 camps located in 23 states in the United States. The Italian POWs were a link to the old country and welcomed by their Italian American brothers and sisters. After an armistice was signed by the Italian government, the Italian POWs in the United States were permitted weekend visitors and sometimes allowed to go off-base when not required to work.

Biografia

In 1938, Enrico Fermi (1901–1954) and his wife, both Jewish, fled from Fascist Italy because of the Racial Laws to conduct research in the United States. He won the Nobel Prize for Physics in 1938 and supervised the first nuclear chain reaction on December 2, 1942. The chemical element 100, Fermium, is named after him.

Biografia

Umberto II (1923–1983), the son of Vittore Emanuelle and Queen Elena, was the last king of Italy. He reigned for 26 days, from May 9, 1946, until June 2 of the same year, when a referendum ended the monarchy.

Italian Americans, feeling a special kinship (since their own sons were fighting in Italy), forged friendships with the young Italian soldiers and brought them to family gatherings. Quite a few of these Italian prisoners of war fell in love and married American women.

Cinecittà

During Mussolini's reign, the largest complex of film studios in Europe was built in Rome in 1935–1936. Called Cinecittà, it served as the sound stage for many classic films during the golden age of Italian cinema.

In the first years of fascism the regime took little interest in the film industry, but when the propaganda campaign was in full swing, the fascists took advantage of the powerful image on *lo schermo grande*—the big screen—and financed historical documentaries and costume dramas.

Biografia

Joe DiMaggio (1914–1999), popular hero, cultural icon, and one of the greatest baseball hitters of all time. The Yankee Clipper enlisted in the armed services in 1942. His parents immigrated from Sicily.

Movies often offer a much better picture of historical events than the printed word can. To understand the effects the wars had on Italy, you may want to watch the Oscar-winning *The Garden of the Finzi-Continis* (1971; directed by Vittorio De Sica) for an excellent depiction of the gradual disintegration of the Jewish community living in Italy at the beginning of World War II. In addition, watch Luchino Visconti's film *Obsession* (1942).

For commentary about the Allied liberation of Italy during World War II, don't miss the movie *Paesan* (1946; directed by Roberto Rossellini and co-written by Federico Fellini). Other films include the award-winning *Life Is Beautiful* directed by Roberto Benigni.

The Least You Need to Know

➤ Benito Mussolini rose to power by taking advantage of the disappointment and disorder that followed World War I.

➤ Fascism was a totalitarian form of government that restricted many rights and repressed free speech and the press.

➤ Many Italian Americans supported Mussolini until his extreme views became more evident.

➤ Italy lost twice in World War II—to both the Germans and Allies.

Chapter 20

Myth and Magic

In This Chapter

➤ Italy chooses democracy

➤ The "Economic Miracle"

➤ The Italian government

➤ The Mafia

After the Allies left, Italy was left to the arduous task of rebuilding her cities and creating a government that would be safe from the extreme politics associated with the totalitarian government of Mussolini and his fascists. It wasn't easy, but within one generation, Italy's economy had become one of the world's largest, with Italians enjoying an unprecedented increase in their standard of living.

Rising Up from the Ashes

The end of World War II left Italy in shock. In the city of Florence, Germans had blown up every bridge across the Arno River with the exception of her renowned Ponte Vecchio ("old bridge").

Allied bombing had left many sections of Naples and Rome reduced to rubble. In the countryside the armed resistance had left villages a barren wasteland of burned buildings and bare or flooded fields with the factories, railroads, power plants, and bridges virtually destroyed.

The familiar silhouette of Florence's Ponte Vecchio was saved from German bombing.

Before any reconstruction could begin, a new government needed to be selected. On June 2, 1946, elections were conducted that allowed women to vote for the first time. When the tallies were in, the results were clear. Italians had voted in favor of a republic.

The *Costituzione della Repubblica Italiana* was approved on December 22, 1947, in the aftermath of World War II and became effective on January 1, 1948. In this new democracy (referred to as the First Republic), elected officials were responsible to the citizens that had put them in office.

For almost 40 years Italian politics were dominated by one party, the Christian Democrats. Eventually, events both in Italy—such as terrorism in the 1970s and widespread political corruption—and on the world stage—such as the thaw in the Cold War and the fall of the Berlin Wall in 1989—ended the status quo. The government instituted electoral system reforms that revamped the entire political system, and the so-called Second Republic came into being.

Biografia

Prince Emanuelle Filiberto (1972–), born and raised in Geneva, Switzerland, and the great-grandson of the wartime king Vittore Emanuelle III, is the man who would be king except for the fact that he has never visited Italy. After the country was abandoned by the cowardly king, a 1948 constitutional amendment barred direct male descendants of the last king of Italy from ever setting foot on Italian soil again. Requests to change the law have been rejected.

Italian Parliament

Similar to the U.S. Congress, there are two houses of Parliament—a Chamber of Deputies and a Senate. Elected by the Parliament, the *Presidente* of Italy functions as the official head of state, though he or she does not run the country. He lives in the Palazzo Quirinale in Rome, originally the summer home of the pope.

Typically, Italians vote for a party. The *Presidente del Consiglio* (prime minister) is chosen by the president based on election results and is the individual responsible for running things.

Biografia

Silvio Berlusconi and the members of Italy's fifty-ninth postwar government were sworn into office in June 2001. Berlusconi is a conservative media tycoon and one of the world's richest men. He is a member of the Forza Italia Party. Since the mid-1990s Umberto Bossi, leader of the separatist political party *Lega Nord* (Northern League) has supported the idea of the "Northern Republic of Padania," even claiming its independence from Italy. A small "security force" of Greenshirts has been recruited, too.

The Parties

Italians have as difficult a time understanding the differences between American Democrats and Republicans as Americans have understanding labyrinthine Italian politics. In the past, parties provided a belief system that largely affected the culture and lifestyles of its members. There were socialists, communists, Christian Democrats, and anarchists, each with clearly outlined principles that often sharply contrasted.

In Italy, there are several parties from which to choose, ranging from the extreme left, such as the *Rifondazione Comunista* Party, to the extreme right, with the *Alleanza Nazionale*, an offshoot of the old Fascist Party but without the totalitarianism.

Cristiano Democratici   Center Right

Alleanza Nazionale   Right (former Fascist Party)

Forza Italia   Center Right

Democratici di Sinistra   Left (former Socialist Party)

Rifondazione Comunista   The leftist of left (Communist Party)

SDI Socialisti Democratici Italiani   Center left (Socialist Democrats)

I Popolari   Center (former Christian Democrat Party)

Lega Nord   Right

L'Ulivo   Center left alliance

I Verdi   Save the Earth Party

The Press

Italian newspapers are often slanted in one direction or another, and Italians usually read the publication that conforms to their political beliefs. In a certain way, this makes uncovering the "real story" easier since the different perspectives offer the reader the opportunity to look at a topic from another angle. To truly understand world headlines, many Italians read several papers.

A few papers you might see people reading include:

Corriere della Sera (similar to *The New York Times*)

La Repubblica (*The New York Times* to the left)

Il Messaggero (center; published in Rome)

Il Secolo (extreme left/fascist)

L'Osservatore Romano (Vatican)

La Stampa (center-right; published in Torino)

Il Manifesto (left)

Il Sole 24 (business; similar to *The Wall Street Journal*)

Constitutional reform, known as *la bicamerale,* is still a hot topic and has yet to be agreed on. These changes would include directly electing the president, more power for the regions, and reform of the judicial system.

The Neorealists

After the 20 years of artistic and cultural repression by the Fascist regime, the climb to economic prosperity was accompanied by a boom in the arts, most particularly in film. While members of the Italian parliament argued and debated, Italian Neorealists such as Roberto Rossellini, Vittorio De Sica, Luchino Visconti, and the realist/surrealist Federico Fellini attempted to depict the realities of life.

Luchino Visconti

Born to an aristocratic family in Milan, the director Luchino Visconti (1906–1976) worked on motion pictures, operas, ballets, and plays. Considered the father of the neorealist movement in Italian cinema, he made films such as *Ossessione* (*Obsession;* 1942) that attempted to depict life as it really was. Visconti used natural lighting, cast local residents, and filmed in the country, outside the controlled stages of the big studios.

Visconti got his start in film by working as an assistant to the French director Jean Renoir on films such as *Une Partie de Campagne* (*A Day in the Country;* 1936). During the war he participated in several anti-fascist, left-wing political campaigns. Later he went onto make dramas such as *La Caduta degli Dei* (*The Damned;* 1969) and neorealist films like *Rocco e i suoi fratelli* (*Rocco and His Brothers;* 1960).

Visconti worked with other important figures of the day, including an adaptation of *Il Gattopardo* (*The Leopard;* 1963) from the book by Italian writer Giuseppe di Lampedusa and a production of the opera *La Traviata* by the well-known Italian composer Giuseppe Verdi.

"*Italia*"

In Italics

1993—*Le Mani Pulite*—Operation Clean Hands—was an investigation into political corruption that implicated thousands of businessmen as well as three former prime ministers. During the corruption trials of the 1990s, the city of Milan was nicknamed *Tangentopoli,* or "Bribesville," because of the prevalence of bribery among the local businessmen.

Roberto Rossellini

The leader of the Neorealist movement was the director Roberto Rossellini (1906–1977). Born in Rome the same year as Visconti, Rossellini's start in film came during the war where he directed patriotic films and shot footage of Rome during the last days of World War II. Movies such as *Open City* (1945) and *Paisan* (1946) depicted the harsh realities of Italian life after the brutal devastation of the war. Handheld cameras, "real" actors, and natural settings became the hallmarks of neorealism.

Other films include *Stromboli* (1949) starring Ingrid Bergman, *Strangers* (1954), and *General Della Rovere* (1959) with another important neorealist film maker, Vittorio De Sica. Rossellini later married Bergman, with whom he had a daughter, *la bella* Isabella.

Vittorio De Sica

The actor, director, producer Vittorio De Sica (1902–1974) was born in Sora, where he launched his career as a comic stage and film actor. When he began directing films in the 1940s, in the film *Sciuscia* (*Shoeshine*; 1946) he chose to focus on the harsh realities facing Italy's orphans after the war. His awarded work, *Ladri di Bicicletta* (*The Bicycle Thief*; 1948), depicted a hard-working man whose bicycle—his only means of transportation to work—is stolen.

Other films include *La Ciocara* (*Two Women*; 1961); *Ieri, Oggi, Domani* (*Yesterday, Today, and Tomorrow*; 1964), the story of a Jewish family during the war; and the Academy Award–winning film *Il Giardino dei Finzi-Contini* (*The Garden of the Finzi-Continis*; 1970).

Federico Fellini

The beloved Federico Fellini (1920–1993) charmed audiences with his surrealistic style and sympathetic characters. Born in the seaside town of Rimini, Fellini began his career as a writer and cartoonist. Soon, however, he was working with Roberto Rossellini on the movie *Open City*.

His film *I Vitellini* (1953) brought Fellini into the limelight. His signature neorealist style depicted the lives of society's transients and included films such as the Academy Award–winning movie *La Strada* starring Giulietta Masina (his wife), *Nights of Cabiria* (1957), and *La Dolce Vita* (1960) starring Marcello Mastroianni.

Marcello Mastroianni

The motion picture star Marcello Mastroianni (1923–1996) was born in Fontana Liri and worked as an extra until his big break came when Luchino Visconti hired him as a member of his theater company. The ever-likable Mastroianni charmed audiences with his performances in movies such as *White Nights* (1957), *Big Deal on Madonna*

Street (1958), and *La Dolce Vita* (1960). Later in his career, he performed opposite Sophia Loren in *Yesterday, Today, and Tomorrow* (1964) and *Marriage Italian Style* (1964); he also starred in the English-language films *A Place for Lovers* (1968) and *Used People* (1992) with costar Shirley MacLaine.

Sophia Loren

The international sex symbol and Academy Award–winning actress Sophia Loren (1934–) was born in Rome and discovered at the age of 15 by the Italian movie producer Carlo Ponti (whom she later married). A beauty pageant winner, Ms. Loren won the hearts of Italy immediately, and by 20, she was a star.

In the wartime tale *La Ciocara* (*Two Women;* 1961), viewers follow Sophia as she plays a mother with her grown daughter during their struggle to survive during World War II. Other films worth mention include *Gold of Naples* (1954), *Houseboat* (1957), and *A Countess from Hong Kong* (1967).

Anna Magnani

The internationally renowned Italian actress Anna Magnani (1908–1973) was best known for her powerful portrayals of lower-class women. Magnani was raised by her grandparents in Rome, where she attended the Academy of Dramatic Arts for a brief time before joining a traveling repertory company. Her entrance into the neorealist film movement began when she was cast by Roberto Rossellini in his film *Città Aperta*. Magnani's ability to portray deep emotion is exemplified in a number of her roles, including a housewife set against black marketeering in postwar Italy in *L'onorevole Angelina* (1947), a naive and blindly optimistic village idiot in *Il Miracolo* (1948), a stage mother in *Bellissima* (1951), and in her first Hollywood film, *The Rose Tattoo* (1955), for which she won the Academy Award for best actress.

The Italian Miracle

Italy had gone from being a country living in a devastated war zone replete with starving masses to one in which fashionably clothed families took vacations with clockwork regularity. The majority—mostly middle-class Italians—now owned homes filled with the latest electrical appliances, parked Fiat Cinquecentos in their garages, bought Vespas for their kids, and went to the movies on a regular basis.

Di Interessa

The "Italian Miracle" refers to the enormous wealth the postwar years of the 1950s and 1960s brought to Italy.

The backbone of the Italian economy's success rested on the back of the small business owner. Quite contrary to the American model of big business and industry, it was the efforts of hardworking, entrepreneurial Italians that created a world-class economy made up of mom-and-pop shops, restaurant owners, butchers, bakers, and vendors.

In the great tradition of their ancestors—the amalgam of cultures that had congregated, conquered, and settled in the peninsula—these industrious, ingenious craftsmen and artists had once more created one of the world's most productive economies.

Di Interessa

The high-tech information age has transformed the area near Catania, Sicily, into the new Silicon Valley thanks to the presence of Italian and international high-tech companies.

A big contributor to the economic prosperity in Italy has been the demand for Italian-made goods. The Italian regions Montepulciano and Chianti are recognized names to most Americans. Italian pasta companies such as Barilla and De Cecco have inundated American supermarkets. Italian fashions by designers Giorgio Armani, Gianni Versace, and Gucci are coveted by trendy dressers.

The list of goods continues. Italian-designed household items (coffee makers, telephones, clocks, toasters, bicycles, etc.) remain the standard for many buyers. Italian marketers have cultivated a willing worldwide audience with the style and tastes that Italy is famous for. You'll read more about the phenomenon in Chapter 25, "Made in Italy."

You Must Go to School

Another key reason for the Italian economic miracle was compulsory education. In Italy, obligatory schooling for elementary school was extended to secondary school and included boys and girls up to the age of 14. In addition, entry to university programs was granted to anyone who wanted to attend.

Compulsory education created an Italian population that was literate and learned, which greatly improved Italy's competitive standing as an industrialized nation. Higher education also gave women new opportunities in professions that were previously closed to them. While in theory, all Italian children should be schooled equally, the typical disparities between the wealthy northern regions and her agrarian southern sisters continue to exist.

Il Sorpasso

Il Sorpasso refers to the economic milestone in the mid-1980s when Italy surpassed Britain (and possibly France, depending on the exchange rate and what statistics were used) to become the fifth largest economy in the world. Many economists believe that if the *economia sommersa* (underground economy) were also included, it would add an additional 25 percent to the total Italian economy.

How did Italy manage all that in so little time? Having a common language really helped and so did the political, social, and economic contributions of Italian women, who had been kept back for so long.

Italians Speak the Same Language

For centuries, leaders such as Napoleon, Garibaldi, and Mussolini all tried to create a new sense of identity for the Italian nation, but with limited success. As charismatic and persuasive as they were, none seemed to be able to forge one national identity.

Television, cinema, and radio were enormously effective in fostering Italian unity. Italians throughout the country could see the same movie or listen to the same show and gain a sense of community in the process. With easy access to movies, television programs, and news from around the world, Italy became part of the global village.

Television also promoted an Italian linguistic unity. News announcers began speaking a standard, noninflected *lingua franca*. The power of the media and its instant accessibility cannot be overestimated. In just 40 years, television accomplished what writers like Dante Alighieri, Alessandro Manzoni, and the *l'Accademia della Crusca* (the national language academy) were not able to do in 400 years: Italians now all spoke the same language.

Burning Their Aprons

Another reason for the economic boom—and perhaps a result of it as well—was the increasing role in economic and political life played by Italian women. No longer limited to the domestic role of *casalinga* (housewife), the opportunities available to Italian women expanded tremendously. Italian women now pursue higher education, are prominent in business and the professions, and can even serve in the military. You'll learn more about the history of Italian women in Chapter 23, "Mamma and the Madonna."

Married to the Mob

Even as Italian women were improving their collective lot in life and contributing positively to society, another group was making headlines, although not in a way that would make their mothers proud.

While modern television shows like *The Sopranos* make it seem like organized crime is a totally American phenomenon, the Mafia actually has been a factor in Italian life for centuries. As you

Di Interessa

The Pizza Connection was a heroin-smuggling Mafia operation that used New York City pizza parlors to distribute the drugs. During the mid-1980s the testimony of Tommaso Buscetta, an Italian Mafia turncoat, resulted in the conviction of hundreds of mobsters in Italy and the United States.

may recall from Chapter 4, "From Shore to Shore," the Italian Mafia was created in response to the constant invasions into Sicily of Arabs and Normans.

Everyone called it something different then: The Sicilian Mafia was called *Cosa Nostra,* the Neapolitan version, the *Camorra,* and the Calabrian criminals were the *Ndrangheta.* Later, Sicilian emigrants exported their special brand of violence to the eastern United Sates where it became a romanticized criminal organization that rebounded in Italy.

Most people don't realize that the Mafia originally worked in the spirit of Robin Hood and was known for stealing from the rich to feed the poor. Just as the Mafia started as a force to fight against invaders, it later attempted to protect peasants and the landless poor against the oppressive practices of the landowners.

Movies such as *The Godfather* demonstrate one of the most crucial values held by the Mafia: Family comes first. As the movie demonstrates, however, that was true only if money-making impetus for the organization was satisfied. The ideas of solidarity, respect, and honor that had been the guiding principles of the Mafia were slowly being eroded, replaced by the values associated with the new wealth pouring in as a result of the Mafia's well-run illegal drug industry in the last decades of the twentieth century.

La Bella Lingua

Pentiti is Italian for "repentants" or stool pigeons, former gangsters turned police informers who squeal on each other, brushing aside their allegiance to *omertà,* or the code of silence which they hide behind for so long.

Basta! *Enough Is Enough!*

Since the late 1970s, the Italian government has been cracking down on the Mafia, enticing members to become informants with promises of lighter sentences and protection. In the 1986 trials that lasted over a year, 19 life sentences were handed out and over 300 more defendants were sent to prison. The fight continues.

The Least You Need to Know

➤ The Italian nation finally became a democracy in 1948.

➤ The postwar economic boom in Italy was fueled by the blood, sweat, and tears of entrepreneurs and family businesses.

➤ The media have radically altered how Italians perceive themselves as a nation.

➤ Northern Italy has continued to outpace the south economically, exacerbating tensions between the two regions.

Part 5

Pizza, Pasta, and Fantasia

Italy's charms are irresistible. Whether you are admiring the classic features of Sophia Loren or sipping on a glass of wine, Part 5 celebrates the things you love most about Italy.

What is Carnevale and where can you go to see it for yourself? What do the Italians do for fun? If you love to go fast, try driving an Italian sports car. If you are a theater buff, learn more about the Nobel Prize winner Luigi Pirandello, one of Italy's most prized dramatists. Consider yourself a film nut? Receive an Italian film starter kit to get you started on the significant Italian contributions to film. Love to eat? Find out what is and what isn't Italian food, and learn to prepare a meal yourself.

Learn about the long road to the women's suffrage movement and how far women have come since ancient Roman times. Delve into the mysterious and the mystical as you study some of the more unusual aspects of Italian culture, including bleeding statues, invisible dancing fairies, and puppets that come to life. Finally, whether a carefully tailored suit or a finely sculpted shoe, Italian design is synonymous with style.

Chapter 21

Life Is a *Carnevale*

> ### In This Chapter
>
> ➤ There's a celebration for every occasion
>
> ➤ Theater
>
> ➤ Il cinema: movies

A common Italian expression used is *Che bello!* (How beautiful!) It is uttered often, to describe anything from a beautiful *tramonto* (sunset) to a fine meal.

It's no exaggeration to say that the Italians embrace life. They love doing everything with style, too. Whether it's zipping along on a *motorino* with the wind through their hair, cheering on their favorite soccer squad, or dancing at a masquerade ball, they have an unquenchable passion and spirit.

How do Italians entertain themselves? What kind of sports do they play and what holidays and festivals do they celebrate?

Carnevale

Carnevale is generally held in February prior to Lent. It energizes Italian towns, large and small alike. It combines ancient pagan rituals and Christian values. Centuries ago it was an officially sanctioned way for people to *festeggiare* one last time before the austerity of Lent had to be observed. It's been celebrated for centuries in Christian countries throughout the world—Rio di Janeiro, Brazil, for instance, has a huge, internationally famous Carnival, and New Orleans, Louisiana, has Mardi Gras. The Italian spin on the event, of course, is what makes *Carnevale* unique.

La Bella Lingua

The word ***carnevale*** originated in Italian and meant "farewell to meat."

The two largest *Carnevali* take place in Venice and the seaside town of Viareggio. Piazza San Marco in Venice draws thousands of visitors from around the world during the cold and bleak *Carnevale* season in February. Costumed revelers partake in any number of venues in the spirit of *Carnevale,* filling the streets and canals. In Viareggio, there are parades for four consecutive Sundays that feature huge, spectacular floats holding elaborate papier-mâché models satirizing political figures and current events.

There are *Carnevale* events held throughout Italy. If you are lucky enough to participate, make sure you bring your dancing shoes, and don't forget a costume. (A mask will do.)

Typical Carnevale *masks.*

226

Italian Holidays and Important Dates

In addition to *Carnevale,* tradition and ritual play a strong role throughout Italian culture, especially during holidays such as Easter and Christmas. On the local level, there are patron saints' days, town festivals, and other *sagre* that are a centerpiece of community life. See Chapter 2, *"Che Panorama!"* for a sampling of fairs and celebrations. On the national level, Italy has a host of days on which everything closes:

January 1 (*Capodanno*—New Year's Day)

January 6 (*Epifania*—Feast of the Epiphany)

Easter Monday (*Pasquetta*—Little Easter)

April 25 (Liberation Day)

May 1 (Labor Day)

August 15 (Ferragosto)

November 1 (*Ognissanti*—All Saints Day)

December 8 (Immaculate Conception of the Blessed Virgin Mary)

December 25 (*Natale*—Christmas)

December 26 (St. Stephen's Day)

I'll Bet You I Win

Betting and gambling are ancient traditions in Italy. Six-sided dice were used by Etruscans and passed on to the Romans around 600 B.C.E. In Caesar's time, lotteries were known to exist, and Roman soldiers bet on the turn of numbered chariot wheels. In 1515, six names were drawn for election to the Senate in Genoa. Later, the names were changed to numbers. And in 1530, a state-run lottery game, *Lo Giuco de Lotto,* was held, which marked the beginning of bingo. The game is still held every Saturday in Italy.

The Palio

One of the most exciting and spectacular festivals in Italy is the Siena Palio, a twice-yearly hell-for-leather race around the Piazza del Campo, the central square. It is named after the painted silk banner that the winner receives. Horses from the seventeen districts—*contrade*—compete. The Palio first took place in 1482 and is accompanied by considerable preparation and pageantry. It's the horse that wins—it doesn't matter if the jockey has been tossed off his mount during the race.

Hope Springs Eternal

Totocalcio, Tototip, Totogol, TotoBINgol, Totosei, SuperEnalotto—all these are names for different gambling games popular in Italy. Sometimes it seems there are more ways for Italians to gamble than there are pasta shapes. There are syndicates, systems, software, and schemes for those who dream of winning a fortune. A recent survey by *Istituta Doxa* indicated that about one third of all Italian adults—i.e., about 16 million people—play either Totocalcio (a soccer pool) or Lotto at least occasionally.

La Bella Lingua

Italian sports fans in Italy are called *tifosi*—derived from "typhoid-fevered." They are raucous and energetic, at times bordering on violent. After a major victory, they often take to the streets in chaotic and spontaneous celebration.

La Bella Lingua

A *passeggiata* is a stroll or walk, from the verb *passeggiare* (to walk).

Il Calcio

In Italy, *calcio* (soccer to Americans, football to Europeans) far surpasses all other sports in popularity. Italians cheer on the local teams, especially those in the Serie A, the highest level of the Italian soccer major leagues. On Sunday afternoons during the season huge numbers of fans either watch soccer on TV or fill the stadiums around the country.

Gli Azzuri (the Blues—for the color of their jerseys) is the nickname of the national team that participates in the World Cup. Italy has won three world championships, most recently in 1982.

La Passeggiata

One moment the streets are empty, the next they are filled with elegant people on a stroll, or *passeggiata*. It's the ritual evening walk, when the townspeople gather to converse with friends, strut their finery, flirt, have an ice cream, and show off their children. The parade of well-dressed people is part of the Italian effort to *fare una bella figure*, "to look good." It's an inherently Italian inspiration to create a civilized world.

Usually the evening promenade takes place in and around the main square. Nearly every town has a main square or piazza, which is the focus for much of the civic activities. It's not only for *la passeggiata*, but also for local festivals and rallies. In most towns, too, there are certain religious and municipal buildings that are usually grouped around the piazza, too.

Having fun in the piazza.

(Photo by Anna Andersson)

A Driving Passion

Italians have a love affair with wheeled vehicles, whether it's a blazing Ducati, a Vespa *motorino,* a Fiat Cinquecento, or a high-performance sports car like a Ferrari, Lamborghini, or Maserati. They also have a reputation for driving *veloce come un razzo—* as fast as a bullet!

How captivated are Italians with their cars, bicycles, and scooters? Every March 9 there's the Blessing of the Vehicles in Rome at the Santa Francesca Romana Church (located next to the Colosseum). On the feast day of Saint Frances of Rome, the patron saint of car drivers (indeed, there's a saint for every occasion!), drivers from all over the region arrive en masse to park as close to the church as possible and receive the full benefits of the saint's blessing for the coming year.

Di Interessa

Consult the Italian Government Travel Office Web site at www.italiantourism.com for more information.

Buzzing Hornets

A *vespa* is a hornet or wasp. It's also an apt name for those buzzing, swarming, darting motor scooters that threaten to take over Italian city centers. *Motorini* are more popular then ever, given the high cost of gas and the difficulty in parking in cramped historic towns.

The Vespa motor scooter is a symbol of Italian style and design. Who can forget Audrey Hepburn and Gregory Peck in *Roman Holiday* (1953), buzzing around on a Vespa? Or Marcello Mastroianni in *La Dolce Vita* (1960)?

The Vespa motor scooter is also a symbol of Italian revival and regeneration. In post–World War II Italy, the brothers Enrico and Armando Piaggio wanted to manufacture a "quick and easy means of transportation" that would also restart their bombed-out factory. They created not only a small, economical scooter, but also a new form of transport that became immensely popular. Italy became known as "Vespa Country," and a new word entered the Italian language, *vespizzare,* to get somewhere on a Vespa. There are even tales of children named Vespino, or "little Vespa."

Prancing Colts

Il cavallino rosso, the high-stepping horse in red, is the symbol of Ferrari, the Italian car that's synonymous with performance, power, and speed. Enzo Ferrari (1888–1988) became a racing driver for Alfa Romeo in 1920 before working as one of their designers. In 1929, he founded the company named after him, launched the famous Ferrari trademark in 1947, and produced a range of high-quality sports and racing cars.

Since the early 1950s Ferraris have won more world championship Grands Prix than any other car. And what better venue to see them than the San Marino Grand Prix, the prestigious Formula One race held every year in the postage stamp–sized state within Italy's borders.

Il Giro d'Italia

Il ciclismo—cycling—is a popular sport in Italy. The Tour of Italy, for instance, is a grueling, month-long bicycle race up and down the mountains of the peninsula that attracts world-class athletes. Italy has many colorful bicyclists, such as Mario "Super Mario" Cipollini and Marco *"Il Pirata"* (the Pirate) Pantini.

Speaking of color, any serious *ciclismo* fan would immediately recognize *celeste Bianchi*—a color halfway between military green and sky blue. The Bianchi bicycle manufacturer, founded over 100 years ago, invented the color that's used on many of their bikes.

Di Interessa

Architect, painter, draftsman ... and bicycle designer? Leonardo da Vinci worked on the design of the bicycle during the 1490s. A crude sketch of a bicycle found in Leonardo's notebooks has been attributed to one of his students but is believed to reflect da Vinci's previous work on the bicycle and its parts. A wooden model of the bicycle can be seen at the Museo Leonardiano in Vinci.

Italian Teatro

The love Italians have for a sporting event is nurtured by the same passion they have for any kind of show, especially if it's theater.

Luigi Pirandello

Considered one of Italy's most prized dramatists during the fascist period between the World Wars, Luigi Pirandello was awarded the Nobel Prize for Literature in 1934.

Born in the ancient city of Agrigento, Sicily, Pirandello was educated at the University of Rome and Bonn. He taught Italian literature from 1897 to 1921 before he was able to devote himself to an exclusively literary career. Pirandello's success rested in his ability to portray the concerns and lives of the lower middle class while delving into the more complex issues of reality, illusion, and disappointment.

Luigi Pirandello's masterpiece, *Six Characters in Search of an Author,* shows six fictional characters who appear on stage searching for their creator. Unfinished and unhappy, the characters invade a rehearsal of another play, insisting on playing out the life they feel is rightfully theirs.

Di Interessa

In the film version of Pirandello's play, Greta Garbo appears in *As You Desire Me* (1932), directed by Georges Fitzmaurice.

Pirandello died in 1936, just two years after he received the Nobel Prize. His plays include *Il piacere dell'onestà (The Pleasures of Honesty;* 1917), *Così è (se vi pare) (Right You Are If You Think So;* 1917),

Enrico IV (*Henry IV;* 1922), and *Come tu mi vuoi* (*As You Desire Me;* 1930). He also wrote the well-known short-story collection *Pensaci, Giacomino* (*Better Think Twice About It;* 1933).

Dario Fo

Another Nobel Prize winner and popular playwright, actor, and director is Dario Fo (1926–). Fo has earned international acclaim for his political satires and ideological attacks on social evils such as capitalism, imperialism, and corruption.

The controversial and charismatic Fo began his career as a live performer in cabaret-style venues that eventually developed into a series of "bourgeois comedies" that mainly poke fun at his middle-class audience. During the 1970s and 1980s under the McClaren Act, Fo was denied a visa to enter the United States due to his political views. Invited by the American Repertory Theater to perform, Fo came to the United States in 1986. Since 1954, he has been married to Franca Rame, his co-star. His plays include *Accidental Death of an Anarchist* and *Orgasmo Adulto Escapes from the Zoo.*

"Italia"

In Italics

1997—Dario Fo is awarded the Nobel Prize for Literature for his cheeky performances while "emulating the jesters of the Middle Ages in scourging authority and upholding the dignity of the downtrodden."

Italy at the Movies

Whether it's a young, sexy starlet or a slap-happy Roberto Benigni, Italian film has contributed widely to international cinema. Cinecittà has produced movies such as *Ben Hur, Cleopatra,* and Sergio Leone's spaghetti westerns. In an interesting twist, the studios were able to accommodate the Italian-American filmmaker Martin Scorsese in the construction of a massive reproduction of nineteenth-century New York for his film *Gangs of New York.*

As you learned in Chapter 20, "Myth and Magic," neorealist cinema emerged with the fall of fascism in the 1940s. Prominent neorealist directors such as Federico Fellini, Roberto Rossellini, and Vittorio De Sica all strived for an almost documentary style, sometimes featuring nonprofessional actors.

Those Wild 1960s

After the low-budget documentary-styled films of the postwar era, directors in the turbulent and troubling 1960s were greatly influenced by the social upheavals affecting Italy and the world at large.

Examples of post-neorealist films include …

➤ *L'Avventura* (1959), *La Notte* (1960), *L'Eclisse* (1962). Michelangelo Antonioni's trilogy about estranged couples and young, hopelessly isolated aristocrats.

➤ *Fellini Satyricon* (1969). A decade before *Caligula,* Federico Fellini crafted this visually stunning look at the decadence and debauchery of Ancient Rome. Based on contemporary accounts, the succession of bizarre beings, orgiastic lifestyles, and amoral attitudes reflects Fellini's views of 1960s youth.

➤ *Death in Venice* (1971). Visconti's brilliant version of Thomas Mann's classic story. A jaded, middle-aged composer on holiday in Venice spots a handsome young boy on the beach. His doomed obsession with the youth renews his interest in living.

Examples of films from this time period include …

➤ *Il Conformista* (1970). Bernardo Bertolucci directed this film about a weak-willed man who becomes a fascist flunky and goes abroad to arrange the assassination of his old teacher, now a political dissident.

➤ *Criso Si È Fermato a Eboli* (1978). Directed by Francesco Rosi. The anti-fascist doctor and painter Carlo Levi is confined to house arrest in a small town during the dark years of fascism.

➤ *Kaos* (1984). Directed by brothers Paolo and Vittorio Taviani. Part fairy tale, part pagan romp, these are five stories by author-playwright Luigi Pirandello. This look at peasant life in turn-of-the-century Sicily ranges from the comedic to the Gothic.

> ## "*Italia*"
>
> ### In Italics
>
> The first feature film in Italy, *La Presa di Roma, 20 settembre 1870,* was shown in 1905 and directed by Filoteo Alberini. The tracking shot was pioneered on the set of Giovanni Pastrone's film *Cabiria* (1914). The intertitles (they didn't have talkies yet) were written by the popular soldier-poet Gabriele D'Annunzio.

Pier Paolo Pasolini

The filmmaker Pier Paolo Pasolini (1922–1975) remains one of Italy's most controversial filmmakers. A politically radical homosexual, Pasolini's filmmaking reflected his perspective on life that blended Marxism, Catholicism, and neorealism.

Pasolini's erotic adaptations of well-known stories are best exemplified in the films *The Decameron* (1970), *The Canterbury Tales* (1971), and *Arabian Nights* (1974).

➤ *Teorema* **(1969).** Is wanderer Terence Stamp, who moves into a middle-class Milan household, a messenger from Heaven or Hell? You decide in this offbeat drama about how the stranger's presence affects those he meets.

➤ *The Gospel According to St. Matthew* **(1964).** A totally original filmed version of the story of Jesus, Pasolini combines nonprofessional actors, magnificent Italian locales, and a stirring classical score for a moving and surprisingly reverent biographical drama.

➤ *The Canterbury Tales* **(1971).** The bawdy humor your English Lit teacher played down is brought back in full force in this quartet of stories, centering around religious hypocrisy and sexual misadventures. Pasolini himself appears as author Geoffrey Chaucer.

Lina Wertmüller

The films made by the Italian filmmaker Lina Wertmüller (1928–) are best characterized by controversial and passionate characters and complicated sexual issues. Born Arcangela Felice Assunta Wertmüller Von Elgg in Rome, Wertmüller worked as a teacher before studying at the Theater Academy. In the 1950s, she worked as a writer, director, and stage actress. Her big break in cinema came when the actor Marcello Mastroianni introduced her to Federico Fellini. She worked as an assistant in his critically acclaimed movie $8^1/_2$ (1963). That same year, Wertmüller wrote her first film, *The Lizards*.

Wertmüller's reputation grew as her films gained more renown. *The Seduction of Mimi* (1972) won her a Best Director award at the Cannes Film Festival. Others of her movies include the powerful film *Love and Anarchy* (1973) starring Giancarlo Giannini, who also appeared in Wertmüller's powerful film *Swept Away,* costarring Mariangela Melato.

Italian Movie Directory

The prestigious *Mostra Internazionale d'Arte Cinematografica* (Venice Film Festival) occurs every September for two weeks and includes filmmakers from all over the world. This brief and incomplete list of contemporary Italian films run the gamut from serious to comedic and serve as an excellent beginning for your Italian film journey. Subtitled or dubbed, they're all great *divertimento*.

The Night of the Shooting Stars (1982)

Il Nuovo Cinema Paradiso (1989)

Mediterraneo (1991)

Johnny Stecchino (1993)

Ciao Professore! (1994)

L'Uomo delle stelle (1994)

Il Postino (1995)

La Vita È Bella (1998)

English Language Movies

These films are either about Italy, set in Italy, or about Italian Americans. And don't forget all those Sergio Leone spaghetti westerns!

A Room with a View (1986)

Moonstruck (1987)

Where Angels Fear to Tread (1992)

Big Night (1996)

Stealing Beauty (1996)

A Midsummer Night's Dream (1999)

The Talented Mr. Ripley (1999)

Tea with Mussolini (1999)

Di Interessa

Who could not fall in love with the expressive Giancarlo Giannini, whose ability to project powerful emotions on the screen moves the viewer in films such as *Le Sette Bellezze* (1976), *Love and Anarchy* (1973), *The Seduction of Mimi* (1972), and *Swept Away* (1975), all directed by another of Italy's great directors, Lena Wertmüller.

The Least You Need to Know

➤ *Carnevale* is celebrated in many ways throughout Italy.

➤ Italians are fanatical about soccer, the national sport.

➤ The Siena Palio is a historic horse race held annually in the town square.

➤ Two of Italy's greatest playwrights, Dario Fo and Luigi Pirandello, won the Nobel Prize for Literature.

Spaghetti Doesn't Grow on Trees

As a child, I really believed that spaghetti grew on trees. I imagined the long strands as they hung off tree branches like the wilted leaves of a weeping willow. Now I know better, and I've learned a few other things along the way.

Food. Everyone loves it, and we all need its nourishing ingredients to survive. When you put an Italian in the kitchen, survival is brought to a new level of art where simple wholesome ingredients are transformed into the favorite *piatti* (dishes) you love so much.

In this chapter, you'll learn more about the subject of food. You'll learn a few terms that will help you decipher an Italian menu. You'll get a crash course on the virtues of *olio d'oliva*. You'll be offered a little lesson on pasta and given recipes you can try at home whenever you feel like eating Italian like the Italians do.

Buon Appetito!

Italian food is as varied as the Italian landscape. Unless you grew up on Mars, you are familiar with a few Italian foods like spaghetti with *pomodoro* sauce, pizza, and cappuccino. Other Italian delicacies may become newly acquired tastes and include salty anchovies, fried *calamari* (squid), artichoke hearts, sausage made from *cinghiale* (wild boar), or the earthly treasure *tartufo* (truffle), a seasonal delight. The enjoyment of a meal is a combination of fresh ingredients, fine wine, and warm hospitality.

Italian hospitality at its best.

(Photo by Anna Andersson)

La Bella Lingua

Pomodoro (tomato) comes from the French words *pomme* ("fruit"—although it is often translated as "apple") and *d'oro* ("of gold"), describing the golden fruit grown in South America and brought back to Europe by traders. It was commonly believed that the sometimes acidic tomatoes were poisonous unless cooked for several hours. Today, we know this is not true, but the myth continues.

Interestingly enough, the order of an Italian meal is just as important as the combination of ingredients used. The same regional differences found in language are found in the *cucina*. And if you are a vegetarian, you'll find lots of options in Italian cuisine. After you order your *primo piatto* (first course), instead of ordering a *secondo piatto* (second course), try having an extra *contorno* (side dish) or a serving of *formaggio* (cheese).

Italians eat their food *alla carta*, one plate at a time.

➤ *L'antipasto* (the appetizer) literally means "before the meal." A typical *antipasto* can be *una bruschetta* (toasted bread with various spreads), or it might be a light Caprese (tomato and mozzarella salad with basil and drizzled with olive oil). (*Psst!* Italians generally save their *insalata* [salad] for after the meal.)

➤ *Il primo piatto* (the first course) is usually a pasta or rice dish. Some menu items include *gnocchi al sugo di pomodoro* (potato dumplings with tomato sauce), *linguine alle vongole* (linguine in clam sauce), *tortellini prosciutto e piselli* (tortellini with prosciutto and peas), and *zuppa di verdura toscana* (Tuscan country soup).

➤ *Il secondo piatto* (the second course) is your protein, usually meat, poultry, or fish. Some favorites are *pollo al limone* (lemon chicken), *ossobuco alla milanese* (veal shank with lemon, garlic, and parsley), *calamari alla marinara* (squid in tomato sauce), and *coda di rospo con carciofi* (monkfish with artichokes).

➤ *Il contorno* is a side dish or *antipasto*. Popular menu items include *insalata mista* (mixed salad), *finocchi al cartoccio* (baked fennel), and *formaggi vari* (varied cheeses).

Il Vino

Wine, the nectar of the gods, is generally consumed as part of the meal but a glass sipped during twilight in good company for pleasure's sake is also part of the Italian tradition.

In Italics

1533—Catherine de' Medici arrived from Florence to marry the heir to the French throne; she brought with her a number of chefs and pastry cooks, thus introducing the French courts to the joys of eating Italian food. So enamored were the French with the Italian recipes, they were soon modified and fed back to the world on silver spoons.

Italy is well known for its vineyards and fine wines.

(Photo by Anna Andersson)

Choosing a Wine

While wine experts may help you figure out the fine points of Italian wines and wine culture, you don't need to be an expert in order to savor a rich Chianti Classico

Riserva with your *bistecca alla fiorentina,* or sip a glass of Prosecco (an Italian sparkling wine) to refresh your palate and get your mouth tingling.

La Bella Lingua

If you want to know what to ask for when ordering your favorite vino, here's a miniature Italian lesson.

red wine il vino rosso

white wine il vino bianco (pronounced *bee-ahn-koh*)

rosé wine il vino rosè

dry wine il vino secco

sweet wine il vino dolce

sparkling wine lo spumante

Red or white? Many people have an innate preference and will drink whatever type of wine they prefer with every cuisine. However, some people think that red wine generally goes well with *la carne* such as beef, duck, and lamb. Affordable red wines you'll easily find include Amarone, Barbaresco, Barbera, Bardolino, Barollo, Brunello di Montalcino, Chianti, Dolcetto, Franciacorta, Grignolino, and Lambrusco.

Many people prefer to pair white wine with fish, poultry, and vegetables. Some whites include Bianco di Pitigliano, Bianco Vergine di Valdichiana, Cinque Terre, Ciro, Colli Albani, Est Moscato d'Asti, Pinot Grigio, Verdicchio, and Vernaccia.

Reading the Label

If you want to take your Italian wine tasting to the next level, begin with the label. Most Italian labels offer the following information:

➤ The name written in big letters across the top is generally the winery or the wine's trademark name, such as Antinori, Brunello, or Villa d'Este.

➤ In slightly smaller letters beneath the wine's name comes the appellation. This describes the region where the grapes were grown such as Chianti, a region in

Tuscany. Wines that meet established standards generally have the words *"Denominazione della Origine Controllata"* (DOC) written below the appellation. Other wines are simply classified as vino da tavola (table wine); these range in quality and are served by many restaurants as *il vino della casa* (the house wine).

➤ The vintage is the year in which the grapes were harvested. In Italian, the word for vintage is *Vendemmia*.

➤ Below the *vendemmia* date is the winery information, which describes where the wine was bottled.

Di Interessa

One of Italy's most popular cocktails, a Bellini, was created by Giuseppe Cipriani of Harry's Bar in Venice.

$^2/_3$ cup (160 ml.) of peach puree
1 tsp. raspberry puree
1 bottle Prosecco (or Asti Spumante or champagne)

In every glass pour 7 teaspoons of peach puree. Add 2 to 3 drops of the raspberry puree. Add the sparkling wine and serve.

Olive Olives

The healthy properties—internal and external—of olive oil are well noted. Until recently, many Italian women used an emulsion of lemon juice and olive oil to keep their skin smooth.

Today, olive oil generally is used in the kitchen. If you have ever wondered what the difference is between all the different brands, read on for a brief summary.

➤ **Extra virgin olive oil.** The result of the first cold-pressing of the olive, extra virgin is the finest and fruitiest of the oils (and the most expensive). Best on salads and when you want the distinctive flavor of olives, it can range in color from gold to green.

➤ **Virgin olive oil.** Also a first-press oil, virgin is considered a notch down from extra virgin due to its slightly higher acidity. Good for cooking.

➤ **Olive oil.** Generally a blend of extra virgin and virgin oils. It can contain refined olive oil in addition to cold-pressed and may contain the oil of several different harvests. Olive oil burns at a higher temperature than other conventional cooking oils, making it ideal for frying.

Olive oil should be stored in a cool, dark place for up to six months.

Favorite Foods: Pasta and Pizza

The love affair the world has with Italian food is not an accident. We're all human, and regardless of taste, there are certain things that just about everyone likes. Pizza and pasta are two of them.

"Italia"

In Italics

1701—The rules of kashrut (eating kosher) set Jews apart from Christians, even in Italy. In 1701, an edict issued in Reggio Emilia prohibited Christians from "receiving and eating the unleavened bread of the Jews."

"Italia"

In Italics

Seventeenth century—Prior to the fifteenth century, most food was eaten with the hands or from the point of a knife. Although it did not become commonly used until the seventeenth century, it appears the Napoletani created the four-pronged fork to aid them in eating spaghetti.

Pizza

There's a funny story about an Italian who comes to America and orders a pizza. He's feeling generous and decides to take his friends out for a meal. When it comes time to order, the Italian asks each friend what he would like on his pizza. One says he'd like peppers, the second mentions broccoli, a third asks for mushrooms. So the Italian orders three pizzas for his friends. When the pizzas come out of the oven, the Italian is astounded. These pizzas are *enorme,* he exclaims. Each one is big enough to feed a family!

The reason for his confusion is simple. Italians eat their own plate-sized pizzas, each one just big enough for one person, and they do so using a knife and fork. In Italy you can also purchase pizza by the pound (or in Italy's case, the *etto*—a hectogram, which is about $^1/_4$ pound). This type of pizza is what Americans often refer to as Sicilian pizza, a thicker crusted pizza that is baked on large trays and is then sliced into rectangles.

How to Eat Spaghetti

Put down the spoon, America. Italians wind their spaghetti onto their forks.

When cooking pasta, remember not to overcook it! It should be *al dente* that the long and super thin *capellini* (angel hair) should be served with a light and thin sauce. Thicker pastas such as ziti are best with heavier sauces.

Di Interessa

The Pasta Museum is located in Rome at:

> Piazza Scanderbeg, 117
> 00187 Rome
> Telephone: 39.06.6991109 (when calling from the United States, dial 011 first, then the number)
> Fax: 39.06.6991109

If you can't make it to Rome this week, visit the museum's Web site at www. pastainmuseum.com.

Many names of pastas and foods in Italian are simply descriptions. For example, the word *spaghetti* comes from the word *spago* meaning "string." Here are some other examples:

➤ **Conchiglie.** "Shells" hold onto the sauce.

➤ **Farfalle.** "Butterflies" are the same as bowties and add a festive element to the table.

➤ **Fettuccine.** "Small ribbons" are great with cheese sauces.

➤ **Fusilli.** The long, twisted "spindles" are wonderful with any sauce.

➤ **Lasagna.** "Lasanium" is Latin for pot, describing how this wide band of pasta is generally prepared.

➤ **Linguini.** "Little tongues" are great with any sauce.

➤ **Manicotti.** "Cooked hands" refers to the stuffed pockets of pasta that are filled with meats and cheeses.

➤ **Orecchiette.** "Little ears" serve like tiny spoons to collect the sauce.

➤ **Penne.** "Quills" look just like tubes.

➤ **Rigatoni.** "Ridged" pasta has grooves and work with all sauces.

➤ **Tagliatelle.** "Ribbons" of pasta.

➤ **Vermicelli.** "Little worms" make for a terrific snack.

➤ **Ziti.** "Bridegrooms" are good for a party or anytime.

If you really want to learn about pasta, try visiting the Pasta Museum in Rome; it's the only one of its kind in the world. It contains exhibitions on the history of pasta, examples of the machinery used in manufacture, and documentation on the evolution of pasta from an economic and industrial point of view.

The museum also has important documents that date to 1154, demonstrating that the method of producing and preserving pasta was discovered in the twelfth century in as many as four different regions of Italy.

Il Caffè

When Venetian traders introduced coffee to Europe, little did they know they would be creating a fad that has spread to every corner of the globe. In Italy, coffee is consumed at *il bar*. Traditionally, Italians drink their coffee standing up (*in piedi*). Always expect to pay more once you sit down for service.

There are a few different ways coffee is served in Italy. *Espresso* is what gets Italians started in the morning. *Espresso lungo* refers to a watered-down version of an *espresso* and is what you should ask for if you prefer the weaker coffee consumed in North America. It's opposite is *espresso ristretto,* about the consistency of rocket fuel with just as much punch. *Caffè Hag* is the equivalent of Sanka and decaffeinated.

Italian Food Facts

Simple ingredients yield great results in the right hands. A few food facts will take you a long way.

➤ Italians drink cappuccino as a morning beverage or sometimes as a pick-me-up during the afternoon. They prefer drinking a shot of *espresso* after a meal, sometimes accompanied by a *digestivo* (digestive) such as the artichoke-based liquore Cynar, or with a snifter of Sambucca.

➤ The term *pastasciutta* ("dry pasta") is the affectionate name used by Italians to describe the box of Barilla or De Cecco or Ronzoni pasta you have up on your shelf.

➤ *Al dente* (to the teeth) is the Italian term describing perfectly cooked pasta. Never overcook your pasta! Better that it be slightly chewy than mushy.

➤ Spaghetti sauce (with meat) is referred to as either the Spaghetti alla Bolognese sauce or ragù.

➤ Italians never order "spaghetti and meatballs." If anything, they order *polpette* (meatballs) as a main course. As a rule, they do not eat fried mozzarella sticks, veal parmigiano, or Italian dressing on their salads.

➤ Italians "dress" their salads with salt, pepper, balsamic vinegar, and olive oil.

➤ In lieu of tips, most Italian restaurants charge a *coperta* for your service and bread.

Good Health Comes First

Fast-food restaurants, frozen food, and microwave cooking are all present in Italy today, and all contrary to a culinary tradition with the popular proverb: *A tavola non si invecchia*—"You never age at the dinner table."

To counteract this distasteful trend, the Slow Food Movement was started in Italy during the 1980s. Essentially, "slow foods" are traditional, fresh, made from local ingredients, and served during leisurely meals. The emphasis is on the pleasure of eating, the companionship of friends and family sitting around the table, and enjoying the company of others while dining on delicious foods and wines.

Italians interested in the environment and the nutritional value of their food have also recently battled against "Frankenfoods," genetically modified foods with many unknown effects. In this case, they've even had public demonstrations to protest against a technology that threatens a centuries-old heritage of food and wine.

Plan a Meal

A book about Italy would not be complete without a few recipes. There are dozens of wonderfully illustrated, glossy-paged recipe books at a bookstore near you. Much of Italian food happens by accident; you look in the refrigerator and see what you have. Often spontaneous, the one magic ingredient is olive oil, a key element in the Mediterranean diet. After that, nothing beats a vine-ripened *pomodoro* drizzled with olive oil.

Italian food is about fresh ingredients and color. The following recipes can be prepared separately or be made into one meal.

Risotto

$1^2/_3$ cups uncooked Arborio rice

1 dash (about a tablespoon) olive oil

6 tablespoons butter

1 small cup onion

1 to 2 chopped garlic cloves

$^2/_3$ cup dry white wine

5 cups chicken or vegetable boiling stock

$^3/_4$ cup grated parmesan cheese

salt and pepper

1. Fry onions and garlic in 4 tablespoons of butter until soft, and then add rice. Cook until grains are coated in oil and beginning to color.

2. Add wine and simmer until it is thoroughly absorbed.

3. Add boiling stock 1 cup at a time. Continue cooking and stirring until liquid is absorbed.

4. Gradually stir in remaining broth 1 cup at a time, cooking and stirring until liquid is absorbed before adding the next cup.

5. When all of the stock is absorbed, the rice should be tender, not soft or soggy. Add parmesan and butter, oil, and seasonings, and simmer for a minute more.

6. Cover the saucepan tightly and let stand for five minutes off the heat and serve immediately.

Pot Roast Leg of Lamb

Serves 4

Preheat oven 350°F.

$3^{1}/_{2}$ pounds leg of lamb

4 to 5 sprigs fresh rosemary

3 slices of bacon

4 tablespoons olive oil

3 to 4 garlic cloves, crushed

2 onions, sliced

2 celery sticks, sliced

1 to $1^{1}/_{2}$ cups dry white wine

1 tablespoon tomato paste

$1^{1}/_{2}$ cups stock

12 ounces tomatoes, peeled, quartered and seeded

1 tablespoon freshly chopped parsley

1 tablespoon freshly chopped marjoram

salt and pepper

1. Trim off any excess fat on lamb and season with salt and pepper, rubbing well into meat. Lay sprigs of rosemary (leaving some for the garnish) over lamb and cover with bacon. Tie everything with a string to hold it all together.

2. Heat the olive oil in a skillet and fry the lamb, turning over until brown. Remove lamb from pan.

3. Transfer the oil from the skillet into a fireproof casserole. Fry the garlic and onions together for three to four minutes. Add carrots and celery and cook for a few minutes longer.

4. Lay the lamb on top of the vegetables. Pour the wine over the lamb, and add the tomato paste. Simmer for four to five minutes more. Add stock, tomatoes, herbs, and seasoning. Bring to boil for three to four minutes.

5. Cover casserole tightly and cook for about 2 to $2^1/_2$ hours in the oven, until the lamb is very tender.

6. Remove lamb from the casserole, take off bacon and herbs, with the string. Strain the juices, skimming any fat. Serve separately. The vegetables may be put around the meat. Garnish with rosemary.

Coffee Granite

$^1/_2$ cup sugar

4 cups strong hot coffee or espresso

whipped cream

Pour sugar and coffee into a shallow metal baking pan and freeze, stirring every half-hour until mixture is a coarse ice mixture (about three to four hours). Scoop into a bowl and top with whipped cream or *crema. Buon appetito!*

The Art of Eating Well

The Art of Eating Well by Pellegrino Artusi (1894) is considered the great-grandfather of all Italian cookbooks.

Artusi was a chef, storyteller, and host who hobnobbed with the popular figures of the times. Filled with recipes that range from simple stews to fabulous desserts, the delights presented throughout its pages will please anyone who loves Italian food. This easy recipe (excerpted from the Random House translation) was offered to readers without specific quantities; just use your better discretion, and add a pinch of this, a drop of that, and enjoy:

ZUPPA SANTE'

This soup is prepared using whatever vegetables are in season such as cabbage, carrots, garden sorrel, celery, and winter celery. Julienne the cabbage and heat it over the fire, then squeeze it dry. The carrots and the celery should be cut into inch long strips. Trim the stems of the garden sorrel, and set all the vegetables to cook in a pot with a bit of butter, seasoning them lightly with salt and pepper. Once the greens have absorbed the butter, add broth and simmer till done. Meantime, take good quality day old bread, dice it, and fry the pieces in butter, oil, or lard. Make sure the fat is hot before you add the bread, or the bread will absorb it. Put the bread in the tureen, pour the broth and vegetables over it, and serve the soup.

There are many Italian expressions related to food, some of which are quite clever. As an antipasto to whet your appetite, here are a few:

Italian	English
bere come una spugna	drink like a sponge
di bocca buona	a good mouth (a good eater)
di pasta buona	of good pasta (good natured)
dire pane al pane e vino al vino	to call bread, bread and wine, wine (to call a spade a spade)
essere un sacco di patate	to be a sack of potatoes (boring!)
In vino veritas.	In wine there is truth.
liscio come l'olio	smooth as oil
mangiare pane e cipolla	to eat bread and onion (to live on bread and water)
una cilegia tira l'altra	one cherry pulls the other (one thing leads to another)

The Least You Need to Know

➤ Food is a national obsession in Italy.

➤ Italian food is made from fresh, wholesome ingredients.

➤ The Italian way of life is linked to their inherent knowledge of how to eat and drink well.

➤ Regional culinary differences enrich the Italian palate.

➤ Wine and olive oil have been essential to the Italian diet since the Roman era.

➤ Pizza and pasta are big Italian favorites worldwide, but there is a huge variety of regional foods and delicious local specialties.

Chapter 23

Mamma and the Madonna

In This Chapter

➤ The history of women in Italy

➤ Women during the Renaissance

➤ The Modern woman

➤ Mamma Mia!

Italian women are body builders and biochemists, physicists and journalists, tennis players and poets, playwrights and professors. Young women today live very different lives than their grandmothers did, and a great deal of this has to do with some of the trailblazers whose contributions to Italian society are outlined in this chapter. To see how far Italian women have come, it's necessary to understand where they are coming from. To do so, let's go back in time, to the Romans.

There's an Exception to Every Rule

During the period of the Roman Republic, few women had any political rights. They were not allowed to vote, directly address the Senate, or hang out in the forum. But some women did hold power, including the vestal virgins.

Chosen from Rome's finest families, a vestal began her service between the ages of 6 and 10. After being selected, in a long ceremony, the young girl was escorted to the home of the vestals behind the Temple where her hair was shorn (similar to nuns), her body draped in white, and a new name taken. The vestals' most important job was to keep the sacred flame of Rome burning day and night. Young vestals apprenticed with older vestals, and each girl had a specific task.

Their power and influence in Rome was great and they could testify in court, accept legacies, and bequeath their belongings in wills. Unlike other women of the time, the vestals were not bound to the *patria potestas* (paternal power). The only catch was that the vestals had to remain virgins, devoting their bodies and souls to Rome.

Although a rare occurrence, if a vestal was caught breaking the sacred law, she would be buried alive with a day's worth of food and water.

After having completed the typical term of service (30 years), vestals maintained their prestige and position in Roman society and were free to marry if they chose to do so.

During the Middle Ages, few women were able to gain the respect and admiration that was given to the Vestals. As you may recall from Chapter 7, "The Medieval Minestrone," St. Clare of Assisi (c. 1194–1253) stands out as an exception when she was able to convince the popes to create a separate Franciscan order for women who wanted to devote themselves to God. In any case, very few women owned land and none were allowed to vote.

Di Interessa

The *Atrium Vestæ* (House of the Vestal Virgins) is located in Rome's Forum, just a stone's throw from the Coliseum. In it, the headless statues of the priestesses encircle a small garden.

Renaissance Women

In Chapter 12, "*Putti*, Painters, and the Arts," you learned that the Renaissance was a time of dramatic change and reformation, a "rebirth" of art and culture in Italy. Among the issues discussed at the patron of the arts Lorenzo de' Medici's roundtable of thinkers, artists, and writers, the humanists struggled with the definition of the perfect woman. Should she be chaste as the Virgin Mother herself or as fertile as the idealized female depicted in the luscious paintings of Titian's *Venus*? Read on to learn more about these Renaissance women.

Isabella d'Este: First Lady of the Renaissance

Born in Ferrara, Isabella d'Este (1474–1539) has a name that sings of royalty. As you may remember from Chapter 11, "Strange Bedfellows," Isabella was an important patron of the arts whose influence on Renaissance culture was profound. (If you find yourself in Italy, visit the beautiful Villa d'Este in Tivoli.)

By the time Isabella was 16, she was fluent in Latin and Greek, well-versed in the writings of Plato and Aristotle, and married to Francesco Gonzaga. After the death of her husband, her success as duchy was undoubtedly a result of her ability to act firmly and make sound decisions, the true qualities of a leader.

An avid musician, Isabella's preference for stringed instruments may have led to the use of the *viola* as a consort instrument. She died in Mantua in 1539 after having collected numerous bronzes, instruments, and a globe she apparently used to track Columbus's voyages across *l'Atlantico*.

This fountain located in Rome's Piazza Navona depicts woman as delightfully effervescent.

(Photo by Anna Andersson)

Caterina de' Medici (Catherine de' Medici)

A great patron of the arts, Catherine de' Medici (1519–1589), was daughter of Lorenzo de' Medici, the duke of Urbino, and Catherine of Bourbon. In 1533, she married the duke d'Orléans, who became king of France in 1547 as Henry II. Catherine was queen of France (1547–1559) and mother of the last three Valois kings of France. She had little power during the reign of her husband and that of her first son,

Francis II, but on Francis's death in 1560, the government fell entirely into her hands. She was a major force in French politics during the 30 years of Roman Catholic–Huguenot wars. She ruled as regent for her second son, Charles IX, until he reached his majority in 1563, and she continued to dominate his policies for the duration of his reign.

Apart from her political role, Catherine loved pretty things, interesting people, and good words. She funded a new wing in the Louvre Museum and initiated construction of the Tuileries Gardens and the Château of Monceau. Her renowned personal library contained rare manuscripts.

Biografia

Elena Lucrezia Piscopia Cornaro (1646–1684) was a noble Venetian woman with the distinction of being the first Italian woman to earn a doctorate in philosophy, which she received from the University of Padua on June 25, 1678. Cornaro was widely respected for her academic discourses, translations, and writings.

Lucrezia, Lucrezia

To some, the name Lucrezia Borgia (1480–1514) conjures up images of a beautiful, heartless, rapacious, carnal, and treacherous femme fatale dancing through the popular consciousness. As you may recall from Chapter 11, Lucrezia's father arranged three marriages for her and while Lucrezia's reputation for foulness achieved mythic proportions, the facts are much less scandalous. Once she inherited the duchy of Ferrara, Lucrezia became one of the most influential patrons of the Italian Renaissance.

Incredible Artist Types

Where there are patrons, there must be artists. Men were getting most of the limelight, but not all of it. The examples of Isabella, Catherine, and Lucrezia set the stage for future generations to make their mark and included painters like Artemesia Gentileschi and Francesca Caccini.

Artemisia Gentileschi

Born in Rome, the Baroque painter Artemisia Gentileschi (1593–1652) was one of the few well-known female artists whose work drew heavily from the techniques used by the artist Caravaggio. The daughter of painter Orazio Gentileschi, Artemisia's bold strokes and accomplished use of *chiaroscuro* gave allegorical works such as *Judith Beheading Holofernes* (1620, Uffizi Gallery, Florence) a dramatic realism. Artemisia's studies continued with a friend of her father, Agostino Tassi, whose actions off canvas led to a scandalous trial whereby the teacher was convicted of having assaulted Artemisia during their lessons.

The trial was a humiliating and scandalous public event that marred Artemisia's reputation as both a woman and an artist. Nevertheless, soon after the trial, Artemisia married a Florentine painter with whom she enjoyed the support of the Medici family among others. In 1616, she became an official member of the *Academie del Disegno*, Florence's prestigious artist academy where she became friends with Galileo Galilei. Today, Artemisia is appreciated as both an artist and an early feminist.

Francesca Caccini

Francesca Caccini (1587–1640) was born in Florence, the eldest daughter of composer Giulio Caccini and wife Lucia, a singer. Francesca enjoyed all the privileges of being born into a famous musical family and growing up in the resplendent Medici court of Florence. Similar to Artemesia, Francesca was taught primarily by her musical father. The young Caccini was encouraged from an early age to participate in the musical entertainment at the Medici court, where she spent most of her life.

Francesca is best known for pieces such as *La Liberazione di Ruggiero* (*The Liberation of Ruggiero;* 1625). She participated in early seventeenth-century operas as both performer and composer. In addition, she published a collection of her own works.

Santa Caterina da Siena

Another prominent female figure during the Renaissance was the Dominican nun St. Catherine of Siena (1347–1380). At the age of six, Catherine—the twenty-fifth child of a wool dyer—claimed to have the first out of many mystical experiences. By the time she was 16, Caterina Benincasa (as she was called before being canonized) had taken an oath of chastity and joined the Third Order of St. Dominic in Siena where spent her time reading, praying, and writing.

Catherine lived during very troubled times. When the Black Death struck in 1374, wiping out almost half of Siena, Catherine remained behind to nurse the sick. The following year, Catherine received the *stigmata*—the five wounds of Christ.

Over time, Catherine's strong opinions, expressed through numerous letters and tracts, made her a prominent leader of the times. Accompanied by a group of followers known as the Caterinati, Catherine made many journeys up to the seat of the papacy in Avignon to persuade Pope Gregory XI to return the papacy from Avignon to Rome. As you may recall from Chapter 8, "Popes, Politics, and Power," upon Gregory's death in 1378, two popes were elected; Catherine supported the Roman pontiff Urban VI against Clement VII of Avignon.

La Bella Lingua

The **stigmata** are marks on the hands and feet that resemble Jesus Christ's crucifixion and can include holes through the wrists and feet, wounds on the forehead, whiplashes on the back, and a spear wound in the side.

253

Almost eighty years after her death, Catherine was canonized in 1461. Today, Italians and Catholics invoke St. Catherine against fire, bodily ills, miscarriages, nurses, and temptations.

Di Interessa

Wealthy widows during the Renaissance were well taken care of by the *commune*. A special investment fund was instituted to ensure a widow might continue to live in the manner to which she was accustomed even after the death of her husband, and performed a service similar to today's life insurance.

Di Interessa

Guests at the wedding feast of Lorenzo de' Medici and Catherine of Bourbon were noted as having consumed 800 calves, 5,000 pounds of sweet-meats, 4,000 hens, and 100 kegs of wine a day for the three–day event.

It's the Convent for You, Young Lady

Catherine's efforts were due, in part, to the fact that she was well read and able to express her message with the diplomacy and insight necessary to sway the Pope's opinion, impossible without the education she received while living in the convent.

The women living in the convents served many functions; they received orphans such as Florence's *Ospedale degli Innocenti* (and a magnificent example of the architect Filippo Brunelleschi's work). They housed collections of books and music. They grew gardens. They prayed. They offered shelter, and sometimes, they became a solution to the growing challenge facing many fathers who lacked the assets to properly dower their daughters in marriage.

One such example was the Ortobello of Florence, a secular organization founded around 1370 to provide free housing to large numbers of older laywomen. (In Italian, the word *ortobello* means "beautiful garden," describing the typical garden grown by the nuns in convents.) The Ortobello served as an asylum for widows and also women with children. What made it exceptional was the fact that, unlike other church-sponsored hospices in Venice and Siena (where the decisions were made by men), the Ortobello was primarily run by women for women.

Won't You Marry Me?

Until recently, marriage has probably been the single most important event in a woman's life, but not necessarily for romantic reasons. Possessing very little authority, legal or otherwise, a woman's power was attached to her husband's position in society. As you just learned in Lucrezia Borgia's case, her father (the pope) used her to form political alliances.

A family of good name might use their daughter to gain the pockets of someone's son. As such, women were the key to success and social mobility. The arrangement of marriages is seen by scholars to be the exchange and transfer of economic and political power. When Caterina de' Medici married into the French courts, she brought the Medici name with her. As a result, preparing a woman for the big day was something that started early on.

Dowry

If you wanted to play, you had to pay, and a woman's dowry determined whether she would be sitting in the front row or high up in the balustrade. Most well-to-do men invested in a state dowry fund; like a bond, it accumulated interest until such time as it was needed by his precious sweetheart. If he had too many daughters, he might send most of them to a convent in order not to spread the money out too thin.

An Italian woman's dowry was mostly cash, but the jewelry, clothes, and silver she kept in a *cassone* (wedding chest) were counted as well. During the Renaissance, a decent dowry for a merchant's daughter was in the 1,000 florin range. To give you an idea of how much buying power that signifies, consider these numbers:

female slave	50 florins
house rental for one year	25 florins
¹/₄ share in wool or silk business	1,500 florins

La Bella Lingua

The Italian word *nubile* refers to an unmarried, "nubile" woman. Bachelors, on the other hand, are referred to as *celibe* (celibate).

Biografia

The Italian porn star and politico Cicciolina is the radical ex-wife of American artist Jeff Koons. Cicciolina became famous during her campaign for a seat in Italy's Lower House where she was a parliament member from 1987 to 1992.

Women for Hire

Toward the end of the Italian Renaissance, woman slowly began to gain respect in the arts and professions, but they needed to be both gifted and very lucky to overcome the daily prejudices of life. Female artists and scientists were often wealthy in their own right and had the means to provide themselves with paint and canvas. This was not the case for most women, however.

The Courtesan

One of the most prominent features of Venice in the seventeenth century was the courtesan, a type of upper-class prostitute, renowned for her extreme beauty and lavish clothing. Venetian courtesans of this period weren't your average prostitutes—many were wealthy members of society. Some were kept by nobles and thus had extravagant homes and clothing fit for royalty. Others were shrewd businesswomen, having a different client every night of the week and making more money than the average merchant did.

As companions for bankers, princes, prelates, and merchants, the courtesans were known for their wit, charm, and elegance. They wrote novels, published poems, and influenced politics, often delivering political messages from pillow to pillow.

Veronica Franco is perhaps the best-known courtesan of the Renaissance. Depicted by the Renaissance painters Jacopo Tintoretto and Moretto da Brescia, this hall-of-famer helped relations between Venice and France by bedding the King of France. Her life was depicted in the 1998 film *Dangerous Beauty* (directed by Marshall Herskovitz).

As courtesans began to establish themselves as escorts to the VIP's of the Renaissance, their styles of dress began to resemble that of noblewomen; and why not? They made the money and enjoyed court life just as much as any aristocrat. As a result of mounting pressure from "honest" women, sumptuary laws forbid courtesans from wearing pearls, the distinguishing quality of a lady.

Di Interessa

To learn more about an organization devoted to highlighting the accomplishments, history, and culture of women of Italian ancestry, contact:

The National Organization of Italian American Women
445 West 59th Street, Suite 1248
New York, NY 10019
212-237-8574
www.noiaw.com

You've Come a Long Way, *Bambina*

An Italian woman living today might easily take for granted her right to vote, own land, or participate in politics. Only a few years ago, life in villages and small towns had the average Italian woman living under close scrutiny by family members. Her acquaintances and her dates were selected and chaperoned. (This is still true in parts of the south and Sicily.)

In addition to being loyal mothers, the twentieth century saw Italian women emerge in contemporary society as dynamic, attractive, and educated, effective in professional life as successful politicians, doctors, lawyers, writers, teachers, and entrepreneurs. Today, women in Italy can belong to any number of organizations dedicated to the advancement of women in the world, including the *La Federazione Italiana Donne Arti Professioni Affari* (FIDAPA; The Italian Federation of Business and Professional Women), a satellite of the International Federation of Business and Professional Women.

I Am Woman, I Am *Forte*

If you were having a dinner party and could invite anyone, past or present, dead or alive, you might consider having one or a few of these outstanding and versatile contemporary women come to the table.

The Muse of Duse

The actress Eleonora Duse (1858–1924) was considered one of the leading ladies of her time and was known for her ability to evoke powerful emotions in her audiences. A contemporary to the French actress Sarah Bernhardt, Duse first appeared in Naples in the French play by Émile Augiuer in *Les Fourchambault* (*The House of Fourchambault*) in 1878. With Cesare Rossi, she toured the world, including appearances in New York City's Fifth Avenue Theater in 1893. In 1897, she began a close relationship with the poet, playwright, and nationalist Gabriele D'Annunzio. Her career would end with ill health and after a brief return to the stage, Ms. Duse died in Pittsburgh, Pennsylvania. She was buried in Italy.

Biografia

The right-wing member of Parliament Alessandra Mussolini is probably best known as the granddaughter of the Duce. She is also niece to Sophia Loren.

Maria Montessori

The renowned teacher Maria Montessori (1870–1952) is best known for developing an educational theory known as the "Montessori Method." Maria's education made her the first female doctor in Italy; as such she was chosen to represent Italy at the first Women's International Congress in Berlin.

Frustrated by the medical approach to treating mental disorders, Maria revolutionized education by stressing that children learned best by actively participating in the learning process, a novel concept at a time when children were taught not to speak until spoken to and rote memorization was the favored method of learning.

"Italia"

In Italics

1912—The first American Montessori School opened in Tarrytown, New York.

Ciao!

La Bella Lingua

The term *divorce* (*divortium*, from *divertere*, *divortere*, "to separate") was employed in pagan Rome for the mutual separation of married people.

"Italia"

In Italics

March 8—Internationally celebrated as Woman's Day. In Italy, the day is marked by gifts of yellow Mimosa flowers.

Natalia Levi–Ginzburg

Known for her simple writing style and clear message, the Italian novelist Natalia Levi–Ginzburg (1916–1991) was strongly moved by the events of World War II that forced her and her husband, Leone Ginzburg, both Jewish, to be confined to a small village from 1940 to 1943. Ginzburg's short stories and novels have been translated into English and, through the depiction of the subtle details of family life, speak of the universal truths and challenges faced by all women. Her best-known novels are *The Road to the City* (translated in 1949), *The Dry Heart* (translated in 1949), *Voices in the Evening* (translated in 1963), and an autobiographical novel *Family Sayings* (1963).

Elsa Morante

The novelist and short-story writer Elsa Morante (1918–1985) is best known for her novels. *L'isola di Arturo,* or *Arturo's Island* (1957), is a story depicting the loss of innocence and disillusions of adulthood. In *La Storia* (*History;* 1947), Morante depicts the life of an Italian-Jewish schoolteacher raising a son born as a result of a rape by a German soldier during World War II. Elsa Morante was married to the successful novelist Alberto Moravia and frequented the literary circles of her day.

Oriana Fallaci

Noted author and journalist Oriana Fallaci (b. 1931) first appeared on the political front while conducting interviews with internationally known figures such as Yasir Arafat, Henry Kissinger, Indira Gandhi, and Golda Meir, among others. Fallaci's highly political novels include *Lettera a un bambino mai nato* (*Letter to a Child Never Born*; 1976) and *Uomo* (*Man: A Novel*; 1980).

The Long March to Equal Opportunity

Since the end of fascism, the Italian woman's movement has made great strides, including the introduction of women's suffrage, legal divorce, and laws protecting a woman's control over her reproductive rights. Here is a brief chronology outlining some of the women's progress made for women:

1946   The right to vote is given to all Italian women.

1950   A bill is introduced concerning working mothers.

1963   A bill admits women to all public offices and all professions.

1970   After a long parliamentary debate, a bill introducing divorce is passed. A referendum results in the eventual implementation of divorce.

1975   The Family Law Reform is made essential as a result of the introduction of divorce, finally made legal.

1977   Equal Opportunity laws are passed in compliance with the recommendations of the European Community due to pressures from women's groups and movements. The law opens jobs to women that had been segregated on gender lines; it cancels many of the protective regulations governing women's work, and it makes discrimination against hiring women illegal. Provisions for extending parental leave to fathers are made.

1978   Abortion is legalized.

1991   The "Positive Actions Law for women" is created to facilitate the advancement of women.

In Italics

February 27, 2001—In a controversial case that had Italian feminists fuming, Italy's highest court ruled that a pensioner could divorce his wife of 50 years on the grounds that she failed to keep their house in proper order.

Di Interessa

The relationship Italian men have with their mothers is explored in the television documentary *Mother Tongues: Italian-American Sons and Mothers* (1999) directed by Marylou Tibaldo-Bongiorno.

Mamma Mia!

What would a chapter about women be without talking about Italian mothers? Go anywhere in Italy and you'll hear the common expression *"Madonna!"* Madonna is the big mamma, the Mother of God, the essence of supreme divinity, purity, and holiness. She is by far the most painted, admired, and depicted female figure in the world. *Maria* is one of the saints officially entrusted with the protection of Italy.

Figures such as this one are a common sight in Italy.

(Photo by Anna Andersson)

Mothers are so central to Italian life, there's even a term—*mammismo*—that refers to a fully capable male who continues to depend on his mother for meals and domestic chores such as laundry and cleaning.

Film and popular culture have depicted *la mamma italiana* as a black-scarved, kitchen-bound, overbearing matron. She is, in fact, one of the most cherished and essential figures in Italy, deeply respected as the pillar of the Italian home.

But among younger women, the role of the "mamma" is changing. Fewer women are having children than ever, and then they're usually having only one. When they do, Italian law mandates that employers give pregnant employees no less than three months paid leave starting in the seventh month of pregnancy. If a woman decides to take time off, her job will be held for up to one year. That's *progresso*, and we're not just talking about a can of soup!

The Least You Need to Know

➤ The right to vote was given to women in 1946.

➤ Divorce was only made legal in 1975.

➤ The key patrons of the Renaissance include Isabella d'Este, Catherine de' Medici, and Lucrezia Borgia.

➤ Saint Catherine of Siena was one of the first females involved with the predominantly male world of politics in the Renaissance.

➤ Maria Montessori changed the face of education.

➤ Natalia Ginzburg, Oriana Fallaci, and Elsa Morante are contemporary authors whose work deserve attention.

Chapter 24

Thanks, it's tough wiping your eyes when your arms are granite...

Weeping Statues and the Blood of San Gennaro

In This Chapter

➤ Saints' days and patrons

➤ Statues that weep and bleed

➤ Padre Pio: a humble friar

➤ Fairy tales and charms

➤ Pinocchio

The rolling hills and medieval castles of the Italian countryside provoke the imagination; this is the place of magic potions and prophetic visions. Where the nymphs of *la foresta* dance while the angels in Heaven sing. It is a place of myths and legends, fairy tales and charms, saints and reliquaries. It is mystical and mysterious, enchanting, delirious, orgiastic, apocalyptic, cryptic.

This chapter covers some of the idiosyncratic and quintessentially unique phenomena that make up an important part of Italian culture and history.

L'onomastico: Saint's Day

In Italy, it's safe to say that just about every festival or *carnevale* celebration is religious in nature and pays homage to a saint. Often a statue representing the saint is carried through the streets amidst the singing and chanting of enthusiastic devotees.

Naples has San Gennaro (the same San Gennaro honored in New York's Little Italy). Florence celebrates the festa di San Giovanni, Padua honors Saint Anthony, and Rome loves Saint Paolo. Saint Mary is honored throughout the country, as is (of course) San Francesco d'Assisi—Italy's patron saint.

Di Interessa

To find out more about your patron saint and other saint news, visit the official Patron Saints Index at www.catholic-forum.com/saints/indexsnt.htm. This site includes profiles, areas of patronage, prayers, links to related sites, and other related information.

Similar to birthdays, Italians often celebrate their *onomastico* ("name day") by exchanging cards and gifts. Giorgio would celebrate the feast day of San Giorgio on April 23, Clara on August 11, Giovanni on August 29, and Gregorio on September 3. There's at least one saint for every day of the year, so you can have your pick.

You don't get to be saint just for being nice. You have to have been martyred, performed a miracle (as you'll soon see with Padre Pio), or in the American saint Mother Cabrini's situation, affected the community in a profound way. For this reason, each saint represents a different virtue or characteristic. Taxi drivers pray to Saint Christopher while animal lovers pray to Saint Francis. St. Lucia is invoked for eye problems. Infertile women pray to St. Antonio of Padua while booksellers may pray to St. John of God on March 8. St. Valentine, as you know, is venerated by lovers and want-to-be-lovers alike.

"Italia"

In Italics

Some of the more celebrated Saints' days include:

San Valentino (Rome) February 14

San Marco (Venice) April 25

Sant'Elisio (Cagliari) May 1

Sant'Antonio (Padua) June 13

San Giovanni (Florence, Genova, Turin) June 24

San Pietro (Rome) June 29

Santa Rosalia (Palermo) July 10 through 15

San Gioacomo (Sicily) July 23 through 25

San Petronio (Bologna) October 4

San Francesco (Assisi, Italy) October 4

Sant'Ambrogio (Milan) December 7

S. LUCIA V. M.

Religious in character, prayer cards are generally found in most Italian churches.

San Valentino: Patron Saint of the Birds and the Bees

Saint Valentine is not necessarily one of the more important saints, but he is certainly one of the most famous. Best known to lovers, St. Valentine's patronage extends to those suffering from epilepsy and fainting spells, and he was invoked against the plague. He is also friend to travelers, beekeepers, and young people (remember those cards you used to give in elementary school?). He is generally represented by the cherubic (and meddlesome) Cupid. St. Valentine is often depicted with birds and roses.

Who was Saint Valentine? Identified with two early Christians, in one story he was a priest in Rome, in another he was the Bishop of Interamna (currently Terni, Italy) who was beaten and beheaded on February 14 on the orders of Claudius II. How did either one of them come to represent immortal love?

Di Interessa

As you may recall from Chapter 6, "Rome Wasn't Built in a Day," the wolf was a common emblem used in Roman and pre-Roman times. A teacher at the *Luperci* College of Priests, the infamous Roman Marc Antony crowned Julius Caesar during the Lupercalia festival in 44 B.C.E. *Lupercalia* (from Latin *lupus* "wolf" and meaning "feast of the wolf") refers to the ancient Roman annual festival held on February 15 that honored Juno (the Queen of the Roman gods and goddesses), whose ceremony was intended to encourage a fertile and plague-free year. The *Lupercalia* festival reflected the earliest pastoral days prior to the she-wolf that gave birth to Romulus and Remus, Rome's founders.

Here again, there are different theories about the origins of Saint Valentine's Day. His attachment to the sentiment and romance of love seems to be linked to the Roman pagan festival of Lupercalia. Among the other festivities, one favorite love game reminiscent of "spin the bottle" involved placing into an urn the names of the young women that were then drawn by the young men. The couples were bound together until the next year.

Under Pope Gelasius (see the pope list in Chapter 8, "Popes, Politics, and Power"), priests replaced the names of the girls with the names of the saints in an attempt to dissuade locals from their pagan superstitions and heathen gods. That's how St. Valentine came to be tied to the holiday. The day also represented the pairing of birds, who were said to choose their mates on St. Valentine's Day.

There is also some mystery over the venerated saint's relics. The Scottish friars at the Church of Blessed St. John Duns Scotus in Glasgow claim they possess St. Valentine's remains. Meanwhile, priests at the Whitefriar Street Church in Dublin claim they were passed on as a gift from Pope Gregory XVI to the Carmelite priest John Spratt.

Saintly Remains: Relics

Italian churches are filled with the bones, ashes, and garments of saints and holy martyrs. The remains of Saint Valentine are only one example. The alter of every

Roman Catholic church contains a *relic,* a rule that dates back to the persecutions in Rome when Mass was spoken over the graves of martyrs.

The veneration of relics as miraculous dates from the third century. St. John of Damascus taught that the earthly body of a saint maintained a sort of permanent grace; the Roman Catholic Church holds that the miracles are performed by the intercession of the saint in Heaven on the prayer of the living. What- ever the case may be, throughout Italy thousands of people attribute numerous miracles to the bones and remains of martyrs and saints.

The most venerated relics include the pieces of the True Cross, the shroud of Veronica, the Holy Nails in the iron crown of Lombardy (Monza), and the Holy Lance at St. Peter's (Rome). One of the more famous relics has to do with the patron Saint of Naples, San Gennaro.

La Bella Lingua

Relic comes from Latin *reliquiae,* which means the re- mains of something, and refers to an object such as a body part or piece of clothing.

San Gennaro's Blood

Three times a year the sealed glass vial that allegedly contains the blood of San Gennaro is brought out in a solemn ceremony. In front of television cameras and the thousands of amazed pilgrims who flock to witness the occurrence, the blood lique- fies, a phenomenon that has been occurring off and on since 1389. The event is well- documented and remains one of the true mysteries that even science cannot seem to explain to everyone's agreement.

San Gennaro (Januarius), the Bishop of Benevento (a small city near Naples), was mar- tyred during the reign of Emperor Diocletian in 305 C.E. As if being thrown into an amphitheater filled with wild animals wasn't enough, the poor bishop was beheaded.

Sometime in the fifth century, or so the story goes, San Gennaro's relics were taken to a catacomb near Naples where he was declared the patron saint of the city. The bones were stolen, taken to Benevento, and hidden for several centuries until they were found beneath the altar at the cloister of Montevergine. Frederick of Aragon took them to Naples, and in 1304 Charles II of Anjou built a silver reliquary for the saint's head. In 1337, ceremonies were instituted by Archbishop Orsini of Naples but it was not until 1389 that the miracle was first recorded in the diary of an anonymous Neapolitan.

Elaborate scientific theories have evolved in an attempt to explain the paranormal phenomenon, the most likely involving a procedure used to simulate blood. Critics say that the miracle is a magic trick and a hoax. Opponents wonder how a secret of this magnitude could be kept for six centuries.

Skeptics argue the substance is a strange amalgam of microorganisms affected when shaken. Again, believers say, prove it. Scientists say that all the compounds necessary for a concoction capable of transmuting from a solid to a liquid form can be found locally (limestone, chalk, eggshell, and volcanic rock) and were widely used by alchemists like Albertus Magnus (1193–1280) and his student Thomas Aquinas (1226–1274).

The big unanswered question is: What would motivate someone to go to all that trouble? Was it a hoax? A collective hallucination? A miracle? We may never know.

Weeping Statues

Although Pinocchio is a myth, there are several incidents involving statues that have come to life during the last 20 years. Recorded miracles and supranatural activities have always been part of the Italian collective consciousness, but what makes these events particularly interesting is the fact they all occurred in front of reputable witnesses, often recorded by television crews and photojournalists.

> ## "*Italia*"
>
> ### In Italics
>
> **1317**—Pope John XXII forbid the study of alchemy in a Papal Bull. "... if any members of the clergy are found among alchemists, they will receive no mercy."

> ### Di Interessa
>
> Written by Enrico Malatest, the book *She Wept Into My Hands* chronicles the sensation surrounding the Virgin statue at Civitavecchia.

In 1995, after a statue of the Virgin Mary (*The Weeping Virgin*) was brought from Medjugorje (Bosnia), she wept tears of blood in Civitavecchia, a port town near Rome. Vatican-appointed authorities responsible with analyzing the blood determined that the DNA of the blood was human and unconfirmed reports indicate the Vatican has accepted the tears as a miracle. As a result, tens of thousands of pilgrims visit Civitavecchia annually.

In a 1987 incident witnessed by a police officer and a journalist, blood streamed from the wooden heart of a Christ statue located in Parma. The examined blood appeared to be human but possessed no platelets. In 1994, at the Sant'Antonio Abate near Naples another miracle took place, this time from a statue of Christ that bled from its head, hands, heart, and feet. Several other weeping and bleeding statues that have appeared in the last ten years were the subject of investigation and included the towns of Potenza (May 1991), Nocere Inferiore (June 1992), and Subiaco (January 1994).

Padre Pio

The miracles attributed to the Italian Capuchin friar and mystic Padre Pio (1887–1968) include the stigmata (the wounds of Christ), prophecy, conversion, and spontaneous healing. The priest had first attracted attention when his hands began to bleed at the age of 31.

For 50 years until his death at the age of 81, the controversial friar had been the subject of many Vatican investigations. In fact, the Church stripped him of his ministerial rights, ordered him not to speak to members of the opposite sex, and had his confessional bugged.

In Italics

1978—During a public exposition of the Shroud of Turin, 44 researchers from several countries were authorized to carry out tests directly on the Shroud for an overall period of one hundred and twenty hours. In 1988 samples of the Shroud were taken for a carbon-14 test that indicated—in contrast with all the previous tests— that the Shroud fabric probably originated between the thirteenth and fourteenth centuries. Other researchers have questioned the reliability of carbon dating.

All in all, however, his good deeds outweighed the bad and believers claim Padre Pio's intercessions have helped heal the infirm around the world. Padre Pio was beatified on May 3, 1999, in a live broadcast in front of St. Peter's Square, by one his most avid supporters—Pope John Paul II. The pontiff described Padre Pio as a "humble friar who had suffered gently."

Padre Pio is entombed at the Santa Maria della Grazie Church in San Giovanni Rotondo. A legend in his own lifetime, thirty years after his death, Padre Pio continues to perform miracles. Seven million people visit the shrine every year and the cult continues to grow. Fact or fiction? You decide.

The hands of Padre Pio show the stigmata.

Cryptic Messages

Speaking of Capuchin monks, one of Rome's stranger attractions can be found underneath the Church of Santa Maria della Concezione. Built in 1626 for Cardinal Barberini, the church itself is unassuming (although the small Caravaggio painting in the chapel is worth a glance), but it is the crypt below that deserves mention.

After paying a donation, visitors are led into a cemetery where five chambers containing the remains of over 4,000 monks are arranged in a series of macabre tableaux and designs. In one room, hundreds of skulls are neatly stacked against a wall. The ceilings are decorated with fibulae; vertebrae make for perfect flowers, ribs as their stems. Hanging from the ceiling, a complete skeleton holds a scythe while others stand vigil dressed in the typical robe worn by the monks. The impression is made even more powerful by the ethereal Gregorian chants that permeate the stone cellars. Inscriptions remind visitors of their imminent mortality: "What you are, we used to be. What we are, you will be." It's a sight worth seeing, and no haunted house can ever come close to this one.

The *Malocchio* and Other Charms

Charms and amulets have been around for thousands of years, designed to ward off evil spirits and protect the wearer from any number of misfortunes. The Italian term *coronet* refers to a cuckolded man. The small amulet *Mann coronet* translates to "hand horn" and refers to the hand gesture made in which the middle and ring fingers are folded into the palm, while the index and pinky fingers are extended, resulting in what appears to be a horned head of a bull. (Remember the bunny ear gesture you learned in Chapter 5, "The Sound of Music"?). The amulet was worn during ancient times to protect against impotency.

Speaking of horns, the *cornice* are usually carved from red coral or cast in silver and gold. Literally meaning "little horn," this charm was worn to protect against the bad luck caused by *malocchio* ("evil eye") and represented the horn used by Amalthea to feed milk to Jupiter.

The Etruscans were accomplished goldsmiths who commonly used delicate filigree around the edges of their jewelry. The Romans adopted many Etruscan crafts, resulting in the tusk, another variation the horn theme used to ward off bad luck.

The ancient *cimatura* was an amulet used to protect infants from the evil eye and is also referred to as the witch charm. Another amulet is the *manofico;* translating to "hand fig," the word *fico* is also slang for a woman's genitals. In this crude gesture that imitates the act of relations between a man and a woman, the hand is made into a fist with the tip of the thumb extending through the index and middle fingers (or between the middle and ring fingers).

Finally, the *bulla* (sharing similar origins with the term "papal bull") refers to a metal charm that was traditionally worn by boys. The *bullae* depicted lions, snakes, and satyrs, again used to defend against the evil eye.

Fairy Tales

Storytellers have been a part of the Italian culture ever since there have been stories to tell. Many of the fairy tales you remember from infancy find their origins in Italian literature.

Many sacred stories focused on the lives and times of important saints and legends, such as the collection written about St. Francis of Assisi, *I fioretti di San Francesco* (*The Little Flowers of St. Francis*) in 1345. Originally written in Latin, it was soon translated into the vernacular Tuscan tongue where it became a favorite.

During the Middle Ages, the tradition of Italian storytelling is seen with the poetry recited by the minstrels, *giulliari* (wandering players), and *cantastorie* (storytellers). Even the Tuscan poet and novelist Boccaccio (see Chapter 9, "Leaving the Middle Ages") drew inspiration from medieval traditions when he wrote his masterpiece, *The Decameron*.

Yet it wasn't until the sixteenth century that many of these stories were finally put into print.

Di Interessa

A wonderful collection of Italian-American writers can be found in the anthology *The Italian American Heritage: A Companion to Literature and Arts*, edited by Pellegrino D'Acierno (1999).

Giovan Francesco Straparola

In what was one of the first collections of written stories, in 1550 Giovan Francesco Straparola di Caravaggio published in Venice *Le Piacevoli Notti* (*Pleasant Nights*). Adopting the same model used by Boccaccio, the 25 stories were written down as if they had been told by twelve women and two young men over a thirteen-night period. Straparola's books were so successful, an additional 48 stories were assembled for a second volume that was published in 1553.

Giambattista Basile

If you want to impress your Italian friends, ask them to talk about the scholar and man of letters Giambattista Basile (1575–1632). This Neapolitan poet and storyteller assembled and wrote the first collection of European tales in his masterpiece *Il Pentamerone, Lo Cunto de li Cunte, overo Trattenemiento de li Peccerille* (*The Pentameron, The Tale of Tales, or Entertainment for the Little Ones*). Basile's fifty stories were told by travelers stopping in an inn during *Carnevale*. Written using the Neapolitan dialect, and recounted over the course of five days, they included early versions of the infamous fairy tales of *Cenerentola* (*Cinderella*), *La bella addormentata* (*Sleeping Beauty*), and *Capucetto rosso* (*Little Red Riding Hood*).

Di Interessa

The literary critic Benedetto Croce was the first to translate Giambattista Basile's masterpiece *The Pentameron* from the Neapolitan dialect into Italian in 1924. To learn more about Italian folktales, begin with the wonderful collection published by Italo Calvino, titled *Fiabe italiane* (*Italian Folktales*; 1956).

Looking Grimm

For a real thriller, pick up an old copy of the Grimms' famous fairy tales where you'll find the requisite tales of love, loss, and adventure. What you probably didn't know is that, while the Grimm brothers deserve credit for transcribing the folktales of the countryside and adapting them to print, they were hardly the creators of the tales, most of which had been passed down from generation to generation through the oral tradition of storytelling.

In their book *Household Tales* (1814), considered by many to be the bible of fairy tales, the Grimm brothers William and Jacob respectfully refer the reader to one of their most important sources—*The Pentameron*—and include a biography of its author, none other than Italy's Giambattista Basile.

Di Interessa

The town of Collodi is located between the Tuscan towns of Lucca and Pistoia and is the inspiration behind Carlo Collodi's adopted pseudonym. To learn more about the *Fondazione Nazionale Carlo Collodi* (National Carlo Collodi Foundation), visit it online at www.pinocchio.it.

Stretching the Truth

Another important and widely recognized author is best known for having created the beloved character Pinocchio. Carlo Collodi (born Carlo Lorenzini) was born in Florence where he remained until his death. Collodi started as a journalist and supported himself while writing reviews for *L'Italia Musicale* (*Musical Italy*), a prestigious periodical. The blending of storytelling with practical lessons was a popular formula used in children's literature, and Collodi was a master. Books he wrote included *L'Abbaco di Giannettino* (*Johnny's Arithmetic Primer*) and *La grammatica di Giannettino* (*Johnny's Grammar Book*).

Pinocchio

"C'era una volta" (Once upon a time) begins most Italian *favole* (fairy tales) and *racconti* (stories). And so it begins with Pinocchio, the classic children's tale about a wooden puppet who aches to become a real boy.

In 1881, the story originally appeared in *Il giornale per i bambini* (*The Children's Magazine*), an Italian weekly, as the first installment of *Storia di un burattino* (*Story of a Puppet*). The name was later changed to *Le avventure di Pinocchio* (*The Adventures of Pinocchio*) and came out in full book form in 1883. The popularity of the book throughout Italy led to its translation into English in 1891, replete with illustrations depicting the puppet's metamorphosis into a human boy.

Pinocchio has been translated into dozens of languages. The book probably made its first appearance in the United States in the arms of a young immigrant child. It would not take long before millions of American schoolchildren fell in love with the mischievous Italian puppet.

In 1911, Pinocchio's image was first animated in a silent hand-colored experimental film created by Count Giulio Cesare Antamoro, an Italian pioneer in the field of early cinema. The puppet has been depicted in 30 shorts and feature-length films by Italians, Americans, English, and Japanese directors.

Di Interessa

Not to be missed for a night of family fun are several films depicting the wooden puppet: the Walt Disney film classic *Pinocchio* (1940), *Pinocchio* directed by Steve Baron (1996), and the soon to be released *Pinocchio* directed by Italy's favorite actor and director Roberto Benigni (2002). If you can, try to obtain the 1911 version starring Italy's beloved actor Polidor (1887–1977), directed by Cesare Antamoro.

La Fata

Just as Peter Pan had his muse Tinker Bell, fairies have always had a place in folklore, often helping guide the mortals toward their *fada*, or destiny. The Italian word for fairy is *fata*, just a letter away from *fada* "fate."

➤ **Aguane.** These are a race of female spirits that dwell in the mountains along the streams and rivers. They are associated with water and wear magic red caps that make them invisible.

➤ **Basadone.** This word probably derives from "bacia donna" and literally means "woman kisser." This little devil rides the breeze, stealing kisses along the way. He is associated with air.

➤ **Caccavecchia.** Also called *linchetto, buffardello* (from the word *buffo,* "funny"). These elves can't stand disorder and are blamed for nightmares and odd noises heard during the night.

➤ **Callicantazaroi.** These little skinny and naked fairies are usually half blind and wandering. They love pork and are associated with Earth.

➤ **Candelas.** Literally meaning "candle," these fairies flicker like fireflies.

➤ **Farfarelli.** The Italian word *farfalla* means "butterfly"; these mischievous winged female creatures love to play in the dust.

➤ **Faunus.** In Roman religion, this woodland deity was the protector of herds and crops, identified with the Greek pastoral god Pan (also a fertility god). The god was said to have been attended by Fauns, the muscular, virile half-goat/half-human creatures. Faunus's female counterpart went by the name Fauna or Bona Dea.

➤ **Gianes.** These solitary female weavers divine while spinning thread.

➤ **Monaciello.** Literally meaning "little monk," these drunken elves are also called *Pandacciu* and *Mamucca.* They are the guardians of the wine cellars in which they live and are often the thieves of those missing socks you never seem to find.

➤ **Orcuili.** Masters at changing their shape, these male dwarves are known for their nasty temperament and horrible stench.

➤ **Querciola.** These friends to lovers generally live in trees (*il quercio* means "walnut tree"), and their element is fire.

➤ **Silvani.** These transparent-winged wood nymphs keep watch over the animals of the wood.

The Least You Need to Know

➤ Italians celebrate their *onomastico* the same as they do birthdays.

➤ Italian churches are filled with the relics of saints and martyrs such as the blood of San Gennaro and the Shroud of Turin.

➤ Giovan Francesco Straparola di Caravaggio published the first written collection of 25 folktales in his book *Le Piacevoli Notti* (*Pleasant Nights*).

➤ The scholar Giambattista Basile (1575–1632) was the first to write the first collection of European tales in his masterpiece *Lo Cunto de' Cunti* (*The Tale of Tales*).

➤ *Pinocchio* originally appeared in 1881 and was written by Carlo Collodi, an Italian journalist and educator.

Chapter 25

Made in Italy

In This Chapter

➤ Milan: fashion capital

➤ Specializing in textiles, jewelry, and design

➤ Clothes encounters

➤ The powerhouse designers today

La moda! Italy is synonymous with fashion, and the Made in Italy label is a password for creativity, quality, and taste. Image-conscious Italians take their clothes seriously, as they have been doing for centuries.

What role has fashion played in the history of Italy, and how is fashion important today?

Art of a Different Sort

Not only was Florence the center of the Italian Renaissance, but did you know that the textile trade was also a stronghold of the Florentine economy since the Middle Ages? Originally, the city was a leader in the mass production of woolen cloth, and by the sixteenth century, smaller and more luxurious fabrics such as silks, brocades, fine linens, embroideries, trimmings, and specialty fabrics were being manufactured. Today, Florence is still a leader in the fashion and interior furnishings industries.

During the age of the Medici Grand Dukedom of Tuscany (1537–1743), quality clothing and textiles were vastly expensive and therefore highly prized. A single court costume for a man or a woman cost as much as a large house, and a set of brocade wall hangings outpriced a whole room of major old-master paintings. Such extravagant creations were daily necessities of life at the Medici court, complementing its brilliant cycle of festivals and ceremonies.

This portrait by the painter Antonio del Pollaiuolo shows the complicated hairstyles and elaborate jewelry worn during the Renaissance. Portrait of a Young Woman *(late 1460s).*

(Milan, Museo Poldi Pezzoli)

Di Interessa

You can see more of Pollaiuolo and other portrait artists of the time at the Museo Poldi Pezzoli in Milan.

The Joy of Jewels

The jeweler's art also flourished in the Renaissance, fuelled by the rivalry between courts and noble families that expressed itself in ostentatious display. Many outstanding artists designed jewelry, among them Botticelli and Giulio Romano. Some, such as Benvenuto Cellini, even initially trained as goldsmiths. Because Renaissance jewelry was so elaborate, the value of the workmanship usually exceeded the intrinsic value of the material, therefore so much of it survives.

Contemporary portraits offer excellent evidence of the opulence and variety of Renaissance jewelry. Women's hair ornaments emphasized the movement of loose hair and braids. Necklaces were particularly popular, either in the form of a heavy gold chain with a central pendant or multiple ropes of pearls; those of extreme length were worn looped up to the bodice. Numerous brooches and rings were worn together, pearls dangled from the points of lace ruffs and stiff caps, and frequently the whole female dress would be jewel-encrusted.

Historic Clothing

In what other country would thousands of people every year wait in line for hours to see an ancient bed sheet, a face towel, or a rumpled medieval sackcloth? In Italy, clothing is not just a covering. For devoted Christians these items provide evidence of faith. For others, they add to the accumulated knowledge about historical figures.

The Shroud of Turin is a relic, preserved at Turin since 1578, that is venerated as the cloth used to wrap Christ's body for burial. It bears the imprint of the front and back of a human body as well as markings that correspond to the traditional stigmata.

Religious pilgrims travel to the Basilica di San Francesco in Assisi, where they can see the tomb of St. Francis, amazing frescoes everywhere, and relics, including his robe. It's in tatters, but there is enough to gain a sense of the man's humility and the power of personal example.

Then there's Veronica's Veil. According to legend, while Jesus was carrying the cross, Veronica stepped forward to wipe the sweat from his brow as he stumbled, and her towel miraculously retained the image of Jesus' face. This relic is preserved in St. Peter's where, once a year, it is displayed.

La Bella Lingua

In Italian, the Shroud of Turin is known as *la Sindone* or *la Sacra Lenzuola,* the Holy Sheet.

Biografia

As part of the vow of poverty, the Franciscan style of dress adopted by St. Francis and his order was purposely simple. The undyed brown wool cloak was held together by a long cord, symbolic of the cross.

No Cutoffs or Exposed Shoulders Allowed

For a culture that prides itself on *"fare una bella figura"* (make a good figure/impression), there have been attempts throughout history to curtail sartorial excess. In ancient Rome, for example, there were laws limiting finery and confiscating excessive gold jewelry.

In the later Middle Ages, clothing became one of the principal indicators of social class and sumptuary laws were in force to ensure that the distinctions were observed. These laws also operated to protect home-produced textiles against encroachments by foreign goods.

Di Interessa

Some churches remain very strict about their dress code and require visitors to keep their legs and shoulders covered.

Di Interessa

Pantalone was a caricature of the Venetian merchant, rich and retired, mean and miserly, with a young wife or an adventurous daughter. He always wore tight-fitting long red trousers or red breeches and stockings, a short, tight-fitting jacket, a loose, long, black cloak with plain sleeves, a red woolen skullcap, and yellow Turkish slippers.

Another area with which sumptuary laws were often concerned was the banning of fashions that might encourage sexual license: low-cut dresses for women, exaggerated codpieces for men. Girolamo Savonarola, the prophet of doom whom you read about in Chapter 11, "Strange Bedfellows," even preached against this type of clothing. Unfortunately for him, the Florentines preferred their finery, and he soon found himself in designer prison wear.

Commedia dell'Arte

Commedia dell'arte, also known as Italian comedy, was a humorous theatrical presentation performed by professional players who traveled in troupes throughout Italy in the sixteenth century. One aspect that made it so popular was the costumes. The audience was able to pick up from each character's dress the type of person he was representing. For elaboration, loose-fitting garments alternated with very tight, and jarring color contrasts opposed monochrome outfits. Except for the *inamorato*, males would identify themselves with character-specific costumes and half masks. The *zanni* (precursor to clown) Arlecchino, for example, would be immediately recognizable because of his black mask and patchwork costume.

While the *inamorato* and the female characters wore neither masks nor costumes unique to that personage, certain information could still be derived from their clothing. Audiences knew what members of the various social classes typically wore and also expected certain colors to represent certain emotional states. Regardless of where they toured, *commedia dell'arte* conventions were recognized and adhered to.

Get Me Wardrobe

Imagine you're a wardrobe designer working on the set of the latest epic movie being filmed at Cinecittà. It's about the history of Italy, and you need to dress certain *tipi fissi,* or fixed social types. Here are some suggestions about what clothing and accessories you'll need before the director yells *"Azione!"*

➤ **Roman Senator.** A toga for this prominent citizen! It was adopted in the sixth century and was off-limits to women, slaves, and non-Romans.

➤ **Medieval Monk.** Austere dark robes, sandals, and a belt made of rope. Don't forget the tonsure hairstyle, too—for that almost-bald look.

➤ **Renaissance Lady.** For the noble lady, you'll need a flowing silk dress trimmed with gold, leather, or soft skin slippers, a linen purse decorated with embroidery, and elegant jewelry.

➤ **Venetian Courtesan.** She'll need a rich crimson gown with a frothy linen undergarment, known as a *camicia.* The low-cut, tight-fitting silk bodice should be embroidered with silver thread and pearls and fringed with a ruffled border. And her accessories should include precious jewels.

➤ **Casanova.** The famous hedonist needs a powdered wig, heavy make-up to cover the pockmarks on his face and a flamboyant brocaded blouse. To emphasize his masculinity, tightly fitted hose, with jewelry to show off his taste.

Di Interessa

When Italians need stockings or socks they go directly to the experts. At the specialty store *la merceria* (millinery) or *negozio di calze* (sock store), shopkeepers will spend hours describing the different fabrics and colors available to the consumer. They also often sell *guanti* (gloves). In Rome you can buy a pair of Cardinal's socks (red only) for less than $10.

Clothing Makes the Politician

Sometimes a shirt is just a shirt. But in Italy, even the color one wears can have great political and ideological significance. In Part 4, "Redshirts, Blackshirts, and Greenshirts," you read about three types of historical movements, all easily recognizable by the color of their shirts.

The Redshirts: During the Risorgimento, Giuseppe Garibaldi and his volunteer force of 1,000 men dressed in bright red shirts, which became the symbol for national unification.

The Blackshirts: *Le camicie nere* were members of Mussolini's Fascist party who goose-stepped their way to power in Rome in 1922 and were feared for their violent methods used to maintain order.

The Greenshirts: Green-clad security force of the separatist political party started in the 1990s with little power that nonetheless stirs up north versus south fears again.

Street Fashion

Walk down the major thoroughfare of any Italian city in the early evening and you'll get swept up in *la passeggiata*, the traditional daily stroll. Young parents push their children in strollers, teenagers gather with their friends, and everyone checks out what their neighbor is wearing. It's a friendly game of one-upmanship, where you can show off your taste and dress to impress.

Style Capital

Milan, Italy's second largest city, is the country's financial and publishing center. But for fashion *cognoscenti*, it's the capital of style, rivaled only by Paris and New York. Many major fashion houses are headquartered here, and it's the city of choice for many aspiring designers. There are fashion shows year-round filled with glamorous supermodels strutting the latest Armani, Dolce & Gabbana, or Valentino fashions and trade fairs for wholesalers.

Institutes of fashion offer courses in design, pattern-making, and styling that draw an international group of students. An entire industry has grown up around the fashion world, including fashion photographers, modeling agencies, public relations firms, and textile firms.

"*Italia*"

In Italics

1909—Futurism, an early twentieth-century movement in art, literature, music, technology, and fashion, was launched by the poet Filippo Marinetti in 1909 and glorified modern machinery, progress, and technology.

Di Interessa

Giorgio Armani has designed the uniforms of the *carabinieri* (the Italian police force) and the Alitalia flight attendants.

Business Is All the Fashion These Days

Italian fashion designers of today are both artists and serious business professionals. The work produced by Armani, Versace, Prada, Missoni, Moschino, Ferrè, Valentino, Gucci, Dolce & Gabbana, and many others have elevated the craftsmanship of fashion into an art form.

Here are just a few of the many Italian fashion designers that have made their mark.

Giorgio Armani

Armani first studied medicine, then worked as a window dresser before becoming a designer for Nino Cerruti in 1961. He then worked for several designers until 1975, when he established his own company and rapidly became one of Italy's best-known ready-to-wear designers for both men and women. Emporio

Armani was launched in 1981, and Armani Exchange shops arrived in the United States in 1981, offering well-designed basics at moderate prices.

Benetton

Giuliana Benetton and her three brothers founded a company that has expanded to become the world's largest knitwear manufacturer. Giuliana, at the age of 13, began working as a skein winder in a knitting workshop. Later she produced her own brightly colored sweaters on a home knitting machine. Her brother Luciano sold her sweaters to local stores, enabling her to start her own business, in 1955, with a collection of 18 pieces. By 1960, Benetton was able to employ a team of young women and to sell wholesale.

The first Benetton factory opened in Treviso in 1965; four years later the first Benetton store opened in nearby Belluno. Giuliana and her three brothers expanded the business throughout Italy in the 1970s before taking on the rest of Europe and the world. By the mid-1990s there were some 7,000 Benetton stores in over 100 countries. The Benetton name, assisted by unusual and sometimes controversial advertising, is now an instantly recognized trademark throughout the world.

Salvatore Ferragamo

When he was 16, Ferragamo (1878–1960) joined his brother in California where he made shoes by hand for Hollywood film companies and on private commissions for actors and actresses. In 1927, he returned to Italy and set up shop in Florence. He claimed to have invented the wedge heel, platform sole, and metal support in high heels. The shortage of leather during the war made him experiment with cork, raffia, and cellophane. In 1947, the "shoemaker of the stars" invented the so-called invisible shoe, made of clear nylon and a black suede heel.

Prada

The Prada fashion house was founded in 1913 in Milan. Originally a manufacturer of leather goods, the company was revived in the 1970s by Miuccia Prada. Prada began producing accessories, including a simple black nylon backpack fitted with leather straps. All these accessories made from black nylon were stamped with the Prada name and were an instant success, a must-have for fashion mavens, and widely copied.

Di Interessa

Shoe buffs can combine fashion with sightseeing when in Florence. Visit the Salvatore Ferragamo Museum, which is on the second floor of the flagship Ferragamo store. It's in the historic Palazzo Spini Feroni and has over 10,000 shoes in its collection.

Valentino

In 1959, Valentino Garavani opened a couture house in Rome. He rapidly became a favorite of aristocracy, during an era depicted so well by Fellini in *La Dolce Vita*. International celebrities, such as Jacqueline Kennedy, wore his elegant, glamorous creations. *Rosso valentino* (Valentine red) is the color of choice for high society.

Versace

His brilliance, his sexiness, his love of strong colors and clean line made him one of the most important designers of the 1980s and 1990s, much loved by stars like Madonna, Sting, and Princess Diana. Gianni Versace, the "prince of fashion," originally worked with his dressmaker mother in Milan and in 1978 opened his own business. Many of his ideas were audacious and carried out with high technical achievement.

Tragically, Versace was killed in 1997 in front of his mansion in South Beach, Miami, Florida. Today the Versace design house is run by Versace's sister, Donatella, renowned in her own right for her innovative style and fashion.

Di Interessa

Every city has a special appeal for different shopping tastes:

Milan: best for that shopping spree

Venice: Venetian-blown glass is world-renowned

Como: factory outlet galore

Deruta: Umbrian town known for its ceramics

Florence: paper goods, fashion, markets, silk

Rome: antique market at Porta Portese

Italian Ambassadors of Fashion

In addition to those designers discussed previously, here is a list of well-known Italian designers:

Laura Biagiotti	Max Mara
Byblos	Missoni
Cerruti	Anna Molinari
Roberto Cavalli	Moschino
Fendi	Pucci
Fiorucci	Schiaparelli
Romeo Gigli	Trussardi
Gucci	Ermenegildo Zegna
Krizia	

Di Interessa

The *viaggio* starts with your thoughts. Check out Made in Italy at www.made-in-italy.com/ and Italian National Tourist Board at www.enit.it/ for information on fashion, travel, and tourism.

Stendhal's Syndrome

In the mid-nineteenth century while on a tour of Italian architecture, the famed French author Stendhal (pseudonym of Marie-Henri Beyle; 1783–1842) found himself so overwhelmed by the beauty of what he was seeing that he slipped into a mysterious fugue state from which it took him days to recover. The term Stendhal's Syndrome refers to that curious phenomenon observed in the late nineteenth century of numb, depressed travelers wandering the streets of the city, stumbling across the Ponte Vecchio, eyes glazed and spirits dazed from an overload of Renaissance splendor.

While traveling through Italy for the first time, if you find yourself suffering from aesthetic overload, don't despair. Blame it on Stendhal's Syndrome and go out for a little retail therapy. (Go on, buy yourself that pair of Ferragamo shoes you've been eyeing all week!)

Don't Forget the Credit Card

There are several major department store chains in Italy. Coin is the trendiest, selling a mixture of both traditional and cutting-edge fashions, accessories, and home furnishings. La Rinascente is one of the largest chains of Italian department stores, with locations in most cities. La Rinascente sells up-market (but not designer) clothes, accessories, toiletries, and things for the home. La Standa and Upim are two off-price department store chains. United Colors of Benetton are just about everywhere and capture the essence of young Italian street fashion.

Shop Till You Drop

In Rome, head for Via Condotti, which runs perpendicular to the Spanish Steps and contains some of the world's most glamorous boutiques. For a dream shopping spree, Via dei Tornabuoni is Florence's version of Rodeo Drive. Milan's fashion district is near the gothic Duomo on Via Monte Napoleone and the surrounding street.

When you shop in Italy, you will probably want to buy everything you see. The number of small, family run boutiques makes the experience much more personal than what most Americans are accustomed to while perusing the mall. To make the best of your time and money, consider these tips:

La Bella Lingua

The **VAT** (value added tax) in Italy is referred to as IVA and is a sales tax attached to all major purchases. Save your receipts—non-European travelers receive VAT refunds once they leave the country.

➤ Dress simply. If you're dripping with gold, chances are the sales merchants won't give you much of a break when you ask them for a *sconto* (discount).

➤ Bring change to markets. At the moment of truth, you'll have much more bargaining power if you don't require change.

➤ Beat the crowds. You know, "the early bird …"

➤ Don't trust anyone to mail you your merchandise unless it's a qualified shipping agent.

➤ Always get a receipt. This is especially helpful when you're passing through customs and want to avoid paying the *VAT*.

Clothing Sizes

The following table will help you determine your size in Italy.

Women's Clothing		Men's Clothing	
Italy	USA	Italy	USA
38	4	44	34
40	6	46	36
42	8	48	38
44	10	50	40
46	12	52	42
48	14	54	44
50	16	56	46
52	18	58	48
		60	50

The Least You Need to Know

➤ Milan is the leading center of fashion design.

➤ The types of clothes worn by people were an indicator of their social and economic status.

➤ Italian designers such as Giorgio Armani, Valentino, and Gianfranco Ferré are world-renowned.

➤ Artists have greatly influenced fashion and vice versa.

Part 6

Italy's Exports

Along with their stories, traditions, and recipes, Italian immigrants brought their ideas, talents, and drive to the United States.

In Part 6, you'll learn about some of the many Italian Americans whose actions and accomplishments have affected us all. Who were the writers and thinkers who influenced our ideas? What medical and scientific advances can be attributed to Italians? Who are the artists who have so beautifully expressed our innermost feelings and desires?

This "Who's Who" of Italian power players and notables includes Nobel Prize winners, educators, athletes, and entertainers, in addition to political and industry leaders.

Chapter 26

Follow Your Muse

> **In This Chapter**
>
> ➤ Letters and then some
>
> ➤ Educators spread the word
>
> ➤ Great achievers in the arts

While Italy is the motherland of the millions of Italian-American immigrants, they in turn are her children. Any parent hopes to see their child succeed, and in this respect, Italians should be proud of the fact they have produced so many prodigies here in the United States!

Writers and Thinkers

Through their words and actions, the Italians have been influencing the thoughts and deeds of humanity for centuries. Humanists such as Marsilio Ficino and Pico della Mirandola explored man's relationship to himself and the world. The works of Machiavelli and the treatises of Baldassare became code for members of the aristocracy. The letters of patroness Isabella d'Este and the notes of Leonardo da Vinci reveal the thoughts and concerns each faced during the Renaissance. The philosophy of Filippo Mazzei inspired Thomas Jefferson. All in all, Italian contributions to the world have been well-documented.

City Lights

Born in Yonkers, New York, Lawrence Ferlinghetti (b. 1919) was a prominent poet of the 1950's Beat Generation (a small group of artists based in San Francisco and New York). After earning a doctorate in poetry, Ferlinghetti moved to San Francisco, where he founded the magazine *City Lights* and published several works by himself and other notable poets (such as Allen Ginsberg's book *Howl*) through the creation of the popular "Pocket Poets Series." Ferlinghetti makes an appearance in Jack Kerouac's 1962 novel *Big Sur* as the sensible Lorenzo Monsanto.

The poet Gregory Corso (1930–2001) was born in the heart of New York City's Greenwich Village. Described by the king of the beat poets Allen Ginsberg as an "aphoristic poet, and a poet of ideas," in 1950, Corso met Allen Ginsberg through whom he became acquainted with Jack Kerouac, William Burroughs, and other New York artists and poets. Works include *Gasoline* (City Light Books, 1958), *Long Live Man* (New Directions, 1962), and *Herald of the Autochthonic Spirit* (New Directions, 1981).

Who's Who

Read on to learn more about some of the many gifted Italian American writers and thinkers of our time. There are many more wonderful writers than listed here; just think of this list as a sampling from across the board. Have a nibble, or go for the whole pie!

Di Interessa

The book titled *The Dream Book: An Anthology of Writings by Italian American Women* (Syracuse University Press, 1985) was called a landmark in American literature for it collected, for the first time, Italian–American women authors and presented them in various literary genres as a cohesive voice.

➤ The writer Helen Barolini is an award-winning novelist, critic, translator, essayist, and one of the first to write a novel about contemporary Italian American women (*Umbertina*, Feminist Press, 1979).

➤ The poet and scholar John Ciardi (1916–1986) created the only English translation of Dante's *Divine Comedy* that reproduces the poem's complex rhyme scheme. Ciardi authored more than 60 books, hosted a weekly radio commentary on National Public Radio in the 1980s, taught at Harvard and Rutgers universities, and was the only American poet ever to have his own television program (*Accent*) on CBS.

➤ A novelist worth mentioning is Pietro di Donato, best known for his book *Christ in Concrete* (Signet, 1939), one of the few proletarian novels written by a blue-collar worker. The son of an Italian immigrant, Donato tells the story of the life and death of his father, a foreman for a construction crew of Italian immigrants.

➤ Don DeLillo was born to Italian immigrant parents in 1936 and has published 11 novels, along with several plays and numerous stories. DeLillo won the William Dean Howells Medal for *Underworld* (Scribner, 1998), described by the American Academy of Arts and Letters as the "most distinguished work of American fiction" published in the last five years.

➤ The contemporary author Barbara Grizzuti-Harrison was raised in Brooklyn. A travel writer and essayist, Harrison is the author of one novel and five books of nonfiction, including *Italian Days* (Atlantic Monthly Press; 1998 winner of the American Book Award). Harrison also wrote *The Islands of Italy, a History, a Memory of Jehovah's Witnesses, The Astonishing World*, and most recently, *An Accidental Autobiography* (Houghton Mifflin Co., 1997).

➤ The writer Jerre (Gerlando) Mangione was born in Rochester, New York, in 1909, the first of six children born to Sicilian immigrants. Mangione is best known for his stories depicting the Italian-American immigrant experience. His fictionalized account of life in a Sicilian ghetto in Rochester became a classic of Italian-American life. The book *Mount Allegro* (Syracuse University Press, 1998) was a portrait of typical immigrant life and became a classic of ethnic American literature. A must-read for anyone interested in the experience of Sicilian immigrants.

➤ The author Ed McBain (1926–) was born Salvatore Albert Lombino and grew up in New York's East Harlem and North Bronx. He wrote the script for the movie *Blackboard Jungle* and invented the police procedural novel. In the course of his lifetime, he wrote 94 novels with 100 million copies in print in many languages. Early in his career, publishers warned him that "Lombino" was too hard to pronounce and might hurt sales. Lombino used several pen names, the most familiar being the Irish sounding "McBain" for his detective stories and "Evan Hunter" for his more literary works.

➤ The author of many feminist-related books, Camille Paglia was born on April 2, 1947, in Endicott, New York. Paglia is a professor of the humanities at the University of the Arts in Philadelphia and is the author of the books *Sexual Personae: Art and Decadence from Nefertiti to Emily Dickinson* (Vintage Books, 1991); *Sex, Art, and American Culture* (1992), and *Vamps and Tramps* (Vintage Books, 1994).

Di Interessa

If you're interested in pursuing a degree program in Italian studies, you can find a comprehensive list of universities and colleges at the Italian embassy Web site at www.italyemb.org.

➤ Mario Puzo (1920–1999) was born in Manhattan's West Side and, following military service in World War II, attended New York's New School for Social Research and Columbia University. Puzo is best known for having written the novel-turned-film *The Godfather* Putnam Pub Group, June 1969. Other critically acclaimed novels include *The Dark Arena* (Ballantine Books, 2001), *Fools Die* (Signet, 1996), *The Sicilian* (Ballantine Books, 1984), and *The Fourth K* (Random House, 1991). Mario passed away July 2, 1999, at his home in Bay Shore, Long Island. His novel *Omerta* (Ballantine Books, 2001) was released a year later.

Di Interessa

Mario Puzo also wrote several screenplays, including *Earthquake, Superman,* and all three of the *Godfather* movies for which he received two Academy Awards. His novel *The Last Don* (1996) was made into a CBS television miniseries.

➤ The writer Gay Talese (1932–) was one of the founders of the 1960's "New Journalism," a type of journalism that weaved fictional elements such as dialogue and scene description into news writing. From 1956 to 1965, Talese was a sports and politics reporter for *The New York Times.* Among his many best-sellers is *Honor Thy Father* (Ivy Books, 1992), the story of crime boss Joe Bonanno and his son Bill; *Thy Neighbor's Wife* (Ivy Books, 1993), which examines America's changing sexual mores; and *Unto the Sons,* a largely autobiographical book about his Italian heritage.

➤ The Emmy Award winner and author Gioia Timpanelli is considered by many to be the dean of America's professional storytellers. She lives in New York and in Italy and travels regularly around the country for storytelling performances, workshops, and seminars. Her works include *Sometimes the Soul: Two Novellas of Sicily* (W.W. Norton & Company, 1998), which won the 1999 American Book Award.

➤ The award-winning author Lewis Turco was born in Meridan, Connecticut. Turco has published 21 collections of his own poems, including *The Shifting Web: New and Selected Poems* (University of Arkansas, 1999) and a book of literary criticism, *Visions and Revisions of American Poetry* (University of Arkansas, 1986). His poetry, fiction, drama, and essays have appeared in most literary magazines and in over 100 books.

➤ Professor and writer Robert Viscusi is president of the Italian American Writers Association at Brooklyn College (CUNY) and has held grants from the National Endowment for the Humanities. Well-known for his essays and studies of Italian-American literature, he has published many books, including *Astoria* (Gaernica Editions, 1995), and the poem "An Oration Upon the Most Recent Death of Christopher Columbus" (1993).

➤ The novelist Frances Winwar (1900–1985) was born Francesca Vinciguerra. Winwar translated and wrote biographies of poets, statesmen, and heroes, including Joan of Arc and Napoleon. Born in Sicily, she came to the United States in 1907 and later anglicized her name on the advice of her editor.

The Italian American Writers Association

The Italian American Writers Association (IAWA) aims to promote Italian-American literature by encouraging the writing, reading, publication, distribution, translation, and study of Italian-American writing.

For more information about the IAWA, contact:

Italian American Writers Association
PO Box 2011
New York, NY 10013
212-625-3499
www.iawa.net

Biografia

Eugenio Montale (1896–1981) is an Italian-born poet, prose writer, editor, and translator who won the Nobel Prize for Literature in 1975 after being one of the chief architects of modern Italian poetry in the 1920s. Montale's dark and obscure poems have been superficially related to those written by his contemporaries Giuseppe Ungaretti and Salvatore Quasimodo, who were part of the hermeneutic school of poetry in Italy.

The Italian Influence on Education

Little has more impact on a society than the education offered its members, yet educators continue to be the unsung heroes. Who were the most important teachers and what were their contributions? Read on!

Maria Montessori

The Italian educator and physician Maria Montessori (1870–1952) developed the famous Montessori Method (1909), an innovative educational system that revolutionized the teaching of infants. During the 1920s and 1930s, she traveled and conducted courses in many countries. Many of her ideas have been incorporated into nursery education in Europe and the United States, and there are Montessori kindergartens and schools around the world.

The idea behind her method of instruction is that children should be allowed greater freedom in the pursuit of their studies, thereby gaining self-confidence.

The Center for Italian Studies

The Center for Italian Studies at the State University of New York, Stony Brook, is one of the few departments devoted to bringing about a better understanding of Italy and Italian Americans.

Through research, conferences, fellowship programs, and classes, students and participants are versed on political, economic, educational, and religious aspects of Italian and Italian-American culture.

The director of the Italian Studies Program, Fred Gardaphe is Associate Editor of *Fra Noi*, an Italian-American monthly newspaper. Gardaphe co-founded *VIA: Voices in Italian Americana*, a literary journal and cultural review. He is currently president of the American Italian Historical Association and served as vice president of the Italian Cultural Center in Stone Park, Illinois, from 1992 to 1998. Gardaphe's books include *New Chicago Stories, Italian American Ways* and *From the Margin: Writings in Italian-Americana*. His study, *Italian Signs, American Streets: The Evolution of Italian American Narrative*, was named an Outstanding Academic Book for 1996 by Choice. He has also published *Dagoes Read: Tradition and the Italian/American Writer* and *Moustache Pete Is Dead!*

Di Interessa

In Italy, literacy for men and women is almost the same (98 percent of males and 96 percent for women). For the first time in world history, women have surpassed men in the field of education: More women between ages 20 and 25 pursue a degree (secondary or higher) than men. Additionally, there are more women in the workforce than men.

The Italian American Program

Founded in 1990, the Italian American Program preserves and interprets the history and culture of people of Italian descent in Western Pennsylvania. It is one of the largest collections of oral histories, artifacts, photographs, and other research materials dealing with Italian immigrants and their descendants in the United States.

Di Interessa

For more information about the Italian American Program and contact:

Italian American Collection
Historical Society of Western Pennsylvania
Senator John Heinz Pittsburgh Regional History Center
1212 Smallman Street
Pittsburgh, PA 15222
412-454-6433

To view its Web page (and find useful links), go to www.wpaitalians.com.

Learned Individuals

Italian Americans have founded some of America's oldest colleges and universities. Two Italian Jesuits founded Santa Clara University in California: John Nobili and Michael Accolti in 1851. The Jesuit priest Joseph Cataldo founded Gonzaga University in Washington State in 1881. Father Pamphilus founded St. Bonaventure College, one of the best and well-known small colleges in New York State, in 1858.

➤ Father Giovanni Grassi served as the president of Georgetown College (now Georgetown University) in Washington, D.C., in 1812.

➤ Father Anthony Ciampi was president of Loyola College in Baltimore, Maryland in 1863.

➤ Father Lawrence B. Palladino was president of Gonzaga University, in Washington State, from 1894 to 1897.

➤ Leonard Covello (1887–1982) was the first Italian-American high school principal in New York City where he served at Benjamin Franklin High School in East Harlem from 1934 to 1956. A pioneer in bilingual education, Covello believed a school should serve the interests of its neighborhood. Covello was also a co-founder of the American Italian Historical Association in 1966.

➤ James Laita was one of seven men chosen by Benjamin Franklin, the University founder, to attend what was then called the College of Philadelphia. Laita was part of the first graduating class of the University of Pennsylvania in 1757.

➤ In 1978 at the age of 38, A. Bartlett Giamatti became the youngest president of Yale University in 200 years. He was also the first president not entirely of Anglo-Saxon heritage. As the New Haven, Connecticut, university's nineteenth president, Giamatti served until 1986 when he resigned to become the president of Major League Baseball (MLB). In January 1989, he became commissioner of Major League Baseball. He died of a heart attack in September 1989 at the age of 49.

➤ Peter Sammartino was the founder, president, and chancellor emeritus of the liberal arts institution Fairleigh Dickinson University in New Jersey, which he began in 1942 with his wife, Sylvia (Sally) Scaramelli. Sammartino also founded the International Association of University Presidents and was the author of 30 books. The Sammartinos died in 1992.

➤ While serving as superintendent of the Baltimore County schools, Anthony Marchione turned the nation's twenty-fifth largest school district with its 105,500 students around by pairing new teachers with experienced mentors and cutting class sizes. In 1993, Baltimore ranked thirteenth out of Maryland's 24 counties. By 1998, it ranked eighth.

Di Interessa

Mario E. Cosena was the first American of Italian birth to become dean of an American college in Brooklyn and launched the campaign to teach Italian language in the high schools and colleges of the nation.

➤ Lina Lantieri cofounded "Resolving Conflicts Creatively," an organization which teaches students how to prevent violence in the classroom in New York City. The private agency, founded in 1985, forms partnerships with public schools to help elementary and high school students develop conflict resolution skills and form friendships.

➤ Angelo Patri was best known for his widely syndicated column devoted to dispensing advice and counsel to parents on how to properly raise children. Patri also wrote numerous books on child psychology and was the first Italian-born educator to become a school principal in the United States.

➤ Joseph V. Calabrese was a member of the Colorado Legislature. He founded a school for exceptional children before becoming President and Director of the National Association for Retarded Children.

The Arts

For centuries, the Italians have enhanced the world we live in through their skill as artists, sculptors, and magic makers. Although there are far too many gifted Italian

Americans to mention here, read on to learn more about some of the talented artists whose works you probably recognize.

➤ Costantino Brumidi (1805–1880) emigrated to the United States in 1852. Considered the Michelangelo of the U.S. Capitol, Brumidi painted the huge Capitol interior dome as well as the President's Room, where Lincoln signed the Emancipation Proclamation. Brumidi started his career in Rome where he became known for restoration of classic works. In 1855 he began working on the Capitol dome and dedicated the rest of his life to embellishing the Capitol.

➤ Attilio Piccirilli and his five brothers carved the Lincoln Memorial in Washington, D.C., along with the stone lions that flank New York's Public Library, statues in Rockefeller Center, and many other works. In 1889, Piccirilli and his brothers established what would become one of the largest sculptures studio in the country.

Di Interessa

Three Italians—Enrico Causici, Antonio Capellano, and Luigi Persico—were sculptors who worked on the early phase of the building and decoration of the U.S. Capitol in 1805 and were the first to introduce American mythology into their sculptures.

➤ Artist Georgia O'Keeffe (1887–1986) was of Italian descent; her mother was Ida Totto and the artist was named for her maternal grandfather, Giorgio Totto. O'Keeffe pursued studies at the Art Institute of Chicago and the Art Students League in New York, where she was quick to master the principles of imitative realism. In 1908, she won the League's William Merritt Chase still-life prize for her oil painting *Untitled (Dead Rabbit with Copper Pot)*. O'Keeffe moved from New York to New Mexico, whose stunning vistas and stark landscape configurations inspired her work.

➤ Painter Giorgio Cavallon (1904–1989) was one of America's first abstract-expressionists whose works won him election to the American Academy and Institute of Arts and Letters. His artworks are part of the permanent collections of major museums of modern art around the world.

➤ Self-taught painter Ralph Fasanella (1914–1997) was known for his paintings that depicted working-class life and ethnic neighborhoods, especially that of his native Bronx in New York City. Fasanella is best known for his paintings *The Supper* and *The Great Strike—Lawrence 1912*.

➤ Painter Robert De Niro (1922–1993) has paintings in the Metropolitan and Brooklyn Museums and other major institutions. He was the father of the famous film actor who bears his name.

➤ Painter and sculptor Frank Stella (1936–) achieved fame in the 1960s. Stella's work ranges from minimalist paintings to abstract expressionism and his paintings hang in America's most prestigious museums, including New York's Museum of Modern Art, Chicago's Art Institute, and San Francisco's Museum as well as in museums in Europe. He was born in Malden, Massachusetts.

➤ Rosemarie Truglio is the director of research for public television's award-winning children's program *Sesame Street*. She develops the program's interdisciplinary curriculum and conducts research to enhance the program's educational and entertainment values. Dr. Truglio is a nationally recognized expert on the effects of television on children and teenagers.

The Least You Need to Know

➤ Italians have excelled in the fields of philosophy and literature.

➤ The contribution to the fields of education have been enormous and include the legendary Maria Montessori.

➤ Italian-American studies have become a regular element at several American universities.

➤ Italian artists such as Georgia O'Keeffe and Frank Stella have inspired future generations.

Science and Medicine

The list of Italian and Italian-American contributions to the sciences and medicine is enormous and finds evidence of greatness as far back as the Renaissance, when the known world was revealed to be far more vast than man had imagined.

Italians have been influencing the way we treat the human body for centuries. Influenced by the Arabs and the Byzantine Greeks, the renowned medical school of Salerno was devoted to scientific study and writing even as far back as the tenth century.

An excellent example of scientific curiosity combining art and science is in a Florence museum. At the Museo di Zoologia there is a section called Cere Anatomiche. Wax arms, legs, body sections, and organs cover the walls, and wax cadavers in various stages of deconstruction recline on satin beds. The artist Clemente Susini and the physiologist Felice Fontana made most of the models between 1775 and 1814 to serve as teaching aids.

Science and Medicine

Whether you're talking about physicists, biologists, physicians, chemists, or humanists, the curious Italians have been asking important questions regarding the very nature of life since Roman times. Read on to learn about a few of these Italians and Italian-American thinkers whose donations to the world have been revolutionary. The list is hardly comprehensive; rather, it hopes to illustrate a range of accomplishments made by Italian Americans.

In Italics

1221—The first autopsies were conducted in the first medical school of the Western world, founded in Salerno (Sicily).

Biografia

"Watson, *vieni qua!*" Those could have been the famous words that everyone associates with the invention of the telephone if Antonio Meucci (1808–1896), a mechanical engineer, had had the money to patent his device. In 1849, Meucci conceived of the idea of a *teletrofono* in Florence, years before Alexander Graham Bell claimed he had invented it.

Alessandro Volta

Alessandro Volta (1745–1827) was an Italian physicist credited with discovering that chemical energy could be converted into electrical energy. For this great discovery, he is considered the cofounder of electrochemistry and the inventor of the battery.

Enrico Fermi

The physicist Enrico Fermi (1901–1954) left Italy in 1938 to receive the Nobel Prize for Physics in Sweden. He never went back. He and his wife moved to the United States to escape Italy's increasing fascism and anti-Semitism.

In 1940, Enrico Fermi continued to conduct nuclear fission experiments at Columbia University. Fermi's team confirmed that absorption of a neutron by a uranium nucleus could cause the nucleus to split into two nearly equal parts, releasing several neutrons and enormous amounts of energy.

Since then, Fermi's theory has been expanded and refined. Nuclear reactors have been built in many countries to supply energy for military uses such as nuclear submarines and civilian uses such as ordinary electricity.

Guglielmo Marconi

The Italian scientist Guglielmo Marconi (1874–1937) was the inventor of a successful system of radiotelegraphy in 1896. In 1909 he received the Nobel Prize for Physics, which he shared with German physicist Ferdinand Braund. Marconi later worked on the development of short-wave wireless communication, which constitutes the basis of nearly all modern long-distance radio.

Not to Mention ...

Throughout the last couple of centuries, Italian Americans have been offering their insights and research to the world. A few of their many contributors are included here.

➤ Avogadro (1776–1856), a chemist and physicist, derived a hypothesis that led to Avogadro's number—6.02252×10^{23}—(the number of atoms in a mole) which is crucial to the study of chemistry. That's a *lot* of atoms!

➤ Stanislao Cannizzaro was a nineteenth-century chemist famous for his discovery of Cyanamid and his method of synthesizing alcohols. He was also responsible for explaining how atomic weights could be determined and distinguished from molecular weights. Together with another chemist, Amedeo Avogadro, he was responsible for defining the modern science of chemistry.

➤ Horticulturist Dr. E. O. Fenzi came to Santa Barbara, California, in 1893 to cultivate the nearly barren soil of that area. He introduced many foreign and exotic plants and was successful in growing them in the very arid territory.

➤ In 1895, Filoteo Alberini applied for a patent for a brand-new machine that could make motion pictures.

➤ Gaetano Lanza was born to Sicilian immigrants. In 1848, he founded the engineering department at the Massachusetts Institute of Technology in Cambridge, Massachusetts, where he taught mechanical engineering for 36 years.

Di Interessa

The Italian word *video* is derived from the Latin "I see" and has become part of television terminology.

➤ Vincenzo Lanciais is the automotive genius credited with inventing the one-piece cylinder block and crankcase, replacing the erratic chain drive with the universal jointed drive shaft-to-axle system, creating the first steel wheels (when everyone else was using wood) and a host of other breakthroughs including the first integral electrical system, the first V engine, and the first V12 engine. If this were not enough, in 1921 two historic innovations were developed by this Italian genius: unit body construction and independent front suspension.

➤ Count Alessandro Dandini patented more than 22 inventions after he arrived in the United States in 1945. Among his patents are the three-way light bulb, the rigid and retractable automobile top, and the spherical system, which concentrates and extracts solar energy.

➤ In 1959, Emilio Serge and Owen Chamberlain were awarded the Nobel Prize for Physics for their experiments that demonstrated the existence of the anti-proton (not to be confused with the anti-popes, about whom you read in Chapter 8, "Popes, Politics, and Power").

➤ In 1969, Rocco Petrone helped make possible the first moonwalk. He was director of Apollo 11 launch operations and oversaw the first lunar landing and five subsequent lunar missions. He was also responsible for the NASA portion of the U.S./Soviet Apollo-Soyuz test project.

➤ Italian physician and poet Francesco Redi (1626–1697) proved, through a series of biological experiments, that life among lower life forms was not a result of spontaneous generations. To prove his theory, he performed some of the first biological experiments ever to employ the use of proper scientific controls.

➤ Albert Sacco Jr., the chairman of the chemistry department at Worcester Polytechnic Institute in Massachusetts, spent 16 days in space in 1995 on the space shuttle *Columbia*.

Biografia

Galileo Galilei was the first to write in Italian rather than Latin in scientific works.

"Italia"

In Italics

Sometime between 1175 and 1230, Ruggero Frugardo wrote the first textbook of surgery ever compiled. The book contained many drawings that demonstrated the latest techniques used by doctors of the day. It was the predominantly used source until the Renaissance.

Jacuzzi

The seven Jacuzzi brothers (Joseph, Frank, Valeriano, Rachele, Candido, Giocondo, and Gelindo) from Pomone, Italy, have an impressive list of inventions. They include the toothpick propeller, the world's first enclosed cabin style monoplane (first used by the Allies and honored in the Smithsonian's National Air and Space Museum), and the jet injector pump for deep wells.

Later developments by this company include jet propulsion units for boats, propeller fans for keeping frost out of orchards, and a variety of jet and submersible pumps. But their most famous invention in involved bathing and became synonymous with their family name, the Jacuzzi whirlpool.

Medicine

The Italian contributions to the fields of immunology and genetic research have helped saved millions of lives.

➤ Lazzaro Spallanzani was the first scientist, in 1780, to theorize and prove that spermatozoa were necessary for the fertilization of a mammal.

➤ Tullio Suzzara Verdi was born in Mantua in 1829 and studied medicine at Hahnemann College in Philadelphia. In 1859, he became the first Italian-American medical school graduate.

➤ Feli Formento was the chief surgeon of the Louisiana Confederate Hospital during the Civil War. He later became president of the American Public Health Association, which educates the public about health issues.

➤ Camillo Golgi received the Nobel Prize for Medicine in 1906. He also developed a method of staining cells with silver nitrate, which allowed the researcher to see clearly all the varied features of nerve elements.

➤ Beginning in the 1930s, Vincent R. Ciccone secured over 20 patents for techniques that contributed to the mass production of penicillin. He revolutionized the way medicine is combined with hard candy, paving the way for the production of cough drops and other medicinal lozenges.

➤ Mariana Bertola, M.D., also known as "Dr. Crusade," was a teacher, obstetrician, political activist, and social reformer who founded women's clubs and settlement houses in California during the first decades of the twentieth century. Through her work with the California Federation of Women's Clubs, she ensured that every county hospital in the state had both children's and maternity wards.

➤ In 1943, Salvador Luria and Max Delbruck wrote a paper on the mutations of bacteria-hosting phages that have been called the starting point of bacterial genetics. In 1969, Luria was the co-recipient of the Nobel Prize for Medicine for discoveries concerning the replication mechanism and genetic structure of viruses.

➤ In 1950, Margaret J. Giannini, M.D., founded the Mental Retardation Institute in New York City. This was the first for the handicapped in the world.

"*Italia*"

In Italics

1859—Tullio Suzzara Verdi, M.D., becomes the first Italian-American medical school graduate after studying medicine at Hahnemann College in Philadelphia. Verdi attended Secretary of State Charles Seward the night President Lincoln was fatally shot. Seward was attacked in his home as part of the assassination plot that killed Lincoln.

➤ In 1951, Raffaele Lattes became director of the laboratory for surgical pathology and has been a professor of surgery and surgical pathology at the College of Physicians and Surgeons of Columbia University.

➤ In 1962, Piero Foa joined the faculty of Wayne State University and the division of research of Sinai Hospital in Detroit; for his research he received awards from the Illinois Medical Society, the Chicago Medical School, and the Council of Chicago Technical Societies in several areas of medicine and physiology.

"Italia"

In Italics

To date, three Italian Americans have received the Nobel Prize for Medicine: Salvador Luria (1969), Renato Dulbecco (1975), and Louis Ignarro (1998).

Di Interessa

Girolamo Fracastoro was a sixteenth-century physician and poet who developed epidemiology, a branch of medical science that deals with control of disease. A humanist, Fracastoro wrote the first textbook on contagious diseases in which he defined infection as the passage of minute bodies from the infected body to another person. You probably know them as "germs."

➤ In 1975, the virologist Renato Dulbecco received the Nobel Prize for Medicine for his research into cancer replication. Born in the region of Calabria in 1914, Dulbecco emigrated to the United States in 1947. The recipient of many academic honors and awards, Dulbecco's pioneering research showed that the key to understanding and eliminating cancer lies in DNA research.

➤ In 1984, Robert Gallo, M.D., a research scientist and virologist in Maryland, co-discovered the AIDS virus and developed a blood test to screen for the disease.

➤ Since 1984, Anthony S. Fauci, M.D., has been the director of the National Institutes of Allergy and Infectious Diseases in Maryland. His research has led to the development of effective therapies for several formally fatal immunological diseases. He has overseen the development and testing of therapies to help people with AIDS and other contagious diseases.

➤ In 1994, the groundbreaking book, *The History and Geography of Human Genes,* was written as the result of 12 years of research. It is the largest collection of genetic information about over 400 populations around the world. The book was written by Luigi Cavalli-Sforza, a genetics professor at Stanford University, and was co-authored with Paolo Menozzi and Alberto Piazza.

➤ In 1999, Catherine De Angelis, M.D., became the first woman to become editor of the *Journal of the American Medical Association (JAMA)* in its 116-year history. This high achiever became dean at Baltimore's Johns Hopkins School of Medicine. De Angelis started as a nurse and then put herself through college and medical school.

➤ Albert D. Pacifico, M.D., is a heart surgeon and director of the Division of Cardiothoracic Surgery at the University of Alabama at Birmingham. He is responsible for developing new techniques and refined surgical methods in adult and pediatric heart surgery.

➤ Pierantonio Russo, M.D., is a pioneer in pediatric cardiac transplant surgery; his work in Philadelphia helps to provide new hearts to newborn infants.

➤ In 1986, Rita Levi-Montalcini and her colleague were awarded the Nobel Prize for Medicine for their cancer research. Montalcini researched tumor and nerve cell growth in an effort to develop new techniques for battling the disease and for regenerating damaged nerves. With a colleague, she discovered a protein from a tumor that could spur new nerve growth.

Di Interessa

In the sixteenth century, Gasparo Tagliocozzi was a professor of anatomy and surgery at the University of Bologna. The most common use of the skills he pioneered is in the field of cosmetic surgery. His repair techniques centered on nasal reconstruction, and he developed procedures to avoid the rejection of transplanted tissue.

The Least You Need to Know

➤ The Italian Enrico Fermi received the Nobel Prize for Physics in 1938.

➤ Guglielmo Marconi is best known as the inventor of the radio and won the Nobel Prize for Physics in 1909.

➤ Italians have excelled in the medical profession through their work in the fields of immunology, biology, and chemistry.

➤ To date, three Italian Americans have won the Nobel Prize for Medicine: Salvador Luria (1969), Renato Dulbnecco (1975), and Louis Ignarro (1998).

Circo Massimo

Ever since the first minstrels tied on their bells and started dancing and singing, the Italians have been big on entertainment.

Along with their recipes and stories, the Italian immigrants brought over a tradition in sports and entertainment that gave us greats like Frank Sinatra, Rudolph Valentino, and Tony Bennett.

The Old-Timers

Before video and television, radio was the main form of entertainment for most American families. Back in the years during the war and after, voice was the link to the world.

They sang to us and expressed the feelings, hopes, dreams, and fears shared by a nation. These were the immigrants and the children of the immigrants. They had come from humble beginnings and made it big. They evoked pride in the Italian-American community and showed the world just how good it could get.

Although today we have television, music videos and CD players, some of those old-timers are still breaking our hearts, and we love them for it!

Tony Bennett

In 1926, the singer Tony Bennett (born Anthony Dominick Benedetto) was born in New York City. He grew up in Queens, New York. His father emigrated from Calabria, while his mother was born in New York's Little Italy.

During the 1950s, the suave Bennett had a series of popular hit singles. In the 1960s, he performed with several swing bands such as those led by Count Basie, Duke Ellington, and Woody Herman. Bennett's signature song, of course, is "I Left My Heart in San Francisco."

Bennett has won several Grammy Awards and had a resurgence in the 1990s, winning the album of the year Grammy Award and becoming the idol of the unplugged MTV generation.

Perry Como

The performer and singer Perry Como (1912–2001) grew up in Conansburg, Pennsylvania. One of 13 children of Italian immigrants, Como left his job as a barber in the 1930s to sing with big bands. In 1945, Como had his first million-selling hit, "Till the End of Time." Best known for his annual Christmas special, he will be remembered as one of the country's most popular entertainers in the post–World War II era.

Henry Mancini

The composer, conductor, pianist, and arranger Enrico Nicola Mancini (1924–1994) composed more than 70 film scores, including *Breakfast at Tiffany's,* with its hit song "Moon River" (1961), *The Days of Wine and Roses* (1962), *The Pink Panther* (1964), and music for the television serials *Peter Gunn* and *The Thornbirds*. In the course of his successful career, Mancini recorded more than 80 albums and won 20 Grammy Awards, two Emmys, and four Academy Awards

Biografia

Guido d'Arezzo (990–1050), an Italian monk, invented the musical notation system do-re-me-fa-sol-la-ti-do. He also popularized the use of colored lines in written music to indicate pitch.

Dean Martin

Dean Martin (1917–1995; born Dino Crocetti) was born in Steubenville, Ohio, and began singing in nightspots in his hometown and later around the country. After teaming up with comedian Jerry Lewis, the Martin-Lewis team was soon one of the hottest successes in show business. Martin was a member of the famed "Rat Pack," he costarred in the early 1960s in several films featuring Frank Sinatra, Peter Lawford, and the gang.

Frank Sinatra: "Ol' Blue Eyes"

The "Chairman of the Board," Francis Albert Sinatra (1915–1998), grew up in Hoboken, New Jersey, to Italian immigrants. Also known as "Ol Blue Eyes", Sinatra began his singing career in the l930s with Tommy Dorsey's band and soon after entered the movies, winning an Academy Award in 1953 for *From Here to Eternity*. During his long career, he became one of the most successful pop music figures of the century and was widely respected for his versatile musical style and rich voice. Sinatra retired from show business in 1971 but returned in several concert tours. He was married four times, to Nancy Barbato (with whom he had three children, Nancy, Frank, and Tina), the actor Ava Gardner, actress Mia Farrow, and until his death to Barbara Marx.

Di Interessa

Italian is the universal musical language for tempo and dynamics, among other things. Words like *allegro* (fast or lively), *andante* (medium pace), and *presto* (very fast) are all used to mark the score of compositions.

Rock My World, Bambino

The voices of Italian Americans are listened to around the world. From the lewd words sung by the rock star Frank Zappa to the triumphant trumpet music of the jazz master Chuck Mangione, to the provocative lyrics of Madonna, you're sure to recognize these happening, hopping, rockin' and rollin' personalities.

Jon Bon Jovi

Jon Bon Jovi (John Frank Bongiovi) was born March 2, 1962, in New Jersey. Bon Jovi is an international rock star and actor who's won several awards with his band of the same name. Arena rock classics like "You Give Love a Bad Name," "Lay Your Hands on Me," and "Keep the Faith," as well as popular videos on MTV, have made his band immensely popular.

Madonna

The pop singer, dancer, songwriter, and actress Madonna (Madonna Louise Veronica Ciccone) was born August 16, 1958. Madonna began as a dancer at the University of Michigan before moving to New York City with $30 in her pocket. Her albums *Madonna* (1983) and *Like a Virgin* (1984) secured her position as a sexual and pop icon. In 1985 she won critical praise for her part in the Hollywood film *Desperately*

Seeking Susan. Truth or Dare (1991) was a revealing backstage performance film that paved the way for her book *Sex* (1992), which garnered enormous publicity. She has her own recording company and produces her own films and videos. Her album *Music* was released in the fall of 2000. Driven by the success of the title track, *Music* received several Grammy Award nominations, including Record of the Year and Best Vocal Pop Album.

Chuck Mangione

Charles Frank Mangione was born in Rochester, New York, on November 29, 1940, the son of an Italian-born grocer. He first attracted attention with his older brother, Gap, in a mainstream jazz band, The Jazz Brothers, in which he played trumpet for which he became so widely known. He has been praised for his musical innovation and performance ability for five decades.

Bruce Springsteen

Born September 23, 1949, in Freehold, New Jersey, Bruce Springsteen has become one of the most popular rock musicians of the past 30 years. Thanks to his rebellious persona, lyrics about small-town outsiders, and memorable pop tunes, he has sold tens of millions of albums and won over legions of loyal fans worldwide. He has been nominated for two Grammys and an Oscar for his song "Philadelphia."

Frank Zappa

The rock and roller Frank Zappa (1940–1992) was one of the great iconoclastic musicians of the twentieth century. He was born in 1940 in Baltimore where his Sicilian-born father was employed. Zappa formed an R&B group called the Blackouts and played drums in his high school band. Zappa's post-modernistic music took inspiration from all kinds of music. By the time of his death after a long battle against prostate cancer, Zappa had recorded over 60 albums. In 1994, Zappa was elected by critics into *Down Beat* magazine's Hall of Fame.

Di Interessa

Many Italian Americans were bandleaders and included notables such as Guy Lombardo, Louis Prima, Ted Fio Rito, Joe Venuti, Frankie Carle, Carmen Cavallero, and Henry Mancini.

At the Metropolitan Opera

The Metropolitan Opera became one of the finest opera companies in the world under the leadership and management of Giulio Gatti-Casazza (1869–1940). Giulio brought to its stage a brilliant array of singers, including Enrico Caruso, Rosa Ponselle, Amelita Galli-Curci, Beniamino Gigli, and Ezio Pinza, as well as the conductor Arturo Toscanini. Gatti-Casazza managed the Met from 1908 to 1935.

Enrico Caruso

Born in Naples, the opera legend Enrico Caruso (1873–1921) was the most admired Italian operatic tenor of the early twentieth century and one of the first musicians to document his voice on gramophone recordings.

The eighteenth of 20 children, Caruso came from a poor family. He received no formal music training until his study with Guglielmo Vergine at age 18. Within three years, in 1894, he made his operatic debut in Mario Morelli's *L'Amico Francesco* in Naples at the Teatro Nuovo. Four years later, Enrico was asked to create the role of Loris in the premiere of Umberto Giordano's *Fedora* in Milan. He was a big hit and soon his calendar was full with world-wide engagements. In 1900, Enrico debuted at Milan's famous opera house La Scala with *La Bohème*.

Caruso became the most celebrated and highest paid of his contemporaries. He made recordings of about 200 operatic excerpts and songs; many of them are still being published. His voice was sensuous, lyrical, and vigorous in dramatic outbursts and became progressively darker in timbre in his later years. Its appealing tenor qualities were unusually rich in lower registers and abounded in warmth, vitality, and smoothness.

La Bella Lingua

Bravo? Brava? Want to cheer, but don't know the right words? To applaud, use *bravo!*—one man; *brava!*—one woman; *bravi!*—two or more people, at least one of them a man; *brave!*—two or more women. The French term *ancor* is short for the Italian *ancora* and means "again."

Anna Moffo

Another Italian-American star of the Met was Anna Moffo, who was born in Wayne, Pennsylvania, on June 27, 1932, to Italian-American parents. She studied singing under Euphemia Giannini-Gregory and later won a Fulbright scholarship and studied in Europe. Ms. Moffo debuted in 1959 with the Metropolitan Opera Company as Violetta in Guiseppe Verdi's *La Traviata*. She had a 17-season career with the Met and sang 220 performances in 18 operas.

Liberace

The flamboyant pianist, singer, and actor Liberace (1919–1987) was born as Wladziu Valentino Liberace in Wisconsin. Famous for the candelabrum he always placed on top of his piano, by the mid-1950s, 192 television stations carried his successful show, *The Liberace Show*. The University of Nevada at Las Vegas houses a collection of Liberace memorabilia at the Liberace Museum.

Gian Carlo Menotti

The composer and writer Gian Carlo Menotti was born on July 7, 1911, in Cadegliano, Italy. In 1923, he began his formal musical training at the Verdi Conservatory in Milan. Following the death of his father, his mother took him to the United States, where he enrolled at Philadelphia's Curtis Institute of Music to study composition under Rosario Scalero.

In 1958, Menotti organized the Festival of Two Worlds, in Spoleto, Italy, a program dedicated to collaboration and one of the most popular festivals in Europe. The festival literally became "of two worlds" in 1977 with the founding of Spoleto USA in Charleston, South Carolina, which Menotti led until 1993 when he became Director of the Rome Opera. In 1984, Menotti was awarded the Kennedy Center Honor for lifetime achievement in the arts. He was chosen the 1991 "Musician of the Year" by *Musical America*, inaugurating worldwide tributes to the composer in honor of his eightieth birthday.

Di Interessa

Italian-American cartoonists have created some of the world's most popular animated characters including Donald Duck, created by Alfred Tagliafero; Woody Woodpecker, a creation of Walter Lantz, (born "Lanza"); and Casper, the Friendly Ghost, the brainchild of Joseph Oriolo.

Cinema

Italians have always loved movies and movie stars. After all, the word *paparazzi* derived from a character in a Fellini movie. In *La Dolce Vita*, Paparazzo is a freelance photographer on a sputtering scooter who pursues celebrities with a big, boxy flash camera.

Although there are far more wonderful and talented actors, directors, and producers than mentioned here, you can start the show with this mini-guide of Italian Americans in cinema. Let's start with the directors.

Albert R. "Cubby" Broccoli

Bond … James Bond. Cubby Broccoli (1909–1996) produced all but one of the 17 *James Bond* movies, launching the wildly successful *007* film series in 1962 with *Dr. No*. His last film was *Golden Eye* in 1995.

Frank Capra

Filmmaker Frank Capra was born May 18, 1897, in Bisaquino, Sicily, and moved to California with his family when he was six years old. He made some of the most memorable films ever, including *It Happened*

Di Interessa

Broccoli, that green vegetable that your mother made you eat when you were growing up, was actually developed and named by Broccoli's ancestors in the nineteenth century.

One Night, Mr. Deeds Goes to Town, Lost Horizon, Meet John Doe, and *It's a Wonderful Life.*

Francis Ford Coppola

Francis Ford Coppola was born April 7, 1939, in Detroit, Michigan. He is one of the most successful and controversial moviemakers in the United States and around the world. His best-known works include *Apocalypse Now* (1979), *The Godfather* trilogy (1972–1990), *Tucker* (1988), and *Bram Stoker's Dracula* (1992).

Brian De Palma

The screenwriter and producer Brian De Palma was born in 1940 in Newark, New Jersey. A master of the psychological thriller, De Palma has consistently demonstrated a fluent, inventive cinematic style. De Palma began making films as a student, first at Columbia, later at Sarah Lawrence. Although De Palma works primarily in the genre of the psychological thriller, elements of romance, horror, and gangster melodramas are explored as well. Films include *Carrie, The Untouchables,* and *Mission: Impossible.*

> **Biografia**
>
> Among the many Italian Americans working in Hollywood is the father-and-son team of Carmine and Francis Ford Coppola, who won four Oscars in 1975 for *The Godfather, Part II.* Carmine, who was a flautist for Arturo Toscanini, composed the soundtrack and Francis, who first won an Oscar for *Patton,* directed the film.

Penny Marshall

Penny Marshall (Carole Penny Masciarelli) was born in the Bronx, New York, on October 15, 1942. She starred in the hit TV series *Laverne and Shirley* before becoming one of the few women directors in Hollywood. Her second film, *Big* (1988) made her the first woman director in American history to direct a film that earned $100 million. Her other films include *Jumpin' Jack Flash, Awakenings,* and *A League of Their Own,* costarring another Italian American, Madonna.

Martin Scorsese

Martin Scorsese was born in Flushing, New York, in 1942 and has been one of America's most critically acclaimed filmmakers for more than 20 years. He achieved cinematic success with movies that reflect his own Italian-American Catholic upbringing. The Oscar-winning *Goodfellas* was adapted from Nicholas Pileggi's book *Wiseguys,* about Henry Hill, a gangster turned informant. A brilliant, bloody study of the Mafia, *Goodfellas* is classic Scorsese. When asked what he thought he would grow up to be, Scorsese is quoted as saying, "I only wanted to be an ordinary parish priest."

Quentin Tarantino

The director and actor Quentin Tarantino was born 1963 in Knoxville, Tennessee. At the age of 2, he and his 18-year-old mother moved to Los Angeles. His mother took him to the cinema from an early age, where he saw the film *Carnal Knowledge* at age eight and *Deliverance* at age nine. From this early introduction Tarantino fell in love with the cinema.

In 1992, Tarantino burst onto the movie scene with his dark and violent crime story *Reservoir Dogs,* which he both wrote and directed. He also directed *Pulp Fiction* (1994) and *Jackie Brown* (1998), and wrote the screenplay for *True Romance* (1993).

Stanley Tucci

The actor and director Stanley Tucci made his film debut with *Prizzi's Honor* (1985) and went on to direct the successful film *Big Night* (1996), a film that portrayed an ambitious Italian-American restaurateur, and *Joe Gould's Secret* (2000), a drama about an eccentric man living on the streets of Greenwich Village. Regarding Italian Americans in film, Tucci is quoted as saying, "I, and 15 million other Italian Americans, suffer from stereotyping all the time. I'm always getting scripts with guys who come from Brooklyn and talk like, 'Hey, whattayadoin'?' It's the only way Italians are portrayed in American film."

Actors

The Italian Americans have been making us laugh and cry for decades.

Marlon Brando

Marlon Brando was born in 1924 in Omaha, Nebraska. The powerful Brando is one of the most celebrated and influential screen and stage actors of the postwar era. A combative and often contradictory man, Brando's many films include *Streetcar Named Desire* (1951), *The Wild One* (1953), *On the Waterfront* (1954), *The Godfather* (1972), and *Apocalypse Now* (1979).

Nicolas Cage

The sex symbol and actor Nicolas Coppola, best known as Nicolas Cage, was born in 1964 in Long Beach, California. A nephew of the director Francis Ford Coppola, Cage graduated from doing teenage parts in films like *Valley Girl* (1983) and *Rumble Fish* (1983) to portraying a series of leading roles. Cage's films include *Moonstruck* (1987), *Raising Arizona* (1987), and *Leaving Las Vegas* (1995). In *Moonstruck,* he plays an Italian American who falls in love with his brother's fiancée. Interestingly, Nic Cage chose a new surname so he'd be evaluated on his own merits and not as part of the Coppola family.

Robert De Niro

Robert De Niro was born on August 17, 1943, and grew up in Little Italy, New York City. De Niro's first big success was in 1973 when he played the treacherous Johnny Boy in Martin Scorsese's movie *Mean Streets*. The very next year, he won the Academy Award for Best Supporting Actor as young Don Vito Corleone in *The Godfather, Part II*.

From that point forward, De Niro's notoriety and masterful performances have increased and indeed continue to grow. Today, he is recognized as one of the greatest actors of the twentieth century.

Susan Lucci

Susan Lucci was born on December 23, 1948, in Scarsdale, New York. Susan Lucci began playing Erica Kane on the soap opera *All My Children* in 1970, winning the daytime Emmy for best actress in 1999.

Al Pacino

Al Pacino was born Alfredo James Pacino in New York City on April 25, 1940. He is best known for his award-winning portrayal of Michael Corleone in all three films made from Mario Puzo's *Godfather*. He was nominated for a Golden Globe and an Academy Award in the film *Glengarry Glen Ross* (1992) and won both the Academy Award and the Golden Globe award for his performance in *Scent of a Woman* (1992).

Susan Sarandon

Born Susan Tomalin in New York City (1946), Sarandon is known for her screen portrayals of mature women with a strong sexuality. Sarandon worked in the theatre and television before attracting growing attention in *The Front Page* (1974), *The Great Waldo Pepper* (1975), and especially *The Rocky Horror Picture Show* (1975).

In 1982, she was named Best Actress at the Venice Film Festival for playing the role of Aretha in *Tempest* (1982). Sarandon has had major parts in a series of successful films, including *The Witches of Eastwick* (1987), *Bull Durham* (1988), *A Dry White Season* (1989), and *Thelma and Louise* (1991). She won the Best Actress Award for her role in *Dead Man Walking* (1996).

Sylvester Stallone

The actor, director, and writer Sylvester Stallone was born July 6, 1946, in New York City. In just three days he wrote the screenplay *Rocky* (1976), a film that would make him a star. Directed by John G. Avildsen, *Rocky* won Academy Awards for Best Picture and Best Director. Stallone was nominated for Best Actor and Best Original Screenplay.

John Travolta

Born February 18, 1954, in Englewood, New Jersey, Travolta has starred in a number of films, such as the blockbuster *Saturday Night Fever, Grease, Urban Cowboy,* and the Brian De Palma thrillers *Carrie* and *Blow Out.* He's been nominated twice for Academy Awards and also starred in Quentin Tarantino's *Pulp Fiction.*

Rudolph Valentino

One of the first immigrants to gain nationwide fame in the United States was Rudolph Valentino, born Rodolfo Guglielmi in southern Italy. He came to New York City in 1913, taking work as a dishwasher, janitor, and gardener. His talent as a tango dancer won him a Hollywood contract. He made only three movies, but they repeated the image of the dark, passionate Latin lover.

Let's Have a *Festa*

Americans love movies and television. Some additional well-known Italian-American performers include the following:

Danny Aiello: actor

Don Ameche: actor

Sonny Salvatore Bono: singer, songwriter, actor, politician

Ernest Borgnine (Ermes Eferon Borgnino): actor

Jerry Colonna: actor, comedian

Lou Costello: actor, comedian

Vic Damone: singer

Tony Danza: boxer, actor, comedian

Dom DeLuise: actor, comedian

Danny DeVito: actor, director, producer, comedian

Leonardo DiCaprio: actor

Jimmy Durante: actor, comedian, singer

Anthony Franciosa: actor

Connie Francis (born Constance Franconero): singer

Annette Funicello: actress

Vincent Gardenia (born Vincente Scognamiglio): actor

Vittorio Gassman: director

Ben Gazzara: actor, director

Dennis James (born Demie James Sposa): actor

Frankie Laine: singer

Julius LaRosa: singer

Jay Leno: talk show host

Ray Liotta: actor

Sal Mineo: actor

Liza Minnelli: singer, actress

Vincente Minnelli: director

Joe Montagna: actor

Joe Pesci: actor

Stephen Segal: actor, director

Mira Sorvino: actress

Marisa Tomei: actress

John Turturro: actor

Di Interessa

The Chicago-based National Italian-American Sports Hall of Fame honors medical, business, and sports professionals who are members of the Italian community and provides local students with scholarship money.

Sports

There's nothing like witnessing perfection in a sport. It must have been something to watch baseball legend Joe DiMaggio in his prime or see boxing champion Rocky Marciano, the "Rock," win the world heavyweight championship. Read on to learn more about some of America's greatest athletes.

Phil Rizzuto

Known as "the Scooter" for his agility as a shortstop, Phil Rizzuto (1918–) played for the New York Yankees from 1941 to 1954, minus two years spent in the Navy during World War II (1943–1945). A key member of ten Yankee pennant-winning teams and nine World Series classics, he had 200 hits in 1950, a Yankee club record for shortstops, which helped earn him selection as the American League's Most Valuable Player that year. After retiring, he became a sports announcer and was known as "the Voice of the Yankees."

Vince Lombardi

Legendary football coach Vince Lombardi (1913–1970) led the Green Bay Packers to five National Football League (NFL) championships (between 1959 and 1967), the first and second Super Bowls (1967 and 1968), and three world titles during the 1960s. The Brooklyn-born former football player and coach introduced the T-formation offense, which he used in 1956 to bring the New York Giants to their first NFL championship since 1938. In 1969, he coached Washington, D.C.'s Redskins, bringing them to their first winning season in more than two decades. He died in 1970 and was elected posthumously to the Football Hall of Fame the same year. His motto was "Winning isn't everything, but wanting to win is."

Di Interessa

The Colosseum in Rome could seat 50,000 people and was used mainly for gladiatorial and wild-beast fights and was frequently flooded for large-scale mock naval battles.

Joe Paterno

Joe Paterno became head coach of the Pennsylvania State University football team in 1965 where he led the team to 22 major bowl games and four perfect seasons. Under his leadership, the team produced many All-American players and 48 players who joined the NFL. Three times honored as Coach of the Year, he has won more than 80 percent of his games.

Dan Marino

Dan Marino (1961–) played for the Miami Dolphins, and was the highest-rated quarterback in the NFL in 1984. He passed for an amazing 47 touchdowns in his first 20 games, a record it took Joe Namath three seasons to accomplish.

Franco Harris

The Pittsburgh Steelers football giant Franco Harris is a black Italian American whose mother came from Lucca. A record-breaking rusher, he led his team to its first divisional title in 40 years and then won two league championships in 1974 and 1975. He held the record for the most yards gained in a Super Bowl—158—against the Minnesota Vikings in 1975.

Brian Piccolo

Brian Piccolo led the nation in rushing when he played for Wake Forest University, totaling 1,044 yards during his senior year in 1964. Drafted by the Chicago Bears, he gained 927 yards and caught 58 passes before his life was cut short by cancer in 1970 when he was 27 years old.

Joe Montana

The greatest Super Bowl drive of all time—eight completed passes in two minutes and thirty seconds—was the work of San Francisco 49er Joe Montana in 1984. Montana quarterbacked the 49ers to four Super Bowl titles before playing for the Kansas City Chiefs. He was the Most Valuable Player of three of those four Super Bowls.

Yogi Berra

Yogi Berra (Lawrence Peter Berra) was born on May 12, 1925, in St. Louis, Missouri, and grew up on Elizabeth Street in a neighborhood called The Hill. As a baseball player he became a 15-time All Star, winning the AL MVP three times, in 1951, 1954, and 1955. He played in 14 World Series and holds numerous World Series records, including most games by a catcher (63), hits (71), and times on a winning team (10), first in at bats, first in doubles, second in RBI's (runs batted in), third in home runs and BOB's (bases on balls). Yogi also hit the first pinch-hit home run in World Series history in 1947. Yogi was elected to the National Baseball Hall of Fame in 1972.

The Yankee Clipper: Joe DiMaggio

Joe DiMaggio (Joseph Paul DiMaggio Jr.) was born in Martinez, California, on November 25, 1914, to Sicilian parents from the island Isola Femmine off Sicily. He grew up in San Francisco's Little Italy and was known as Joltin' Joe when he was a star of the New York Yankees team from 1936 to 1951. DiMaggio was renowned for his outstanding batting ability and for his outfield play. In 1941, Joltin' Joe broke the previously held record of 44 games with a hit. He went on to create a 56-game hitting streak, which still holds today. During World War II, Joe missed three years of baseball while performing military service. He was briefly married to Marilyn Monroe in 1954.

Di Interessa

Seven Italian-American football players have won the Heisman Trophy, college football's highest honor. They are Alan Ameche (Wisconsin), Gary Beban (UCLA), Joe Bellino (Navy), Angelo Bertelli (Notre Dame), John Cappelletti (Penn State), Gino Torretta (Miami), and Vinny Testaverde (Miami). Cappelletti, an all-American running back, gave his trophy to his younger brother, Joey, who was dying of cancer.

Di Interessa

Italy now has a professional basketball league. Many former and aspiring NBA players have played for the teams—but it doesn't threaten to eclipse the popularity of *calcio* (soccer) any time soon.

All-Time All-Star Italian-American Baseball Team

There are so many incredible Italian-American baseball players it would be impossible to list all of them here. The following players are best known for the positions they held during the course of their very successful careers. Some include ...

Managers

Tony LaRusso

Tommy Lasorda

Phil Cavarretta

Billy Martin

Manuel Pesano

Joe Altobelli

First Basemen

Lee Mazzilli

Joe Pepitone

Second Basemen

Craig Biggio

Tony Lazzeri

Shortstops

Phil Rizzuto

Rico Petrocelli

Catchers

Yogi Berra

Roy Campanella

Third Basemen

Sal Bando

Ron Santo

Outfielders

Tony Conigliaro

Rocky Colavito

Joe DiMaggio

Buttercup Dickerson (born Lewis Pessano)

Pitchers

Dave Giusti

Sal Maglie

Vic Raschi

Dave Righetti

Designated Hitters

Ed Abbaticchio

Joe Torre

Jennifer Capriati

Born March 29, 1976, tennis player Jennifer Capriati became the youngest Grand Slam semi-finalist ever when she won the French Open at the age of 14, the same year she became the youngest player to win a match at Wimbledon. After some time off from the game due to personal challenges, Capriati won the Australian and French Opens in 2001.

Biografia

The first Italian–American base-ball player in the major leagues was Buttercup Dickerson. Born Lewis Pessano (1858–1920), he began playing for Cincinnati in 1878 as the starting outfielder.

Mario Andretti

Racecar driver Mario Andretti was born in 1940 in Montona, Italy, in an area now part of Slovenia. He grew up in Lucca, where he began racing at age 13. In 1955, his family moved to Nazareth, Pennsylvania. As a racecar driver, he won the USAC championship in 1965, the year he entered the Indianapolis 500 for the first time. He repeated as USAC champion in 1966, won the Daytona 500 (a stock-car event) in 1967, and won the Indianapolis 500 in 1969. Andretti has also raced with—and against—his sons Michael and Jeff, who also became professional automobile racers. Andretti retired from competition in 1994.

Rocky Graziano

The American boxer Rocky Graziano (Thomas Rocco Barbella, 1922–1990) was the world middleweight boxing champion (1947–1948). The resourceful Graziano retired from boxing in 1952 and became a beloved comic actor. In 1956, his autobiography *Somebody Up There Likes Me* was made into a film. Graziano was inducted into the Boxing Hall of Fame in 1971.

Rocky Marciano

The popular boxer Rocky Marciano (Rocco Francis Marchegiano, 1923–1969), "the Rock," was born in Brockton, Massachusetts, and was the only undefeated champion boxer. He began boxing in the United States Army in 1943. In September 1952, Marciano won the heavyweight championship, and successfully defended his title six times between 1952 and 1956. Unquestionably one of the world's great boxers, Marciano died in a plane crash in 1969.

Charles Atlas

The strongman and physical fitness buff Angelo Siciliano (1892–1972) was born in Acri, Calabria, and immigrated to the United States when he was still young. Atlas invented the bodybuilding technique called *isometrics* and gave hope to the proverbial "97-pound-weakling." Nicknamed "The World's Most Perfectly Developed Man," Atlas created a hugely successful mail-order muscle-building business. From the 1920s to 1960s, he was a media superstar renowned for performing many astounding feats of strength and heroism.

Mary Lou Retton

Mary Lou Retton (1968–) doesn't fool around. During the 1984 Olympic games in Los Angeles at the age of 16, Mary Lou became the first American woman to ever win the Gold Medal in the All-Around in women's gymnastics. Her five medals were the most won by any athlete at the 1984 Olympics. Retton was named *Sports Illustrated* magazine's "Sportswoman of the Year" in 1984. In 1993, almost a decade after her Los Angeles triumph, an Associated Press national survey named her the Most Popular Athlete in America. In 1997 she was inducted into the International Gymnastics Hall of Fame.

The Least You Need to Know

➤ Italian-American entertainers have been successful in many fields.

➤ The universal language of music is Italian.

➤ In the American film industry a number of Italian Americans have stood out as actors and directors.

➤ Italian Americans have excelled in sports, winning World Series rings, gold medals at the Olympics, and boxing titles.

Friends and Favors: Powerful Players

The Roman Senate, *la signoria,* family dynasties, and monarchies. The banking industry during the Renaissance, centuries-long trade dominance in the Mediterranean, and the Italian economic miracle of the twentieth century. All this leads to one thing: Italian Americans are part of a greater tradition that finds its roots in ancient times.

Well-trained in government and public service, enterprising in business, and concerned about the welfare of society, Italian Americans have made their mark in America.

Who are these captains of industry and top government? Read on to learn more about some of the many Italian Americans who have made significant contributions to society, particularly in the fields of government and industry, and through education and philanthropy.

Great Rulers, Now and Forever

The U.S. government has adopted the structure and many of the social policies that find their origins in the Roman Empire. The bicameral legislative body and laws protecting the lives and rights of citizens are just some of these traditions. In the United States, Italian Americans have always played major roles in government and upholding law-and-order.

Fiorello La Guardia: The Little Flower

The beloved mayor of New York, Fiorello La Guardia (1882–1947) was born in New York City on December 11, 1882, to immigrant parents. Fiorello was mayor of New York for three terms from 1934 to 1945. During his long and successful law career, Fiorello fought vigorously to improve workers' rights and eliminate child labor. The five-foot, three-inch mayor was affectionately called the "Little Flower," the translation of his name.

Alfred E. Smith

The Democrat Alfred Smith (1873–1944) was born in New York City as Alfred Emanuele Ferrara. Elected in 1919, Smith was the first Italian-American governor of New York. Smith was a popular governor and worked hard to improve conditions for factory workers, gain better housing for the poor, and preserve state lands.

Smith was governor for three terms and was the first Italian American to run for the presidency, which he lost to Herbert Hoover in 1928.

Di Interessa

The great seal of the United States—the bald eagle grasping an olive branch in one claw and 13 arrows in the other—was modeled on the Roman Republic symbol. That also had an eagle with outstretched wings perched above laurel leaves and arrows. And just in case the imagery isn't strong enough, the great seal of the United States also contains the Latin words *E Pluribus Unum* (*Out of Many, One*), which originated with the Roman poet Horace.

Mario Cuomo

Mario Cuomo was born in New York City in 1932 to parents who had emigrated from the Provincia di Salerno (just outside Naples). He is married to Matilda, with whom he has five children. In 1982, he was elected governor of New York State, and remained so for several successful terms.

Schooled at St. John's University, Cuomo graduated summa cum laude and went on to practice law, representing members of the community in their dealings with the government. In 1975, Governor Hugh Carey appointed him secretary of state.

The governor's book, *Reason to Believe* (Simon & Schuster, 1995), is described as being "an analysis of where this country has been, where it is now, and where it should go." Governor Cuomo is currently practicing law at the New York City firm of Willkie Farr & Gallagher and lecturing nationwide. In the summer of 1995, he began hosting a weekly national radio talk show, "Me and Mario," that discusses issues of the day.

Mario Cuomo's son Andrew Cuomo was born in 1957 and followed in his father's political footsteps when he joined the cabinet of President Bill Clinton. As one of the youngest cabinet secretaries ever, Cuomo received kudos for his aggressive reforms at the Department of Housing and Urban Development.

Mario Cuomo has done a great deal to instill pride in the Italian-American community. A thoughtful writer and eloquent speaker, listen to what he had to say about Italian Americans:

> From Roman times, Italian contributions to the arts, politics and culture have civilized the Western world; the Italian legacy is surpassed by no other culture. Think of Italians' contributions to the United States alone: an Italian discovered America. Named for another Italian. And the statue which symbolizes freedom and liberty to people throughout the world was designed by yet another.

Di Interessa

New York has the greatest number of Italian Americans, estimated at approximately 1,882,396. Other cities with Italian Americans include:

➤ Philadelphia (497,721)

➤ Chicago (492,158)

➤ Boston (485,761)

➤ Pittsburgh (316,351)

Rudy Giuliani

The charismatic mayor of the Big Apple, Rudolph (a.k.a. "Rudy") Giuliani was born in New York City in 1944 as the grandson of Italian immigrants who arrived in the wave of the 1880s. He became a United States attorney in Brooklyn, New York, where he successfully prosecuted a number of organized crime leaders. From 1994 to 2001, Giuliani was mayor of New York City. Under the leadership of Giuliani, New York City crime went down by over 50 percent, making the city one of the safest large urban centers in the country.

Rick Lazio

Republican Congressman Rick (born Enrico) Lazio was born in 1958 in Amityville, New York. Lazio was elected to his house seat in November 1992. Lazio graduated from Vassar College and earned a law degree from American University. In 1999, Lazio was named Chairman of the National Italian-American Convention. He resides in Brightwaters, Long Island, with his wife, Patricia, and their two daughters, Molly Ann and Kelsey.

Biografia

Maria Teresa Cafarelli de Francisi was the model for "Miss Liberty," which appeared on the one-dollar silver coins that circulated in the United States during the 1920s and 1930s. The coins are now valued at about $100 each. Her husband, Antonio de Francisi was the coin's engraver. He emigrated from Palermo in 1903 at age 16.

Quite a Resumé

A few more Italian-Americans who stand for justice are included in this list of prominent figures.

➤ Michael Musmanno (1897–1968) served on the Supreme Court of Pennsylvania and on the bench of the Nuremberg War Crimes Tribunal, which tried the Nazi officers after World War II.

➤ Anthony J. Celebrezze (1910–1998) was secretary of Health, Education and Welfare. Chosen by President Kennedy and retained by President Johnson, Celebrezze was a successful lawyer who was elected to the State Senate of Ohio and then made mayor of Cleveland.

➤ Peter W. Rodino Jr. (1909–1973) was Chairman of the House Judiciary Committee and the U.S. congressman to lead the Committee recommendation to impeach Richard M. Nixon. As a young man, the Newark-born Rodino wrote poetry and hoped to become a professional songwriter. He discovered that although he churned out "songs galore," the money just wasn't there. He traded his dream of stardom for a daytime factory job and attended night school, earning a law degree in 1937. Elected to Congress in 1948, Rodino supported the law that made Columbus Day a national holiday in 1973.

➤ The conservative Antonin Scalia was born in an Italian neighborhood of Trenton, New Jersey, in 1936. The son of a Sicilian immigrant, in 1986, he became the first Italian-American Supreme Court Justice.

➤ Jack Joseph Valenti was special Assistant to President Lyndon Johnson and, since 1995, he has served as president and CEO of the Motion Picture Association of America. Valenti is best known for pioneering the movie ratings system.

➤ Judge John Sirica (1904–1992) made the historic ruling that forced President Nixon to hand over tapes and other material subpoenaed by the grand jury during the Watergate scandal. Sirica successfully argued that executive privilege did not take precedence over constitutional requirements.

➤ Charles Joseph Bonaparte (1851–1921) was a direct descendent of the Bonaparte or Buonaparte family, originally from Florence. He founded the Federal Bureau of Investigation in 1908 and was the first Italian American appointed to a cabinet position. He served as Secretary of the Navy and later as U.S. Attorney General during Theodore Roosevelt's administration.

Italian-American Power Women

The same impetus that has brought us so many successful Italian-American men is what has driven a few special women to push past historical barriers and rise to the top of their field.

Geraldine Ferraro

Geraldine Ferraro (1935–) was the first woman nominated by a major political party as its candidate for vice president of the United States. Born in Newburg, New York, in 1935, she grew up in Queens after the death of her father, who was an immigrant from a town north of Naples.

As an attorney, Ferraro worked in the Queens, New York, District Attorney's office, where she started the Special Victims Bureau. Ferraro ran successfully for Congress from New York City's 9th District in 1978. There, she was a women's and human rights advocate, working for passage of the Equal Rights Amendment, sponsoring the Women's Economic Equity Act ending pension discrimination against women, and seeking greater job training and opportunities for displaced homemakers.

In 1984, Ferraro was picked to run as vice president of the United States on the Democratic Party ticket, with former Vice President Walter Mondale as the candidate for president. In her acceptance speech, she spoke of the realization of the American dream: "Tonight, the daughter of an immigrant from Italy has been chosen to run for vice president in the new land my father came to love ..." The ticket lost, but Ferraro's candidacy forever reshaped the American political and social landscape.

Ella Tambussi Grasso

Ella Tambussi Grasso (1919–1981) spent her life in her home state of Connecticut and won her first election—to the General Assembly of the state—in 1952; she never lost an election thereafter. She became Secretary of State of Connecticut, and then served two terms in the U.S. Congress. She served as governor until illness forced resignation in 1980.

Having overcome religious prejudice and sexism to succeed, Ella was a champion for those who needed help, including minorities, women, young people, working people, and the elderly. She inspired affection and trust as she improved the state's economy and created a more effective government.

In Italics

1974—Ella Tambussi Grasso was elected governor—the nation's first woman elected state governor.

Eleanor Cutri Smeal

Born in Ashtabula, Ohio in 1939, Eleanor Cutri Smeal was elected president of the National Organization for Women (NOW) in 1977. As an Italian-American woman who had experienced discrimination, Smeal dedicated her life to empowering women in society. In 1987, she founded the Feminist Majority Fund and Foundation, an organization devoted to education and research projects designed for the advancement of women.

Industry Leaders

In business and commercial trading, Italian-American power players have had starring roles in the banking, publishing, and financial industries.

Di Interessa

One important business motto of the United States, "caveat emptor," is a Latin phrase that means "let the buyer beware." Originally, it was a popular Roman saying that first appeared in a central marketplace in the city of Rome.

Generoso Pope Sr.

Generoso Pope Sr. (1891–1950) was the owner and publisher of the newspaper *Il Progresso Italo-Americano*. Mr. Pope purchased *Il Progresso* in 1928 and built it into the largest Italian language newspaper in the United States. After Pope's death, his son Generoso Jr. became *Il Progresso*'s publisher. Generoso Jr., who also created the weekly tabloid *The National Enquirer*, sold *Il Progresso* in 1980.

Amadeo Pietro Giannini: The Bank of Italy

Giannini (1870–1949) was an American banker and the founder of the California-based Bank of Italy—later the Bank of America—which, by the 1930s, was the world's largest commercial bank. He was a major pioneer of branch banking (refer to Chapter 10, "Can You Spare a Florin? Banking and Commerce," to learn how Italian bankers created the modern banking system) and made loans to small farmers and businessmen, which was unusual at the time. During the 1930s and 1940s, Giannini's banks continued to make loans to both large and small enterprises, notably to the young motion-picture industry. His farm mortgage policies also helped in the phenomenal expansion of agriculture in central and northern California.

Richard A. Grasso

The ebullient chief executive and chairman of the New York Stock Exchange Richard A. Grasso was born in Queens, New York, to immigrant parents. Mr. Grasso's humble beginnings seem far removed from his role on Wall Street. He grew up in a five-story walkup in Queens. A favorite warm-up joke of his on the luncheon circuit refers to the source of the family's wealth: "The oil, the rubber, and airline industries. My family ran an Exxon station near LaGuardia Airport."

Lee Iacocca

Quoted as saying, "The only rock I know that stays steady, the only institution I know that works, is the family," Lee Iacocca was born Lido Anthony Iaccoca in Allentown, Pennsylvania, in 1924. His parents were immigrants from a town north of Naples. Iacocca was known as the King of Detroit, having served as president of the Ford Motor Company from 1970 to 1978 and then president (1978), CEO, and chairman (1979) of the Chrysler Corporation until 1992. He volunteered to be chairman of the Statue of Liberty–Ellis Island Foundation to plan the celebration of the statue's centennial in 1986.

Biografia

Lee Iacocca's modern day-counterpart in Italy is Gianni Agnelli (1921–) who was the chairman of Fiat for more than thirty years and one of Europe's leading industrialists. Considered one of the elder statesmen of Italy, he is known as L'Avvocato (the lawyer) to his countrymen, and was appointed a senator for life.

Enterprising Italian Americans

A few more Italian-American entrepreneurs have had great success in a number of different business ventures. A few are listed here.

➤ Bernard Castro (1904–1963) will go down in history as the manufacturer of the famous "Castro Convertible" soft bed. Castro started as a humble upholsterer and became the multimillionaire head of the greatest company of its kind in America.

➤ Steve Geppi is the owner of the world's largest distributor of English-language comic books. Today, Geppi's Baltimore-based Diamond Comic Distributors, Inc., delivers 1,300 comic book titles (out of 1,600), and has a 52 percent market share of this $500 million industry.

➤ Antonio Pasin was an immigrant Italian carpenter who came to America in 1914 at the age of 16. In 1917, he created the popular Radio Flyer red wagon. Today, his three grandsons run the Chicago-based Radio Flyer, Inc., whose 100 employees still manufacture about 8,000 wagons a day. The name "Radio" was inspired from the technological innovation of the time, invented by fellow Italian Guglielmo Marconi. "Flyer" was a nod to the wonder of flight.

➤ Louis R. Perini is founder and president of a large construction firm who bought the financially unprofitable Boston Braves, transporting them lock, stock, and barrel to Milwaukee. As the owner, he helped the team set new attendance records in the league as they won several pennants and even a World Series title. Currently, the Braves are in Atlanta, Georgia, and owned by media mogul Ted Turner.

➤ Leonard Riggio (1941–) is the founder and chairman of Barnes & Noble, the original mega-bookstore concept, which is also the nation's largest operator of video game and entertainment software stores. The company is also a pioneer in electronic commerce, with a sophisticated Web site. Riggio is listed in the Forbes 400 and on the *Forbes* list of "America's Top CEOs."

Di Interessa

If it weren't for the Italian immigrants, there would be no Prince Spaghetti Day, because there would be no pasta. Italians, along with their dreams, brought along the simple recipe for pasta: flour, water, and eggs.

Food Giants

Not surprisingly, Italian Americans have had more than their fair share of influence on *gastronomia*. From Planters peanuts to rich Ghirardelli chocolates, from sandwich shops to world-famous restaurants, Italian Americans have fed a lot of their fellow citizens.

Vince Marotta: Mr. Coffee

Vince Marotta invented the best-selling coffee maker in the world as well as the paper coffee filter. Interestingly enough, Joe DiMaggio, after retiring from baseball, became the spokesperson for the company. Many people nowadays remember Joe DiMaggio as "Mr. Coffee" rather than for his achievements as a baseball player.

Wednesday Is Giuseppe Pellegrino Day

Giuseppe Pellegrino emigrated from Sicily as a youngster and was originally a partner and sales manager for the Roman Macaroni Co. of Brooklyn, New York. In 1941, he bought out the Prince Macaroni Manufacturing Company, whose slogan "Prince Spaghetti Day" became nationally recognized as it attempted to introduce non-Italians to pasta products. Through Pellegrino's hard work and innovation, Prince would become one of the largest pasta-producing companies in the United States.

Ernest and Julio Gallo Know Wine

After Prohibition was lifted in 1933, the brothers Ernest and Julio Gallo took all of their savings and invested in their father's California vineyards. It marked the beginning of the California wine industry. Today, E. & J. Gallo have become one of the world's foremost wineries in the art and science of grape-growing and winemaking; in keeping with the Italian tradition, their wines have received numerous prestigious awards such as "Best in Show" and "Winery of the Century."

Di Interessa

Anyone who watched television in New England in the 1970s probably remembers the "Wednesday is Prince Spaghetti Day" commercial. Anthony, a young boy, comes running home through the narrow streets of Boston's North End (Boston's Little Italy) after hearing his mother yelling for him to come home for a supper of Prince spaghetti.

Boy That's Good: Chef Boyardee

The man behind the nation's leading brand of ready-to-eat spaghetti dinners, pizza, sauce, and pasta was Ettore Boiardi. An Italian immigrant, Boiardi began as a chef's apprentice at age 11. He eventually opened a restaurant in Cleveland, Ohio, and in the 1930s, began selling his pasta and sauce in cans. During World War II, Chef Boyardee was the largest supplier of rations for the U.S. and Allied Forces.

You Sure Know How to Make a Good Panino (Sandwich)

Anthony Conza founded the first Blimpie in New Jersey in 1975. There are now over 2,000 Blimpies in the United States and 13 foreign countries with a net worth of $38 million.

Fred De Luca founded Subway after he borrowed $1,000 at age 17 to start his first sandwich shop. Today, there are 13,136 Subways in 64 countries. De Luca is currently worth $3 billion. That's a lot of lire.

Anthony T. Rossi: Fresh Squeezed

Anthony Rossi (1900–1993) founded the Tropicana Juice Company in 1947 as a Florida fruit packaging company. In 1954, Anthony Rossi developed a pasteurization process for orange juice. It was the first time that orange juice made from 100 percent fruit (not-from-concentrate) was available in a ready-to-serve pack. Today, Tropicana is the world's leading producer and marketer of branded fruit juices.

What's Cooking?

Italians are very good at making sure America is well-fed. Indeed, it's easy to love Italian food. The combination of fresh ingredients and attention to detail makes every meal a delight! You'll probably recognize most of the products these enterprising Italian Americans have brought to the table.

➤ Domingo Ghirardelli left a successful confectionery business in Peru to seek his fortune in the gold fields of California. But his venture in the gold fields proved unsuccessful, forcing him to return to chocolate in 1852. His San Francisco Ghirardelli Chocolate Company now houses many restaurants and exclusive boutiques, and is a major tourist attraction located near San Francisco's Fisherman's Wharf.

➤ Luisa Leone was born in Bazzano, Italy, and founded Mamma Leone's restaurant on 48th Street in New York City in 1906. Mamma Leone's has attained world-wide fame for the quality and quantity of food at reasonable prices.

➤ Celeste Lizio came to America during the 1930s and opened a restaurant with her husband in Chicago. She is best known as the founder of Mama Celeste's Pizza, a line of frozen Italian foods that she later sold to Quaker Oats.

➤ Melchiorre Pio Vincenzo Sardi opened the famous New York City haunt, Sardi's restaurant, in 1922. Sardi's is probably unmatched in America as a rendezvous for luminaries of state, screen, and radio.

➤ Amedeo Obici and Mario Peruzzi, both Italian immigrants, created Mr. Peanut and the Planters Peanut Company in 1887 in Pennsylvania. By 1930, the partners had four huge factories, and raked in over $12 million annually. Obici was called "The Peanut King."

➤ Leonardo ("Lee") Rizzuto is the man who put a handheld hair dryer in every beauty salon and American home. Chairman and president of Conair Corporation in Connecticut, Rizzuto

Biografia

Next time you bite into a Big Mac, you can thank an Italian American for the meal. James Delligatti invented the sandwich in 1967, and since then, McDonald's has sold billions of the hamburgers.

and his parents founded the company in 1959 with $100 and their invention of hot rollers. In 1971, Conair perfected the professional pistol-grip hair dryer. Today, Rizzuto is sole owner of this multimillion-dollar corporation, which also owns Cuisinart, a leading name in kitchen appliances and cookware.

➤ The Di Giorgio brothers were two Italian Americans who started the Di Giorgio Corporation, one of the world's largest shippers of fresh fruit.

Italian Americans Commemorate Italian Americans

A few special people have dedicated their lives to preserving Italian culture and commemorating the achievements of Italian Americans. Whether you're talking about the Sons of Italy or the Garibaldi Museum, there are plenty of opportunities for Italian Americans to get in touch with long-lost family members, meet new friends, and establish business networks.

Di Interessa

For one-stop shopping and interesting news related to Italian-American organizations in your area, you can visit The Ultimate Italian Community at www.ultimateitalian.com/site4/community/organizations.html.

Di Interessa

To get in touch with your heritage, check out the Sons of Italy Web site at www.osia.org.

Or write for more information about their magazine, *Italian America,* a quarterly full-color magazine with original feature articles ranging from the Italian influence on American wines to travel pieces about Italy's most beautiful sites.

OSIA
219 E Street, NE
Washington, DC 20002
202-547-2900

The Father of Sons of Italy

Dr. Vincenzo Sellaro (1868–1932) developed the idea of uniting the Italians into one great organization that would enable them to become the masters of their own destinies. In 1905, Dr. Sellaro founded the Order Sons of Italy in America, the largest established Italian-American organization in the country. *"L'Ordine Figli D'Italia,"* the Italian version of the Sons of Italy, actually refers to the "Children of Italy." Women make up half of the Sons of Italy.

Its purpose is to enrich heritage nationwide through programs in education, cultural preservation, grass-roots initiatives, and charitable fund-raising, and by strengthening the ties between the United States and Italy.

Una Storia Segreta (A Secret Story)

Una Storia Segreta is a traveling exhibit created by the American Italian Historical Association that tells the story of Italian-American internment during World War II. This program led to the passing of House Resolution 2442, a bill calling for official acknowledgement of these atrocities by the U.S. government through the "Wartime Violations of Italian-American Civil Liberties Act," a bill supported by Congressmen Rick Lazio (R-NY) and Eliot Engel (D-NY).

For those of you who don't remember the war, the bill honors the Italian Americans who were treated as enemy aliens during World War II. Families were subjected to curfews, forced to leave their own homes, and moved into internment camps. In the meantime, many of them had sons fighting in the armed services.

The civil liberties abuses of Italian Americans suffered during World War II are not well known. But they did occur, and *Una Storia Segreta* tells the truth about the story.

Di Interessa

To learn more about the Meucci-Garibaldi Museum, contact:

The Order Sons of Italy in America
420 Tompkins Avenue
Staten Island, NY 10305
718-442-1608
www.osia.org/public/museum.htm

The Meucci-Garibaldi Museum

The Meucci-Garibaldi Museum, located in Staten Island, New York, commemorates the two Italian-American men for whom it is named: Antonio Meucci, known for inventing the first telephone (but failing to patent it before Alexander Graham Bell), and Giuseppe Garibaldi. Today, the house is a National Landmark owned and administered by the Sons of Italy Foundation, a philanthropic organization dedicated to fostering a positive image of Italian Americans.

Visitors may view the documents, historic telephone models, and hand-hewn furniture of Meucci's home and learn more about how Meucci discovered he could transmit a human voice over a copper wire charged with electricity.

Museo ItaloAmericano

Established in 1978, the Museo ItaloAmericano is devoted exclusively to Italian and Italian-American art and culture. The mission of the Museo ItaloAmericano is to research, collect, and display works of Italian and Italian-American artists, and to promote educational programs for the appreciation of Italian art and culture in order to preserve the heritage of Italian Americans for future generations.

Share Your Talents

Commerce and initiative is in the blood of Italians, and it's no different with Italian Americans. They've have been part of the American political scene for more than 200 years, and have built some of America's largest industries and corporations.

If you are an Italian American, you have reason to feel proud. If you are one of the many who simply happen to love an Italian American and everything Italian, join the crowd. Be all you were meant to be, and share yourself with the world! *Arrivederci!*

Di Interessa

For more information about the Museo ItaloAmericano, contact:

Museo ItaloAmericano
Fort Mason Center, Building C
San Francisco, CA 94123
415-673-2200
www.museoitaloamericano.org

The Least You Need to Know

➤ Italian Americans have been involved in American politics since the country was formed.

➤ A number of Italian Americans have served as mayors, governors, political appointees, and judges.

➤ Major corporations have been headed by Italian Americans.

➤ Popular food products such as Prince spaghetti, Tropicana orange juice, Gallo wine, Planter's peanuts, and Chef Boyardee SpaghettiOs were all created by Italian Americans.

Glossary

abbazia Abbey.

Aiuto! Help.

al dente "To the teeth"; refers to perfectly cooked pasta.

allegro "Quick and lively"; used in music direction.

ancora The French term *ancor* is short for the Italian *ancora* and means "again."

andante Medium pace.

anfiteatro Amphitheater

Anniversario della Liberazione Liberation Day (April 25).

antipasto Literally translates to "before the meal" and denotes an appetizer.

arco Arch.

artisti Artists.

L'Atlantico Atlantic Ocean.

Azzunzione Feast of the Assumption (August 15); celebrates the ascent of the Virgin Mary to Heaven and marks the beginning of the Italian summer holidays.

Azzuri Literally signifies "the Blues" and refers to Italy's World Cup soccer team.

banca Bank.

bancarotta Literally "bank broken," it means bankrupt.

baroque Describes the art and architecture of the sixteenth and seventeenth centuries.

battistero Baptistery.

bel canto "Beautiful singing"; describes an operatic style of music that blends composition with vocal technique.

Bel Paese "Beautiful country"; an affection term used to describe Italy.

la bella lingua The beautiful language.

benandanti   "Good walkers"; describes members of an ancient agrarian cult in the Friuli region of northern Italy.

bere come una spugna   Idiomatic expression that means "drink like a sponge."

bistecca   Beefsteak.

bizzocche   Refers to the Tertiary Sisters, a group of laity associated with a religious order within the Roman Catholic Church.

borghetto   The word *ghetto* probably derives from the Italian *borghetto*, a diminutive for the word borgo and related to the English word *burg*, which originally referred to a walled town.

braccianti   Comes from the Italian word *braccia* (arm) and refers to the fact that day laborers were the "arms" of the land.

brava!   This is what you cheer to applaud female opera stars.

bravo!   This is what you cheer to applaud male opera stars.

brindisi   A toast such as "Cincin!" or "Alla salute!"

buon giorno   Good day.

buona notte   Good night.

buona sera   Good evening.

caboto   A coastal seaman.

calcio   Soccer to Americans, football to Europeans.

camera degli sposi   Wedding chamber.

le Camicie Nere   "The Blackshirts" refers to members of Mussolini's Fascist party.

campanile   Bell tower.

campanilismo   A strong attachment to one's village or birthplace; derives from the word *campanile* (bell tower).

capisco   I understand.

Capodanno   New Year's Day.

La Cappella Sistina   The Sistine Chapel.

i carabinieri   The Italian military police force.

carne   Meat.

Carnevale   Literally "farewell to meat," refers to the festival of Mardi Gras.

cartone   "Cardboard." The word *cartoon* derives from the Italian word *cartone* (cardboard) and refers to the full-scale drawings used to prepare for a painting.

castrati   Singers who were castrated to maintain their treble voices; usually played women's roles.

celeste   Sky blue.

celibe   Unmarried man; bachelor.

che bello   How beautiful.

che panorama   What a view.

chi esce riesce   An idiomatic expression used to describe the fleeing immigrants meaning, "He who leaves succeeds."

chiesa   Church.

ciao   Hi/Bye (familiar).

ciclismo   "Cycling," which is a favorite pastime for Italians.

classico   Classic.

cognoscenti   Connoisseurs.

commedia dell'arte   Popular during the sixteenth to eighteenth centuries, refers to a form of Italian comedy that used improvised dialogue and masked characters.

condotte   Contracts.

contadini   Peasant farmers who often owned a small plot of land.

contorno   In Italian cooking, refers to any side dish.

contrade   Refers to the different competing "districts" that participate in the famous Palio horse race conducted in Siena.

contrapposto   "Set against"; refers to a method whereby parts of the body are set in opposition to each other around a central vertical axis.

cornuto   "Cuckold"; refers to a fool, a commonly used Italian insult.

cortile   Galleried courtyard or cloister.

di bocca buona   An idiomatic expression that means "a good mouth" and refers to a good eater.

di moda   In fashion.

dialect   A regional variety of a language.

dire pane al pane e vino al vino   Common idiomatic expression that means literally "to say bread to bread and wine to wine" and translates to the American expression "to call a spade a spade."

DOC   "Denominazione della Origine Controllata" refers to wines meeting established standards.

la dolce vita   "The sweet life."

dov'è?   Where is?

è buono   That's good.

Epifania   Feast of the Epiphany (January 6).

essere un sacco di patate   Idiomatic expression that means "to be a sack of pota-toes" or a bore.

fare una bella figura   "To make a good figure" refers to the impression one makes upon others.

fascism   Practiced by the dictator Benito Mussolini between 1922 and 1943, refers to a system of government based on a totalitarian philosophy that glorifies state and na-tion and assigns to the state control over every aspect of national life; characterized by repression of all opposition and extreme nationalism.

fata   Fairy.

Ferragosto   Coinciding with the religious feast of the Assumption of Mary on August 15, refers to the vacation taken during the month of August.

Festa della Arancie   "The orange festival"; a popular event characterized by the throwing of oranges.

Festa della Primavera   "Spring Festival."

feste   Holidays, festivals.

festeggiare   To celebrate.

Firenze   Florence.

gastronomia   Gastronomy.

Genova   Genoa.

gettoni   Refers to the telephone tokens used before phone cards became popular.

girasole   Sunflower.

grignoni   "Green horn"; a common reference made to newly arrived immigrants.

Immacolata Concezione   Immaculate Conception of the Blessed Virgin Mary (December 8) refers to the Roman Catholic doctrine that the Virgin Mary's soul was free from the stain of original sin from the moment of her soul's conception.

in vino veritas   An idiomatic expression that signifies "in wine there is truth."

inquiro   Latin for "inquire into."

Isola Della Lacrime   "The Island of Tears" was the Italian name for Ellis Island.

libretto   "Little book" used in opera for following the story line.

liscio come l'olio   An idiomatic expression that means "smooth as oil."

loggia   A covered gallery or balcony.

lunette   Semicircular space in a vault or ceiling.

lupa   A slang term for prostitute.

Lupercalia   From Latin lupus "wolf" referred to ancient Roman festival held in February.

La Madonna   Jesus' mother, the Virgin Mary.

la madre patria   The Mother-land; this was what Italian immigrants used to refer to Italy.

mammismo   Refers to the relationship between a grown son and his doting mother.

mangiare pane e cipolla   An idiomatic expression that literally means "to eat bread and onion" and translates to the English expression "to live on bread and water."

maschio   Male.

Mediterraneo   Mediterranean.

mi dispiace   I'm sorry.

la Miseria   Refers to the poverty that characterized southern Italy during the mass emigrations.

motorino   Motor scooter.

Napoli   Naples.

Natale   Christmas.

nave   The central body of a church.

nipotismo   "Nepotism" refers to the favoritism shown by a person in power to relatives and friends, especially in appointing them to favored positions.

non capisco   I don't understand.

nonna/nonno   Grandmother/grandfather.

nubile   Unmarried woman.

nuovo   New.

Ognissanti   All Saints Day, November 1.

opera   Refers to a work of music and describes the music that developed during the sixteenth century.

oratorio   A musical religious work performed without scenery.

ortobello   It was common practice for there to be a "beautiful garden" in back of most convents.

Padova   Padua.

paesani   Country folk.

paese   Country; nation; land; place.

pane   Bread.

pantalone   A caricature of the Venetian merchant.

pantaloni   Pants, trousers.

pappagallo   "Parrot"; refers to Italian wolf-whistlers.

Paradiso   Paradise.

Pasqua   Easter Sunday, refers to the Christian festival commemorating the resurrection of Jesus Christ.

Pasquetta   Little Easter (Easter Monday).

passeggiata   A stroll or walk, a simple Italian pleasure.

passione   Passion.

pastasciutta   Refers to dry pasta, as opposed to fresh.

pellegrino   Pilgrim, wanderer, wayfarer.

i pentiti   "Repentants"; stool pigeons.

per favore   Please.

piatto   Literally "plate" and refers to an Italian meal or course, as in *primo piatto* (first course), *secondo piatto* (main course).

pizzicato   A musical direction used to describe the "plucking" of a violin's strings.

pomodoro   This "fruit of gold" refers to a tomato.

porcospino   "Porcupine"; one of the animals represented at the Palio horse race

portico   The covered entrance to a building.

praeficae   Professional mourners who are more often than not strangers to the deceased.

presto   A musical direction indicating that something should be played very fast.

Primo Maggio   Labor Day (May 1).

primo piatto   First course.

putti   Cherubic babies and angels often used in Renaissance painting.

Pyrrhic victory   Sometimes used when a winner's losses are greater than his gains.

quanto?   How much?

Quattrocento   Literally "four hundred" and refers to the fifteenth century.

relic   Usually religious in nature, refers to the remains of something or someone such as an object or body part.

Renaissance   Literally "rebirth"; refers to the period of European history running from roughly 1400 to 1600.

riserva   Reserved.

Risorgimento   The movement for, and period of, political unification in Italy during the 1800s; also came to mean "a past Italian greatness awaiting revival."

Roma o Morte   "Rome or Death." Garibaldi's battle cry after his defense of the city against the French in 1849.

ruota   The "wheel" (similar to a lazy Susan) built into the thick monastery walls where unwanted babies and orphans could be left.

sagre   Sacred.

salve   Greetings.

Santo Stefano   Saint Stephen's Day (December 26).

santuario   Sanctuary.

scudi   Ducats, a form of money used in Italy during the Renaissance.

serie   Series.

la spiaggia   The beach.

SPQR   Stands for "Senatus Populus Que Romanus" and translates to the Senate and the People of Rome; the symbol is found emblazoned on light posts, mailboxes, street signs, and other municipal fixtures throughout modern-day Rome.

spumante   Sparkling wine.

stigmata   Refers to the marks on the hands and feet that resemble Jesus Christ's crucifixion wounds.

Stil Novo   The use of the vernacular in literature begins with the "Stil Novo" ("new style") poets from Sicily and Tuscany where, for the first time, the spoken language was put into written form, allowing for the development of a specific set of rules.

sul mare   At sea.

tarocchi   Tarot cards.

taverna   Tavern.

tifosi   Literally "typhoid-fevered"; refers to the impassioned Italian sports fans who frequent soccer games.

Torino   Turin.

la torre   The tower.

totocalcio   A soccer betting pool.

tramonto   Sunset.

umanista   Humanist; (1) a Renaissance student or follower of classical learning; (2) one concerned with the welfare of human beings; (3) originally referred to a teacher of Latin and Greek.

un sacco di soldi   An idiomatic expression that literally means "a sack of money"; is used to describe someone with a lot of the stuff.

una cilegia tira l'altra   An idiomatic expression that translates to "one cherry pulls the other" and signifies "one thing leads to another."

vendemmia   Refers to the vintage of a wine.

Veni, vidi, vici   Latin for "I came, I saw, I conquered."

Vespa   "Wasp"; Italian-made motor scooter.

vespizzare   To get somewhere on a Vespa.

via dolorosa   "Sorrowful way" was how immigrants described the ocean voyage to America.

video   I see; the Italian word *video* is derived from the Latin "I see" and has become part of television terminology.

vieni qua   Come here.

vino   Wine.

vino dolce   Sweet wine.

vino rose   Rosé wine.

vino rosso   Red wine.

vino secco   Dry wine.

Vitelù   Oscan term for the Italian peninsula and is probably connected to the word for calf (seen in Latin "vitulus," and Umbrian "vitlu") and originally used to refer to the Greek colonies in Italy; a form of the ancient word survives today in the modern name Italia.

Vulgar Latin   The spoken Latin that eventually evolved into Italian.

zanni   Traditional character in the *commedia dell'arte*.

Web Resources

If you have access to a computer, you'll find more than you need to know about Italy if you visit these Italian and Italian-American Web sites.

Culture

About Italian Culture
www.italianculture.about.com

All about Italian art history, sports, architecture, current events, and more. Includes an extensive database of Italian surnames.

American Academy in Rome
www.aarome.org

American overseas center for independent study and advanced research in the fine arts and the humanities.

American Family Immigration History Center
www.ellisislandrecords.org

A useful tool when doing geneological research about family members who passed through Ellis Island, with useful links.

Ciao! New York
www.ciaony.com

An online meeting place for Italophiles who live and work in New York City. With restaurant recommendations, links to cultural events, and a bulletin board.

DolceVita
www.dolcevita.com

Features articles on fashion, travel, cuisine, design, and events in Italy.

***F & L Primo* Magazine**
www.flprimo.com

Online version of the print magazine dedication to Italian-American culture with a preview of the current issue, letter from the editor, and a collection of recipes.

H-Itam
www2.h-net.msu.edu/~itam/about.html

An interactive network/forum for scholars and activists relating to the Italian-American experience and, more generally, the ethnic culture of the Italian diaspora worldwide.

Italian Folk Art Federation of American
www.italian-american.com/ifafa/

Promotes interest in Italian folk arts, folklore, traditions, costumes, dances, songs, and instruments. The IFAFA also conducts conferences and publishes a newsletter.

Italian Culture on the Net
www.italicon.it

Multilingual site with information on the Italian language, art, and culture.

***Italy Italy* Magazine**
www.italyitalymagazine.com

Online version of profusely illustrated English-print magazine with lifestyle and Italian culture features, articles on history, and off-beat travel tips.

Food

About Italian Food
italianfood.about.com

Learn about the regional styles of Italian cooking, fresh ingredients, and download hundreds of recipes.

Eat Eat Hurrah!
www.eateathurrah.com

Everything about *la cucina italiana:* recipes, regional menus, healthy eating, diets, and a special vegetarian section. Send a postcard and check the food horoscopes, too.

Italian Cooking and Living
www.italiancookingandliving.com

Online recipes; information about Italian food, wine, travel, and culture; and the opportunity to participate in culinary events and trips to Italy.

Toscana Saporita Cooking School
www.toscanasaporita.com

Italian cooking school based in a Tuscany villa offers small classes and hands-on instruction in English. Browse itineraries, register for a class, and learn more about their tours.

About Italian Language
italian.about.com

Regularly updated feature articles, an Italian For Beginners section with grammar lessons, vocabulary-building drills, interactive workbook exercises, quizzes, and a word of the day audio download.

It Schools
www.it-schools.com

Database containing a comprehensive list of schools that arrange courses in Italian as a foreign language.

Italian Yahoo! Group
groups.yahoo.com/group/Italian/

Free e-mail group service for beginners to advanced who are learning the Italian language. Discussions include Italian music, culture, art, and food.

Università per Stranieri a Perugia
www.unistrapg.it

Study in a university setting with traditional college-level courses and programs.

La Bella Lingua Language and Culture
www.labellalingua.com

Italian language and culture related information with postings for cultural tours in Italy.

Music

Italian Music Heritage
www.cilea.it/music/

Information on Italian music, educational institutions, exhibitions, concert halls, and conferences.

Opera Web
www.opera.it

Extensive resource for opera with news, interactive quiz, biography of singers, articles from conductors, and history.

News

CNN Italia.it
www.cnnitalia.it

Italian-language-based version of the CNN news site.

Italy Daily
www.italy-daily.com

Headline news, business, and politics gathered from a variety of European sources.

Organizations

Casa Italiana Zerilli-Marimò at New York University
www.nyu.edu/pages/casaitaliana

Cultural institute at NYU has information on scholarships, events in New York City, and Italian studies.

FIERI
www.fieri.org

Italian-American service organization dedicated to preserving the Italian culture and encouraging the study of Italian and Italian-American history

Italian Embassy in the United States
www.italyemb.org

Washington, D.C.–based office with information on passports, trade, and the Italian government.

Italian Sons and Daughters of America
www.orderisda.org

Fraternal benevolent organization devoted to serving those of Italian-American heritage. Contains information on membership, life insurance, and annuities.

National Italian American Foundation
www.niaf.org

This organization's mission is to preserve and protect Italian-American heritage and culture and to encourage the teaching of Italian language and culture in U.S. schools.

Permanent Mission of Italy to the United Nations
www.italyun.org

Learn about the activities of the mission in New York and about UN activities in Italy.

Travel

Italian State Tourism Board
www.enit.it

Multilingual government-run site with information on tour operators, travel agencies, and links to regional tourist offices in Italy.

Italy for Visitors at About
goitaly.about.com

Trip planning, tips on Italian hotels, transportation, sights, events, and more.

Time Out Florence
www.timeout.com/florence/

Accommodations, sightseeing, essential info, entertainment, eating and drinking, and more in the city identified most closely with the Italian Renaissance.

Time Out Rome
www.timeout.com/rome/

Accommodations, sightseeing, essential info, entertainment, eating and drinking, and more in the Eternal City.

Time Out Venice
www.timeout.com/venice/

Accommodations, sightseeing, essential info, entertainment, eating and drinking, and more in the city on the lagoon.

Suggested Films and Books

There's so much to learn and so little time! If you want to pursue your Italian studies further, check out the following list of films and books.

Films

The rich Italian history is a popular subject for filmmakers. Drama, intrigue, love, betrayal, victory, defeat ... you name it, and it's here!

English Language Films About Italy and Italians

The Agony and the Ecstasy (1965, Carol Reed). The biographical story of Michelangelo's troubles while painting the Sistine Chapel at the urging of Pope Julius II.

Big Night (1995, Campbell Scott and Stanley Tucci). A failing Italian restaurant run by two brothers gambles on one special night to try to save the business.

Enchanted April (1992, Mike Newell). This slow-paced gem centers on the civilizing influence of Italy on beleaguered Londoners, both male and female, and has its own civilizing influence on the viewer. It's almost like taking a little mini-trip to Italy, a gorgeously filmed enchantment.

The Godfather Trilogy (1992, Francis Ford Coppola). A Mafia boss's son, previously uninvolved in the business, takes over when his father is critically wounded in a mob hit.

Goodfellas (1990, Martin Scorsese). Henry Hill and his friends work their way up through the mob hierarchy.

It Started in Naples (1960, Melville Shavelson). Marietto, also known as Carlo Angeletti, is the little star in this movie who steals the limelight from Clark Gable and Sophia Loren. He plays the super cute little street urchin who may or may not be the real nephew of a rich American lawyer from Philadelphia.

The Italian Job (1969, Peter Collinson). Comic caper movie about a plan to steal a gold shipment from the streets of Turin by creating a traffic jam.

Moonstruck (1997, Norman Jewison). While waiting for her timid fiancé to decide between her and his mother, Cher falls in love with the fiancé's estranged brother (Nicolas Cage), a bakery worker with a love of opera and life.

Roman Holiday (1953, William Wyler). A young princess, tired of the constraints her position brings, runs away. She doesn't know the man who befriends her is a reporter out for a story. Audrey Hepburn at her Oscar-winning best in an immortal comedy-romance!

A Room with a View (1986, James Ivory). When Lucy Honeychurch and chaperone Charlotte Bartlett find themselves in Florence with rooms without views, fellow guests Mr. Emerson and son George step in to remedy the situation. Meeting the Emersons could change Lucy's life forever but, once back in England, how will her experiences in Tuscany affect her marriage plans?

The Talented Mr. Ripley (1999, Anthony Minghella). Ripley is sent to Europe to retrieve a rich and spoiled millionaire playboy, but when the errand fails, Ripley kills the playboy and assumes his life.

Tea With Mussolini (1999, Franco Zeffirelli). Pseudo auto-biographical tale from the early life of director Franco Zeffirelli looks at the life of a bastard son (Charlie Lucas as a child, Baird Wallace as the teen) of an Italian businessman, whose mother has died and is raised by an Englishwoman (Joan Plowright) in pre–World War II Mussolini Italy.

Where Angels Fear to Tread (1991, Charles Sturridge). The widow Lilia Herriton meets and marries a young man when she visits Italy. The man is only a dentist without a good name, and Lilia's relatives are clearly unhappy with her choice. Lilia dies while giving birth to a son, and two relatives travel to Italy to take care of the baby, expecting no trouble from the father.

Italian Language Films

If you really want to understand the Italians from the inside-out, try these Italian language films directed by some of Italy's most important directors.

The Bicycle Thief (1948, Vittorio De Sica). The film that changed the face of Italian cinema. In postwar Italy, even schlepping movie posters looks good to a jobless man, worth pawning the sheets to get that bike out of hock.

Big Deal on Madonna Street (1958, Mario Monicelli). Peppe, formerly a boxer, organizes the break-in of a pawnshop. Tiberio, an unemployed photographer, Mario, a receiver, the Sicilian Michele and Cafanelle, an ex-jockey, are the other members of the gang. Though they are advised by Dante, a retired burglar, the task is not so easy.

Cinema Paradiso (1988, Giuseppe Tornatore). A famous film director returns home to a Sicilian village for the first time in almost 30 years. He reminisces about his childhood at the Cinema Paradiso where Alfredo, the projectionist, first brought about his love of films. He is also reminded of his lost teenage love, Elena, whom he had to leave before he left for Rome.

Dear Diary (1994, Nanni Moretti). The Italian actor-writer-director Nanni Moretti plays a self-conscious Italian whose life reads like an artist's sketchbook.

Divorce Italian Style (1961, Pietro Germi). Marcello Mastroianni stars as a self-centered Sicilian nobleman facing a mid-life crisis. He's lost all romantic interest in his wife and becomes obsessed instead with marrying his teenage cousin.

General Della Rovere (1959, Roberto Rossellini). Grimaldi is a swindler pretending to be a colonel in the Italian army during World War II.

Ginger and Fred (1986, Federico Fellini). One of Fellini's last films, and starring Guilietta Masina and Marcello, this movie explores how television has infected the brains of Italians.

Una Giornata Particolare (*A Special Day;* 1977, Ettore Scola). Sophia Loren plays the housewife and mother of six children during Mussolini's Italy who befriends a suicidal neighbor who happens to be homosexual.

Ieri, Oggi, Domani (*Yesterday, Today, and Tomorrow;* 1963, Vittorio De Sica). Starring Sophia Loren, this film chronicles three very different women and the men they attract.

Il bell'Antonio (1960, Mauro Bolognini). Women love handsome Antonio because they think of him as the perfect lover … little do they know.

Il sorpasso (1962, Dino Risi). Roberto, a shy student, meets Bruno, a 40-year-old man, who takes him for a drive through the Roman countryside.

Johnny Stecchino (1991, Roberto Benigni). Good-hearted but not very bright, Dante finds himself involved in a case of mistaken identity in this Italian comedy.

La Caduta degli Dei (*The Damned*). The dramatic collapse of a wealthy, industrialist/ Junker family during the reign of the Third Reich.

La Dolce Vita (1960, Federico Fellini). Marcello is a young playboy journalist who spends his days between celebrities and rich people.

La Notte di San Lorenzo (1982, Paolo and Vittorio Taviani). The Night of San Lorenzo, the night of the shooting stars, is the night when dreams come true in Italian folklore. In 1944, a group of Italians flee their town after hearing rumours that the Nazis are coming.

La Strada (1954, Federico Fellini). Gelsomina is sold for a few coins by her very poor mother to Zampano, a fairground wrestler. She follows him on the road ("la strada") and helps him during his shows.

La Vita È Bella (*Life Is Beautiful;* 1997, Roberto Benigni). An Italian Jew uses an involved story to protect his son in a Nazi death camp during World War II.

Lamerica (1994, Gianni Amelio). Immigrants from Albania meet in Italy after being sealed off from the West under the draconian communist dictatorship.

Love and Anarchy (1973, Lina Wertmüller). Tonino is a sad-faced, freckled peasant who comes to Rome to kill Mussolini.

Marriage Italian Style (1964, Vittorio De Sica). Domenico, a successful businessman with an eye for the girls, begins an affair with Filumena when she is 17 years old.

Mediterraneo (1991, Gabriele Salvatores). Somewhere near Greece during World War II, an Italian ship leaves a handful of soldiers on a little island where they pass most of the war.

Mille Bolle Blu (1993, Leone Pompucci). This movie tells the stories of a group of Roman families who live in the same building during a total eclipse of the sun in 1996.

Rocco e i suoi fratelli (*Rocco and His Brothers*) (1960, Luchino Visconti). A widow moves to Milano with her four sons, one of whom is Rocco.

Roma: Citta Aperta (*Rome, Open City;* 1946, Roberto Rossellini). Resistance leaders hide from the Nazis.

Sciuscia (*Shoeshine*) (1946, Vittorio De Sica). A heartwrenching commentary on impoverished children's lives, friendship, corruption, and betrayal.

The Seduction of Mimi (1972, Lina Wertmüller). Actor Giancarlo Giannini plays a Sicilian during the 1970s who leaves Sicily to look for work in the North.

Stromboli (1949, Roberto Rossellini). A young woman from a Baltic country marries a fisherman in a small village to escape from a prison camp.

Une Partie de Campagne (*A Day in the Country*). The family of a Parisian shop owner spends a day in the country.

Books

Naturalmente, these are but a few of many titles that offer insight, wisdom, and entertainment related to Italy. (Publication dates include reprint editions and may not indicate when the book was first published.)

Alighieri, Dante. *La Divina Commedia* (*The Divine Comedy*). (Translated by Allen Mandelbaum, Everyman's Library, 1995)

Ariosto, Ludovico. *Orlando Furioso.* (Oxford University Press, 1998)

Artusi, Pellegrino. *The Art of Eating Well.* (Random House, 1996)

Barolini, Helen. *Umbertina.* (Feminist Press, 1999)

Barzini, Luigi. *The Italians*. (Simon & Schuster Trade, 1996)

Bastianich, Lidia. *Lidia's Italian Table*. (William Morrow & Company, 1998)

Bianchi, Anne. *Italian Festival Foods: Recipes and Traditions from Italy's Regional Country Food Fairs*. (Hungry Minds, Inc., 1999)

Boccaccio, Giovanni. *The Decameron*. (Translated by G. H. McWilliam, Penguin, 1996)

———. *Famous Women*. (Harvard University Press, 2001)

Calvino, Italo. *If on a Winter's Night a Traveler*. (Harvest Books, 1982)

Castiglione, Baldassare. *Il Cortegiano* (The Book of the Courtier). (Translated by George Bull, Penguin USA, 1976)

Costantino, Mario, and Lawrence Gambella. *The Italian Way: Aspects of Behavior, Attitudes, and Customs of the Italians*. (McGraw Hill, 1996)

D'Acierno, Pellegrino. *The Italian American Heritage: A Companion to Literature and Arts*. (Garland Publishing, 1998)

da Vinci, Leonardo. *The Notebooks of Leonardo da Vinci*. (Editor, Jean Paul Richter, Oxford University Press, 1998)

Eco, Umberto. *The Name of the Rose*. (Harcourt Brace, 1983)

Euvino, Gabrielle. *The Complete Idiot's Guide to Learning Italian, Second Edition*. (Alpha Books, 2001)

Fallaci, Oriana. *Lettera a un bambino mai nato*. (*Letter to an Unborn Child,* Simon & Schuster Trade, 1977)

Gardaphe, Fred. *From the Margin: Writings in Italian Americana*. (Purdue University Press, 1990)

Hoobler, Dorothy, and Thomas Hoobler. *The Italian American Family Album*. (Oxford University Press Children's Books, 1998)

La Sorte, Michael. *La Merica: Images of Italian Greenhorn Experience*. (Temple University Press, 1985)

Laurine, Maria. *Were You Always an Italian?* (Norton & Company, 2001)

Levi, Primo. *If Not Now, When?* (translated by William Weaver, Penguin USA, 1995)

Machiavelli, Niccolo. *Il Principe (The Prince).* (Distribooks International, 1999)

Mann, Thomas. *Death in Venice.* (Buccaneer Books, 1983)

Mayes, Frances. *Under the Tuscan Sun: At Home in Italy.* (Broadway Books, 1997)

Neighbor, Travis; and Monica Larner. *Living, Studying, and Working in Italy.* (Henry Holt, 1998)

Parks, Tim. *Italian Neighbors or a Lapsed Anglo-Saxon in Verona.* (Fawcett Books, 1993)

Pope John Paul II. *Breakfast with the Pope: Daily Readings.* (Charis House Press, 1995)

Pirandello, Luigi. *Six Characters in Search of an Author.* (Signet Classic, 1998)

Radomile, Leon J. *Heritage Italian-American Style.* (Vincero Enterprises, 1999)

Stone, Irving. *The Agony and the Ecstasy.* (Doubleday, 1961)

Talese, Gay. *Honor Thy Father.* (Ivy Books, 1992)

Timpanelli, Gioa. *Sometimes the Soul: Two Novellas of Sicily.* (Vintage Books, 1999)

Weaver, William, ed. *Open City: Seven Writers in Postwar Rome: Ignazio Silone, Giorgio Bassani, Alberto Moravia, Elsa Morante, Natalia Ginzburg, Carlo Levi, Carlo Emili.* (Steerforth Press, 1991)

Map of Italy

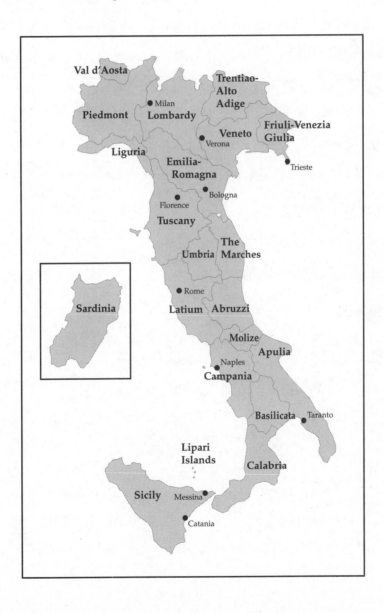

Val d'Aosta

Trentiao-
Alto
Adige

Milan

Piedmont   Lombardy

Veneto   Friuli-Venezia
Giulia

Verona

Liguria

Emilia-
Romagna

Trieste

Bologna

Florence

Tuscany

The
Umbria Marches

Rome

Sardinia   Latium   Abruzzi

Molize

Apulia

Naples

Campania

Basilicata   Taranto

Lipari
Islands

Calabria

Sicily   Messina

Catania

Index

Q–R

V

Valenti, Jack Joseph, 329
Valentino, Rudolph, 318
value added tax. *See* VAT
Vandals, 62
VAT (value added tax), 286
Vatican City, 13
Vatican City State, 74
vehicles
    Blessing of the Vehicles,
        229
    Ferraris, 230
    Vespa motor scooters, 230
Venetians
    floods, 18
    organization of one of first
        banks of public debt, 103
Verdi, Giuseppe, 189
Verdi, Tullio Suzzara, 305
Vergil (Roman poet), Aeneid,
    51
Verrazano, Giovanni da,
    140-141
Verrocchio, Andrea del, 127
Versace, Gianni, 284
Vespa motor scooters, 230
Vespucci, Amerigo, 139
virgin olive oil, 241
Visconti, Luchino
    (Neorealist), 217
Viscusi, Robert, 294
Vita Nuova, 93
Vivaldi, Antonio, 161
Volta, Alessandro, 302

W

W.O.P. (without official
    papers), 33
waterways, 16
    Appius Claudius' Aqua
        Appia aqueduct, 16
    Roman baths, 16
waves of immigration, 193
    customs inspection, 196
    Ellis Island inspection and
        interrogation, 195-196
    Island of Tears, 194-195

National Origins Act, 199
networking and organiza-
    tions, 198-199
search for employment,
    196
    Boss System, 197
    successful individuals,
        197-198
Web sites (resources), 347
    culture, 347-348
    food, 348-349
    music, 349
    news, 349
    organizations, 350
    travel, 350-351
*Wedding Chamber. See Camera
    degli Sposi*
wedding chest (cassone), 255
weeping statues, 268
Werewolf of Pavia legend, 153
Wertmüller, Lina, 234
wines, 239
    choosing a wine, 239-240
    Ernest and Julio Gallo, 333
    labels, 240
Winwar, Frances, 295
witch charm, 270
witch hunts, 153-154
witchcraft, Giovanni Giacomo
    Casanova, 155
without official papers. *See*
    W.O.P.
women, 249
    artists, 252
        Artemisia Gentileschi,
            252
        Francesca Caccini, 253
    contemporary society, 257
        Eleonora Duse, 257
        Elsa Morante, 258
        Maria Montessori, 257
        Natalia Levi–Ginzburg,
            258
    hired, courtesans, 255-256
    Italian woman's move-
        ment, 259
    marriage, 254
        dowrys, 255
    mothers, 260-261

political figures, 329
    Eleanor Cutri Smeal,
        330
    Ella Tambussi Grasso,
        330
    Geraldine Ferraro,
        329-330
Renaissance, 250
    Caterina de' Medici, 251
    Isabella d'Este, 250
    Lucrezia Borgia, 252
    Santa Caterina da Siena,
        253-254
role of Italian women,
    "Italian Miracle," 221
Roman Republic period,
    249-250
World War II, fall of Benito
    Mussolini, 209
writers, 291-295
    IAWA (Italian American
        Writers Association), 295

X–Y–Z

Zappa, Frank, 312
Zecca (mint), 105
zucchetto, 86

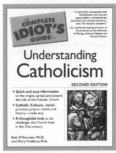

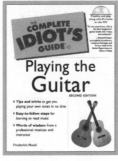

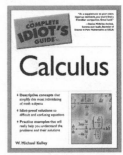